THE NEW ADVISOR GUIDEBOOK

THE NEW ADVISOR
GUIDEBOOK

THE NEW ADVISOR GUIDEBOOK

Mastering the Art of Academic Advising

Pat Folsom, Franklin Yoder, and
Jennifer E. Joslin

JOSSEY-BASS™
A Wiley Brand

NACADA
The Global Community for Academic Advising

Published by Jossey-Bass
A Wiley Brand

One Montgomery Street, Suite 1000, San Francisco, CA 94104-4594—www.josseybass.com

Jossey-Bass books and products are available through most bookstores. To contact Jossey-Bass directly call our Customer Care Department within the U.S. at 800-956-7739, outside the U.S. at 317-572-3986, or fax 317-572-4002.

Wiley publishes in a variety of print and electronic formats and by print-on-demand. Some material included with standard print versions of this book may not be included in e-books or in print-on-demand. If this book refers to media such as a CD or DVD that is not included in the version you purchased, you may download this material at http://booksupport.wiley.com. For more information about Wiley products, visit www.wiley.com.

Library of Congress Cataloging-in-Publication Data

The new advisor guidebook : mastering the art of academic advising / [edited by] Pat Folsom, Franklin Yoder, Jennifer Joslin.
    1 online resource.
    Includes index.
    Description based on print version record and CIP data provided by publisher; resource not viewed.
    ISBN 978-1-118-82358-3 (pdf) – ISBN 978-1-118-82360-6 (epub) – ISBN 978-1-118-82341-5 (cloth)   1. Counseling in higher education.   2. Faculty advisors.   I. Folsom, Pat, editor.   II. Yoder, Franklin L., editor.   III. Joslin, Jennifer, editor.
    LB2343
    378.194–dc23   2015019132

Printed in the United States of America
SECOND EDITION
HB Printing   SKY10032195_122821

The Jossey-Bass Higher
and
Adult Education Series

This book is dedicated to all embarking on the journey
to master the art of academic advising.

CONTENTS

PART ONE
Mastering the Art of Advising

PART TWO
Foundations: The Conceptual Component

PART THREE
Foundations: The Informational Component

PART FOUR
Foundations: The Relational Component

PART FIVE
Delivering Advising

PART SIX
Advisor Development for Foundational Mastery

APPENDIXES

PREFACE

This is an exciting time to become an academic advisor—a time in which global recognition of the importance of advising is growing, and research affirms the critical role advising plays in student success (Klepfer & Hull, 2012). This positive attention to the field also means that advisors, regardless of their specific responsibilities, face the intense challenge to deliver quality services responsive to the specific contexts of the institution and the changing needs of students (Wallace, 2013, ¶3). This second edition of *The New Advisor Guidebook* is specifically designed to help first-time advisors meet this challenge. As the first of three books in the newly developed academic advisor core resource library, it also prepares advisors to meet the students' advising needs over time and within a continuously changing higher education environment.

Changing Emphases in Higher Education

State, provincial, federal, and national parliamentary bodies are compelling post-secondary institutions to focus on degree completion, financial affordability, career attainment, the worth and efficacy of higher education, and the burden borne by citizens, students, parents, and governments. The resulting focus on college completion has increased the scrutiny of policies extant before the global financial crisis in the late 2000s and inspired new policies; for example, performance-based funding has replaced enrollment-based funding. This reprioritization is associated with increased involvement of government entities and higher education foundations.

Agents of change are paying attention to graduation rates and progression, career and work readiness, appropriate major choices, and careers in science, technology, engineering, and math as well as service-oriented business environments. The Georgetown Center on Education and the Workforce, The Lumina Foundation, and other nonprofit organizations stress that college-bound students should consider financial aid responsibilities, graduation and progression rates, and majors that lead to the best job postgraduation (e.g., Carnevale, 2013; Carnevale, Smith, & Strohl, 2010). In the United States, President Obama has called for greater institutional transparency such that students and their parents can access information helpful for making optimal choices for the postsecondary experience.

As the burden for higher education has shifted from taxpayers to students and parents in the United States, the United Kingdom, and elsewhere, institutions have redoubled efforts on effective academic advising, personal tutoring, and other student support services (Field, 2015; Organisation for Economic Co-operation and Development, 2012; Thomas, 2012). Advising administrators as well as practitioners have responded to the new demands by highlighting the importance of adequate staffing, state-of-the-art technology tools, assessment, and training and ongoing professional development for long-term effective advising.

Current State of Advisor Training and Development

The increased attention on the importance of effective academic advising leads to greater recognition of the importance of and need for advisor training and ongoing professional growth and development. To deliver advising that enhances students' educational experiences, aids in fulfilling institutional missions and goals, and meets the changing emphases in higher education, advisors must participate in opportunities for professional growth.

The first edition of this *Guidebook* (Folsom, 2007) offered a vision for a comprehensive approach to advisor training and development, calling for programs that include "year-long new-advisor development programs" (Folsom, 2007, p. 8) and "that provide ongoing training support" to ensure that newcomers to the field "fully develop as advisors" (p. 8). More recently, Julie Givans Voller (2011) explicitly outlined the requisite components of a comprehensive approach to advisor training and development:

> Comprehensive programs include pre-service training for new advisors as well as ongoing support throughout a new advisor's first year in the field. Moreover, they include continuous professional development through multiple delivery methods for experienced advisors at all stages of their careers. (¶3)

However, upon review of the *2011 NACADA National Survey of Academic Advising*, Givans Voller (2013) noted that "fewer than one half of the respondents indicated receiving pre-service training and individualized development and nearly one tenth received no training or development" (¶3). She also pointed out, "Even though the success of advising hinges upon the strength of training provided from pre-service until the end of an advisor's career, the number of institutions supporting comprehensive training and development programs for advisors is low" with "fewer than one half (47%) of institutions [offering the components] . . . , which embody the definition of *comprehensive*" (Givans Voller, 2013, ¶3).

Recent publications indicate that despite making some progress in training content, institutions need to substantially improve access to extensive initiatives (Fusch & Phare, 2014). An Academic Impressions survey of advising directors (Fusch & Phare, 2014) indicated that the content of training has improved since the publication of the first edition of the *Guidebook*: "Most formal training programs remain short, heavily information-driven sessions" (Folsom, 2007, p. 7, summarizing from Gordon & Habley, 2000). In fact, the Academic Impressions survey revealed that most directors of advising offer "some training in developmental and intrusive advising, rather than merely prescriptive [*sic*] advising" (Fusch & Phare, 2014, ¶4) and that "approximately

65% provide training in the other skill sets: relational (establishing trust, communication, questioning, mentorship), conceptual (the theory and practice of advising, student rights/responsibilities), and personal (including personal growth and professional development)" (¶2). Although conceptual and relational components of advising are incorporated into initiatives at some institutions, in general, training programs appear to remain information heavy: "More than 90% of directors provide some training on informational skills" (Fusch & Phare, 2014, ¶2).

The amount of training advisors may receive remains discouraging. According to the Academic Impressions survey, "Only 61% offer an orientation for new advisors" and "a sizeable minority offers no training at all" (Fusch & Phare, 2014, ¶6). These findings indicate little, if any, improvement since 2011, when the *NACADA National Survey of Academic Advising* revealed that 40% of institutions provide pre-service training (Carlstrom & Miller, 2013). As Givans Voller (2013) explained, these findings "suggest that college students may know more about the institution than their advisors do" (¶8).

In fact, ongoing training and development efforts fall short of the continuous professional development critical for comprehensive programs (Givans Voller, 2013). According to the Academic Impressions survey, ongoing training and development—a critical component of comprehensive programs—is not being maximally offered by advising directors (Fusch & Phare, 2014, ¶7):

- o 65% . . . offer occasional workshops.
- o 62% facilitate some form of peer advising or mentorship.
- o . . . 51% offer a structured series of ongoing trainings (which may, or may not, be mandatory).

Most of the directors responding to the 2014 Academic Impressions survey worked with professional advisors, but an earlier survey targeting academic deans and department chairs as well as advising directors paints an equally alarming picture of training for faculty advisors (Fusch, 2012). Survey results indicate that "three quarters of the institutions surveyed rely heavily on faculty advisors," yet "faculty advisors often receive little or no training" even at institutions where "there were many resources available for training and developing professional staff" (Fusch, 2012,¶2).

Results from the Academic Impression surveys (Fusch, 2012; Fusch & Phare, 2014) suggest that institutions are not fulfilling goals for preparing and developing effective academic advisors. The question posed by directors in the latest Academic Impressions survey may reveal much about the work left to do: "How do you move training beyond just an information dump, and ensure that advisors will be equipped and driven to implement what they're learning?" (Fusch & Phare, 2014, ¶8). In the long term, this question can be addressed by the implementation of comprehensive advisor training and development programs at all institutions of higher education. More immediately, leaders in the advising field must (a) create a common advising curriculum delineating the knowledge and skills new advisors must acquire, (b) provide advisors with the resources to study this curriculum, and (c) give advisors the tools to manage their development. The academic advisor core resource library offers effective tools for new advisors, even for those without access to formal training programs.

The Academic Advisor Core Resource Library

The academic advisor core resource library supports all advisors in their development over time: as they enter the field, gain proficiency, and master the art of advising. The resource library is composed of three books, each of which addresses one of the three essential components of advising (Habley 1987, 1995; chapter 2):

- o The informational component includes knowledge advisors must acquire.
- o The relational component reflects the communicative skills and approaches advisors must master.
- o The conceptual component refers to the ideas and theories that advisors must understand.

The *Guidebook* offers the informational component. It introduces readers to and provides the foundational basis for all three components of advising. The book also offers guidelines for meeting goals related to the three components in the advisor's first year through foundational mastery (three or more years). The *Guidebook* is Advising 101 and serves as the entry point to the core resources for most new advisors.

Academic Advising Approaches: Strategies That Teach Students to Make the Most of College (Drake, Folsom, & Miller, 2013) focuses on the relational component. As they grow more proficient in their craft, academic advisors expand their relational skills to include a variety of approaches and strategies that help students understand and take advantage of the college experience. *Approaches* provides a comprehensive examination of the communicative strategies advisors invoke, as appropriate, to address the diverse and sometimes difficult issues students bring to advising sessions. The *Approaches* book is considered Advising 201, the second-level core resource for advisors (Year 2 and beyond).

Beyond Foundations: Becoming a Master Advisor (Grites, Miller, & Givans Voller, forthcoming) concentrates on the conceptual component of academic advising, including a variety of topics that experienced, master advisors must understand to make a difference for their students, campus, and profession. *Beyond Foundations*, Advising 301, is targeted to advisors who have been practicing the craft for more than three years.

The New Advisor Guidebook: Audience, Focus, and Aims

The audience for the updated *New Advisor Guidebook* extends to faculty or professional advisors new to the field. We anticipate that those establishing or refining training programs will utilize the *Guidebook* as a resource for advisors, and it will serve as the primary resource for advisors managing their own development. We encourage those institutions and associations worldwide to use the *Guidebook* as a curriculum guide for those new to the profession, especially those responsible for their own self-development.

Advisors develop excellence through formal study, training, practice, and observation (The American Heritage College Dictionary, 1993). As experiential learners, academic advisors remain students in their fields to gain mastery and achieve excellence (chapter 1). The content and design of the new *Guidebook* support the experiential learning journey advisors take to master the art of advising.

Each chapter focuses on foundational content: the basic terms, concepts, information, and skills advisors must learn in their first year and upon which they will build expertise over time. In addition, within each chapter, contributors have created pathways to practice for new advisors: strategies, questions, guidelines, examples, and case studies that help them connect foundational content to their work with students. For example, Kim Roufs (chapter 4) describes a number of student development theories and demonstrates ways they may be employed in advising sessions; Karen Archambault (chapter 10) identifies five questions advisors can use to gain awareness of their biases and avoid making assumptions about students and then illustrates their use in student situations; Jayne Drake (chapter 12) presents case studies to demonstrate various advising approaches. Additional practice-oriented materials are included in Applications and Insights, such as Peggy Jordan's checklist for listening, interviewing, and referral skills (chapter 11), and Voices From the Field, that feature advising concepts in practice; for example, Anna Chow (chapter 10) applies Archambault's self-knowledge questions to advising international students.

In addition to pathways to practice, we embedded other key elements of advising within chapter content. The authors integrated concepts of diversity as they apply to the advising field (e.g., student populations, advisor role, and institutional type) into their chapters. They also integrated the use of technology, focusing on ways it affects practice. Contributors aimed to keep the full scope of advising practice in their specialized treatises. Those who have served as trainers recognize that new advisors often focus on the mastering of information and the acquisition of communication as the goals for development. As editors, we wanted new advisors to understand that fundamental knowledge and skills provide the tools to use in helping students succeed.

The *Guidebook* also offers new advisors a framework as well as strategies and tools for managing their own development. An updated New Advisor Development Chart (chapter 1) outlines the knowledge and skills practitioners must acquire to effectively advise students. In the Chart, advisors will find two sets of expectations: those realistic for mastering knowledge and skills at the end of one year and those for foundational mastery at the end of three years (chapter 1). The first chapter also includes a learning taxonomy (Anderson et al., 2000) advisors can use to benchmark their development. Aiming for Excellence activities at the end of each chapter give advisors concrete ideas and strategies for expanding their knowledge and improving their skills. Franklin Yoder and Jennifer E. Joslin (chapter 17) present advisors with a framework, guidelines, and a calendar template to manage their growth through a year-long self-development program.

Organization

The first and final chapters of the book identify the knowledge and skills advisors must master. These chapters also present frameworks for setting goals, benchmarking progress, and creating self-development plans. Between these two chapters lies the heart of the book—the content advisors need to read, learn, and apply, as well as use for reflection, as they begin to work with students. This core material is divided into four parts. The first four individual parts present the three essential components of academic advising: conceptual, informational, and relational. Parts four and five address the various ways in which advisors deliver advising: one-to-one, in groups, and online. The book concludes with a section on training and professional growth. Readers will find that the New Advisor Development Chart (chapter 1) closely aligns with this organizational scheme.

Definitions

We made an editorial decision to use Linda Higginson's (2000) framework for the informational component of advising—institutional, external, and self-knowledge as well as student needs—in part three of the book. The use of this framework provides consistency across chapters in addressing various aspects of the informational component. We offer a new feature in this edition: a glossary of terms specific to the advising field (part two). The glossary offers new advisors a quick, easy-to-use point of reference as they read chapters or seek to refresh their understanding of advising terminology.

In addition to chapters, we include practice-based features: Applications and Insights, Voices From the Field, and Aiming for Excellence activities. These terms may be applied differently in other NACADA materials. For the purposes of this publication they are defined as follows:

- o Applications and Insights are short, practice-based materials that assist advisors in thinking about or applying concepts outlined in the chapters. They may include checklists, questions, outlines, and brief descriptors or strategies (e.g., characteristics of effective advisors).

- o Voices From the Field feature information, concepts, and theories applied to the practice of advising as explained by seasoned practitioners.

o Aiming for Excellence activities and queries offer concrete strategies and ideas for advisors to use in managing their growth and development.

Final Thoughts

We congratulate readers on entering this vibrant and rewarding field. We, too, were once new, and we remember how excited—and nervous—we were at the prospect of getting to know and work with our students. We assure readers that they are not expected to possess the knowledge and skills they need to be master advisors on their first day or even in their first year. Advisors achieve excellence through an experiential learning process over many years.

This book sends the advisor on the first leg of the journey. It is designed to help new advisors gain proficiency in advising and to chart their growth as they do so. Although the content focuses on the knowledge and skills advisors need to acquire in their first year, the practice-based materials offer guidance for the years leading to foundational mastery. As advisors apply knowledge they have gained from this book and reflect on their specific experiences in the field, they should return to various chapters and features to document their progress and set new goals. Like the editors and contributors to the first edition of the *Guidebook*, we hope that each advisor's personal copy of this edition "has notes in the margins and becomes dog-eared" (Folsom, 2007, p. 9). We wish all new advisors a rewarding and successful journey!

PAT FOLSOM
FRANKLIN YODER
JENNIFER E. JOSLIN

References

The American Heritage College Dictionary. (1993). [Art]. Boston, MA: Houghton Mifflin.

Anderson, L. W., Krathwohl, D. R., Airasian, P. W., Cruikshank, K. A., Mayer, R.E., Pintrich, P. R., . . . & Wittrock, M. C. (2000). *A taxonomy for learning, teaching, and assessing: A revision of Bloom's taxonomy of educational objectives*. New York, NY: Pearson, Allyn & Bacon.

Carlstrom, A. H., & Miller, M. A. (Eds.). (2013). [Table 8.1]. *2011 NACADA national survey of academic advising*. Retrieved from http://www.nacada.ksu.edu/Portals/0/Clearinghouse/documents/Chapter%208%20-%20Professional%20Advisor%20Development%20-%20FINAL.pdf

Carnevale, A. P. (2013). *Getting more bang for our college bucks*. Retrieved from https://cew.georgetown.edu/wp-content/uploads/2013/06/Carnevale_Spotlight_05312013-to-post.pdf

Carnevale, A. P., Smith, N., & Strohl, J. (2010). *Recovery: Job growth and education requirements through 2009*. Washington, DC: Georgetown University, Georgetown Public Policy Institute.

Drake, J., Folsom, P., & Miller, M. A. (Eds.). (2013). *Academic advising approaches: Strategies that teach students to make the most of college.* San Francisco, CA: Jossey-Bass.

Field, K. (2015, January 20). 6 years in and 6 to go, only modest progress on Obama's college-completion goal. *Chronicle of Higher Education.* Retrieved from http://chronicle.com/article/6-Years-in6-to-Go-Only/151303/?cid=at&utm_source=at& utm_medium=en

Folsom, P. (2007). Foreword. In P. Folsom (Ed.), *The new advisor guidebook: Mastering the art of advising through the first year and beyond* (Monograph No. 16) (pp. 7–9). Manhattan, KS: National Academic Advising Association.

Fusch, D. (2012, July 6). *Improving faculty advising.* https://www.academicimpressions .com/news/improving-faculty-advising

Fusch, D., & Phare, C. (2014). *Survey report: Training academic advisors.* Retrieved from http://www.academicimpressions.com/news/survey-report-training-academic-advisors

Givans Voller, J. (2013). *Implications of professional development and reward for professional academic advisors.* In A. H. Carlstrom & M. A. Miller (Eds.), *2011 NACADA national survey of academic advising* (Monograph No. 25). Retrieved from http://www.nacada.ksu.edu/Resources/Clearinghouse/View-Articles/Implications-for -professional-development-2011-National-Survey.aspx

Gordon, V. N., & Habley, W. R. (Eds.). (2000). *Academic advising: A comprehensive handbook.* San Francisco, CA: Jossey-Bass.

Grites, T. J., Miller, M. A., & Givans Voller, J. (forthcoming). *Beyond foundations: Becoming a master academic advisor.* San Francisco, CA: Jossey-Bass.

Habley, W. R. (1987). *Academic advising conference: Outline and notes* (pp. 33–34). Iowa City, IA: The ACT National Center for the Advancement of Educational Practices. Retrieved from www.nacada.ksu.edu/Portals/0/Clearinghouse/advisingissues /documents/AcademicAdvisingConferenceOutlineandNotes.pdf

Habley, W. R. (1995). Advisor training in the context of a teaching enhancement center. In R. E. Glennen & F. N. Vowell (Eds.), *Academic advising as a comprehensive campus process* (Monograph No. 2) (pp. 75–79). Manhattan, KS: National Academic Advising Association.

Higginson, L. C. (2000). A framework for training program content. In V. N. Gordon & W. R. Habley (Eds.), *Academic advising: A comprehensive handbook* (pp. 298–307). San Francisco, CA: Jossey-Bass.

Klepfer, K., & Hull, J. (2012). *High school rigor and good advice. Setting up students to succeed.* Retrieved from http://www.centerforpubliceducation.org/Main- Menu/Staffingstudents/High-school-rigor-and-good-advice-Setting-up-students-to- succeed/High-school-rigor-and-good-advice-Setting-up-students-to-succeed-Full- Report.pdf

Organisation for Economic Co-operation and Development. (2012). *Education at a glance 2012: Highlights.* Retrieved from http://www.oecd.org/edu/highlights.pdf

Thomas, L. (2012). *Building student engagement and belonging in higher education at a time of change: Final report from the What Works? Student Retention & Success*

programme. Retrieved from https://www.heacademy.ac.uk/sites/default/files/What
_works_final_report.pdf

Wallace, S. (2013). Implications for faculty advising. In A. H. Carlstrom & M. A. Miller
(Eds.), *2011 NACADA national survey of academic advising* (Monograph No. 25).
Retrieved from http://www.nacada.ksu.edu/Resources/Clearinghouse/View
-Articles/Implications-for-faculty-advising-2011-National-Survey.aspx

ACKNOWLEDGMENTS

The first edition of *The New Advisor Guidebook: Mastering the Art of Advising Through the First Year and Beyond* (Folsom, 2007) served as an introduction for professional advisors new to the field. In this revision, we expanded the scope to include all advisors worldwide while maintaining the focus on first-year knowledge and skills acquisition. We consider this edition Advising 101 and the first in the academic advisor core resource library from NACADA: The Global Community for Academic Advising.

Like professors who must choose the content and format for an introductory course in psychology or biology, we started the revision by asking questions: What information will give students the best understanding of the field? What formats and activities will best help students learn and apply their knowledge? What topics will provide students with the best foundation upon which to build a comprehensive base of knowledge and skills? The answers to these questions have evolved over time, the result of multiple reviews, comments, suggestions, and chapter drafts by experts in advising. The creation of this book has been a journey, and we appreciate the efforts and contributions of every person who traveled with us, kept us moving forward, and brought this project to a successful conclusion.

Review Panel for *The New Advisor Guidebook*, First Edition

We thank members of the review panel who re-addressed the original text of *The New Advisor Guidebook* (Folsom, 2007). Your insightful analyses, thoughtful comments, and useful suggestions on the first publication challenged us as we deliberated about changes needed to update the book and to meet new advisors' training and development needs. We found ourselves continuously returning to your comments as we addressed the book's content and format. We added a learning taxonomy, improved the alignment between chapters and the New Advisor Development Chart, and specifically targeted Voices From the Field components as results of your review. We so appreciate the strong support of the NACADA: The Global Community for Academic Advising Publications Advisory Board, New Advising Professionals Commission, and Faculty Advising Commission that provided such a talented team of reviewers.

Karen Archambault, Drexel University

Catherine Coe, University of Florida

Christopher Cuccia, Seton Hall University

Khaseem Davis, Northern Virginia Community College

Rafael de la Pena, Alberta College of Art and Design

Sara Herkes, University of Colorado–Boulder

Kayla Hotvedt, University of North Dakota

Bob Hurt, California State Polytechnic University Pomona

Mark Mannheimer, Northern Virginia Community College

Alison McElfresh, Northern Virginia Community College

Cynthia Pascal, Northern Virginia Community College

Content Review Panel for *The New Advisor Guidebook*, Second Edition

We also thank members of the content review panel for your assistance in the early phases of the second edition of *The New Advisor Guidebook*. Your comments and suggestions helped us identify content gaps, define the key questions, and clarify our direction.

Taylor Adams, Utah State University

Sarah Beebe, Kansas State University

Michelle Ciesielski, Missouri State University

Brad Cunningham, Kansas State University

Julie Givans Voller, Phoenix College

Theresa Harper, Oregon State University

Chelsa Jensen, Kansas State University

Cheri Kau, The University of Hawaii–Manoa

Lauren Layton, University of Nevada–Las Vegas

Joey Lynch, University of Nebraska–Lincoln

Denise Malloy, Montana State University

Craig McGill, Florida International University

Liz Morningstar, University of Colorado–Boulder

Kasandrea Sereno, University of South Florida

Janet Spence, University of Louisville

George Steele, retired from The Ohio State University

Janie Valdes, Florida International University

Damian Whitney, University of Nebraska–Lincoln

Authors

Your expertise, feedback at the annual meeting, and ongoing drafts helped us identify the most important and foundational information to include for new advisors. We appreciate your extensive time and effort to meet our requests to include pathways to practice, integrate diversity (advisor, institutional, and student), and explain uses of technology in chapter content. We along with new and future advisors thank you for your contribution to this important project. We encourage readers to check out The Authors section to find out more about the contributors and their passions for helping new advisors succeed.

Executive Office

We thank the Executive Office of NACADA: The Global Community for Academic Advising for their superb support on this book. We offer a special thanks to Marsha Miller, Assistant Director for Resources and Services, whose knowledge of advising research and resources is unparalleled and who, even when we experienced bumps in the road, stepped in and found ways to move us forward. We also extend a very special thanks to Nancy Vesta, NACADA copy editor, for her keen eye and ability to polish our prose to professional standards.

Finally, we dedicate this book to all new advisors and wish them success in their journey to master the art of advising.

PAT FOLSOM
FRANK YODER
JENNIFER E. JOSLIN
EDITORS

Reference

Folsom, P. (Ed.). (2007). *The new advisor guidebook: Mastering the art of advising through the first year and beyond* (Monograph No. 16). Manhattan, KS: National Academic Advising Association.

THE EDITORS

Pat Folsom is the retired Assistant Provost for Enrollment Management and Director of the Academic Advising Center at the University of Iowa. Folsom has 30 years of experience in academic advising including overseeing an exemplary practice advisor development program and serving on the design team for the building in which the Center is housed. Folsom implemented a number of programs for first-year students at the University including IowaLink, a first-year program for at-risk students; The College Transition, a first-year seminar; and College Success Seminar, a course for first-year students on probation. As Assistant Provost, she also worked on initiatives for undergraduate student success including strategic planning for the needs of international students, restructuring the content and format of student orientation programs, and implementing academic support service programming for students. In addition to NACADA: The Community for Academic Advising conference presentations and a webinar, she was the editor of *The New Advisor Guidebook: Mastering the Art of Advising Through the First Year and Beyond* (2007) and has contributed chapters to *Academic Advising: A Comprehensive Handbook (2nd edition)* (2008), *Comprehensive Advisor Training and Development: Practices that Deliver* (2010), and *Academic Advising Administration: Essential Knowledge and Skills for the 21st Century* (2011). Folsom has served as Chair of the Advisor Training and Development Commission, Chair of the Professional Development Committee, and member of the NACADA Board of Directors. Folsom earned a BA in 1969 from Ohio Wesleyan University and an MLS from SUNY, Geneseo in 1973.

Franklin Yoder has been at the Academic Advising Center at The University of Iowa since 1992. He is currently an Associate Director at the Advising Center where he is responsible for new advisor training. In the past several years, he has been involved with NACADA: The Global Community for Academic Advising by leading workshops for new advisors, co-presenting a webinar on advising theory, writing monograph chapters, and presenting at sessions on training and technology and other related topics. He received his PhD in history from the University of Chicago and also serves as an adjunct professor in the History Department at The University of Iowa.

Jennifer E. Joslin was appointed the Associate Director for Content Development of NACADA: The Global Community for Academic Advising in September 2013. She had served as the Director of the Office of Academic Advising at the University of Oregon and as the Senior Associate Director for Training and Development at the University of Iowa. Joslin is a Past President of NACADA and former board and council member.

In addition to serving as Coeditor for the second edition of the *New Advisor Guidebook* along with Pat Folsom and Franklin Yoder, Joslin coedited, with Nancy Markee, *Academic Advising Administration: Essential Knowledge and Skills for the 21st Century* (2011).

In 2012, she was awarded a University of Oregon Officer of Administration award acknowledging inspired leadership and commitment to fostering an inclusive campus climate. In 2011, she was awarded the NACADA Region 8 Advising Administrator Award, which recognizes demonstrated excellence in advising administration.

Joslin has presented at regional and national advising conferences, consulted at institutions in the United States and Australia, and presented three national webinars for NACADA on the topics of social media, LGBTQA issues, and advising administration. She has written for the *NACADA Journal* and several NACADA books including *Advising Special Populations* (2007); *The New Advisor Guidebook (1st edition)* (2007); and *Comprehensive Advisor Training and Development* (2011). In addition, she has served on the Content Review Boards for the *Academic Advising Handbook (2nd edition)* (2008); *Academic Advising Today*; and *Foundations of Academic Advising CD 3: Understanding Cultural Identity and Worldview Development*.

Joslin currently teaches graduate courses in the Kansas State University College of Education in the Department of Counseling and Educational Psychology. A native Californian, Joslin received her PhD from the University of Iowa in 2002. She is a proud member of the Jane Austen Society of North America. Tweet (@jenniferejoslin), befriend, and connect with her at http://about.me/jenniferjoslin.

THE AUTHORS

Karen L. Archambault, EdD, served as Executive Director of Drexel Central, a one-stop shop for financial aid, bursar, and registration services for Drexel University in Philadelphia, Pennsylvania. Prior to her arrival at Drexel, Archambault served as Director of Student Services for the Branch Campus and Higher Education Centers for Brookdale Community College, supervising a cross-functional team that supported student success through admissions, registration, financial aid, academic learning assistance, advising, and student life. While Archambault's experience spans a wide range of functional areas, her primary interests are in transfer student preparation and retention as well as in cross-campus intersections that support student success. She is an active member of NACADA, serving on the National Council, the Publications Advisory Board, and the Administrators' Institute Advisory Board.

Patrick Cate is the Dean of Student Success at Plymouth State University in Plymouth, New Hampshire. He holds a BA in Biology from Keene State College and a MEd from Plymouth State University. He is active with NACADA at the state and region levels as a liaison and a conference co-chair and nationally as a member of the NACADA Academic Advising Consultants and Speakers Service. He is the creator of the Targeted Advising Approach and has consulted with institutions nationally on the subject. He has presented numerous times at NACADA regional and annual conferences and has won a Best of Region Award. He has led graduate course work as well as state drive-in and pre-conference workshops on introduction to advising theory and practice.

Yung-Hwa Anna Chow is the Assistant Director of the College of Arts and Sciences, General Studies and Advising Center, at Washington State University. Her accomplishments include writing for *Academic Advising Today* and serving as a member of the NACADA Research Committee and Finance Committee. She regularly presents at regional and annual conferences and served as a webinar panelist on the topic of advising international students from China. She is the recipient of a 2011 NACADA research grant and spent that summer in Shanghai, China, conducting research for the project. In 2012–13, she served as Chair of the Global Engagement Commission for NACADA, and in February 2013, she led a second NACADA webinar on advising international students.

Joanne K. Damminger, EdD, is the Assistant Vice President for Student Affairs at Delaware Technical Community College and Past President of NACADA. Damminger's work focuses on creating a shared vision for student affairs and leading professionals dedicated to student success and creating positive first-year student experiences centered on learning, engagement, and completion. Damminger presents nationally and internationally on career advising, ethics in advising, first-year experience, living–learning communities, and helping students to become intentional learners. She has published in several books and publications related to career advising and ethics in advising. She earned her EdD in Educational Leadership, MA in Student Personnel Services, and BA in Elementary Education from Rowan University.

Jayne K. Drake is a former President of NACADA and has served in many other roles in the Association including the Council and Board of Directors. As a member of the NACADA Academic Advising Consultants and Speakers Service, Drake travels nationally and internationally to provide keynote addresses and to conduct workshops on a number of advising-related topics, among them faculty advising, advising administration, and advising as teaching. She also serves as a consultant and reviewer to a number of colleges and universities regarding the development and reorganization of advising services. She has been published widely in the field of advising. She is the recipient of NACADA's 2012 Virginia N. Gordon Award for Excellence in the Field of Advising and the 2014 Bobbie Flaherty Service to NACADA Award.

David Freitag, after a career in the computer software industry, earned an MS in Academic Advising from Kansas State University, taught at the University of Arizona, and has been an advisor and more recently an instructor at Pima Community College. He enjoys writing software and articles for the academic advising community.

Jody Johnson is a former Senior Associate Director in the Undergraduate Advising Center (UAC) at the University of Kansas. He received his ME in Social Foundations of Education at Rutgers University and has worked in advising and enrollment management for 26 years. He led the development of a six-week training program for the UAC that was featured as an exemplary practice in NACADA's 2010 monograph, *Comprehensive Advisor Training and Development: Practices that Deliver*. He has presented at various conferences on training, creativity in the workplace, and using institutional mission in everyday life.

Peggy Jordan is a professor of Psychology at Oklahoma City Community College (OCCC), where she has worked for 15 years. She is a faculty advisor for approximately 250 students and serves on OCCC's training team for cooperative learning. Jordan has served as Chair of the NACADA Publications Advisory Board and Two-Year Colleges Commission. She has contributed to numerous NACADA publications and presented at numerous state, regional, and national conferences. Jordan received a PhD in Counseling Psychology from Oklahoma State University and an MEd and a BA from the University of Central Oklahoma. Before serving in higher education, she worked as a psychotherapist in agencies and in a private practice.

Susan Kolls has enjoyed a career at Northeastern University in Boston for almost 30 years, most spent as an academic advisor. In 2011 Kolls became Associate Director, Student Account Services, a position that allows her to bring advising theory into the Student Financial Services realm.

NACADA is an important part of Kolls's professional life. She is especially proud of her service on the Board of Directors, 2009–2012. She has presented over 50 times since 1997, winning three Best of Region Awards. Together with Jose Rodriguez, Kolls presented a NACADA webinar in 2010. Kolls continues to serve NACADA as a member of the Region 1 Conference Committee.

Kolls lives outside of Boston, where she spends time at soccer games, writing, painting pottery, and enjoying music.

Marsha A. Miller began her academic career as a history major at the University of Missouri. She has graduate degrees from the University of Iowa and Emporia State University and advised and taught at Cloud County Community College for 14 years. At Cloud she served as Chair of the Faculty Committee that restructured Cloud's advising program and was director of that program when it received the NACADA Advising Award and the Noel-Levitz citation for Excellence in Student Retention.

Miller currently is NACADA's Assistant Director for Resources and Services. She regularly presents at conferences and publishes articles. She is the managing editor for NACADA-produced books and established the *NACADA Clearinghouse of Academic Advising Resources*. Miller is the NACADA Director on the Board of the Council for the Advancement of Standards in Higher Education (CAS) and answers member questions regarding advising-related concerns.

Dorothy Burton Nelson, a nationally certified counselor, holds her terminal degree in Career and Workforce Development. She serves as director of a student success center and has devoted her professional life to working with students in their academic and career pursuits. Her current work includes managing a staff of professional academic and career advisors in a total-intake center for first-year students. Burton Nelson has developed and taught two levels of undergraduate career planning courses and currently teaches a first-year success course and a graduate-level career development class that helps future advising professionals integrate career development information into academic advising practices. Burton Nelson has been a member of NACADA since 1991 and has contributed to the organization through teaching, writing, and consulting.

Charlie L. Nutt was appointed as the Executive Director of the National Academic Advising Association in October 2007. Prior to this he served as the Associate Director of the Association for 5 years. Additionally, he was Vice President for Student Development Services at Coastal Georgia Community College for 9 years and Assistant Professor of English/Director of Advisement and Orientation for 6 years. He received his AA from Brunswick College, BSEd from the University of Georgia, and MEd and EdD in Higher Educational Leadership from Georgia Southern University.

Nutt has had vast experience in education. In addition to his 15 years as a teacher and administrator at Coastal Georgia Community College, where he originated the college advisement center and orientation program that was awarded a Certificate of Merit by NACADA in 1995, he has taught English in grades 9–12, served as a department chair and assistant principal in a high school, and served as Director of Development and Admission at a private K–12 institution. Presently, he teaches graduate courses in the College of Education in the Department of Counseling and Educational Psychology. He has also been instrumental in the development of the NACADA/ K-State Graduate Certificate in Academic Advising and several other NACADA professional development initiatives.

Jeanette Pellegrin has been working in education since 1991, when she began teaching history at Panama Canal Community College. Upon moving to Kansas in 1993, she worked as a coordinator for the Herington Education Center at Cloud County Community College, where she advised college students of a variety of ages and skill levels. She continued to advise students at the Geary County Campus and eventually became the sole advisor dedicated to serving students attending through online programs. Pellegrin now works as the Dual Enrollment Coordinator at Paul D. Camp Community College in Franklin, Virginia. She earned a BA in History from the University of Maryland at College Park, Maryland, served as an officer in the United States Air Force, and completed an MLS (Master's of Liberal Studies) from Fort Hays State University in December 2014.

Kathleen (Kim) Roufs is Director Emerita of the Advisement Coordination Center at the University of Minnesota Duluth. She received her EdD in Higher Education Policy and Administration from the University of Minnesota. Long interested in the application of theory to practice, at her former institution she developed advising assessment models that examined advisors' application of theory to practice as they related to persistence and completion as well as facilitated faculty seminars on applying theory across disciplines in academic advising. Roufs currently serves as a Mentor in the Higher Learning Commission Academy for Student Persistence and Retention.

Matthew M. Rust serves as the Director of Campus Career and Advising Services at Indiana University–Purdue University Indianapolis. In this role, he coordinates professional development, technology incorporation, and outcomes assessment within academic advising and career development. His professional background includes academic advising, career exploration, outcomes assessment, and first-year seminar teaching. Rust earned a BA in Political Science and Philosophy/Religion from Butler University, an MS in Student Affairs in Higher Education from Miami University, and a JD *cum laude* from North Carolina Central University School of Law. Admitted to the North Carolina State Bar in 2011 (currently inactive), Rust regularly presents on legal issues in advising as well as liberal education and assessment. Rust currently serves on the Editorial Board of the *NACADA Journal*.

Rebecca Ryan is the Undergraduate Program Coordinator for the Institute for Environmental Studies at the University of Wisconsin–Madison. Ryan has been active in NACADA since 1996, including as a presenter in numerous concurrent sessions and pre-conference workshops at the annual conference, a regional representative, a faculty instructor for Summer Institutes, and member of NACADA's Professional Development and Awards Committee. She has also served as Chair for a NACADA regional and a Wisconsin Academic Advising Association (WACADA) state conference, President of WACADA, and Wisconsin State Liaison to NACADA (two terms). Ryan has authored contributions for the first *New Advisor Guidebook* in 2007 and for *Academic Advising Today*. Her favorite topics include advisee management, advisor training, advising curricula, collaborative relationships, undecided students, integrating academic and career advising, and the value of liberal arts.

Jennifer Santoro is a certified professional coach through the Institute for Professional Excellence in Coaching. She is passionate about studying and supporting the human potential. She received her BA in Communication and her MA in Integrated Marketing Communication and Management from Florida State University. During her studies she also earned a certificate in Project Management. She believes in the power of reflection and living a life with purpose. She had the honor of working with Florida State University for 6 years as a higher education professional. With over 10 years of professional experience in the nonprofit, higher education, and private sectors, Santoro combines her marketing, public relations, advertising, and project management experience with her coach training and experience to assist clients in reaching their full business and personal potential. She currently specializes as a strategy coach for entrepreneurs and serves as Chief Happiness Officer of InVidz. With her perspective from the private sector, she continues to partner with colleagues at Florida State University to further work in the development of self-aware graduates.

Misti Dawnn Steward earned her BA in Mass Communications from Reinhardt University, and after interning as a career coach graduate assistant and obtaining her MEd in College Student Affairs from the University of West Georgia, she now works as a college life coach at Florida State University, and while focusing on retention, guides incoming students through their freshman year transition. She has also taught the living-learning community class Exploration and Discovery, co-instructed a class on career development, served as a ropes course facilitator and group-dynamic leader on weekends, and has recently finished a contribution to the NACADA webinar *Integrating Academic and Career Advising*. Steward is passionate about the connection between higher education, career readiness, and student success through self-exploration and -awareness.

Beverly A. Wallace, PhD, has extensive experience as a faculty member and advisor for graduate and undergraduate majors and undeclared students. She received a PhD and MEd in Educational Psychology from the University of Alabama and an MA in English Education (secondary) from Southeastern Oklahoma State University. Beverly Wallace has served as a faculty member in the Departments of Teacher Education and English at the University of Maryland University College European Division (Germany), Mansfield University of Pennsylvania, and the University of Central Missouri. She currently teaches a first-year course, works as a faculty advisor for conditionally admitted students, and serves as the Coordinator of Academic Recovery Programs at Shippensburg University of Pennsylvania. She has given numerous presentations in the areas of student development, retention, and critical thinking, and she has been published in several NACADA venues.

A lifelong learner, **Stephen O. Wallace**, PhD, has earned four graduate degrees including an MEd in Higher and Adult Education Administration and a PhD in Educational Administration. His broad professional experiences have included serving in various student service and faculty positions at the University of Maryland University College European Division (Germany), the University of Alabama, and the University of Central Missouri. Stephen Wallace currently teaches a first-year course and serves as a faculty advisor for conditionally admitted and undeclared students and serves as the Coordinator of Advising Development at Shippensburg University of Pennsylvania. He has presented at the NACADA Annual Conference and been published in several NACADA venues.

Donald Woolston led the undergraduate advising and student affairs office at the University of Wisconsin–Madison College of Engineering from 1991 until 2010. He has served as a NACADA Board member and as Chair of the STEM Advising Commission. Between 1999 and 2010 he presented at annual and regional NACADA conferences with Rebecca Ryan. He is the coauthor of a book on writing for scientists and engineers and a book for high school students on how to choose the right engineering school. In 2010 he retired from engineering and now works as a consultant in distance education and professional communication.

THE NEW ADVISOR GUIDEBOOK

THE NEW ADVISOR
GUIDEBOOK

PART ONE

MASTERING THE ART OF ADVISING

Mastering the art of advising is a long-term developmental process for every advisor. Although new advisors sometimes feel overwhelmed and inadequate during their initial years in practice, they need to recognize that mastering all aspects of advising requires years of study, observation, and experience. As they track their progress through the primary tool for setting goals and assessing progress, the New Advisor Development Chart, advisors will see tangible developmental changes that match up with the processes undertaken by their colleagues, including those who have successfully achieved the goals that new hires seek to accomplish. Although no two advisors will follow the exact same path to mastery, the New Advisor Development Chart provides touch points that apply generally to everyone entering the dynamic field of advising.

1

MASTERING THE ART OF ADVISING

GETTING STARTED

Pat Folsom

Watching a skilled [advisor] help a student is like watching an artist at work. Each makes their craft look easy. The artist applies paint to canvas with a seemingly effortless ease, and the work of art magically appears. [Master] advisors . . . conduct conferences with an equal ease and fluidity.

—Pat Folsom (2007, p. 13)

Master advisors, deftly adapting approaches and strategies within a conversation, teach students to solve problems and make decisions, challenge them to think in new ways, and help them to articulate and create pathways to their educational goals.

> Of course, the ease or effortlessness with which advisors and artists practice their craft creates a false impression; both advisor and artist are seamlessly integrating [and thoughtfully applying] multiple components of their respective crafts that took years to learn. For advisors in training or new advisors, observing an experienced advisor can be simultaneously inspiring and overwhelming. New advisors see the advisors that they want to become and recognize that they have a long way to go to master the craft. (Folsom, 2007, p. 13)

Contributors to this revised and updated edition of *The New Advisor Guidebook: Mastering the Art of Advising Through the First Year and Beyond* (Folsom, 2007) encourage new advisors by examining the constructs underpinning the magic of advising and by providing the tools for advisors to manage their first three years of training and development. Advisors' desire to become excellent practitioners and to master the art of advising drives their motivation to grow professionally. The understanding that mastery matters propels them toward successfully meeting their advising goals.

Mastering the Art of Advising

Excellence in advising matters to the students with whom advisors work and to the institutions they serve. Students report that academic advising is important to them (Noel-Levitz, 2009). Specifically, the advising relationship contributes to their satisfaction and persistence (Folsom & Scobie, 2010; Habley, 2009; Kuh, 2008; Noel-Levitz,

2009). George Kuh (2008), citing results from the 2005 *National Survey of Student Engagement*, noted that "students who rate their advising as good or excellent . . . are more satisfied with their overall college experience" (p. 73) and that the "quality of academic advising is the single most powerful predictor of satisfaction with the campus environment for students at four-year schools" (p. 73). In addition, a recent study by Kasey Klepfer and Jim Hull (2012) showed that "both four-year and two-year students who reported talking to an academic advisor either 'sometimes' or 'often' had significantly higher persistence rates than those who did not" (p. 11).

According to Kuh (2008), academic advisors play an important role in "promoting development and success" (p. 81), and defined broadly, student success includes "academic achievement, engagement in educationally purposeful activities, satisfaction, acquisition of desired knowledge, skills, and competencies, persistence, and attainment of educational objectives" (Kuh, Kinzie, Buckley, Bridges, & Hayek, 2007, p. 1). Pat Folsom and Nora Scobie (2010) noted that "strong academic advising contributes to and supports every component" of this definition of student success (p. 15). Advisors help students delineate a clear pathway to success (Kuh, Kinzie, Schuh, & Whitt, 2005) by assisting "in ways that encourage them to engage in the right kinds of activities, inside and outside the classroom" (Kuh, 2008, p. 69). Advisors also contribute to student satisfaction (Schreiner, 2009) and persistence (Klepfer & Hull, 2012). Furthermore, advisors connect students to sources of academic support, teach them to solve problems, and help them make academic decisions.

In addition to being important to student satisfaction, persistence, and success, the quality of academic advising exerts an important effect on institutions. Specifically, advising "is integral to fulfilling the teaching and learning mission of higher education" (NACADA: The Global Community for Academic Advising [NACADA], 2006, ¶7) because the "academic advising relationship is where some of the best teaching and learning can occur within the academy" (Hunter, McCalla-Wriggins, & White, 2007, p. 1).

As Folsom and Scobie (2010) explained, "To guide students effectively on clear pathways to success, advisors must be knowledgeable about the institution, its resources, and the student body" (p. 17). To help students develop critical-thinking skills, solve problems, and make important decisions, advisors must develop strong communication and interpersonal skills. Therefore, "to provide advising that elicits high student satisfaction, they must be able to establish positive working relationships with students" (Folsom & Scobie, 2010, p. 17). Furthermore, "to meet their strategic goals, institutions need strong advising by well-trained personnel who understand the mission and goals of the institution" (Folsom & Scobie, 2010, p. 17). To contribute to these levels of student and institutional success, new advisors must seek excellence, and their first step is to gain appreciation of academic advising as an art.

The Art of Advising

The art of teaching. The art of medicine. The art of advising. Webster's (1989) defines *art* as the "exceptional skill in conducting any human activity." The term also describes occupations that require the acquisition of a knowledge and skill set "attained by study, practice, or observation" (The American Heritage College Dictionary, 1993). Professionals in teaching, medicine, and advising share these defining occupational characteristics. In addition, those who teach, provide healthcare, and advise must be able to use their knowledge and skills effectively with their students, patients, and advisees. Practitioners will not find a magic formula for establishing successful interpersonal interactions because each class, patient, and advisee presents a unique situation. The art of teaching, medicine, and advising lies in the nuanced application of practitioner knowledge and skills in complex human interactions.

Effective teachers, for example, acquire an extensive knowledge base and skill set. They thoroughly grasp their subject area(s) and student learning theory. They gain information about student development through academic study and learn about the culture, socioeconomic status, and learning styles of their students. Furthermore, they develop strong relational skills that enable them to interact effectively with students and successfully implement teaching and learning strategies. For example, high school instructors of the American Civil War must demonstrate full understanding of the conflict: the causes, battles, important figures, immediate and long-term repercussions, and importance within American history. From this knowledge base, they develop learning outcomes for their students.

Excellent teachers apply their familiarity with their students' learning styles, developmental skills, and specific needs to develop classroom strategies that promote student engagement with the material and achieve the desired learning outcomes. In the classroom, instructors synthesize their knowledge and skills, using relational skills to bring quiet students into the conversation as well as recognize and support students struggling with concepts. They ask questions that challenge students to explore ideas more fully. Their complex and nuanced synthesis and application of knowledge, skills, and relationships constitute the art of teaching.

Healthcare professionals use a similarly integrated application of competencies as they interact with patients. Physicians, for example, sift through their expansive knowledge of diseases and symptoms to arrive at specific diagnoses. Equally important to the diagnostic process, doctors must know their patients; for example, symptoms of heart attack may differ according to gender. Furthermore, to prescribe treatment, they must know their patients' potential reactions to it, which may vary according to age and gender as well as other preexisting factors such as other prescribed medications or known allergies. Physicians undertake years of academic study and acute, informed observation, but the critical pieces of their understanding come directly from the individual patient. A physician's strong relational skills contribute to a patient's trust, without which the patient may not be forthcoming and the doctor will lose information crucial for a proper diagnosis. Creating trust and opening lines of effective communication require cultural competency because beliefs and attitudes toward medicine vary among peoples such that patients may selectively share important information or follow a specified treatment. The art of medicine, like the art of teaching, lies in a complex synthesis and nuanced application of knowledge, skills, and relationships.

Advisors, too, use a complex and extensive knowledge base and skill set as they interact with students. They must gain in-depth knowledge about academic programs, institutional structures, and policies and procedures to help students "define, plan, and achieve their educational goals" (Council for the Advancement of Standards in Higher Education [CAS], 2013, ¶5) and "teach students the basic information they need to navigate the institution . . . and understand the curriculum" (Folsom & Scobie, 2010, p. 16). In addition, advisors "help students weigh options and make good academic decisions and challenge students to grow by asking questions that make students think more critically about who they are and how the institution can help them reach who they want to become" (Folsom & Scobie, 2010, p.16); they also assist students in understanding the rationale behind and the value of their education (Folsom & Scobie, 2010).

Like teachers, advisors must build a foundation in student development theory and also become knowledgeable about the specific students with whom they work; they need to know their advisees' academic strengths and challenges as well as the ethnic, cultural, socioeconomic, and personal factors that inform their worldviews and life experiences. Advisors must select and artfully apply the advising approach best suited for each student and unique situation. Like physicians, advisors acquire critical pieces of information on students' goals and circumstances through direct communication with advisees. That is, they must establish positive working relationships with each student by demonstrating awareness of the human dynamics that characterize the advising conversation. Each time they meet with a student, master advisors invoke their deep understanding of the role of advising, extensive knowledge base, and relational skills to "seamlessly synthesize and apply information about the student and the institution in ways that help students grow and make the most out of their college experience" (Folsom, Joslin, & Yoder, 2005, ¶1). Mastering this art "begins with advisors' desire to become the best possible advisor" (Folsom, 2007, p. 13).

Deconstructing the Magic: Essential Components and Competencies

Unraveling the complex intersection of knowledge, skills, and human dynamics to make mastery of the art easier for new advisors involves breaking advising down into its components. Habley (1995) identified and grouped the foundational knowledge and skills required for advising into three essential components:

- o The conceptual component includes the ideas and theories that advisors must understand to effectively practice the art.
- o The informational component refers to the knowledge that advisors must gain to guide the students at their institution.
- o The relational component involves the communicative skills and interpersonal approaches advisors must build including those critical to establishing advising relationships with students.

The three essential components include all the knowledge and skills that all advisors must master regardless of their individual responsibilities.

The essential components of advising (NACADA, 2006) serve as a foundation for development of advisor competencies. A competency

> is a measurable pattern of knowledge, skills, abilities, behaviors, and other characteristics that an individual needs to perform work roles or occupational functions successfully. Competencies specify the "how" of performing job tasks, or what the person needs to do the job successfully. (U.S. Office of Personnel Management, n.d., ¶1)

NACADA (2014) presented such a performance-based set of competencies:

- o Foundations knowledge (conceptual)
  - o Advising philosophy
  - o Theoretical frameworks
  - o NACADA core values
  - o Knowledge of higher education issues including legal and ethical issues
- o Knowledge of college student characteristics (informational)
  - o General knowledge of college students
  - o Specific knowledge of population(s) advised
- o Career advising knowledge and skills (informational)
  - o Knowledge of academic major
  - o Knowledge of occupational, workplace relationships
- o Communication and interpersonal skills (relational): Ability to relate to individuals and groups of designated students through the use of basic communication, helping, and problem-solving skills
  - o Knowledge of application of advising at local institution (informational)

The academic advisor competencies (NACADA, 2014) and essential components of advising "give novice advisors clear goals to strive for" (Gordon, 2003, ¶1). Competencies also "give administrators external standards to refer to on the hiring, evaluation, and promotion of academic advisors" (Gordon, 2003, ¶1).

New advisors who acquire the foundational knowledge and skills for the three essential components of advising are developing academic advisor competencies. For example, advisors who develop their relational skills, gain self-knowledge, work across diverse student populations, and understand their ethical responsibilities to students, colleagues, and the institution are advancing their knowledge of occupational and workplace relationships. Advisors who establish strong interviewing and communication skills and become adept in applying multiple advising approaches are also learning ways to help students think critically, develop problem-solving skills, and make decisions.

Advisors acquire an operational repertoire of the essential components over a sub-stantial period of time. The contributors to this guidebook called on years of experi-ence to offer this focus on the foundational mastery of the conceptual, informational, and relational components of advising.

Gaining Mastery

The mastery of any art depends upon experiential development through long-term study, practice, and observation. The art of advising, for example, "is in large part learned in the advising chair. Advisors develop excellence over time, student by stu-dent, through an experiential synthesis of the conceptual, informational and relational components of advising" (Folsom et al., 2005, ¶1).

Experiential learning for academic advisors, however, differs from that of teaching and medicine in a significant way. In addition to traditional classroom and text-based study, formal educational programs for teachers and healthcare professionals include substantial opportunities for learning through observation, practice, and experience. New academic advisors come from a wide variety of academic backgrounds, and many take the chair without formal observation, practice, and experiential learning opportunities in the field. Instead, advisors typically acquire the basic knowledge and skills to master the art of advising on the job.

To achieve excellence, advisors must understand the three essential components of advising—conceptual, informational, and relational—as well as synthesize and apply them in advising interactions. However, a new advisor may find mastering even one component (informational) or one aspect of a component (listening skills) daunt-ing; the integration of unfamiliar or unpracticed competencies into an advising ses-sion may overwhelm the newcomer. At some institutions, training and development programs guide advisors through this experiential process, but where such help is unavailable, advisors can self-manage their learning and development by setting real-istic short- and long-term goals that intentionally allow for reflection and learning from their advising experiences. This chapter provides both a framework and a road map to guide advisors in their experiential journey as well as the means to chart their growth.

The New Advisor Development Chart: A Developmental Framework

The New Advisor Development Chart, an update of that offered in the 2007 version of *The New Advisor Guidebook* (Folsom, 2007), gives new advisors a framework to use as they start their journey toward mastery of the art of advising. The Chart identi-fies essential topics and proficiencies for effective advising—the knowledge and skills advisors need to demonstrate in effective practice. Three of four sections address the essential components of advising as delineated by Habley (1995): conceptual, infor-mational, and relational.

- The conceptual component of the Chart identifies theories and concepts advisors use to answer key questions asked of them: What is an academic advisor? What is the role of academic advising at the institution? What is the advising unit's mission? What are advisors' responsibilities? Why is academic advising important? What does student development theory convey about students? What ethical and legal theories and circumstances affect practice? The answers to these and similar questions create the context within which advisors work.

- The informational component of the Chart identifies the knowledge advisors must acquire to guide students effectively. Advisors can use the following categories of knowledge to organize and process the needed information in a workable framework: internal (institutional) and external (Higginson, 2000), student needs, and self-awareness.

- The relational component of the Chart identifies the communication skills and interpersonal strategies necessary to effectively interact with students. The Chart addresses listening, interviewing, and referral skills as well as approaches to advising.

The fourth section of the New Advisor Development Chart identifies the skills and knowledge advisors need to deliver advising in one-to-one advising sessions, in group meetings, or through electronic means. It helps advisors determine the most effective means (e-mail, group, one-to-one) to deliver advising for various situations. Taken as a whole, the Chart provides a comprehensive outline of the skills and knowledge necessary for advisors to master the art of advising.

The Developmental Journey

At first glance, new advisors may find the scope of the Chart overwhelming; however, it was designed on the premise that mastering the art of professional practice requires experiential development over time. Upon close examination of the Chart, advisors will find that the focus does not indicate need for immediate proficiency in every advising skill they will one day need to apply, but rather provides guidance on learning the foundations of advising over approximately three years of practice. In the Chart, advisors also will find both a starting point and a destination for their foundational development. For each topic or skill, the Chart sets realistic expectations for the advising skills and knowledge that advisors can master during their first year as well as for gaining foundational expertise in basic knowledge and skills of advising at the end of three years.

Chart Example: The General Education Program

The section on the general education program (GEP) (informational component) illustrates the developmental nature of the two sets of featured learning outcomes and expectations.

Year One: Knows the categories of the GEP. Understands the rationale as written in institutional policy and articulates rationale in advising session. Uses resources to explain the GEP requirements and describe courses to students. Reviews student progress on the GEP using institutional monitoring tools.

Year Three and Beyond: Demonstrates detailed, experience-based knowledge of GEP and courses. Creates course descriptions for GEP classes and rationales for GEP. Recommends GEP courses that enhance individual student programs of study or serve as exploratory courses for majors and build foundations for postgraduate professional programs. Synthesizes knowledge of student (e.g., academic profile, major and cultural factors, student development theory) and adapts GEP rationale and course descriptions to meet specific student situations. Evaluates and selects best advising approach to facilitate GEP discussion with each student.

In the GEP illustration, the expectations for advising after three years differ substantially from the first-year goals and reflect the new, more complex, higher-level skills and knowledge advisors have gained through study, observation, experience, and practice. Between the beginning of their first and the end of their third year, for example, advisors

- acquire GEP course syllabi and discuss them with students.
- observe a few sessions of the GEP courses commonly taken by the students they advise.
- ask students open-ended questions about their GEP classes such as "What books are you reading in your literature class?" "Which assignments do you look forward to and which assignments are you concerned about?" "Are the lectures and discussions interesting?"
- inquire of other advisors about their students' experiences in specific GEP classes (e.g., the characteristics and academic profiles of successful students in the class).
- research various theories germane to advising (e.g., student development, learning, identity) and intentionally incorporate this knowledge into advising sessions.
- learn about various advising approaches and gradually but intentionally incorporate a variety of them into advising sessions.
- observe other advisors in appointments with students, each time focusing on specific issues such as the articulation of purpose and value of the GEP, articulation of GEP course descriptions, advising approaches, student development theory in practice, or relational skills.
- reflect on their own advising interactions with students.

New advisors develop foundational mastery of advising through the incremental synthesis and internalization of these activities and experiences. Advisors should use the New Advisor Development Chart to identify the skills and knowledge they need to gain as well as to set goals for the learning outcomes or expectations during each subsequent year in practice. As they embark on their journey toward mastery, new advisors need metrics or benchmarks to help them document their progress and identify successful completion of these objectives after three years; that is, they need a developmental road map.

The Learning Taxonomy: A Developmental Road Map

Advisors move from first-year expectations to mastery of the foundational aspects of advising on a continuum though a learning taxonomy: a hierarchy of learning and behaviors built on the simplest concepts and practice and extending through degrees of difficulty toward the most complex actions (Clark, 2015). A learning taxonomy particularly appropriate for the active, interactive process of academic advising is Bloom's revised taxonomy (Anderson et al., 2000), which is composed of six levels that advisors can use to guide them in their development. Don Clark (2015, ¶10) explained the learning stages, as originally put forth by Anderson et al. (2000), that represent appropriate hierarchal benchmarks applicable to advising development:

1. Remembering—recalls previous learned information.
2. Understanding—comprehends the meaning, translation, interpolation, and interpretation of instructions and problems. States a problem in one's own words.
3. Applying—Uses a concept in a new situation or uses an abstraction when unprompted. Applies classroom learning to novel situations in the workplace.
4. Analyzing—Separates material or concepts into component parts to explain organizational structure. Distinguishes between facts and inferences.
5. Evaluating—Makes judgments about the value of ideas or materials.
6. Creating—Builds a structure or pattern from diverse elements. Puts parts together to form a whole with emphasis on generating a new meaning or structure.

The following example of a new advisor's acquisition and application of advising approaches illustrates the developmental movement through the learning stages:

1. The advisor attends a training presentation about the various advising approaches described by Jayne Drake in chapter 12, including advising as teaching, prescriptive, proactive, and strengths-based advising, as well as motivational interviewing and self-authorship theory.
2. At the end of the presentation, the advisor can list the approaches (remembering).

3. In a discussion with colleagues following the presentation, the advisor practices summarizing or explaining each approach and offers examples for each strategy (understanding).

4. Subsequently, by observing advising sessions of experienced advisors, participating in simulation exercises, or viewing videos, the advisor learns to distinguish among various methods used in practice (applying).

5. While appreciating that no single tactic will work in all situations, the first-year advisor may select and more fully develop skill in one approach by incorporating the relevant questioning techniques and key strategies into the advising sessions (applying).

6. By regularly reflecting on the strategies that worked as well as those less successful with specific students (analyzing), the advisor gradually integrates various approaches, building an advising repertoire and becoming adept at assessing the best strategy to use with specific students or circumstances (analyzing, evaluating).

7. Finally, the advisor combines approaches within individual advising sessions (creating).

To gain exceptional skill in their advising interactions with students and develop academic advisor competencies, practitioners need to reach the complex levels of learning for each essential component of advising. For example, at the highest levels of Bloom's revised taxonomy (Anderson et al., 2000; Clark, 2015)—evaluating and creating—advisors incorporate the knowledge they have gained about student characteristics and development theory as well as the relational skills they have acquired into their decisions of the most appropriate advising approaches to use for each student. Advisors can use the learning stages to document their development in the essential components of advising from their first training endeavors through foundational mastery.

Self-development

Experience and the Learning Taxonomy

Advisor progression from Year 1 expectations to foundational mastery requires time as engaged practitioners and students of advising, and Bloom's revised taxonomy (Anderson et al., 2000; Clark, 2015) offers advisors a tool to understand the characteristics of this learning progression. The process mirrors that of acquiring a second language in that the "ability to use and apply vocabulary and rules of grammar lags behind" the "acquisition of the language itself. . . . [One gains] fluency by becoming immersed in it—hearing it, speaking it, and living it" (Folsom et al., 2005, ¶1). An advisor's ability to apply knowledge and skills requires prior mastery at a lower level on the hierarchy: remembering or understanding. New advisors can expect that their ability to apply specific knowledge and skills will develop relatively slowly as they immerse themselves in advising, internalize key concepts, and gain greater understanding of advising practice and their students.

Student–advisor interactions provide a context for the knowledge and skills that advisors have learned through training, and advisors continually build on the understanding acquired through interactions as they move toward higher levels of learning. Students of their art, advisors return multiple times to the topics and skills learned early in the process. Like adults who reread books introduced in high school, advisors use life experiences to reinterpret and rediscover themes, recognize and make connections, and grasp the language in ways that bring new insights to concepts once only grasped in the simplest of ways. Through training, advisors learn the concept of advising as teaching and can articulate its components. Subsequently, they apply this knowledge in their direct work with students. When they revisit the concept after time spent with students, they find the intervening experiences give them a much more nuanced understanding of it than they had acquired in training. Advisors use the knowledge they have gained from their experience with students to closely analyze the approach, examine its various components, and evaluate areas that need improvement (e.g., integrating new relational components of advising) and set goals for moving higher up the hierarchy of Bloom's revised learning taxonomy (Anderson et al., 2000; Clark, 2015).

As students of their practice, advisors should reflect frequently and regularly about their advising experiences with students and evaluate these interactions with respect to the first-year expectations and foundational mastery found in the New Advisor Development Chart. Specifically, they use the Chart to identify the knowledge and skills they need to build, and they employ Bloom's revised taxonomy (Anderson et al., 2000; Clark, 2015) to set goals and chart their growth. Above all else, those seeking to become master advisors must intentionally engage in their own learning and development.

Advisors will not necessarily progress toward mastery at the same pace in all components (Folsom, 2007, p. 14). A learning hierarchy builds upon the preexisting knowledge and skills of new advisors as well as those they gain through training and their work with students. An advisor with a counseling degree and background will likely start at a relatively high level of Bloom's learning taxonomy (Anderson et al., 2000; Clark, 2015) regarding relational skills. A new faculty advisor returning to his or her undergraduate alma mater may start at a relatively high level for institutional knowledge or understanding the role of advising at the institution. Realistically, new advisors

> should think of advisor development as multiple journeys toward excellence and not try to accomplish every goal simultaneously. Instead he or she should determine an initial destination (set goals), map out a route, and take a trip. Upon reaching the first destination, the advisor should choose a new destination and begin planning the next trip. (Folsom, 2007, p. 15)

The New Advisor Development Chart and Learning Taxonomy

The comprehensive overview of the essential components of advising in the New Advisor Development Chart informs both new faculty and professional advisors working with all types of student at all varieties of institution; likewise, Bloom's revised taxonomy (Anderson et al., 2000; Clark, 2015) provides a guide for learning regardless of advisor or institutional type. However, advisors must adjust their learning and development goals to their unique advising responsibilities. For example, a faculty advisor responsible for advising senior nursing students may initially focus on external information, such as certification requirements and exams, to build a career-related knowledge base. A professional advisor with a caseload of first-year undecided students may focus on the GEP and developing strong listening and questioning techniques to help students evaluate their academic goals and assess their academic strengths.

Furthermore, although the Chart provides a comprehensive framework for types of advising knowledge and skills, it is not exhaustive; some advising positions may require skills or knowledge not represented in it. Therefore, new advisors may want to embellish the Chart by adding specific knowledge of students, majors, regulations, and other information that reflect their advising responsibilities and their institution.

New advisors need to identify the topics, strategies, and activities that will help them achieve the learning outcomes in the Chart. They will find the information, tools, and ideas in subsequent chapters of this book to aid them in this quest. The Chart is arranged according to the chapters in the book, and advisors are encouraged to review the Chart prior to reading each chapter. In addition to contributions focused on the conceptual, informational, and relational components of advising, the book includes chapters on the delivery of advising (one-to-one, group, and online) to assist new practitioners as they move from training to working with students. The final chapter outlines a framework for self-development during the first three years. When used in combination, the New Advisor Development Chart, Bloom's revised taxonomy (Anderson et al., 2000; Clark, 2015), and subsequent chapters in this book give new advisors the means by which to manage their training and development from the first day of their first year through their third year; however, to achieve and maintain excellence, advisors must commit to ongoing professional development via study, observation, and practice (The American Heritage College Dictionary, 1993) throughout the many years they work with students. Like other educators and healthcare professionals, advisors work in a continuously changing environment and must be aware of new curricular developments as well as emerging research on advising approaches and student development. *Beyond Foundations: Becoming a Master Academic Advisor* (Grites, Miller, & Givans Voller, forthcoming), the third book in the academic advisor core resource library, outlines strategies for advisors' long-term professional development.

Mastery Matters

Marc Lowenstein (2006) observed that

> an excellent advisor does for students' entire education what the excellent teacher does for a course: helps them order the pieces, put them together to make a coherent whole, so that the student experiences the curriculum not as a checklist of discrete, isolated pieces but instead as a unity, a composition of interrelated parts with multiple connections and relationships. (¶5)

Advisors immersed in the daunting task of achieving foundational mastery of advising practice can lose sight of the reason such achievement is important. Advisors must remember that mastery of the knowledge, skills, and essential components of advising is not an end unto itself; mastery gives advisors the tools to help students persist. Acquiring the ability to help students make meaning of their educational experiences and achieve their academic goals culminates in the truly exciting and rewarding result of foundational mastery: student success.

References

The American Heritage College Dictionary, 3rd ed. (1993). [Art]. Boston, MA: Houghton Mifflin.

Anderson, L. W., Krathwohl, D. R., Airasian, P. W., Cruikshank, K. A., Mayer, R. E., Pintrich, P. R., . . . & Wittrock, M. C. (2000). *A taxonomy for learning, teaching, and assessing: A revision of Bloom's taxonomy of educational objectives.* New York, NY: Pearson, Allyn & Bacon.

Clark, D. (2015). *Bloom's taxonomy of learning domains.* Retrieved from http://nwlink.com/~donclark/hrd/bloom.html

Council for the Advancement of Standards in Higher Education. (2013). *Academic advising programs.* Retrieved from http://standards.cas.edu/getpdf.cfm?PDF=E864D2C4-D655-8F74-2E647CDECD29B7D0

Folsom, P. (2007). Setting the stage: Growth through year one and beyond. In P. Folsom (Ed.), *The new advisor guidebook: Mastering the art of advising through the first year and beyond* (Monograph No. 16) (pp. 13–31). Manhattan, KS: National Academic Advising Association.

Folsom, P., Joslin, J., & Yoder, F. (2005). *From advisor training to advisor development: Creating a blueprint for first-year advisors.* Retrieved from http://www.nacada.ksu.edu /Resources/Clearinghouse/View-Articles/Training-Blueprint-for-New-Advisors.aspx

Folsom, P., & Scobie, N. A. (2010). The case for investing in advisor training and development. In J. Givans Voller, M. A. Miller, & S. L. Neste (Eds.), *Comprehensive advisor training and development: Practices that deliver* (2nd ed.) (Monograph No. 21) (pp. 15–18). Manhattan, KS: National Academic Advising Association.

Gordon, V. (2003, September). Advisor certification: A history and update. *Academic Advising Today*, 26(3). Retrieved from http://www.nacada.ksu.edu/Resources /Academic-Advising-Today/View-Articles/Advisor-Certification-A-History-and-Update.aspx#sthash.4y4BoXvn.dpuf

Grites, T. J., Miller, M. A., & Givans Voller, J. (Eds.). (forthcoming). *Beyond foundations: Becoming a master academic advisor*. Manhattan, KS: NACADA: The Global Community for Academic Advising.

Habley, W. R. (1995). Advisor training in the context of a teaching enhancement center. In R. E. Glennen & F. N. Vowell (Eds.), *Academic advising as a comprehensive campus process* (Monograph No. 2) (pp. 75–79). Manhattan, KS: National Academic Advising Association.

Habley, W. R. (2009, October 14). *Advising and retention. Retaining students in Iowa through academic advising* [webcast]. Retrieved March 31, 2010, from www.public.iastate.edu/ ~registrar/IowAAN/drweshabley.pdf

Higginson, L. (2000). A framework for training program content. In V. N. Gordon & W. R. Habley (Eds.), *Academic advising: A comprehensive handbook* (pp. 298–307). San Francisco, CA: Jossey-Bass.

Hunter, M. S., McCalla-Wriggins, B., & White, E. R. (Eds.). (2007). *Academic advising: New insights for teaching and learning in the first year* (Monograph No. 46). Columbia: University of South Carolina, National Resource Center for the First-Year Experience and Students in Transition.

Klepfer, K., & Hull, J. (2012). *High school rigor and good advice. Setting up students to succeed*. The Center for Public Education. Retrieved from http://www.centerforpubliceducation.org/Main-Menu/Staffingstudents/High-school-rigor-and-good-advice-Setting-up-students-to-succeed/High-school-rigor-and-good-advice-Setting-up-students-to-succeed-Full-Report.pdf

Kuh, G. D. (2008). Advising for student success. In V. N. Gordon, W. R. Habley, & T. J. Grites (Eds.), *Academic advising: A comprehensive handbook* (2nd ed.) (pp. 68–84). San Francisco, CA: Jossey-Bass.

Kuh, G. D., Kinzie, J., Buckley, J. A., Bridges, B. K., & Hayek, J. C. (2007). Piecing together the student success puzzle: Research, propositions, and recommendations. In K. Ward & L. E. Wolf-Wendel (Series Eds.), *ASHE Higher Education Report*, Vol. 32, No. 5. San Francisco, CA: Jossey-Bass. Retrieved from https://nces.ed.gov/npec/pdf/Kuh_Team _ExecSumm.pdf

Kuh, G. D., Kinzie, J., Schuh, J. H., & Whitt, E. (Eds.). (2005). *Student success in college: Creating conditions that matter*. San Francisco, CA: Jossey-Bass.

Lowenstein, M. (2006, September). The curriculum of academic advising: What we teach, how we teach, and what students learn. *Proceedings from the Fifth Annual Professional Development Conference for Academic Advising*. Retrieved from www.psu.edu/dus /mentor/proc01ml.htm

NACADA: The Global Community for Academic Advising (NACADA). (2006). *NACADA concept of academic advising*. Retrieved from http://www.nacada.ksu.edu/Resources /Clearinghouse/View-Articles/Concept-of-Academic-Advising-a598.aspx

NACADA. (2014). *Academic advisor competencies*. Retrieved from http://www.nacada.ksu. edu/Resources/Clearinghouse/View-Articles/Academic-advisor-competencies.aspx

Noel-Levitz. (2009). *Report: Academic advising highly important to students (Excerpted data from the* 2009 Noel-Levitz National Student Satisfaction and Priorities Report). Retrieved from https://www.noellevitz.com/documents/shared/Papers_and_Research /2009/AcademicAdvisingHighlyImportant09.pdf

Schreiner, L. A. (2009). *Linking student satisfaction and retention*. Retrieved from https://www.noellevitz.com/papers-research-higher-education/2009/student-satisfaction -retention

U.S. Office of Personnel Management. (n.d.). *Assessment and selection: Competencies*. Retrieved from http://www.opm.gov/policy-data-oversight/assessment-and-selection /competencies/

Webster's Encyclopedic Unabridged Dictionary of the English Language. (1989). [Art]. New York, NY: Gramercy.

NEW ADVISOR DEVELOPMENT CHART: BUILDING THE FOUNDATION

CONCEPTUAL COMPONENT: *GUIDEBOOK* PARTS ONE AND TWO

Foundations	Year One	Year Three and Beyond: Foundational Mastery
Pillars of Academic Advising The NACADA Concept of Academic Advising The NACADA Statement of Core Values of Academic Advising The CAS Standards for Academic Advising Programs (Council for the Advancement of Standards in Higher Education, 2013; NACADA: The Global Community for Academic Advising, 2005, 2006)	Reads, understands, explains, and summarizes CAS Standards and NACADA Statement of Core Values of Academic Advising. Explains and provides examples of ways individual, unit, and institutional advising practice relate to the Pillars of Advising.	Reviews Pillars of Advising annually, analyzing and evaluating individual, office, and campus-wide advising practices to set goals for individual improvement. Uses analysis to recommend changes in office or campus advising practice. Participates in revisions to office or campus advising practice.
Advisor roles and responsibilities	Outlines, explains, and summarizes evolution of advising and advisor roles and responsibilities. Identifies institutional and unit advising models. Understands institutional and office missions. Describes and provides examples of how individual advising responsibilities and practice relate to and support these missions, including student retention, persistence, and completion. Creates personal mission statement for individual advising practice. Locates or creates definition for academic advising.	Reviews institutional, office, and personal mission statements annually, analyzing and evaluating individual advising practice to set goals for growth and improvement. Revises personal advising practices to meet new goals. Uses analysis to recommend changes in current individual, office, or campus practices, roles, and responsibilities. Participates in revisions to office or campus-wide advising practices. Understands issues in higher education that affect academic advising and advisor roles and responsibilities.

Foundations	Year One	Year Three and Beyond: Foundational Mastery
	Explains and provides examples for ways individual, unit, and campus advising practices support student success. Describes, explains, and outlines office expectations and evaluation system. Receives (or requests) feedback throughout the first year. Becomes familiar with professional development opportunities offered by the institution, NACADA, and other advising organizations.	Uses feedback from evaluation tools to set goals for professional growth and improvement. Offers feedback and recommendations on evaluation process as appropriate. Actively involved in professional development activities both within the institution and NACADA.
Ethical issues in advising	Reads, describes, explains, and summarizes advisor ethical responsibilities to students, colleagues, and institution as outlined in NACADA Statement of Core Values of Academic Advising and institutional documents. Describes and summarizes best practices in delivery of advising per CAS Standards. Demonstrates appropriate use of ethical principles in practice. Recognizes potential ethical dilemmas in advising situations. Follows ethical and institutional guidelines for resolution, consulting supervisors before, during, and after advising interaction for assistance in analyzing, evaluating, and resolving situations.	Regularly reviews and analyzes advising practice for ethical delivery of advising per NACADA Statement of Core Values of Academic Advising and CAS standards. Advises unit on existing ethical practices and participates in creation of unit policies and procedures. Develops individual or unit guidelines for ethical advising. Resolves ethical issues independently, needing consultation only per institutional policies. Creates standard set of steps for analyzing and resolving ethical issues. Trains new advisors on ethical issues.
Theory	Reads and summarizes foundational student development theories. Places student behavior in simulations, advising notes, case studies, or advising observations into a theoretical construct.	Consistently applies a number of theories in advising. Analyzes and evaluates the most appropriate theories to use based on student's questions and behaviors. May use multiple theories in one

Foundations	Year One	Year Three and Beyond: Foundational Mastery
	Selects one theory to apply regularly in advising sessions to gain skill in the questioning techniques and advising strategies associated with it. Reads, understands, describes, and summarizes one career model. Recognizes career-related questions and applies career model in advising sessions, returning to the model as needed to clarify phases and questioning techniques as necessary.	session. Continues to add to repertoire of theories. May serve as model, mentor, or trainer for new advisors on the application of theory. Fully integrates advising theories and career model(s) and their respective strategies into advising practice. Analyzes student situation and selects most appropriate model or theory.
Philosophy of advising	Creates initial philosophy of advising using self-developed definition of advising and conceptual resources (pillars, mission statements, theories, and ethical principles).	Annually revisits, analyzes, and revises philosophy to reflect knowledge and skills gained through advising practice, study, and observation.

INFORMATIONAL COMPONENT: *GUIDEBOOK* PART THREE

Internal (Institutional) Knowledge (Higginson, 2000)	Year One	Year Three and Beyond: Foundational Mastery
Policies, regulations, procedures, and deadlines	Understands and knows where to find (most important, frequently used, most likely to affect student) institutional policies, regulations, procedures, and important deadlines. Uses resources and demonstrates understanding by using one's own words to describe, explain, or outline information to students. Consults or refers to appropriate person when unable to answer student questions.	Knows basic policies, regulations, and procedures. Understands details, nuances, and varied interpretations of basic institutional policies. Knows the basis on which exceptions and appeals are granted or denied as well as the process and deadlines for appeals. Knows or can find specialized (pertaining to specific student populations, majors, colleges, or programs) policies, procedures, and regulations. Uses knowledge of student and student situation for choosing advising approaches to explain and provide rationales and select appropriate policy or regulation to resolve problems.
Academic program requirements	Understands, knows, or can find the requirements for majors and programs for which one has advising responsibility. Outlines and explains requirements and course sequences to students (with resources visible). Seeks information from appropriate faculty and staff for exceptions or unusual course sequencing. Can identify and address career-related questions or refer students to appropriate career materials or campus resources.	Knows requirements for the majors and programs for which one has advising responsibility. Generates methods to outline and explains requirements clearly and succinctly. Develops plans to graduation, including exceptions to standard course sequencing. Combines multiple programs into long-term planning and suggests ways to enhance major through electives. Uses knowledge of student and student situation to select explanations and explain rationales. Integrates career-related information into discussion of program requirements. Evaluates best advising approach or career model to answer student questions based on analysis of student's need and development.

Internal (Institutional) Knowledge (Higginson, 2000)	Year One	Year Three and Beyond: Foundational Mastery
General education program (GEP)	Knows the categories of the GEP. Understands the rationale as written in institutional policy and articulates rationale in advising session. Uses resources to explain the GEP requirements and describe courses to students. Reviews student progress on the GEP using institutional monitoring tools.	Demonstrates detailed, experience-based knowledge of GEP and courses. Creates course descriptions for GEP classes and rationales for GEP. Recommends GEP courses that enhance individual student programs of study or serve as exploratory courses for majors and build foundations for postgraduate professional programs. Synthesizes knowledge of student (e.g., academic profile, major and cultural factors, student development theory) and adapts GEP rationale and course descriptions to meet specific student situations. Evaluates and selects best advising approach to facilitate GEP discussion with each student.
Courses	Locates course descriptions in majors and programs for which one has advising responsibility. Knows where to find course descriptions for GEP classes and elective courses. Knows or can find prerequisites (courses, placement scores, year in school) for courses. Uses resources to help students select classes and plan subsequent semesters.	Demonstrates detailed knowledge about courses in programs for which one has advising responsibility, including prerequisites, course expectations, ways in which course meshes with others in the program and fits into a balanced schedule, variations in course content and format among professors, and the student pool in specific courses (e.g., upper level, mixed graduate and undergraduate). Integrates knowledge about student (development, academic profiles, learning styles, academic goals) when discussing course selection and choosing advising approaches.

Internal (Institutional) Knowledge (Higginson, 2000)	Year One	Year Three and Beyond: Foundational Mastery
Institutional resources: counseling, office for students with disabilities, tutorial or learning labs, student organizations, health clinics, career centers, and services for specific student populations	Knows or can locate referral and contact information about campus resources. Identifies resources relevant to student situation or need. Uses vetted, institutionally issued information to explain specific services. Can locate office on a campus map for student.	Has gained detailed knowledge about university resources and services. Explains the policies and procedures of the resource units. Directs student to personal contacts in each office. Analyzes specific needs and developmental stage of each student in selecting resources and providing descriptions. Evaluates and selects appropriate advising approach to prepare student for referral and inspire student to follow through on referral.
External (Noninstitutional) Knowledge (Higginson, 2000)	Year One	Year Three and Beyond: Foundational Mastery
Academic issues related to professional certification and licensure requirements (e.g., for education, nursing, social work, CPA) as well as graduate and professional programs (e.g., pre-medicine, pre-law)	Knows or can find external academic programs, requirements, and admissions processes in areas for which one has advising responsibility. Uses resources to outline and explain requirements, course sequences, as well as admissions requirements and processes (with resources visible). Consults appropriate external institutions and licensing bodies regarding exceptions or unusual course sequencing.	Demonstrates detailed knowledge about academic requirements. Continually updates knowledge. Works in established relationships, including personal contacts, with external institutions, organizations, and accreditation bodies. Analyzes admission data to identify students who may seek certification or licensure. Also reviews successful admissions and program completions to help those in current caseload meet goals. Selects most appropriate advising approach to meet the needs of each student.

External (Noninstitutional) Knowledge (Higginson, 2000)	Year One	Year Three and Beyond: Foundational Mastery
Legal issues in advising	Understands the general legal principles that affect advising: privacy of student information (e.g., Family Educational Rights and Privacy Act [FERPA], U.S. Department of Education, 2014), advisors as agents of the institution, as well as equal rights and due process for students. Acquires understanding of institutional policies and procedures associated with legal principles. Can explain to advisees legal issues that affect the advisor–student relationship (e.g., FERPA, mandatory reporting). Recognizes situations in which legal issues may arise. Knows when to consult appropriate policies and legal counsel of the institution.	Demonstrates experience and nuanced understanding of advising-relevant legal principles and associated institutional policies and procedures. Anticipates situations in which legal issues may arise. May recommend advising policies and procedures to satisfy new or changing law. May serve as initial resource for new advisors on legal issues.
Community resources (e.g., volunteer opportunities, religious organizations, and health, mental health, and social services)	Knows or can find referral and contact information about community resources. Identifies resources relevant to student situation or need. Uses vetted information to explain specific services. Can locate office on a city or county map for student.	Knows and explains in detail services and operations of community resources. Introduces student to personal contacts in each office whenever possible. Analyzes specific need and developmental stage of each student in selecting resources and providing descriptions. Evaluates and chooses appropriate advising approach to prepare student for referral and inspire student to follow through on referral.

External (Noninstitutional) Knowledge (Higginson, 2000)	Year One	Year Three and Beyond: Foundational Mastery
World of work (careers)	Knows or can find information on world of work and specific careers. Uses resources to outline, describe, and explain necessary academic preparation for internships and careers (with resources visible). Consults with or refers students to appropriate office for detailed information about careers. Explains to students how academic skills relate to skills required for careers.	Prepares students for assessments, and may administer and interpret results. Understands workforce trends and changes. Explains to student the role of career advising services in preparing for workforce changes. May participate in or organize career recruiter visits on campus. May train or serve as mentor or resource for new advisors on career advising, assessment instruments, and world of work. Makes recommendations regarding career advising delivery to better meet the needs of students.
Knowledge of Student Needs	Year One	Year Three and Beyond: Foundational Mastery
Institutional level academic and demographic profiles and retention data	Reads, understands, and summarizes data regarding institution's student body: ACT/SAT scores (admission standards); average high-school class rank; the geographic types (rural or urban) of home communities; commuter or residential status (percentage); gender, ethnic, racial, and international makeup; and retention and completion statistics. Describes similarities and differences between students in advising caseload and the general institutional student body.	Demonstrates deep, experiential understanding of the demographics of the student body and understands their implications for advising. Uses understanding of student needs to offer ideas and make recommendations for changes in academic policies and advising services.

Knowledge of Student Needs	Year One	Year Three and Beyond: Foundational Mastery
Advising caseload, academic and demographic profiles, and retention data	Knows basic information about institutional population and individuals for which one has advising responsibility. For example, understands specific needs of first-year students such as transition to college, expectations for freshman year, and so forth, or knows that seniors need career referrals, graduate school applications, and degree applications. Acquires knowledge from reading vetted data resources.	Demonstrates deep, experiential understanding about the population for which one has advising responsibility. Analyzes experience and incorporates data with operational knowledge about population into advising: Integrates and applies knowledge about institution as appropriate for specific student and student populations (e.g., understands that not all undeclared majors are developmentally identical). Selects and integrates appropriate advising approaches for specific student and student populations.
Needs of special populations: students of color, at risk, on probation, in honors curricula or other special academic programs; athletes; students with disabilities; those identifying as LGBTQ; and military veterans	Understands basic unique needs of special student populations through research with vetted data and readings. Locates referral and contact information about resources that support special student populations. Describes services to students referred to the resources.	Demonstrates deep, experiential knowledge about the needs of special student populations. Uses analysis of advising special populations and incorporates data into advising. Integrates and applies knowledge about institution as appropriate for specific student and student populations (e.g., understands that not all military veterans with college adjustment issues are experiencing posttraumatic stress). Fully integrates cultural competency in advising and selects and integrates appropriate advising approaches for specific student and student populations.

Self-knowledge	Year One	Year Three and Beyond: Foundational Mastery
Awareness of one's own attitudes, beliefs, and values	Understands and describes facets of cultural competency. Understands role of self-knowledge in cultural competency and describes its importance for advising. Understands and delineates own diversity with respect to unit and institution. Employs a framework to develop introductory awareness of attitudes, beliefs, and values with respect to institution and students one advises.	Reflects on experiences with diverse populations, and applies knowledge-based clarity about these populations and an increased level of self-awareness to practice. Automatically integrates self-awareness checks into advising sessions, adapting approaches to specific needs of each student.
Advising Tools and Resources: Managing Information	**Year One**	**Year Three and Beyond: Foundational Mastery**
General information on programs, majors, and policies and procedures: catalog and other institutional, collegiate, or departmental publications, handouts, and web sites	Demonstrates familiarity with printed and electronic resources relevant to one's position for use with students; that is, locates information quickly and bookmarks frequently used materials.	Demonstrates in-depth knowledge about printed and electronic resources. Integrates tools seamlessly into practice and teaches students how to use them.

Advising Tools and Resources: Managing Information	Year One	Year Three and Beyond: Foundational Mastery
Advising technology: e-mail, student information systems, degree audits, social media, and organizational systems	Uses basic functions in advising technology, such as electronic transactions required to obtain necessary information about students (grades, ACT/SAT scores, current registration) and university resources, conduct student conferences, maintain student caseload files, manage communication with students, make referrals, and exchange information with colleagues.	Demonstrates mastery in basic functions of advising technology. Uses technology efficiently in advising conferences and to manage student caseloads and traffic (e.g., sends specific student populations targeted e-mail). Uses advanced aspects of systems effectively (e.g., moves easily among multiple technologies within advising session and organizes e-mail for efficient access). Uses advanced aspects of communication management systems to maximize advising contacts and appointments.
Advising tools: checklists, handouts, and degree audits	Locates and distributes paper or electronic handouts to students as appropriate. Uses standard handouts (e.g., checklists for specific types of student appointments) as necessary in advising situations.	Efficiently targets use of resources to individual students. Fully integrates use of materials in conferences. Develops informational handouts as appropriate for new majors, programs, and special student populations.
Organizational system	Develops initial, rudimentary system for organizing information in a way that allows for retrieving information efficiently when working with students via phone, by e-mail, or in a face-to-face appointment.	Establishes well-developed organizational systems to manage both print and electronic information. Accesses information quickly when working with students via phone, by e-mail, or face-to-face.

RELATIONAL COMPONENT: *GUIDEBOOK* PART FOUR

Communication Skills	Year One	Year Three and Beyond: Foundational Mastery
Interviewing, communication, and referral skills: questioning techniques and active listening	Understands and describes components of effective communication. Engages in active listening. Creates a repertoire of questions that elicit solid information from students. Builds set of communications skills that help students think critically, resolve problems, and make decisions. Recognizes student questions and situations beyond scope of expertise. Uses active listening, clarifying questions, and statements with student to ascertain the need for referral. Consults with supervisor as necessary. Recognizes career-related questions from students. Uses established frameworks to interview students.	Demonstrates well-developed questioning, interviewing, and listening skills that elicit specific, germane information from students. Readily grasps nuanced student reactions and responses (verbal and nonverbal) and responds to them appropriately and effectively. Fully integrates components of cultural competency and uses multiple advising approaches when advising. Selects communication techniques, approaches, and strategies most appropriate to determine the need for referrals and to help each student think critically, solve problems, and make decisions. Integrates career and advising interview techniques seamlessly into advising sessions, adapting them to each student and student situation.
Career decision-making strategies	Recognizes that students may struggle with decision making. Uses career-model questioning strategies to help students make sound academic and career decisions.	Applies various decision-making strategies as appropriate to individual student needs and situations. Seamlessly integrates decision-making discussions, approaches, and strategies into student conferences and adapts them to the needs of each student. Applies strategies to decision making unrelated to careers.

Advising Approaches	Year One	Year Three and Beyond: Foundational Mastery
Approaches and strategies for working effectively with students	Reads, understands, and describes a variety of advising approaches. Distinguishes among approaches in practice. May employ multiple approaches but focuses on mastering one approach, incorporating strategies and questioning techniques into advising sessions. Uses approach to model problem solving and help students address problems.	Fully integrates multiple approaches into advising repertoire and adeptly assesses the best approach to use with specific students or in specific situations. Uses multiple approaches, combining them in one session if necessary, to help students address problems.

DELIVERING ADVISING: *GUIDEBOOK* PART FIVE

Advising Delivery	Year One	Year Three and Beyond: Foundational Mastery
One-to-one advising sessions	Understands, lists, and describes the components of an advising session and begins to integrate components into practice. Ensures student questions are addressed while covering topics and information that student needs. Typically stays within time parameters. Establishes expectations for students to meet (e.g., making and keeping appointments).	Fully integrates relational and informational components, advising approaches, and skills in sessions. Adapts information appropriately for individual students according to their developmental stage, needs, concerns, and situations. Facilitates guidance of the conference conversationally (i.e., appointment does not feel like a question-and-answer session). Integrates teaching and other advising approaches seamlessly into sessions. Combines one-to-one advising with other delivery methods to effectively meet student needs. Regularly analyzes and evaluates effectiveness of advising sessions.
Group advising sessions	Understands, lists, and describes characteristics, benefits, and challenges of group advising. Uses established unit or departmental structures and learning outcomes suitable for groups. Ideally co-conducts groups while developing presentation and group facilitation skills.	Regularly analyzes and evaluates advising program to identify advising activities best delivered through group advising. Creates learning outcomes for group sessions. Determines structure and content of groups. Evaluates effectiveness of groups for achieving learning outcomes. May train or facilitate groups with new advisors. Combines group advising with other delivery methods to effectively meet student needs.

Advising Delivery	Year One	Year Three and Beyond: Foundational Mastery
Online advising sessions	Understands, lists, and describes characteristics, benefits, and challenges of advising students online. Uses established criteria to identify activities and functions most suitable for online advising. Uses established unit or departmental guidelines for online advising, technology choices (e.g., e-mail), and communication and caseload management.	Regularly analyzes and evaluates advising delivery to identify advising activities that could be effectively delivered online. Evaluates and selects most appropriate technology for delivery. Develops necessary communication and caseload management organization to support advising. Creates learning outcomes for online sessions. Evaluates effectiveness of online advising for achieving learning outcomes. May train new advisors. Combines online advising, whenever possible, with other delivery methods to effectively meet student needs.
Documentation	Meets minimal unit documentation standards (e.g., decisions, actions taken, referrals) and adheres to institutional legal guidelines for advising notes. Develops enhancements to documentation (e.g., standard checklist for referrals)	Has well-developed conference-documentation skills that exceed minimum office expectations (e.g., notes that give a more robust description of students as well as their needs and situations).

Advising Delivery	Year One	Year Three and Beyond: Foundational Mastery
Effective referrals	Matches student with appropriate referral and provides standard information (i.e., gained via vetted printed resources and web sites). Seeks information and asks for help to ensure effective match of student and referral.	Demonstrates advanced referral skills. Fully integrates detailed knowledge of resources and working knowledge of students to match services quickly and accurately to specific student needs. Prepares student for referral. Selects appropriate advising approach to help ensure student follows up on referral.
Difficult students and student situations	Recognizes when outside expertise is needed to deal with a difficult interpersonal interaction or an unusual or exceptional student situation. Seeks such assistance (e.g., veteran advisor, supervisor) using established protocols. Recognizes emergency situations (e.g., student is dangerous to self or others). Seeks assistance using established protocols.	Adeptly handles difficult student situations, but consults other advisors, administrators, and staff as appropriate using established protocols. Follows established protocols for emergency situations. May participate in development of protocols.

References

Council for the Advancement of Standards in Higher Education (CAS). (2013). *Academic advising programs*. Retrieved from http://standards.cas.edu/getpdf.cfm?PDF=E864D2C4-D655-8F74-2E647CDECD29B7D0

Higginson, L. C. (2000). A framework for training program content. In V. N. Gordon & W. R. Habley (Eds.), *Academic advising: A comprehensive handbook* (1st ed.) (pp. 298–307). San Francisco, CA: Jossey-Bass.

NACADA: The Global Community for Academic Advising (NACADA). (2005). *Statement of core values of academic advising*. Retrieved from http://www.nacada.ksu.edu/Resources/Clearinghouse/View-Articles/Core-values-of-academic-advising.aspx

NACADA. (2006). *Concept of academic advising.* Retrieved from
http://www.nacada.ksu.edu/Resources/Clearinghouse/View-Articles/Concept-of-
Academic-Advising-a598.aspx

U.S. Department of Education. (2014). *Family Rights and Privacy Act (FERPA).* Retrieved
from http://www2.ed.gov/policy/gen/guid/fpco/ferpa/index.html

PART TWO

FOUNDATIONS: THE CONCEPTUAL COMPONENT

By understanding the history and concept of advising, those new to the field lay the foundation for excellent practice. Discussions of theories adapted to advising, including those of student development and from other fields, the history of the field as it evolves into a profession, and the ethics that guide practice compose this section on the conceptual component of advising. This primer introduces topics that provide a broad understanding of advising, grounding it within a larger framework that has shaped higher education. Through these concepts readers gain an appreciation for advising as an outgrowth of a larger and deeper knowledge base.

2

ACADEMIC ADVISING WITHIN THE ACADEMY

HISTORY, MISSION, AND ROLE

Patrick Cate and Marsha A. Miller

A Short History of Academic Advising

Four distinct chronological eras characterize academic advising history. In the first period (1636–1870), academic advising did not occupy a separate role within American higher education (Kuhn, 2008, p. 3). Students during this time had few curricular choices; "The mind was viewed as a tool to be sharpened, and (required) subjects like Latin, Greek, and mathematics were the favored sharpening stones" (Kuhn, p. 4). As they needed answers, students consulted with their professors or looked to the books used in their studies.

The century between 1870 and 1971 made up the second era of academic advising. During this time many colleges and universities added vocational programs (e.g., agriculture and teaching) to undergraduate curricula. To supplement the new career-related courses of study colleges included electives to assure that vocational students became well-rounded contributors to society. In response to curricular offerings growing more complex, Daniel Coit Gilman, President of The Johns Hopkins University, coined the term *adviser* to refer to anyone (usually a faculty member) who prescribed advice to students concerning academic, social, or personal matters (Kuhn, 2008, p. 5). During this time, most prescribed advice focused on aiding students in making curricular choices.

The third era of academic advising (1972–2002) dawned with the publication of two seminal articles that informed the advising field: Burns Crookston's "A Developmental View of Academic Advising as Teaching" and Terry O'Banion's "An Academic Advising Model." Crookston (1972/1994/2009) identified the *developmental advising* era when he said that "advising is concerned not only with a specific personal or vocational decision but also with facilitating the student's rational process, environmental and interpersonal interactions, behavioral awareness, and problem-solving, decision-making and evaluation skills" (2009, p. 78). According to Crookston and his like-minded contemporary, O'Banion (1972/1994/2009), academic advisors should not simply prescribe students with a course of action; rather, they should discern the root cause of student concerns and help them identify and develop the skills necessary to address challenges.

In light of this new thinking about advising, practitioners became more proactive (Glennen, 1975), reaching out to students early and often in the hope of catching potential problems before they caused students to leave the institution. Initiatives focused on student retention, especially from the freshman to sophomore year. During this historical period, Wes Habley (1987) delineated three components of advising used to help students succeed: informational (what advisors must know), relational (what advisors must do), and conceptual (what advisors must understand).

In addition, many campus administrators recognized that the time and skill sets needed to help students tackle an ever-widening range of academic, environmental, and interpersonal issues may not be addressed in the training received by faculty members schooled in an academic discipline. As a result, they hired more full-time professional advisors, some (especially in 2-year colleges) with training in counseling to deliver academic advising (King, 2002). The percentages of campuses utilizing at least some professional staff advisors increased from 2% in 1979 (Carstensen & Silberhorn, 1979) to 72% in 1997 (Habley & Morales, 1998).

In 2003, initial steps taken toward making academic advising a recognized profession ushered in the fourth and current era of academic advising. The National Academic Advising Association Past President Virginia Gordon explained that the newly formed NACADA Certification Task Force was "assigned the task of recommending the specific categories of advising competencies that all effective advisors should be able to demonstrate" (Gordon, 2003, ¶2). Subsequently, the NACADA Certification Task Force (2003) articulated five academic advisor competency areas:

o foundations knowledge (conceptual),

o knowledge of college student characteristics (informational),

o career advising knowledge and skills (informational),

o communication and interpersonal skills (relational), and

o knowledge of application of advising at local institutions (informational).

The need to create these competencies inspired Kansas State University to offer the graduate certificate in academic advising and the first master's degree program for advising. The influence of the competencies first articulated by Habley (1987) and codified by NACADA: The Global Community for Academic Advising (NACADA) are featured in the New Advisor Development Chart in chapter 1.

Also in 2003, Charlie Nutt, then NACADA Associate Director, popularized the phrase *advising is teaching* (chapter 12) first coined in the developmental advising movement of the 1970s (Crookston, 1972/1994/2009). In 2005, then NACADA President Jo Anne Huber named a task force to craft a concept of academic advising; it subsequently defined academic advising as an activity "based in the teaching and learning mission of higher education" with three distinct and intentional parts: "a curriculum (what advising deals with), pedagogy (how advising does what it does), and student learning outcomes (the result of academic advising)" (NACADA: The Global Community for Academic Advising [NACADA], 2006, ¶7). The curriculum section of the concept outlines a variety of issues leaders should consider when crafting a campus definition for academic advising.

Defining Academic Advising

The definitions of academic advising equal the numbers of postsecondary institutions. Each campus reflects unique characteristics that require advisors to assume specific job responsibilities (Carlstrom & Miller, 2013c, 2013d) to meet the needs of students. The intended purposes, resources, and program outcomes of advising influence the definition on a particular campus; that is, features such as online versus residential delivery, Carnegie classification (Carnegie Classification of Institutions of Higher Education, n.d.), non- or for-profit status, and credentials offered (e.g., vocational certificate or associate's, bachelor's, or postbaccalaureate degrees) factor into the definition.

The choice of advising personnel strongly influences a campus-specific definition of academic advising. Casey Self (2013) expounded on the shift begun during the third era of advising as institutions moved away from a faculty-only model to embrace a shared system of advising that relies on an all-hands-on-deck approach to adjust to tightened budgets and increased focus on retention and graduation rates (¶3). The purposeful sharing of advising duties between personnel with divergent backgrounds meant that practitioners drew from a plethora of theories to create a variety of approaches for advising students.

Advising, which takes many forms, can look very different from campus to campus and even from department to department on a single campus. Although historically pictured as a face-to-face activity, advising is also undertaken online or in group settings that range from credit-bearing traditional classroom courses to required noncredit workshops. Advising information can be delivered passively through publications (e.g., flyers, bulletins, posters) or actively through discussion boards within learning management systems accessed asynchronously (e.g., Blackboard). Changes in student populations and available technologies allow for the facilitation of advising through many venues; therefore, a definition of advising may not be connected to a mode of delivery, although it certainly can be influenced by it.

Over the years many have tried to craft a uniform definition for academic advising; samples of their attempts are listed in the history and philosophy index in the NACADA Clearinghouse of Academic Advising Resources. A review of these sample definitions show that although the tasks accomplished within advising vary, the core components of advising remain universal (Habley, 1987). Three documents based on these components serve as pillars for the foundation of advising.

The Pillars of Academic Advising

Three documents serve as NACADA's Pillars of Academic Advising:

o The NACADA Concept of Academic Advising (NACADA, 2006),

o The NACADA Statement of Core Values of Academic Advising (NACADA, 2005), and

o The Council for the Advancement of Standards in Higher Education (CAS) for Academic Advising Programs (AAPs) (CAS, 2013).

The NACADA Concept of Academic Advising (NACADA, 2006) lays out the three intentional parts of advising: the advising curriculum, ways advisors teach that curriculum (pedagogy), and the knowledge students gain from the curriculum (learning outcomes). These elements serve as discussion points for campus leaders defining academic advising in their situation.

The NACADA Statement of Core Values of Academic Advising (NACADA, 2005) undergird the ethical foundation of advising:

> The Statement of Core Values provides a framework to guide professional practice and reminds advisors of their responsibilities to students, colleagues, institutions, society, and themselves. Those charged with advising responsibilities are expected to reflect the values of the advising profession in their daily interactions at their institutions. (¶4)

The oldest pillar, CAS AAPs, first appeared in 1986. Today, campus administrators use CAS Standards to leverage for needed resources and to assess whether the institution's academic advising program meets vetted standards within the field (CAS, 2012, p. 9). The CAS mission states that an AAP exists "to assist students as they define, plan, and achieve their educational goals. The AAP must advocate for student success and persistence" (¶1). In view of the CAS Standards, academic advisors must promote policies and procedures that encourage student success as defined at the departmental, collegiate, and institutional levels. Advisors must be involved in the planning and implementation stages as interpersonal and educational advocates for student persistence and success. Practitioners and scholars (Frost, 2000) have dichotomized this proactive involvement into developmental (third era) versus prescriptive (second era) advising. In the fourth academic advising era, practitioners take responsibility for advising as a functional and integral part of student learning.

Each campus definition for academic advising gets at the heart of institutional needs and desires for advising. Therefore, advisors must adhere to both the institutional definition of and the campus mission for academic advising.

Mission and Vision Statements

Although CAS (2013) provides a global mission for advising, the AAP Standards specifically state that "academic advising programs must develop, record, disseminate, implement, and regularly review their [own] missions" (¶2). Susan Campbell (2008) explained that an academic advising mission statement not only articulates the values and purpose of the program but sets the immediate and future direction of it (p. 235).

Each advising program mission statement must be drawn from the institutional mission. Therefore, if an institutional mission includes "the intellectual and cultural . . . development of our . . . citizens" (University of Louisville Board of Trustees, 2006, ¶1), then the mission for the undergraduate advising program might be "an on-going, intentional, education partnership dedicated to student success . . . that guides students to discover and pursue life goals, . . . advances students' intellectual and cultural development" (University of Louisville Undergraduate Advising, n.d., ¶1).

Advising is an intentional activity; therefore, a well-crafted advising mission statement helps advisors discern the level to which their efforts contribute to student and institutional success. Thus planners must create it with the advisor's daily practice in mind. Consequently, they must describe the target population (e.g., undergraduates), the advising program purpose (e.g., "advance students' intellectual and cultural development" (University of Louisville Undergraduate Advising, n.d., ¶1), and the desired outcomes (e.g., student graduation).

Vision statements help advisors understand the goal of the advising program. Campbell (2008) suggested that vision statements "result from reflection on the organization and its present and future" (p. 234). While the mission statement provides useful information, a vision statement often serves to inspire by describing the ideal situation: "The UNLV [University of Nevada, Las Vegas] Academic Success Center advising unit strives to be recognized nationally for its student success model of academic advising. The unit will employ academic and developmental advising best practices that positively impact the lives of students at the institution" (University of Nevada, Las Vegas, 2014, ¶4). A vision statement helps advisors understand the caliber of advising needed to achieve the programmatic goal.

As with the mission and vision statements, the creation of a campus definition of advising should involve everyone affected by practice (including students). The resulting description should remain readily available and be featured prominently in advising offices, web sites, syllabi, and any advising spaces. All academic advisors must familiarize themselves with the institutional definition of advising as well as those mission and vision statements that relate specifically to practice. New advisors, in particular, may need to ask supervisors or other advisors where these documents can be accessed. All advisors should consider ways their practice supports the mission of their institution and program.

Roles and Responsibilities of Advisors

Definitions of academic advising can differ greatly depending upon institution type, size, and locale. Thus the roles academic advisors play on campuses also vary greatly. Of 21 options listed on the *2011 National Survey of Academic Advising* (Carlstrom

& Miller, 2013c, 2013d), the following were among the top-reported responsibilities of advisors:

- ○ Course scheduling
- ○ Course registration
- ○ Help students develop a plan of study
- ○ Assist with new student orientation
- ○ Serve on committees
- ○ Help students select a college major

Survey respondents indicated that advisors at their institutions undertake responsibilities ranging from assisting with exploring career interests (more than 80% of respondents from 4-year institutions) to coordination of study abroad programs (5% on 2-year and 22% on 4-year campuses) (Carlstrom & Miller, 2013c, 2013d).

Jo Anne Huber and Marsha A. Miller (2013) pointed out that the responsibilities advisors assume often are determined by the definition, mission, and reporting channels for academic advising (¶12). The institutional reporting line used by advisors (e.g., academic affairs, student affairs, or enrollment management) sometimes colors the way others on campus view the role of advising.

Academic Advising Reporting Channels

The results of the *2011 National Survey of Academic Advising* (Carlstrom & Miller, 2013b) showed that 57% of respondents report to academic affairs and 21% report to student affairs. Other reporting lines include academic and student affairs jointly (11%), enrollment management (7%), and the registrar (2%). Nancy King (2013) explained that advisors who report through academic affairs are more likely to be "directly linked with the academic curriculum and practices within academic affairs. For example, a growing number of institutions are creating an advising syllabus and identifying learning outcomes for advising" (¶2).

Tonya McKenna Trabant (2006) described an advising syllabus as "a tool which allows individual advisors or offices to outline the advising relationship and experience for their advisees" (¶2). Additionally, advising syllabi often include the institution's definition of advising, the advising program mission and vision, important dates, and the advisor's contact information. New advisors should ask to see samples of advising syllabi used on campus and featured on The NACADA Clearinghouse of Academic Advising Resources.

Because public focus and funding are tied to retention and graduation rates, institutions increasingly demonstrate advising as an important initiative (Doubleday, 2013). As a result, advising outcomes will be concomitantly linked to various areas of the academy. For example, some institutional leaders have turned to enrollment management as a purposeful fusion of "recruitment, admissions, financial aid, orientation, career planning, retention, and other areas" (Hossler & Bean, 1990, cover). As a result of fourth-era trends and accountability standards, campus stakeholders are studying academic advising organization and delivery models (Complete College America, 2013; Klepfer & Hull, 2012).

Organizational Structures for Academic Advising

King (2013) observed that "advising reporting lines may also be influenced by the type of advising organizational structure employed" (¶5). Once they understand ways an advisor helps them reach their learning goals, students must know how to contact and personally connect with an advisor, which can vary by department, college, and institution.

Marsha A. Miller (2013, ¶4) suggested four questions to address when discussing academic organizational models:

o Who is advised?

o Who advises?

o Where is advising done?

o How are the advising responsibilities divided?

Kenneth E. Barron and Darcey N. Powell (2014) added a fifth question: When does advising occur? (p. 16).

Few advisors work with all students enrolled at an institution. Typically students are grouped for advising purposes. Some institutions organize them by major, others by year in college (e.g., first-year students). Those with multiple advising delivery systems may use one set of rules to assign students taking classes on campus and apply a different rubric to assign distance learners to advisors.

Furthermore, Celeste Pardee (2004) categorized advising delivery systems as either centralized or decentralized (¶4). As the name suggests, in centralized models advisors' offices are located in one physical space (e.g., an advising center). In decentralized paradigms, offices are spread throughout campus. Online advising may complicate the system of advising delivery. However, regardless of the type of personnel or space for advising, student accessibility to an academic advisor is an important logistical issue for advising administrators and planners.

Self (2013) noted that "results from the *2011 NACADA National Survey of Academic Advising* confirm that full-time professional and faculty advisors continue to be the most frequently utilized advising personnel" with over one half of respondents indicating their utilization (¶2) (see also, Carlstrom & Miller, 2013a). Miller (2013) pointed out that, in addition to professional and faculty advisors, counselors, peers, graduate students, and administrators or staff may offer some form of advising, with 10% of institutions reportedly utilizing peer advisors (¶7) (Carlstrom & Miller, 2013a). Regardless of personnel employed to advise, the nature of the assigned duties has changed since 2003 such that no advisor can know all aspects of a student, an institution, or a community.

Furthermore, advisors demonstrate unique skill sets. In general, faculty members know their discipline, the courses within it, and job prospects in the field. Professional advisors, some of whom have been schooled in student development theory, work with the myriad of institutional procedural issues on a daily basis. However, students often find peer advisors more approachable and "able to relate more directly to the experiences of the students with whom they work" (Johnson & Martin Jenkins, 2005, p. 59). As result of these specific and important competencies, one should not be surprised that the *2011 NACADA National Survey of Academic Advising* shows that almost 60% of respondents indicated that their institutions assign advising responsibilities to personnel who hold multiple roles on campus (Carlstrom & Miller, 2013a).

No matter the advising organization or reporting lines, advisors must connect throughout the institution to effectively "teach students how to make the most of their college experience" (Miller, 2013, ¶1). Regardless of personal or professional perspective, one finds advising at the intersection of academic and student affairs (Miller & Alberts, 1994), and advisors need to send students down the proper path to the institutional personnel who can best help them meet their educational objectives.

The Role of Academic Advising in Student Success

For many years, advisors have shared anecdotal evidence demonstrating the link between quality academic advising to student retention, persistence, and completion (i.e., student success). They intuitively know that students who work with them will more likely complete their educational programs. However, the claims of the connection between academic advising and student success remained empirically unsupported until 2012.

In a landmark study sponsored by the Center for Public Education (National Association of School Boards), Kasey Klepfer and Jim Hull (2012) found that

> for both four-year and two-year students, talking to an academic advisor in college either "sometimes" or "often" significantly improved their chances to persist. Students in two-year institutions increased their chances of staying on track by as much as 53 percent by meeting frequently with their academic advisor. (¶8)

In addition, academic advising emerged as one of only three predictors of academic success (along with the number of completed Advanced Placement courses and students' mathematics background). Klepfer and Hull's study brought increased attention to academic advising, the only predictor under institutional control, both inside and outside the academy.

The contextual statement preceding the CAS Standards (CAS, 2013) for AAPs points to "the increasing public attention placed on college completion means increased visibility for academic advising" (¶2). Reports such as *Guided Pathways to Success* (Complete College America, 2013) claimed that academic advising is vital to degree completion. As institutions seek to increase and diversify enrollments, academic advisors help ensure appropriate matriculation and transfer, which lead to degree completion. The evolving manner by which students complete college degrees, including the blending of courses offered on a variety of campuses and online, places new challenges on academic advisors, who must possess the tools needed to meet the demands of students in virtual space and across multiple institutions (CAS, 2013, ¶8). As academic advising moves to the forefront of college completion discussions, recognition of advisor contributions makes acknowledgment of advising as a profession a timely topic.

Promoting the Professional Status of Academic Advising

With the increased focus on academic advising within the academy, the second decade of the fourth advising era has been defined by individuals' concerted efforts to demonstrate academic advising as a recognized profession. Leigh Shaffer, Jacqueline Zalewski, and John Leveille (2010) compared the field of academic advising to the five standards sociologists use for discerning a field as a profession. These researchers (who also have served as faculty advisors) found that although advising has met four of the sociology-defined standards, it lacked the fifth: the research body necessary to provide a curriculum of study for graduate degrees. Marsha A. Miller (2011) noted that such a curriculum must be established and used in the study of academic advising before any certification credential can be developed, tested, and issued (¶10).

Since 2010 many scholar-practitioners have contributed to the development of the broad, deep, and vibrant literature base needed for academic advising to ascend as a profession in higher education. Contributors to *Scholarly Inquiry in Academic Advising* (Hagen, Kuhn, & Padak, 2010) detailed the steps needed to conduct research within the field. NACADA grants fund research of and about advising, and the *NACADA Journal* "advance(s) scholarly discourse about the research, theory, and practice of academic advising in higher education" (Kuhn & Padak, 2008, p. 2). *Academic Advising Approaches: Strategies That Teach Students to Make the Most of College* (Drake, Jordan, & Miller, 2013) delineated several strategies used to address the relational component and competency.

The time needed to develop an extensive literature base depends upon the number and dedication of the scholar-practitioners (Freitag, 2011) who step forward to contribute. Practicing academic advisors must conduct research surrounding practice and theory, and then they must connect that research to establish a professional curriculum to study (Shaffer et al., 2010):

> The biggest need for the future of an emerging field is the establishment of curriculum content for training. . . . Academic advisors need to acquire the type of education that will legitimatize their claim to recognition of advising as a profession . . . by other constituencies within the academy and by stakeholders outside the university itself. (p. 75)

The authors of this book offer starting blocks for new advisors to get engaged in building their own practice and making contributions to the field. We challenge readers to reflect on the material presented in the chapters and implement the Aiming for Excellence activities that follow each chapter. See also the Glossary of Terms (chapter 4).

References

Barron, K. E., & Powell, D. N. (2014). Options on how to organize and structure advising. In R. L. Miller & J. G. Irons (Eds.), *Academic advising: A handbook for advisors and students: Volume 1 Models, students, topics, and issues.* Retrieved from http://www.teachpsych.org/Resources/Documents/ebooks/advising2014Vol1.pdf

Campbell, S. M. (2008). Vision, mission, goals, and program objectives for academic advising programs. In V. N. Gordon & W. R. Habley (Eds.), *Academic advising: A comprehensive handbook* (2nd ed.) (pp. 229–241). San Francisco, CA: Jossey-Bass.

Carlstrom, A. H., & Miller, M. A. (2013a). *Advising personnel* [table 4.1]. In A. H. Carlstrom & M. A. Miller (Eds.), *2011 NACADA national survey of academic advising* (Monograph No. 25). Retrieved from http://www.nacada.ksu.edu/Portals/0/Clearing house/M25/M25%20Chapter%204%20Tables%20with%20Intro%204-7-15.pdf

Carlstrom, A. H., & Miller, M. A. (2013b). *Advisor reporting lines* [table 14.1]. In A. H. Carlstrom & M. A. Miller (Eds.), *2011 NACADA national survey of academic advising* (Monograph No. 25). Retrieved from http://www.nacada.ksu.edu/Portals/0/Clearing house/documents/Chapter%2014%20-%20Advisor%20Reporting%20-%20FINAL.pdf

Carlstrom, A. H., & Miller, M. A. (2013c). *Job responsibilities for 2-year institutions* [table 10.1]. In A. H. Carlstrom & M. A. Miller (Eds.), *2011 NACADA national survey of academic advising* (Monograph No. 25). Retrieved from http://www.nacada.ksu.edu/Portals/0/Clearinghouse/documents/Chapter%2010%20-%20Job%20Responsibilities%202yr%20-%20FINAL.pdf

Carlstrom, A. H., & Miller, M. A. (2013d). *Job responsibilities for 4-year institutions* [table 11.1]. In A. H. Carlstrom & M. A. Miller (Eds.), *2011 NACADA national survey of academic advising* (Monograph No. 25). Retrieved from http://www.nacada.ksu.edu/Portals/0/Clearinghouse/documents/Chapter%2011%20-%20Job%20Responsibilities%204yr%20-FINAL.pdf

Carlstrom, A. H., & Miller, M. A. (Eds.). (2013e). *2011 NACADA national survey of academic advising* (Monograph No. 25). Retrieved from http://www.nacada.ksu.edu/Resources/Clearinghouse/View-Articles/2011-NACADA-National-Survey.aspx

Carnegie Classification of Institutions of Higher Education. (n.d.). *Carnegie classification of institutions of higher education.* Retrieved from http://carnegieclassifications.iu.edu/

Carstensen, D. J., & Silberhorn, C. (1979). *A national survey of academic advising: A final report.* Iowa City, IA: American College Testing.

CAS. (2013). *CAS standards for academic advising programs.* Retrieved from http://standards.cas.edu/getpdf.cfm?PDF=E864D2C4-D655-8F74-2E647CDECD29B7D0

Complete College America. (2013). *Guided pathways to success: Boosting college completion.* Retrieved from http://cl.s4.exct.net/?qs=5070f0ff3e10c3924002ca86e228acbd43cb18 c55cf53cadcf2211cd38d4367f

Council for the Advancement of Standards in Higher Education (CAS). (2012). *CAS professional standards for higher education* (8th ed.). Washington, DC: Author.

Crookston, B. B. (2009). A developmental view of academic advising as teaching. *NACADA Journal, 29*(1), 78–82. (Reprinted from *Journal of College Student Personnel, 13,* 1972, pp. 12–17; *NACADA Journal, 14*[2], 1994, pp. 5–9)

Doubleday, J. (2013, December 2). With an eye toward retention, colleges amp up advising. *The Chronicle of Higher Education.* Retrieved from http://chronicle.com/article/Under-Pressure-to-Hit-Learning/143303/

Drake, J., Jordan, P., & Miller, M. A. (Eds.). (2013). *Academic advising approaches: Strategies that teach students to make the most of college.* San Francisco, CA: Jossey-Bass.

Freitag, D. (2011, March). Freedom to choose: Advisor classifications and internal identities. *Academic Advising Today, 34*(1). Retrieved from http://www.nacada.ksu.edu/Resources/ Academic-Advising-Today/View-Articles/Freedom-to-Choose-Advisor-Classifications -and-Internal-Identities.aspx

Frost, S. H. (2000). Historical and philosophical foundations for academic advising. In V. N. Gordon & W. R. Habley (Eds.), *Academic advising: A comprehensive handbook* (1st ed.) (pp. 3–17). San Francisco, CA: Jossey-Bass.

Glennen, R. E. (1975). Intrusive college counseling. *College Student Journal, 9*(1), 2–4.

Gordon, V. (2003, September) Advisor certification: A history and update. *Academic Advising Today, 26*(3). Retrieved from http://www.nacada.ksu.edu/Resources/Academic-Advising-Today/View-Articles/Advisor-Certification-A-History-and-Update.aspx

Habley, W. R. (1987). *Academic advising conference: Outline and notes* (pp. 33–34). Iowa City, IA: The ACT National Center for the Advancement of Educational Practices. Retrieved from www.nacada.ksu.edu/Portals/0/Clearinghouse/advisingissues/documents /AcademicAdvisingConferenceOutlineandNotes.pdf

Habley, W. R., & Morales, R. H. (1998). *Current practices in academic advising: Final report on* ACT's Fifth National Survey of Academic Advising (Monograph No. 6). Manhattan, KS: National Academic Advising Association.

Hagen, P. L., Kuhn, T. L., & Padak, G. M. (Eds.). (2010). *Scholarly inquiry in academic advising* (Monograph No. 20). Manhattan, KS: National Academic Advising Association.

Hossler, D., & Bean, J. (1990). *The strategic management of college enrollments.* San Francisco, CA: Jossey-Bass.

Huber, J., & Miller, M. A. (2013). Implications for advisor job responsibilities at 2-and 4-year institutions. In A. H. Carlstrom & M. A. Miller (Eds.), *2011 NACADA national survey of academic advising.* Retrieved from http://www.nacada.ksu.edu/Resources/Clearinghouse/View-Articles/Advisor-Job-Responsibilities-a3045.aspx

Johnson, D., & Martin Jenkins, K-M. (2005). Recruiting, selecting and developing peer advisors. In H. Koring & S. Campbell (Eds.), *Peer advising: Intentional connections to support student learning* (Monograph No. 13) (pp. 51–59). Manhattan, KS: National Academic Advising Association.

King, M. C. (2002). *How does advising differ at a community college from that at a four-year institution?* Retrieved from http://www.nacada.ksu.edu/Resources/Clearinghouse/View-Articles/Two-year-college-advising.aspx

King, N. (2013). Implications for advising reporting lines. In A. H. Carlstrom & M. A. Miller (Eds.), *2011 NACADA national survey of academic advising* (Monograph No. 25). Retrieved from http://www.nacada.ksu.edu/Resources/Clearinghouse/View-Articles/Implications-of-advisor-reporting-lines.aspx

Klepfer, K., & Hull, J. (2012). *High school rigor and good advice: Setting up students to succeed (at a glance).* Retrieved from http://www.centerforpubliceducation.org /Main-Menu/Staffingstudents/High-school-rigor-and-good-advice-Setting-up-students-to -succeed

Kuhn, T. L. (2008). Historical foundations of academic advising. In V. N. Gordon, W. R. Habley, & T. J. Grites (Eds.), *Academic advising: A comprehensive handbook* (2nd ed.) (pp. 3–16). San Francisco, CA: Jossey-Bass.

Kuhn, T., & Padak, G. (2008). From the co-editors: What makes research important? *NACADA Journal, 28*(1), 2.

Miller, M. A. (2011). *Laying the foundation for advisor certification: An open letter to NACADA Emerging Leader Janice Williams.* Retrieved from http://nacada.wordpress .com/2011/10/13/laying-the-foundation-for-advisor-certification-an-open-letter-to-nacada -emerging-leader-janice-williams/

Miller, M. A. (2013). Structuring our conversations: Shifting to four dimensional advising models. In A. H. Carlstrom & M. A. Miller (Eds.), *2011 NACADA national survey of academic advising* (Monograph No. 25). Manhattan, KS: National Academic Advising Association. Retrieved from http://www.nacada.ksu.edu/Resources/Clearinghouse/View-Articles/Structuring-Our-Conversations-Shifting-to-Four-Dimensional-Advising-Models.aspx

Miller, M. A., & Alberts, B. M. (1994). Developmental advising: Where teaching and learning intersect. *NACADA Journal, 14*(2), 43–45.

NACADA Certification Task Force. (2003). *Academic advisor competencies.* Retrieved from http://www.nacada.ksu.edu/Resources/Clearinghouse/View-Articles/Academic-advisor-competencies.aspx

NACADA: The Global Community for Academic Advising (NACADA). (2005). *NACADA statement of core values of academic advising.* Retrieved from http://www.nacada.ksu.edu/Resources/Clearinghouse/View-Articles/Core-values-introduction.aspx

NACADA. (2006). *NACADA concept of academic advising.* Retrieved from http://www .nacada.ksu.edu/Resources/Clearinghouse/View-Articles/Concept-of-Academic-Advising-a598.aspx

O'Banion, T. (2009). 1994 (1972): An academic advising model. *NACADA Journal, 29*(1), 83–89. (Reprinted from *Junior College Journal, 42,* 1972, pp. 62, 63, 66–69; *NACADA Journal, 14*[2], 1994, pp. 10–16)

Pardee, C. F. (2004). *Organizational structures for advising*. Retrieved from http://www.nacada
.ksu.edu/Resources/Clearinghouse/View-Articles/Organizational-Models-for-Advising.aspx

Self, C. (2013). Implications of advising personnel of undergraduates. In A. H. Carlstrom &
M. A. Miller (Eds.), *2011 NACADA national survey of academic advising* (Monograph
No. 25). Retrieved from http://www.nacada.ksu.edu/Resources/Clearinghouse/View-
Articles/Implications-of-advising-personnel-of-undergraduates-2011-National-
Survey.aspx

Shaffer, L. S., Zalewski, J. M., & Leveille, J. (2010). The professionalization of academic
advising: Where are we in 2010? *NACADA Journal*, 30(1), 66–77.

Trabant, T. M. (2006). *Advising syllabus 101*. Retrieved from
http://www.nacada.ksu.edu/Resources/Clearinghouse/View-Articles/Creating-an-
Advising-Syllabus.aspx

University of Louisville Board of Trustees. (2006). *University of Louisville's mission
statement*. Retrieved from https://pda.louisville.edu/undergraduatecatalog/previous-
years-catalogs/f08_u09/generalinfo/university-of-louisvilles-mission-statement.html

University of Louisville Undergraduate Advising. (n.d.). *Advising resources for students*.
Retrieved from http://louisville.edu/advising/students

University of Nevada, Las Vegas. (2014). *Academic Success Center: Vision statement*.
Retrieved from http://www.unlv.edu/asc/advising

Aiming for Excellence

o Develop a working definition of academic advising. Use information in chapter
2, your job description, and knowledge gained in training. Ask others in the
department, office, or unit how they define academic advising as a process.
At developmental benchmarks (3, 6, 9, and 12 months), revisit your own
definition. Reflect on changes in your concept of advising made during the first
year and revise your definition accordingly.

o Access institutional mission and vision statements as well as institutional
definitions of advising. Determine the practices that support the goals
articulated in official statements and discuss them with others on campus. If no
statements exist, consider ways to promote the creation of a definition, mission,
or vision statement for advising.

o Attend or host a brown bag lunch where campus advisors discuss the 2012
Center for Public Education study, *High School Rigor and Good Advice: Setting
Up Students to Succeed*, by Klepfer and Hull (2012). Discuss institutional
efforts to help students succeed. Discuss ways in which this study can inform
these institutional efforts as well as the ways in which the study informs
advisors in helping students meet their educational goals.

o Choose an Implications for Practice article from the *2011 NACADA National
Survey of Academic Advising* (Carlstrom & Miller, 2013e) web site and post a

link to it on a campus advising discussion board. Discuss the questions at the end of the selected article with others via the Internet or in person.

○ Use reports from outside agencies (e.g., the Gates Foundation, Complete College America, the Lumina Foundation) to learn about the completion agenda. Then reflect on how your own advising responsibilities contribute to this agenda. Ascertain whether the strategies or support suggested by these reports would help you in practice.

○ Attend advisor training and development activities that extend beyond shared procedural information. If the campus does not currently offer professional development activities, partner with others to create workshops, lectures, or other gatherings that address conceptual and relational issues in advising.

○ To discover the ways in which advising is organized on your campus, ask: Who is advised? Who advises? Where is advising done? How are the advising responsibilities divided? (Miller, 2013, ¶5). Visit other people and units who advise on campus to gain a deeper understanding of their missions, roles, and responsibilities and to explore how advisors in the different models could learn from one another and collaborate to help students succeed.

○ Discuss the Shaffer et al. (2010) article "The Professionalization of Academic Advising" with others across campus. Perhaps a veteran advisor can host a common reading to promote academic advising as a profession.

○ Join a NACADA Listserv or other electronic mail list to gather input on advising topics not addressed by campus networks.

Applications and Insights

Characteristic Responsibilities of Academic Advisors

o Listen, plan, study, learn, share, receive, and ask questions.

o Teach and model decision making and problem solving.

o Challenge students to do their best and expand their horizons.

o Teach success strategies to students.

o Develop educational plans that empower students to achieve their objectives.

o Teach students to navigate the institutional system.

o Assist students in discovering their academic interests.

o Demonstrate resourcefulness.

o Assist students with orientation and registration.

o Keep records of student interactions (one-to-one, group, and online advising).

o Research academic programs and careers.

o Refer students to appropriate resources.

o Advocate to effect policy changes on behalf of students with advising units, academic departments, colleges, and faculty members.

o Collaborate with department and office personnel to implement programs for students.

o Train other advisors.

o Consult with parents.

o Participate in campus events.

o Develop presentations and programs.

Adapted with permission from NACADA: The Global Community for Academic Advising: Folsom, P. (Ed.). (2007). *The new advisor guidebook: Mastering the art of advising through the first year and beyond* (Monograph No. 16) (p. 44). Manhattan, KS: National Academic Advising Association.

3

ETHICAL ISSUES IN ADVISING

Joanne K. Damminger

Effective advising revolves around meeting individual student needs, which can make each working day in the life of an advisor interesting and different from the day before. Issues arise that require advisors to act upon and resolve new situations, and academic advisors must choose specific courses of action while remaining cognizant of their ethical responsibilities to insure students and colleagues are treated fairly and equitably. Usually the advisor can discern the best way to rectify a problem. However, sometimes complex situations arise that require advisors to think carefully about ways to proceed ethically; that is, they seek the resolution that yields the most good and minimizes harm for the involved students, colleagues, and their institutions.

In these complicated circumstances, often called "dilemmas," advisors may recognize more than one applicable resolution and thus must use ethical guidelines to determine the optimal course of action. This chapter introduces advising-related resources to assist in decision making involving ethics: the NACADA Statement of Core Values of Academic Advising (NACADA: The Global Community for Advising Association [NACADA], 2005a, 2005b, 2005c, 2005d) and the guidelines from the Council for the Advancement of Standards in Higher Education (CAS) (2013). The guidelines, and the ethical principles on which they are based, apply to dilemmas challenging all professional and faculty advisors regardless of years of experience, institution type, or geographic location.

Defining Ethics

According to Webster's (1992), *ethics* is "the study and philosophy of human conduct with emphasis on the determination of right and wrong." Marc Lowenstein (2008) explained ethics as the process of thinking critically about right and wrong and good and bad as each relates to an individual's behavior as directed by moral choices. The difficulty in determining the best course of action stems from the basic principles of right versus right behaviors; that is, more than one possible action may effectively resolve a dilemma. In other cases, a particular course of action may resolve one part of a dilemma but create other unforeseen problems. The complexities associated with moral choices make reading, writing, and thinking about ethics both interesting and confusing at times.

Advisors must know the ethical issues that affect their face-to-face or technology-based interactions. Ethical complexities vary by country, as reflected in laws related to confidentiality and access for students with disabilities, and they differ for various types of institutions within the same country. Despite these situational differences, most advisors clearly understand their responsibility to students. However, they may not have intentionally considered their ethical responsibilities to colleagues and institutions. That is, the nature of the profession translates into an implied role for advocating for students, which advisors readily accept, but advisors are also charged with making decisions that maximize the good and minimize harm to colleagues and their institutions as well (Lowenstein, 2008). New advisors can learn about ethical issues related to advising by learning the NACADA Statement of Core Values of Academic Advising (NACADA, 2005a, 2005b, 2005c, 2005d) and the advising standards outlined in the CAS Standards (CAS, 2013).

NACADA Core Values and CAS Standards

The NACADA Statement of Core Values of Academic Advising (NACADA, 2005a) emphasizes the importance of advising within higher education and the critical impact of advising on students, staff, and institutions. It "provides a framework to guide professional practice and reminds advisors of their responsibilities to students, colleagues, institutions, society, and themselves" (¶3). NACADA (2005b, ¶6) "communicates the expectations that others should hold for advisors in their advising roles." As a result, NACADA and the key ideals articulated in the core values can inform advisors in their quests to conduct ethical decision making. The following tenets characterize the values outlined by NACADA (2005c): Advisors are responsible

- to the individuals they advise (¶1).
- for involving others, when appropriate, in the advising process (¶4).
- to their institutions (¶5).
- to higher education (¶6).
- to their educational community (¶7).
- for their professional practices and for themselves personally (¶8).

NACADA core values guide advisors' professional practice and responsibilities in communicating information related to institutional policies, procedures, and processes. They also inform advisors as they learn the best times in the advising process and the resources for making appropriate referrals.

The NACADA Statement of Core Values of Academic Advising (NACADA, 2005a, 2005b, 2005c, 2005d) identifies and outlines responsibilities and best practices for individual advisors in relationship with advisees, colleagues, and others. The CAS Standards (CAS, 2013) focus on responsibilities and best practices in the delivery of advising and advisor training. CAS designed the standards to enhance student development and learning through the continual improvement of programs and services. In general, the CAS Standards state that an advising program must adopt or develop and implement appropriate statements of ethical practice that must be reviewed periodically. Related to an advisor's ethical responsibilities to students, colleagues, and institutions, the following CAS (2013) directives apply to academic advising program staff members:

- Must uphold policies, procedures, and priorities of institutions and departments.
- Must publish ethical practice and ensure periodic review by relevant constituencies.
- Must orient new staff members to relevant ethical standards and statements.
- As appropriate, must inform users of services of ethical obligations and limitations brought about from codes, laws, or licensure requirements.
- Must be aware of, and avoid, conflicts of interest that could adversely influence judgment or objectivity and, when necessary, recuse themselves from the situation.
- Must perform their duties within the limits of their position, training, expertise, and competence. Individuals in need of further assistance must be referred to others with appropriate qualifications.
- Must provide promotional and descriptive information that is accurate and free of deception.
- Must adhere to institutional policies related to ethical and legal use of technology.
- Must recognize their responsibility to ensure the privileged, private, or confidential nature of advisors' interactions with students is not sacrificed. (pp. 12–13)

CAS also offers guidelines for creating and adopting ethical standards for an advising program, such as through the directive to respect privacy and maintain confidentiality in all records and communications as determined by relevant privacy laws. Together, the NACADA Statement of Core Values of Academic Advising and CAS Standards identify and describe responsibilities and set expectations for professional advising practice, but they do not give advisors specific protocols for resolving ethical dilemmas (CAS, 2013; NACADA, 2005a, 2005b, 2005c, 2005d).

Ethical Guidelines for Resolving Dilemmas

Advisors benefit from knowledge of ethical principles that apply to life in general and those that assist specifically in the advising process. These ideals have evolved over centuries and direct ethical behavior (Lowenstein, 2008). According to Lowenstein

(2008), the following ethical ideals can be applied in advising situations and inform related courses of action:

o beneficence,

o nonmaleficence,

o justice,

o respect, and

o fidelity.

Beneficence refers to facilitating as much well-being as possible among all the people affected directly or indirectly and in the short and long term by an action (Lowenstein, 2008). The case of Ariel and Chris illustrates beneficence in action. The advisor, Chris, discovers that Ariel, a student preparing to graduate at the conclusion of the semester, has not taken the math class needed for graduation. Although not Ariel's previous advisor, Chris does not make any negative comments about the person who gave the erroneous information to Ariel, but empathetically explains the situation. Chris apologizes that a mistake was made and researches all possible solutions that would allow Ariel to graduate on time, such as a short-term independent study course, a waiver, or a substitution for the class. Chris considers arranging for Ariel to walk with the intended graduation class on the condition that Ariel finish the course before the degree is conferred the following semester, and Chris looks into securing payment, as a good faith effort, by the institution for the needed course.

Nonmaleficence refers to avoiding or minimizing the harm directly and indirectly affecting people in both the short and long term (Lowenstein, 2008). Individuals practicing nonmaleficence avoid negative effects to the greatest degree possible; nonmaleficence relates to beneficence in that under both ethical approaches one aims to maximize the good and minimize the harm in all situations.

Devon inadvertently misadvises Dani about a required composition course. Although embarrassed about the mistake, Devon practices nonmaleficence by promptly calling and e-mailing Dani to provide the information on the correct class.

The ethical principle of *justice* refers to treatment of all individuals fairly or equitably such that no one is granted special rights or privileges not open to all. *Equitable* does not necessarily mean that individuals receive identical treatment or reap similar outcomes; it means that any differences in the treatment of others do not create inequalities. Equitable treatment has a defensible basis (Lowenstein, 2008).

Although the concept of justice is easily understood, the practice of it can be compromised, often inadvertently, as an advisor helps one student without recognizing the injustice of the remedy to other students, colleagues, or the institution. For example, Ashton and some close friends attend the same school where Ashton's parent, Kai, works in advising administration. Prior to registration, Kai provided academic advising for Ashton and company, and Kai then used professional contacts to register all the students for their classes prior to the opening of registration to the general student body. Ashton's friends were thrilled and appreciated the advantage of avoiding long lines, online registration hassles, and classes reaching capacity. However, Kai has acted unethically by using a protocol unavailable to all students who need to register. In the attempt to benefit one group of students, Kai violated several ethical guidelines, including specific principles that inform the profession of advising, such as upholding institutional registration procedures, and acted unjustly. Unlike Devon, who admitted a mistake, Kai failed to show *respect for persons*, including other advisors, who follow the appropriate institutional policies.

One should always treat individuals as unique and important, never solely as means to one's own end (Lowenstein, 2008). Advisors should always treat others as rational, autonomous agents, not as things that can be manipulated. Behaviors related to respect include, but are not limited to, always telling the truth regardless of the consequences, respecting the privacy and confidentiality of students and staff, and supporting individual autonomy.

Although most advisors do not have the connections to abuse the system as Kai has done, they can show lack of respect in more mundane ways. For example, an advisee comes to an appointment neither well dressed, well groomed, nor well spoken. In a gross lapse of both respect and judgment as well as disregard for Family Educational Rights and Privacy Act (FERPA) regulations (U.S. Department of Education, 2014; chapter 8), the advisor steps into the doorway of a colleague's office after the student leaves and begins to poke fun at the advisee's appearance and poor communication skills. This unprofessional dialogue created other, practical problems: First, the advisee returns to the advisor's office to pick up forgotten paperwork and overhears the conversation between the two advisors. Offended and embarrassed, the advisee not only chooses to avoid this advisor for further mandated sessions but fails to see any positive aspects of the advising process. Second, anyone in the hallway who also overhears the comments unwillingly becomes party to comments that should have remained unsaid or confidential. Third, the colleague on the receiving end of the conversation grows mistrustful of the advisor and feels uneasy participating in conversations and collaborations. Advisors must model respectful behavior and act as advocates for advisees and trusted colleagues, at all times, whether in earshot of unintended listeners or not.

By not taking seriously their obligations to meet explicit and implicit commitments, both Kai and the advisor making disparaging comments failed to show *fidelity* (Lowenstein, 2008). Implicit commitments, such as those made by promises, characterize one's role to the same degree as those explicitly stated in a contract. Advisors must satisfy many implicit and explicit commitments to advisees, colleagues, and the institutions that employ them. Fulfilling responsibilities to all these constituencies can become challenging, especially when they conflict with one another.

For example, at a new student orientation session, an advisor is explaining several institutional publications to the students in the audience. Kendall, the advisor waiting to give additional information, realizes the speaker has provided inaccurate information about one of the publications. Kendall considers interrupting to correct the record, but does not want to embarrass the presenter or risk the audience subsequently doubting the accuracy of the entire orientation. However, Kendall believes that allowing the inaccurate information to stand may yield negative consequences for the students. No solution seems a perfect way to maximize the good and minimize the harm for the largest number of people in the short and long term.

After the presenter finishes an otherwise flawless speech, Kendall diplomatically refers back to the publication, accurately explaining updated content. Kendall purposefully avoided interrupting, demeaning, or calling negative attention to the previous presenter. In an additional statement of fidelity, some advisors in this situation, especially if the error indicates a greater misunderstanding or the presenter has little experience in the subject area, may respectfully and privately elaborate on the correction and offer additional assistance as deemed necessary.

In choosing courses of action in the aforementioned case, one readily notices a degree of overlap between the guiding principles found in the NADADA Statement of Core Values of Academic Advising (NACADA, 2005a, 2005b, 2005c, 2005d), the CAS Standards (CAS, 2013), and other ethical directives. These fundamentals sometimes contribute to the complexity of the study of ethics, but they can also serve as checks and balances for an advisor trying to determine the best course of action.

New advisors, in particular, benefit from having a myriad of overlapping resources in their toolbox when solving complex ethical dilemmas. Effectively resolving ethical dilemmas in advising is integral to daily advising practice and calls for consideration of all existing relevant ethical principles to arrive at the best solution.

Ethical Decision-Making Steps

As new advisors consider all the principles and perspectives related to ethical advising, the following steps may prepare them to make the best possible decisions:

1. Determine the real issues. Advisors need to look at the situation from many perspectives and determine the issues at the core of the dilemma, sorting out drama from the root problem.

2. Research and consider all relevant policies, rules, procedures, and laws that apply to the dilemma. Advisors should be informed and knowledgeable of when and how to consult legal counsel should the need arise.

3. Review all ethical principles. Advisors need to consider the many ethical ideals, such as justice and beneficence, that could inform their final choice of action before resolving a problematic situation. They should look to resources that offer guidance such as the NACADA Statement of Core Values of Academic Advising (NACADA, 2005a, 2005b, 2005c, 2005d) and the CAS Standards (CAS, 2013).

4. Distinguish ethical from unethical behavior. Advisors must discern the courses of action that most maximize good and minimize harm.

5. Be honest. An advisor who does not have the answer is obliged to consult with others or refer the student to someone who can better resolve the dilemma.

6. Consider all possible solutions and the consequences of each.

7. Document all actions related to the situation, not just problematic ones; keep all written and electronic files confidential and secure.

8. Act in a timely manner.

9. Follow up as necessary.

10. Continue to review personal ethics and their relevance for the advising environment.

Although these steps will help advisors appreciate and apply ethical principles, sometimes the best ethical decision may not clearly emerge from clear-cut steps. In these cases, the decision maker must determine the best course of action from several that seem equally ethical.

The following case study provides an example of a fairly typical situation that a new advisor faces and the subsequent dilemma created for the advising supervisor, outlines the ethical principles in conflict, and offers an ethical resolution to the multiple issues at stake. The aforementioned checklist, which includes guidelines for ethical practice, could assist in unraveling the multilayered problems facing Tracy, Lindsay, and Peyton.

The Case

An experienced advisor and unit supervisor, Tracy, receives a call from a new advisor working in another location. Lindsay is facilitating an advising session with a parent and student who are still in the room. Lindsay asks for permission to contact the academic dean and request a postdeadline withdrawal for Peyton, who is not performing well in a class. Peyton attributes the academic problems to poor teaching techniques, an unintelligible instructor, and a general dislike for the class. Lindsay affirms on the phone (with Peyton and parent in earshot) that other students have complained about the instructor, and thus Lindsay agrees that Peyton needs to withdraw from the class past the deadline.

Considerations

Before calling Tracy, Lindsay may have been able to handle this situation better by independently employing ethical principles for a resolution and following the related steps for decision making:

o Upon a superficial look, Lindsay sees that asking the dean for the withdrawal represents beneficence in action for Peyton, who is experiencing extreme frustration in the class. However, upon deeper reflection and investigation, Lindsay may have recognized that Peyton has experienced difficulties in similar classes. By looking only at Peyton's complaints, Lindsay failed to recognize that the proposed resolution (late withdrawal) does not speak to the real problem (Peyton's recurring frustration in challenging courses), and in fact, may not benefit Peyton's development and thus not deliver the beneficence sought.

o As per the NACADA Statement of Core Values of Academic Advising (NACADA, 2005a), advisors are responsible not only to the individuals they advise, but also to their institutions and educational community. Lindsay has a responsibility to uphold the policies of the institution, such as the withdrawal deadlines, and to follow the procedures for applying such deadlines.

o The proposed course of action clearly violates the ideals of justice and respect. Allowing Peyton to withdraw would not be just, fair, or equitable to other students who may have difficulty in the same class or experience similar difficulties in another class but are not granted special permission to withdraw.

o To establish nonmaleficence, Lindsay should have considered the reputation of the instructor. Derogatory comments made in the advising session, particularly when not investigated for legitimacy, potentially cause harm to the instructor and the institution. Lindsay failed to distinguish ethical from unethical behavior.

o Lindsay consults with Tracy, not to discuss the matter, but only to request permission to pursue the withdrawal.

Lindsay's actions create a potential dilemma for Tracy, who must employ nonmaleficence in deciding the best means of correcting Lindsay and helping Peyton without creating further damage to the instructor or the institution. Tracy first recognizes that Lindsay has not offered legitimate and vetted proof of a problem that requires immediate action or that helps Peyton in both the short and long term. She also refuses to participate in Lindsay's violation of fidelity to the colleague and the institution and does not engage in the negative discussion of the instructor or invoked pedagogy.

Resolution

Although unable to simultaneously follow each guideline of ethical behavior in this complicated situation, Tracy must respond ethically and practicably to Lindsay's request. Tracy must first address Peyton's perceived crisis and then resolve the complications that Lindsay has created by speaking negatively about a colleague in the presence of the advisee.

Tracy needs to demonstrate that Peyton's situation has been heard and considered. Tracy rephrases Lindsay's request on Peyton's behalf and then explains that a full analysis of the situation will take time. Therefore, Tracy asks Lindsay to instruct the advisee and parent that they will receive a decision by phone in short order. In a subsequent private conversation with Lindsay, Tracy explains that the request to waive the withdrawal deadline may violate explicit obligations of fidelity to the institution, other students, and colleagues.

In their conversations, the advisors address precedent and Peyton's situation further so that Lindsay can address the waiver request and share the decision with Peyton.

Specifically, in this case, without mitigating medical or personal (e.g., family tragedy) reason, Peyton's withdrawal request cannot be ethically granted. Instead, Tracy suggests that Lindsay assist Peyton with problem-solving and personal development skills by encouraging Peyton to meet with the instructor to discuss the class. Lindsay may also point out the myriad of campus resources that might contribute to Peyton's success in challenging classes as well as ask Peyton to return with an update on progress made in working through the class and with the professor.

After conferring with Tracy, Lindsay promptly calls Peyton and explains the necessary action and offers to help Peyton with a productive approach to the professor. In this way, Lindsay models beneficence, nonmaleficence, NACADA Statement of Core Values of Academic Advising (2005a, 2005b, 2005c, 2005d), and CAS Standards (CAS, 2013).

After they have ethically resolved the advisee's dilemma, Tracy, as the seasoned advisor and supervisor, has an implicit obligation to mentor Lindsay on the aspects of an ethically facilitated meeting. Tracy spends considerable time explaining to Lindsay appropriate respect for the privacy and confidentiality of advisees, families, and colleagues. Both Lindsay and Tracy agree that these types of situations could make for productive discussions in staff meetings so that all advisors can continuously review ethics as they apply in their advising environment.

Using Ethical Practice in Appointments

The case of Tracy, Lindsay, and Peyton illustrates the complex situations advisors face. It shows the twofold dilemma of the senior advisor and the ethical missteps taken by the new practitioner. Ethical behavior benefits the most people (i.e., creates the most good) when undertaken at the earliest points of contact, which for the advisor often means the advising appointment. With greater awareness of ethical guidelines, Lindsay may have avoided creating complications (i.e., inflicted the least harm) for the advisee, the senior advisor, the faculty member, and the institution.

The following practices help advisors interact in a way that helps elicit ethical behaviors by all parties:

o An advisor should conclude the advising session by rephrasing the student's request or concern to demonstrate that the advisor was actively listening and understands the student's situation. An advisor who needs to consult with a colleague informs the student when to expect an answer using the advisee's preferred contact information. The advisor offers encouragement that helps the student stay focused and positive while awaiting further information. In this situation the advisor shows use of beneficence, fidelity, and the NACADA Statement of Core Values of Academic Advising (2005a, 2005b, 2005c, 2005d).

o Largely with respect to fidelity, when an advisor deems a consultation necessary, he or she must consider the ethical principles of respect and fidelity when deciding whether to contact a colleague in person, over the phone, or by e-mail (or other electronic interface).

○ In addition, the advisor must decide whether the colleague-to-colleague consultation should be conducted in front of the advisee; for example, an advisee may benefit from hearing the request for referral to another department, but may not be privy to a conversation in which an advisor expresses confusion over or disagreement with a policy.

○ In a similar directive on respect and fidelity, as illustrated in the NACADA Statement of Core Values of Academic Advising and CAS Standards (CAS, 2013), an advisor must not allow the transference of personal opinions and biases to influence resolution of a dilemma. For example, an advisor's personal opinion of an instructor's approach to teaching is not reason to assist one student with a postdeadline withdrawal but not another in a class with an instructor who uses teaching and learning approaches the advisor admires.

○ As an act of nonmaleficence, an advisor should not negatively comment in the presence of students or family members about a colleague's behavior. Only positive, factual information should be revealed. An advisor who believes that a student would benefit from taking a class with one instructor over another explains the reasons the class might best contribute to the student's development and learning. An advisor who conveys derogatory comments about another person shows a disregard for the ethical standards of beneficence, nonmaleficence, respect, fidelity, NACADA Statement of Core Values of Academic Advising, and CAS Standards.

○ An advisor should investigate a situation sufficiently to make an informed and ethical decision. Such diligence shows beneficence, nonmaleficence, respect, and fidelity.

○ An advisor must remind students of all policies, procedures, and processes that might inform a student's request and choice of action; in this way, the advisor models beneficence, nonmaleficence, respect, fidelity, NACADA Statement of Core Values of Academic Advising, and CAS Standards.

New advisors quickly ascertain that ethical decision making is not an exact science; more than one solution may ethically resolve a dilemma. Therefore, they should avoid haphazard or rushed decisions, consider all perspectives, consult with more experienced colleagues, ensure thoroughness in the deliberations, consider consequences in both the short and long term, and follow up with everyone involved. Advisors should apply beneficence (doing the most good), nonmaleficence (reducing harm), respect, justice, and fidelity (loyalty to implicit and explicit promises) to the greatest extent possible for the greatest number of people.

Summary

Advisors should not take full responsibility for advisee appointments until they have been properly trained and have developed reasonable confidence about the myriad of skills needed to effectively and ethically advise. Even at institutions without formal training programs, advisors must pursue and take ownership of their own training and development by asking quality questions that inform their practice (chapter 17). An advisor unsure about the best way to proceed needs to consult with appropriate supervisors and colleagues. In addition, certain serious situations fall into dangerous territory for the advisor, institution, or advisee. Therefore, all advisors need to know the protocol for consulting with legal counsel (chapter 8).

Advisors handle dilemmas and unresolved student concerns daily, and for many of these issues, the advice from longstanding practitioners who have contributed to this *Guidebook* will prove useful. In addition, the NACADA Statement of Core Values of Academic Advising (2005a, 2005b, 2005c, 2005d) and CAS Standards (CAS, 2013), available online, should be bookmarked and frequently reviewed.

References

Council for the Advancement of Standards in Higher Education (CAS). (2013). *Academic advising programs*. Retrieved from standards.cas.edu/getpdf.cfm?PDF=E864D2C4-D655-8F74-2E647CDECD29B7D0

Lowenstein, M. (2008). Ethical foundations of academic advising. In V. N. Gordon, W. R. Habley, & T. J. Grites (Eds.), *Academic advising: A comprehensive handbook* (2nd ed.) (pp. 36–49). San Francisco, CA: Jossey-Bass.

NACADA: The Global Community for Academic Advising (NACADA). (2005a). *NACADA statement of core values of academic advising*. Retrieved from http://www.nacada.ksu. edu/Resources/Clearinghouse /View-Articles/Core-values-of-academic-advising.aspx

NACADA. (2005b). *NACADA statement of core values of academic advising: Introduction*. Retrieved from http://www.nacada.ksu.edu/Resources/Clearinghouse /View-Articles/Core-values-introduction.aspx

NACADA. (2005c). *NACADA statement of core values of academic advising: Declaration*. Retrieved from http://www.nacada.ksu.edu/Resources/Clearinghouse /View-Articles/Core-values-declaration.aspx

NACADA. (2005d). *NACADA statement of core values of academic advising: Exposition*. Retrieved from http://www.nacada.ksu.edu/Resources/Clearinghouse /View-Articles/Core-values-exposition.aspx

U.S. Department of Education. (2014). *Family Educational Rights and Privacy Act (FERPA)*. Retrieved from http://www2.ed.gov/policy/gen/guid/fpco/ferpa/index.html

Webster's Dictionary: Including Thesaurus of Synonyms and Antonyms. (1992). [Ethics]. New York, NY: PMC.

Aiming for Excellence

o Meet with other advisors in the unit and draft a checklist for solving ethical dilemmas. Share these ideas with administrators for final approval and store with other advising guidelines for easy reference and consistent utilization within the department. Include proven resources such as the NACADA Statement of Core Values of Academic Advising (NACADA, 2005a, 2005b, 2005c, 2005d) and the CAS Standards (CAS, 2013).

o Identify the institution's legal counsel and the protocol for retaining an attorney. Communicate about or create the appropriate steps for obtaining legal advice. Do not wait until counsel is needed to research recommended procedures (chapter 8).

o Meet informally with other advisors to discuss complex advising sessions or dilemmas, share ideas, and identify resources for ameliorating specific problems.

o Attend or develop a professional development workshop series focused on ethics in advising. Use case studies introduced by participants and role play to share ways to resolve dilemmas.

o Gather advisors together to discuss confusing and inconsistent policies, practices, and procedures. Seek clarification by consulting with appropriate administrators. Simplify language and statements for students and staff.

o Document procedures and resources used to resolve ethical dilemmas. Include histories of successful and less-than-satisfactory outcomes.

4

THEORY MATTERS

Kathleen (Kim) Roufs

Advisors who understand developmental and advising theory will become better practitioners. Whether faculty members, professionals, or peers, advisors who understand
and apply theory in their practice challenge themselves to understand their advisees'
psychosocial, cognitive, and identity development.

Furthermore, theories help advisors achieve positive and satisfying interactions
as they work with their advisees. Historically, developmental theories—such as
those articulated by Burns Crookston (1972/1994/2009), Terry O'Banion (1972/
1994/2009), William Perry (1968), Arthur Chickering and Linda Reisser (1993), and
Vincent Tinto (1993), among others—have provided the foundation for applied theories in academic advising because they describe, explain, and help predict student
behaviors; offer a framework for interactions with students; and generate a solid basis
for advisors' questions, advice, and actions. Developmental theory makes a connection between the dictate of classes to take and the guidance of a student toward decisions that help define and clarify immediate and lifelong values, goals, and objectives.
Advisors who bring theory into practice lay the foundation for strong and productive
advisor–advisee relationships.

Theories change, grow, and evolve. No single paradigm characterizes academic
advising; in fact, myriad theories frame it, and understanding and applying them in
practice elevate the profession of academic advising. Furthermore, attempts to simplify theories may obscure the ability to see their applicability and utility. Therefore,
the primer offered in this chapter presents relatively few of the foundational and current theories most common to sound advising. As they gain experience and curiosity,
advisors will discover dozens more. Moreover, they will recognize that many overlap,
build on others, and exhibit similarities within categories of theories. The ambiguities
and fuzzy boundaries between and among theories and models of advising, advising approaches, methods, and styles may initially confound an advisor but prove to
inspire further exploration as the new advisor grows.

Although it offers no guarantee of the outcomes of an advisor–advisee interaction,
theory provides

- a framework for advisors to guide their practices and to construct appropriate
  responses to advisees;
- a process that helps advisors systematically develop their own professional
  skills;

- o a means of assessing students' levels of development and cognitive stages, enabling advisors to guide them in their personal and intellectual growth; and
- o a context for a broader understanding of advisees as developing adults, adult learners, and as applicable, members of underrepresented populations.

Foundational Developmental Theorists and Theories

One of the often cited theories of advising, *developmental advising,* refers to a "systematic process based on a close student–advisor relationship intended to aid students in achieving educational, career, and personal goals through the utilization of the full range of institutional and community resources" (Winston, Miller, Ender, & Grites, 1984, p. 19). Developmental advising evolved from cognitive structural theories used to examine the way people think, theories used to look at the psychological and social development of individuals, and those that focus on specific populations (King, 2005). Alexander Astin (1985), Marcia Baxter Magolda (2010), Arthur Chickering and Linda Reisser (1993), Burns Crookston (1972/1994/2009), Terry O'Banion (1972/1994/2009), William Perry (1968), Nancy Schlossberg (1984, 1989), and Vincent Tinto (1993) are classical and contemporary theorists with whom advisors should be acquainted, but new advisors would benefit from further examination of additional developmental, cognitive, and identity theories. The more one knows about a theory, the more relevant it becomes.

Burns Crookston and Terry O'Banion

In the early 1970s, Burns Crookston created a broad definition of advising that gave birth to the application of developmental theory to practice: "Advising is concerned not only with a specific personal or vocational decision but also with facilitating the student's rational processes, environmental and interpersonal interactions, behavior awareness, and problem solving, decision making, and evaluation skills" (Crookston, 1972, p. 12). According to Crookston, developmental academic advising involves progression toward goals and evolves from constructive discourse between the advisor and the advisee in the context of the campus, social, and academic environments. By applying developmental theories, advisors recognize their advisees' states of psychosocial development and can best guide them toward growth in intellectual, psychological, and social areas.

Crookston (1972/1994/2009) believed that, in addition to guiding students toward degree completion, advisors need to help advisees examine personal values and implement plans to lead satisfying, gratifying, and productive lives. Furthermore, this developmental advising visionary made the point that if it contributed to student growth, then advising could not be divorced from teaching. Along with O'Banion (1972/1994/2009), Crookston is largely credited with suggesting that the advisor and the advisee share responsibility for advising, a stark contrast to previous practices that had placed the advisor in an authoritative role.

Terry O'Banion (1972/1994/2009) also framed the concept of shared responsibility between the advisor and the advisee. His model, as originally described, applies developmental theory to advising in a top-down linear regression: exploration of

o life goals,

o vocational goals,

o program choice,

o course choice, and

o class schedule.

In this process, the advisor and advisee address the large questions about life goals and values such that the advisee can later freely concentrate on vocational goals. Over time, the conversational scope of the advisor and the advisee narrows as they focus increasingly toward the major, the courses, and finally, the scheduling of classes. As advisors gain experience, they recognize that the advisee does not always proceed linearly through the O'Banion (1972/1994/2009) model and that developmental advising takes time and a trusting relationship. In addition, the distinctions between progressions may be unclear; for example, a student may be self-assured about a major, but may not have asked the in-depth questions about the reasons the major is appealing, the extent it fits with the advisee's life goals, or the student's ability to logistically manage the program to degree completion.

A student named Armani loves dramas—TV shows, books, and movies about physical anthropology and archeology—and thus declares the intent to work as a forensic anthropologist. However, Armani takes little interest in anatomy, chemistry, formal logic, data analysis, or theory—disciplines necessary for sound academic and scientific inquiry in the field. Applying O'Banion's (1972/1994/2009) model, the advisor, Morgan, explores life goals with Armani: "What do you know about the profession?" "Why is the field important?" "Why is it important to you?" "What are the professional opportunities?" As they work through the subsequent levels of inquiry, Armani demonstrates a lack of knowledge about the academic preparation necessary to become a forensic anthropologist. These advising dialogues eventually reveal to Armani a passion for, knowledge about, and commitment to art history. This insight has culminated in Armani's vision to work in a museum or gallery and has, in turn, informed the subsequent discussions with Morgan about selection of an appropriate major and courses.

A commonly accepted symbol for O'Banion's (1972/1994/2009) model is the funnel, with life goals at the top and the scheduling of courses at the narrow end. O'Banion's model created the basis for further evolution of advising theory.

William Perry

In the late 1960s, William Perry (1968) developed a psychosocial theory on college student intellectual and moral development. Simply stated, by having their truths and beliefs challenged, advisees grow and adapt. Perry noted that students typically progress from a simple, dualistic view of their worlds to an awareness of ambiguity. Eventually they acknowledge the relativity in peoples' values and affirm one's own commitments and values.

According to Perry (1968), in the early stages of personal development, dual realities exist in a paradigm of either-or situations: They are right or wrong, black or white, good or bad. Such clear boundaries result in relatively easy, prescriptive decision making. As young adults mature, their dualism evolves into subjective multiplicity and they begin to recognize the grey areas that shade some circumstances, the validity of others' points of view, and acceptable ranges of ambiguity. Finally, in the relativism stage, individuals construct their own truths, based on their values, experiences, and knowledge; they appreciate the complexity of questions and answers at multiple levels as well as their own ethnocentricities and those of others.

Leslie was facilitating a group advising session for new transfer students and referenced the spectrum of attendance policies put forth by faculty members, departments, and collegiate units. One advisee in attendance took a dualistic position and asked, "Well, do I have to attend every day or don't I?" Another advisee, who saw the multiplicity in the statement, thought "I suppose I'll need to check each syllabus." A third advisee, who had reached a position of relativism, showed no surprise that absenteeism was not regarded with absolutes and appreciated faculty members' exercise of academic freedom in determining attendance policies. A fourth attendee recognized that an absence could be excused under certain circumstances, and in other instances, the cost of missing a class unexcused might be worth the opportunity gained, for example, to attend an interview for a prestigious internship.

Alexander Astin and Vincent Tinto

In the 1980s, Alexander Astin's (1985) practical theory of involvement illustrated ways to maximize the intellectual and social development of students. He hypothesized that students perform better academically when they are involved in cocurricular campus activities. Astin posited that engaged students, on one hand, show more commitment to academic programs, develop more campus relationships, participate in student or campus organizations and committees, and seem comfortable interacting with faculty members and administrators. On the other hand, uninvolved students tend to demonstrate relatively poor academic performances and seem less likely to form supportive student and campus relationships, which include members of the faculty and the administration (Astin, 1985).

Astin built his theory of involvement on three core elements. The *inputs* include students' demographics, socioeconomic backgrounds, and experiences. They frame the environmental element and the way in which students view their academic situations. *Outcomes* reflect the maturity, knowledge, attitudes, and values of students and ways they choose to live after they graduate.

A first-generation freshman (inputs), Shea set up a meeting with Casey, a faculty advisor. Shea divulged the lackluster nature of this semester's academic performance, reported having made few friends, and appeared to feel isolated (environment). Casey noted that the Student Center needs board members and suggested that Shea apply for a position. Shea reluctantly took Casey's suggestion and was appointed to a seat on the board. Soon after joining the board, Shea started making friends, going to meetings, developing leadership skills, and connecting with others on campus. Shea, whose grades subsequently improved, led a productive life on campus and became a champion of involvement and engagement for first-generation students (outcomes).

Astin's (1985) theory applies in many ways to the advisor–advisee relationship. His work has provided one of the strongest arguments for cocurricular student involvement and the positive correlation it shows with student persistence.

In 1993, Vincent Tinto addressed student departure in community colleges, but now scholars recognize his theory as universally applicable to persistence and degree completion among students in a variety of higher education institutions. Tinto identified three key causes of student departure, in no particular order: academic difficulties; the dissonance students experience when they are unable to identify, articulate, and pursue their educational goals; and a failure or inability to become involved in the fabric of campus intellectual and social environments. To persist, Tinto argued, students should integrate into formal and informal campus and social activities. Tinto, similar to Astin (1985), hypothesized that negative experiences, such as social isolation and poor academic performance, lead to marginalization and withdrawal; positive experiences, such as involvement in campus activities and utilization of academic support programs, when necessary, contribute to the growth of engaged, successful college students.

Tinto's (1993) theory clearly plays out in the experiences of some military veterans returning from active duty. Feeling isolated and uncomfortable in a campus world made up largely of 18- and 19-year-olds, Loren, a nontraditional-aged veteran recently returned from overseas, began to withdraw and disconnect from the 4-year university, feeling it was not a good fit. Kelly, the academic advisor for most military veterans and service personnel, encouraged Loren to join the Veterans Club. Upon attendance, Loren experienced formal and informal involvement, in and out of class, as advocated by Tinto (1993) and Astin (1985) at multiple levels: meeting staff members similar in age and others with comparable life experiences both in and out of the military. Loren increasingly felt more connected and subsequently engaged more confidently with nonveteran and younger students. To encourage a student such as Loren, advisors must recognize signs of marginalization, be sensitive to the interactions that help students persist, and acknowledge advisees' unique experiences and talents.

Arthur Chickering and Linda Reisser

In 1993, Arthur Chickering, along with Linda Reisser, revised his 1969 theory of identity development in college students. Advisors frequently apply Chickering's work to discussions of growth in college students. The revised theory features seven dimensions, or vectors, of student development:

o developing intellectual, physical, and interpersonal competence;

o managing emotions;

o developing emotional autonomy and recognizing interdependence;

o developing healthy interpersonal relationships;

o establishing identity;

o developing purpose; and

o developing integrity.

At first glance, Chickering and Reisser's (1993) ideas of development appear much more complicated than Astin's (1985) or Tinto's (1993) theories. However, as advisors become acquainted with the vectors, they visualize each on a continuum along which a student's development progresses. Most advisees, as young adults, undergo the process of developing their intellectual, physical, and interpersonal competencies; learning to manage their emotions, thus gaining emotional maturity; and entering healthy relationships—all prerequisites for successfully establishing identity, purpose, and integrity. The academic advisor fosters forward movement on the continuum.

Shelby, a freshman with a cocksure attitude, questioned the reason for consulting with an advisor before registration: "This is a waste of time—I already know what classes I have to take" came through loudly and clearly through body language in the advising appointment with Dana. Moreover, Shelby did, indeed, know exactly which classes to take next semester.

Chickering and Reisser's (1993) theory, built on Chickering's previous research, explains the reason an effective, engaged advisor does more than help students pick classes. Dana recognized that Shelby was struggling at multiple levels; specifically, the over-the-top attitude suggested that Shelby may be dealing with issues other than academics. By asking a leading question, Dana scoped Shelby's position in regard to the first vector, developing competencies: "How was your last exam?" Shelby answered with obvious irritation, "The study questions didn't have anything to do with the test questions, so I blew the test." This unsurprising response—the inability to connect study questions to the exam—indicated that Shelby needs to work on intellectual competence. Reinforcing the first vector, developing intellectual, physical, and interpersonal competence, Dana asked questions that pointed toward Shelby's responsibility for the exam results: "Why do you think the study questions did not set you up for a successful exam?" "Did other students in the class have the same problem?" Shelby's subsequent communication with Dana and with classmates propelled Shelby's intellectual and interpersonal growth, and eventually Shelby could see and apply the relationships between study points and broader examination questions.

During these conversations about the test, Dana noticed Shelby's limited advancement in the third vector: developing emotional autonomy and recognizing interdependence in relationships. Shelby's response to Dana's simple question of "Have you talked with your professor?" confirmed these suspicions. Dana encouraged Shelby to disengage from peer influence and accept responsibility for performance, initially by establishing a relationship with the professor so that Shelby controlled future events instead of allowing them to dictate the circumstances that contribute to a poor attitude and performance.

In a developmentally oriented response to Shelby's projections, Dana opened their first session with conciliatory dialogue: "Okay, let's not talk about the classes since you appear to be set in that area. Let's talk about other aspects of your experiences here." Dana followed up with inquiries such as "Where, at this institution, do you find answers when you need them?" "Do you know any faculty members personally?" or "Are you involved in any activities?" The answers to the questions told Dana, who considered the responses in light of Vectors 3 and 4, whether Shelby was making any connections or meaningful relationships on campus.

Dana also recognized that Shelby needed coaching in the second vector. Shelby's haughty demeanor suggested an inability to manage emotions. Dana gave Shelby permission to discuss weaknesses and fears by asking, "Is there anything I can say that will make you smile?" Some students may respond to a carefully couched statement such as "I suspect under that attitude there is a really nice young person. Am I right?" Beginning in the advisor–advisee relationship, Dana steered Shelby toward better management of emotions and attitude.

Development in the first four vectors is a prerequisite for development in the fifth vector: establishing identity. As Dana asked about Shelby's values, peer groups, talents, interests, and friends, over time, Shelby's identity progressed from that of an emotionally needy high schooler to an independent, committed, college student. Gaining real confidence, Shelby laid the groundwork for development in the fifth, sixth, and seventh vectors. After a few semesters, Shelby had developed a solid sense of identity and appreciation for intellectual and cultural diversity. As a result, Shelby's relationships became more stable and a personal moral code by which to live emerged. Shelby consulted with Dana and professors on a regular basis and engaged in student government. By graduation, Shelby was much further along the continuum than upon arrival at Dana's office several semesters earlier.

Dana's thoughtful questions—such as "How committed are you to the courses you are taking?" or "How will these courses help you after college?" and "How do you want to live your life?"—encouraged Shelby to think about important life goals and values. The questions motivated Shelby's development of the sixth and seventh vectors: purpose and integrity.

By engaging in a holistic conversation, Dana let Shelby know that success in college includes more than completing degree requirements. Understanding and helping a student move through the vectors helped produce a responsibly engaged citizen, one whose relationships and identities extend beyond self to impact the workforce and the community.

In another example of Chickering and Reisser's (1993) theory in action, Corey, a sophomore, admitted, "Nothing is going right." A formerly home-schooled student, Corey now floundered academically, had not found a niche, and did not know where to go for help. Corey told Blair, the advisor for undecided students, about discomfort with a particular study group Blair had recommended. In addition, Cory had gained weight and lost confidence, disengaging from educational opportunities and verbalizing intentions for departure.

Corey's intellectual and interpersonal competencies, learned through home schooling, had apparently arrested. Specifically, Corey needed to acknowledge an inability to independently take on every college challenge. With the first, third, and fourth vectors in mind, Blair helped Corey recognize the reality and importance of interdependency. Corey needed to rely on a tutor, a study group, or consultations with professors. By connecting with any or all of the people available as resources in the college environment, Corey developed mature interpersonal relationships. Furthermore, Blair encouraged Corey to get involved in an activity or club to nurture leadership skills, which subsequently contribute to the competence and confidence Corey needed to continue progressing in the fourth vector: identity development.

As an advisor becomes familiar with Chickering and Reisser's (1993) vectors, he or she can usually see a student's development on the continuum. Then the advisor must find the appropriate levels of challenges and supports for the advisee. With time and experience, the advisor often finds Chickering and Reisser's vectors helpful in fostering an advisee's personal growth.

Nancy Schlossberg

In 1989, Nancy Schlossberg outlined a position that advisors should embrace: the theory of mattering and marginality. Schlossberg's work supports that of other theorists who believe that disengagement leads to student departure from the institution. By applying Schlossberg's theory to practice, the advisor recognizes the discomfort of some students within the academy; that is, students easily become marginalized if they fail to connect with an individual or a group. When students know they matter, confidence replaces feelings of marginality. As simple and straightforward as this theory appears, Schlossberg bolstered its credence through her research showing the importance of mattering. She found that for a successful academic experience, students must believe someone or some group finds them important. When they believe they do not matter, students disengage and withdraw. Therefore, for advisors, advisees matter.

Advisors can easily apply Schlossberg's theory by practicing good relational skills. They should focus on advisees, welcome and listen to them, demonstrate patience, show comfort with silence, and remain relaxed. As the relationships evolve, advisors let advisees know that ideas, questions, and initiatives matter, and most important, advisors can easily apply Schlossberg's theory by genuinely feeling that each advisee matters.

Before explaining the values of mattering and marginality, Schlossberg (1984) had created a transition theory that applies to college students who experience major life changes—departure from home or returning to college as adults, making new friends, becoming independent or changing family roles, and questioning their place in an emerging new personal world. Schlossberg (1984) framed transitions in adults' lives as a change in circumstances or relationships in response to an event that pushes one out of comfort zones. Therefore, in addition to applications to traditional-aged students who matriculate from high school or other colleges, transition theory can help advisors understand international student experiences and the new social and academic environments that influence all their advisees' innermost and outer selves. It can also inform advisors about the challenges of nontraditional students reentering the academic world.

Marcia Baxter Magolda

Nowadays, Marcia Baxter Magolda's (2010) idea of self-authorship is a common theme in advisors' discussions about theory. Baxter Magolda divided self-authorship into three domains: epistemological (how one knows), intrapersonal (listening to inner voices), and interpersonal (listening to the voices of others). Self-authorship easily complements Perry's (1968) theory on intellectual and social development because it reflects psychosocial development. In the advising process, by discovering their own truths, responsibilities, and values, advisees develop the ability to think critically at multiple levels, understand and examine the complexities and construction of their decisions and knowledge, and appreciate the complexities, their experiences, and themselves. Advisees who have reached a degree of self-authorship no longer rely on others to define their knowledge and values.

Adia, a student from an immigrant family, entered the university as a freshman undeclared major over a year after her high school graduation and after a year of working in the family business. Adia had one foot in her family's traditional collectivist culture, in which the family or parents make decisions, and one foot in the 21st century individualistic western world, in which individuals are seen as responsible for their own decisions.

Adia's parents agreed that an accounting degree would be beneficial to the family business. However, Adia had positive role models in mathematics and science courses in a large urban high school and was motivated to be a computer scientist. Because of her respect for parental authority, Adia experienced dissonance in trying to balance traditional cultural values, the family business her parents expected her to join after graduation, and her newly discovered personal academic and professional goals.

Adia's advisor, Tristen, applied the epistemological domain of Baxter Magolda's (2010) theory of self-authorship by suggesting that Adia spend 30 minutes each day for a week collecting images and articles about women in science, technology, engineering, and mathematics (STEM) fields. Tristen also asked Adia to interview three female faculty members in STEM disciplines, including computer science. Because Adia was uncomfortable having conversations with authority figures, Tristen explained the best way to contact professors and presented ways to begin and continue conversations with them. For example, Tristen suggested appropriate interview questions that would elicit responses Adia could use to obtain a realistic picture of the problems and promises of a career in computer science. With her interview questions in hand, Adia felt more confident in interviewing the professors.

Adia returned the collection of images, articles, and interview results to Tristen. The following semester, Adia, having acquired a more complete understanding of the challenges of a computer science student and professional, and at the behest of Tristen, visited Career Services to research opportunities in computer science, graduate school aspirations, and other advice on how best to prepare for this career choice. The information gleaned from visits to Career Services built on the foundation of first semester research and interviews. The process elevated Adia's knowledge and ways of thinking to a more complex level: the intrapersonal domain.

By the end of her freshman year, equipped with knowledge about the promise, obstacles, and options of the major and career choice, Adia declared a computer science major, fully aware of the challenges ahead. With increased confidence, she returned to her parents and fully explained the research she had conducted and the plan she had outlined to pursue her new career goals as a computer scientist.

Student Identity

Many identity theories—such as those related to gender, sex, race, ethnicity, and disability, to name only a few—apply to young adults in general and advisees in particular. A long and complex process, identity development typically commences during adolescence and young adulthood. Circumstances and events, coupled with normal psychosocial development, manifest in physical, psychosocial, emotional, and intellectual based self-inquiries such as "Who am I?" and "How and where do I fit in this world?" Advisors must be knowledgeable about and sensitive to the theories and stages of identity development to understand the advisees' experiences, provide a safe environment for those struggling with their identities, and guide them to a more secure stage in their development.

Advisors understand that advisees, especially those of traditional age and new matriculants to higher education, are figuring out who they are, and most identity theories suggest movement, not always smooth, along a continuum. However, they may not fully appreciate the unique aspects of identity development for those not in majority populations, such as those who identify as transgender, gay, bisexual, or lesbian, and those with disabilities or in underrepresented cohorts of race or ethnicity. International advisees also experience atypical transition issues and question their fit into the U.S. culture. In addition to looking for meaning in their new home, these students may also be experiencing challenges with language and cultural barriers.

When advisors first meet an international advisee they should recognize the years of dedication and preparation undertaken for his or her American academic experience. They also must remember that, despite their interest in a U.S. education, international students have established their identity through the traditional cultural values of their home countries. Furthermore, they may have recently dealt with family pressure in selecting the appropriate college to attend and major to pursue to secure a high-profile, high-income profession. They may have intensely competed with others to gain the opportunity to study in the United States. International students typically experience a variety of concerns as they settle into their new academic environments. They might worry about food differences, living arrangements, weather, money, health, academic performance, and sociocultural and psychosocial issues such as culture shock and homesickness (Kim, 2012).

Helena left her home country, where community is valued over the individual, and family relationships are emphasized over achievement, especially for females. She landed in a culture with vastly different values than those with which she was raised. Fortunately for Helena, the U.S. university she attends offers a strong international student program that welcomed her and walked her through the initial registration process.

Despite little proficiency in conversational English, Helena understood all that her advisor, Lee, said to her, and Lee knew that Helena's relatively poor spoken English skills did not reflect her academic ability. Helena slowly demonstrated increased independence, and began, with Lee's encouragement, to make self-directed decisions about her academic program and social life, some of which would have been questioned by those living in her home country.

Lee suggested that Helena move outside her comfort zone, but Helena continued to surround herself with friends from her homeland. Helena declared a business major, and Lee encouraged her to meet students with other majors, but Helena resisted. Lee then recommended that Helena take a particular business ethics course, which required group work, in the hope that it might challenge her traditional worldviews. Helena took the course, which proved a turning point in her identity. She saw herself no longer as a traditional young woman practicing her country's values, but rather as an international student witnessing plural points of view in a multicultural setting. Other international advisees, however, had difficulties resolving the conflicts between their former, traditional ways of life and the new, different environment with unfamiliar rules and social mores, and they needed more time and advisor support than Helena to recognize and resolve their identity crises.

Eventually, Helena limited herself neither to her group of culturally similar peers nor to the values of her native region; she did not divorce herself from either. Helena recognized her independence and interdependence, appreciated multicultural values, and distinguished herself as an engaged international student. Helena benefited from the advice of a persistent advocate who understood the many challenges international students confront in identifying who they are and where they fit in their new global environment.

Ying came to the United States as an international student determined to succeed. He was an only child, and his parents and four grandparents had directed nearly all their resources into Ying's education in mathematics. Ying's advisor, Tory, knew Ying's secondary school preparation would help him excel in his math and science classes, but recognized that Ying did not understand the value of general education courses, which do not receive much credence in Ying's home country. Tory registered Ying for 12 credits in math and science fields and one 3-hour general education course because the learning required in the humanities course represents an approach to academics foreign to Ying and would require some mastery in a language other than numbers. That semester, Ying earned three As and one C.

Ying was ashamed of the C he earned in the humanities course and felt immense relief upon learning that neither his parents nor grandparents could access his grades. Tory consistently supported Ying, explaining to him that his experience in the humanities course would help him earn higher grades in other general education courses, but Ying's deflated ego had affected his confidence in his overall academic abilities. Therefore, in addition to continued encouragement and explanations about general education requirements, Tory connected Ying with one of the math professors from his home country who had overcome the same challenges that Ying faced.

Advisors need to learn about the academic and cultural identities of international students. What would have happened to Ying if he had registered for the traditional 10 or 12 credits of general education and perhaps one 5-credit course in a STEM discipline? He had formed his identity in multiple ways: as a proud citizen of his country, as an only son, as an accomplished math major. With one C, however, Ying fell short of his own expectations, and he felt like a failure. Fortunately, Tory understood the nuances of Ying's identity development initiated in a culture unlike that nurtured in the United States and proffered advice that would ease Ying into the American educational environment and allow him to adjust to new academic experiences.

Social Constructivist Theory of Appreciative Inquiry

Appreciative advising brings together multiple psychosocial theories, but it is primarily rooted in the social constructivist theory of appreciative inquiry and positive psychology. Using appreciative advising, practitioners ask advisees positive, probing, open-ended questions that assist them in capturing their own stories, strengths, educational goals and objectives, and accomplishments (Bloom, Hutson, & He, 2008).

Positive-focused theories apply to all advisees, but an advisor familiar with appreciative advising knows intuitively when such a positive approach may specifically enhance an individual's college experience. For example, Stevie, an adult student on academic probation, sits in Kelsey's office expressing frustration at attempts to balance work, family, and school. Over time, and by applying the six phases of appreciative advising (disarm, discover, dream, design, deliver, and don't settle) (Bloom et al.,

2008), Kelsey helps Stevie optimize an educational plan, maximize time that Stevie can spend on campus, and recognize the strengths, abilities, and accomplishments that Stevie contributes to all realms of life.

In their initial meeting, Kelsey affirms the advisor–advisee relationship by making positive inquiries and actively listening to Stevie's responses. Specifically, in the disarm phase, Kelsey asks about family, goals, work, challenges, hobbies, and children. By establishing trust and coming to know Stevie as a whole person, not just a nontraditional business major, Kelsey welcomes Stevie to come to the office with concerns. Then, invoking the discovery phase, Stevie, who feels safe talking with Kelsey, reveals strengths, skills, and accomplishments—raising a family, serving as a volunteer fire fighter, and coaching a youth league sports team—in which Stevie takes pride. Because Stevie has chosen to attend college, Kelsey realizes that at least one of Stevie's dreams remains unfulfilled and helps Stevie articulate it.

In the deliver phase, Kelsey and Stevie assemble a realistic, doable plan built on Stevie's strengths and dreams. Finally, in the don't settle phase, Kelsey encourages Stevie to persist, not just to graduation, but in honing the learning style that has proven most effective to achieving goals, growing efficient in studying and time management, and keeping the vision that stems from Stevie's dream, even when the inevitable roadblocks seem to stop progress.

In some cases, advising encounters do not go smoothly or relationships are not established easily, but advisor employment of appreciative inquiry and positive psychology, over time, helps advisees to recognize their strengths and accomplishments. Appreciative advising helps them see that they possess the drive and ability to keep going when they hit bumps in the road.

Advice for Advisors

Advisors, whether faculty, professional, or peer, bring multiple experiences and backgrounds to their advising practices. Applying theory to practice may challenge new advisors, but when theory begins to make sense, many will find it fascinating and will seek further exploration.

Pragmatic reasons for knowing theory include initiating reasoned and appropriate conversations; that is, an advisor with some knowledge of theory will more efficiently and effectively ask questions that lead to greater understanding of the advisee's experiences and expectations. A theory-based process also places the decision-making responsibility on the advisee because the advisor guides the advisee toward making appropriate choices rather than prescribes actions; the advisor coaches the advisee rather than mandates instructions.

Even as they gain confidence in use of theory, advisors learn that student development stages remain fuzzy. The theories do not support a pristine, singular approach to leading students toward good academic and life decisions. The art and the science of advising embody developmental, cognitive, and identity theories as well as stages of transition and appreciative inquiry. Advisors apply these and other approaches in a workable fashion for themselves and their advisees, building on the experience of each to create satisfying and meaningful relationships in the process of student persistence and degree completion. Theory matters in effective advising because, to advisors, advisees matter.

Aiming for Excellence

o Invite a faculty member to provide an overview of developmental theories followed by a discussion in which advisors brainstorm about application of those theories to case studies provided by advisors.

o Attend or organize a common reading program focused on advising theories used or being discussed on campuses, such as Baxter Magolda's (2010) theories on self-authorship or Bloom et al.'s (2008) application of appreciative advising.

o Hold informal gatherings to discuss applying theory; best practices; and the intersections of teaching, learning, and developmental theories. Encourage participants to dig deep to conceptualize one or two new ideas to subsequently share with the group. Create a list of the ideas and begin a scholarly deconstruction of them using publications from NACADA: The Global Community for Academic Advising.

o Discuss with other advisors how foundational theories apply to current student demographics. For example, address ways that Chickering's development vectors (Chickering & Reisser, 1993) specifically apply to first-generation or recently immigrated students.

o Use an advising journal to evaluate the anticipated and realized outcome of theories used in practice. At the end of the first semester of advising, read through the journal and look for ways in which your advising style reflected your understanding of theory.

o Review appointment notes for one of your students. Try to determine where the student falls on Chickering and Reisser's (1993) seven vectors of development. Discuss your conclusions with experienced advisors or your supervisor. Consider questions to ask the student in your next session.

o Observe an appointment with a veteran advisor. Discern where the student might fall on the continuum created by Chickering and Reisser's (1993) vectors. Discuss your observations with the veteran advisor.

o Read through the case studies in Appendix B and apply Chickering and Reisser's (1993) vectors in analyzing the situations. Consider ways to prioritize the conference and the questions you would ask the student; that is, plan and visualize the advising session.

o Consider situations in which O'Banion's (1972/1994/2009) top-down regression theory proves useful. Review a student's file or look to a case study offered in this *Guidebook* or elsewhere and generate a list of appropriate questions for the student in the situation presented.

o After reading about Schlossberg's (1989) theory of mattering, list the ways you can indicate to students that they matter to you.

References

Astin, A.W. (1985). *Achieving educational excellence: A critical assessment of priorities and practice in higher education.* San Francisco, CA: Jossey-Bass.

Baxter Magolda, M. B. (2010). The interweaving of epistemological, intrapersonal, and interpersonal development in the evolution of self-authorship. In M. B. Magolda, E. F. Creamer, & P. S. Meszaros (Eds.), *Development and assessment of self-authorship* (pp. 25–43). Sterling, VA: Stylus.

Bloom, J. L., Hutson, B. L., & He, Y. (2008). *The appreciative advising revolution!* Champaign, IL: Stipes.

Chickering, A. W., & Reisser, L. (1993). *Education and identity* (2nd ed.). San Francisco, CA: Jossey-Bass.

Crookston, B. (2009). 1994 (1972): A developmental view of academic advising as teaching. *NACADA Journal, 29*(1), 78–82. (Reprinted from *Journal of College Student Personnel, 13, 1972,* pp. 12–17; *NACADA Journal, 14*[2], 1994, pp. 5–9)

Kim, E. (2012). An alternative theoretical model: Examining psychosocial identity development of international students in the United States. *College Student Journal, 46*(1), 99–113.

King, M. C. (2005). *Developmental academic advising.* Retrieved from http://www.nacada .ksu.edu/Resources/Clearinghouse/ViewArticles/DevelopmentalAcademicAdvising.aspx

O'Banion, T. (2009). 1994 (1972): An academic advising model. *NACADA Journal, 29*(1), 83–89. (Reprinted from *Junior College Journal, 42, 1972,* pp. 62, 63, 66–69; *NACADA Journal, 14*[2], 1994, pp. 10–16)

Perry, W. G., Jr. (1968). *Forms of intellectual and ethical development in the college years: A scheme.* New York, NY: Holt, Rinehart, and Winston.

Schlossberg, N. K. (1984). *Counseling adults in transition: Linking practice with theory.* New York, NY: Springer.

Schlossberg, N. K. (1989). Marginality and mattering: Key issues in building community. In D. C. Roberts (Ed.), *Designing campus activities to foster a sense of community.* New Directions for Student Services, No. 48 (pp. 5–15). San Francisco, CA: Jossey-Bass.

Tinto, V. (1993). *Leaving college: Rethinking the causes and cures of student attrition* (2nd ed.). Chicago, IL: University of Chicago Press.

Winston, R. B., Jr., Miller, T. K., Ender, S. C., & Grites, T. J. (Eds.). (1984). *Developmental academic advising.* San Francisco, CA: Jossey-Bass.

VOICES FROM THE FIELD

CAREER ADVISING: A NEW PARADIGM

Jennifer Santoro and Misti Dawnn Steward

A major does not equal a career. No one currently serving as an academic advisor has earned a bachelor's degree in the discipline because, as of this writing, a major for academic advising does not exist. In fact, many careers that students will eventually populate do not exist and do not directly correlate with a specific major. Instead, a major translates into a set of skills upon which a career can be built. All college academic advisors and coaches are living proof of this fact.

In terms of career readiness, 93% of employers regard the capacity to think critically, communicate clearly, and address complex problems effectively as more important than an undergraduate major (Hart Research Associates, 2013). Furthermore, a major does not directly prepare a student for the career readiness criteria identified by these surveyed employers; rather, the skill sets they described best characterize students who have developed self-awareness and can clearly articulate their desires in life. Therefore, advisors need to support students in reconsidering the notion that a career equals a major and instead guide their development as individuals with the proper competencies to design a career for themselves.

The foundation of higher education theory makes apparent that self-exploration and self-awareness are the key components of a student's college experience. It is human nature for individuals to ultimately seek self-actualization and thus inherently move toward increased development and aptitude (Deci & Ryan, 2002; Deci & Vansteenkiste, 2004; McLeod, 2007). Higher education professionals are charged to develop and provide an environment of balanced challenge and support for students to reach their optimal growth and potential. The postsecondary environment should be designed to empower students to learn outside of their comfort zones and into spaces of self-exploration (Sanford, 1962, 1966). Graduates who have developed a full understanding of self-identity will likely be effective in any field of their choosing, and college educators, including advisors and coaches, are called to assist students in their identity development in the following areas proposed by Chickering (Chickering, n.d.; Chickering & Reisser, 1993):

o developing competence,

o managing emotions,

- moving through autonomy toward interdependence,
- developing mature interpersonal relationships,
- establishing identity,
- developing purpose, and
- developing integrity.

In the process of developing self-awareness, as per Chickering's vectors, one undergoes a process of self-evaluation to identify disparities and fears (Duval & Wicklund, 1972). Eventually, an emphasis on self-awareness and self-actualization plays a fundamental role in a student's growth and development, and it exerts a direct impact on the student's state of readiness for a career.

In response to the general acceptance of self-identity theory as foundational knowledge for informing educators, Richard Arum and Josipa Roska, authors of *Academically Adrift* (2010), asserted that Americans are losing faith in the higher education system because colleges are not delivering on their promises of student career readiness as based on directly applicable in-class experience and immediate job placement. However, this promise of career readiness is rooted in the student's demonstrated levels of higher learning or in evidence of self-exploration and discovery. Therefore, we suggest shifting the paradigm through building on the foundational theories of identity development. Specifically, we emphasize another key factor for advisors and coaches to consider when addressing advisee career readiness: the individual's desires.

LaPorte's Model of Core Desired Feelings

Danielle LaPorte serves as a modern leader in a new paradigm of life based on self-awareness. To create the premise for her theory, she asks, "What if, first, we got clear on how we actually wanted to feel within ourselves, and *then* we designed our to-do lists?" (LaPorte, 2012, p. 64).

LaPorte explained that human beings are driven to act by the desire to feel a certain way. She contends that a feeling is stronger than a thought; therefore, feelings are essential to a human's well-being, and desires may be the strongest motivator toward success (LaPorte, 2014). If they accepted LaPorte's premise to establish desires before writing to-do lists, advisors would not solely direct students to research career titles and check boxes, but would first help them focus on the way they want to feel; that is, advisors would encourage students to explore their core desires, which may be described by the terms in Figure 4.1.

LaPorte's (2012, 2014) ideas that feelings and inner desires create the compass that leads to a meaningful life reflect our own career experiences. We were both drawn to the field of higher education, and coaching in particular, because of our desire to help others, extend generosity, exert influence, and create connections. No matter where our careers may take us, we know that the satisfaction of all our present and

---

Figure 4.1. Listing of terms related to core desires

Adventure	Acceptance	Passion	Trust	Love
Generosity	Creativity	Justice	Security	Safety
Beauty	Connection	Expression	Influence	Intelligence

future needs will be found on the paths we take by following this compass. Ultimately, satisfaction and success in a career come when inner desires align with daily work.

Therefore, based on Maslow's hierarchy tenet of the ultimate human need for self-actualization (McLeod, 2007), LaPorte's (2012, 2014) treatise on core desires, and our own experiences, we contend that a meaningful career, as one of the key elements of a life well lived, best evolves from the fulfillment of a person's desires. For this paradigm shift to take effect, those in higher education need to return, in a modern way, the field back to its foundational purpose: the development of self-actualized graduates. To accomplish this retrofit, academic advisors and coaches need to create an environment that challenges and supports students to start critically thinking about and exploring their own lives (self-awareness). Advisors need to make a substitution in the equation such that the old form,

A College Degree = All-Encompassing, Satisfying Career is reiterated as

A College Degree = Foundational Skills on Which to Build Satisfaction.

Therefore, advisors need to encourage students to articulate their feelings and desires before they choose a major. As one of our first-year students stated, "I learned that it is one thing to know *what* you want to do, but it is much more important to know *why* you want to do it." We have found that when a student becomes clear on his or her inner desires such that a change in major results, the student does not experience the traumatic feelings often associated with transition because he or she has made the decision based on an identification with an inner desire, not with a major.

Theory to Practice Activities

Although numerous activities prove useful for establishing career readiness, we recommend three specific exercises that refocus the efforts on self-exploration and self-awareness to improve career readiness.

Focus Shifting

Building on the theoretical framework set by LaPorte (2012, 2014), focus shifting helps spark conversations about a student's long-term goals. Advisors need to engage students to adequately challenge and support them through the process of self-exploration as used to clarify and solidify their goals. The following activity, from the Institute for Professional Excellence in Coaching (iPEC), has been adapted to the academic field in the following way:

1. Instruct the student to write the Nos. *1*, *2*, and *3* on a sheet of paper.

2. Ask the student to write a specific goal next to No. 1. Explain that instead of listing a general objective, such as "graduating," the student should provide more details: "graduating with a BS in marketing," or instead of "getting a job," the student should clarify by expanding the statement as applicable: "getting a job with Google," "getting a job in Seattle," or "getting a job in the medical field."

3. Tell the advisee to write down his or her anticipated feelings after accomplishing the goal in No. 1. Suggest that specific words such as *brilliant, intelligent, prestigious*, or *artistic* make better choices than generic terms such as *successful, accomplished,* and *confident*. Encourage the advisee to dig deep: "Everyone wants to feel successful, accomplished, and confident, but what would make you individually feel successful, accomplished, or confident?"

4. For completing No. 3, prompt the student to estimate the time necessary to accomplish the goal identified in No. 1. The student will generate a filled-out sheet that looks like the following example:

   1. Graduating with an engineering degree
   2. Brilliant
   3. Five to seven years

Based on the instructions given, many students will interpret the listing on the sheet as No. 1 being the goal, No. 2 as the effect of accomplishing that goal, and No. 3 as the time line to accomplish the goal. However, by altering the student's interpretation of this list, the advisor invokes the paradigm shift: No. 2 shows the goal; No. 1 explains an optional path toward the goal; No. 3 explains the amount of time the person is willing to deny her- or himself in achievement of the goal.

Advisors can broach some important topics after the students complete this exercise, such as changing majors. Once a student sees *brilliant* as the goal, he or she can appreciate that a major in education, engineering, or music may lead to the advisee feeling brilliant, at which point a change in major often becomes a less stressful process.

The result may also inspire the student to get involved in the short term. Realizing that five to seven years is a long time to wait before feeling brilliant, the student may recognize that current involvement on campus may reap valuable immediate rewards. The advisor can help the student identify the activities, clubs, awards, or actions that would help her or him feel brilliant in the short term.

Values Clarification

Within this ever-changing economy and workforce, the jobs for which students are preparing may not exist tomorrow. However, values remain consistent and lasting.

The values clarification activity, which can be completed in a session or as homework, helps a student identify and articulate values.

1. Ask the student to write down as many values as possible. Recommend use of a thesaurus, and accept a list of approximately 25 words or terms.

2. Help the student narrow the list down by pointing out synonym pairs and, as in the shifting focus exercise, general terms that should be revised for more specificity (e.g., *well-respected* instead of *successful*).

3. Instruct the student to cross out the values that resonate the least and point out terms that may encompass other qualities. For example, an advisee who lists originality and creativity as values may need help identifying the one that evokes more meaning or any terms with overlapping characteristics. Could creativity be considered part of originality, or does originality fit more properly under the category of creativity?

4. End the exercise when the student has honed the list to three to seven values. Explain that these values may serve as a new compass that leads toward career preparation.

This activity may take more than one meeting to complete. However, advisors can offer brief explanations during a session that apply to assigned homework for a student to bring to future appointments.

Questions That Lead to Clarity

Following the same thoughts created in the shifting focus and values clarification activities, the questions that lead to clarity emphasize critical-thinking skills, self-awareness, and articulation of desires. The advisor, as with all interactions, need only provide a safe space and attentive listening to encourage a student to reflect on the following questions:

o "Without mentioning job titles or career paths, what are your goals for life?"

Most students have unique and fascinating interests, but may not know the language to translate these interests into careers. For example, a student who likes math, money, strategy, consulting, and risk management exhibits interests that align with aspects of a career as an actuary. However, the advisee who knows nothing about a career as an actuary may latch, inflexibly, onto the idea of being an accountant.

o "What are your natural strengths?"

Much like the query about interests, the question on strengths could stimulate a conversation about career paths. Because the student may not know the extent of his or her innate talents, the advisor may recommend further exploration through instruments such as *StrengthsQuest* (Gallup, 2010), *The Myers-Briggs Type Indicator* (CPP, 2009; The Myers-Briggs Foundation, 2015), *John*

Holland's Self-Directed Search (PAR, Inc., 2013), or *True Colors Online Assessment* (True Colors International, 2015).

o "What do you like to read?"

In a culture of pervasive social media and instant gratification, one needs to make a genuine effort to read. So whatever materials one chooses to consume may subconsciously indicate a desire in a career.

o "What classes do you like (or do not mind) studying?"

Classes that do not require onerous effort may indicate the topics or processes that fit with a career.

Summary

Higher education professionals assist students in readying themselves for a career. In the paradigm shift we have proposed, academic advisors and coaches can utilize the foundational and modern theories that explain the importance of self-awareness development in college students by creating an environment that challenges and supports students to critically think about and explore their own lives (self-awareness) with a focus on core desires. Under this tutelage, students learn to articulate their feelings and wishes before they choose a major, which we believe will inspire a student to reach her or his optimal growth and provide the preparation needed to serve as an active, empowered, and self-aware member of society. This implementation of self-exploration into everyday work will enhance advising and coaching efforts, and it relieves some of the pressure of helping students reach career readiness. In conclusion, by remembering that organizations do not hire majors—they hire people—advisors will stay focused on development of the individual.

Aiming for Excellence

o Determine the best way to discover the desires that serve as a student's life compass.

o Conduct the focus-shifting self-exploration activity on yourself and a colleague. Were you able to identify your goal? Discuss your insights with your colleague.

o Make a list of clarifying questions to ask students. Keep track of the questions that best helped students identify desires and clarify values. Keep your list nearby for quick reference.

References

Arum, R., & Roska, J. (2010). *Academically adrift*. Chicago, IL: University of Chicago Press.

Chickering, A. (n.d.). *Seven vectors: An overview by Arthur Chickering*. Retrieved from https://www.cabrini.edu/communications/ProfDev/cardevChickering.html

Chickering, A., & Reisser, L. (1993). *Education and identity* (2nd ed.). San Francisco, CA: Jossey-Bass.

CPP. (2009). *The Myers-Briggs Type Indicator (MBTI)*. Retrieved from https://www.cpp .com/products/mbti/index.aspx

Deci, E., & Ryan, R. (Eds.). (2002). *Handbook of self-determination research*. Rochester, NY: University of Rochester Press.

Deci, E. L., & Vansteenkiste, M. (2004). Self-determination theory and basic need satisfaction: Understanding human development in positive psychology. *Ricerche di Psichologia, 27*, 17–34.

Duval, S., & Wicklund, R. (1972). *A theory of objective self awareness*. Oxford, England: Academic Press.

Gallup. (2010). *StrengthsQuest*. Available from http://www.strengthsquest.com/home.aspx

Hart Research Associates. (2013, April 10). *It takes more than a major: Employer priorities for college learning and student success*. The Association of American Colleges and Universities. Retrieved from https://www.aacu.org/leap/documents/2013_EmployerSurvey.pdf

LaPorte, D. (2012). *The fire starter sessions: A soulful + practical guide to creating success on your own terms*. New York, NY: Crown Archetype.

LaPorte, D. (2014). *The desire map: A guide to creating goals with soul*. Boulder, CO: Sounds True.

McLeod, S. (2007). *Maslow's hierarchy of needs*. Retrieved from http://www.simply psychology.org/maslow.html

The Myers-Briggs Foundation. (2015). *The Myers-Briggs Type Inventory*. Retrieved from http://www.myersbriggs.org/

PAR, Inc. (2013). *John Holland's Self-Directed Search* (SDS). Retrieved from http://www.self -directed-search.com/

Sanford, N. (1962). *The American college*. New York, NY: Wiley.

Sanford, N. (1966). *Self and society: Social change and individual development*. New York, NY: Atherton.

True Colors International. (2015). *True Colors Online Assessment*. Available from https://truecolorsintl.com/assessments/

VOICES FROM THE FIELD

CREATING A PERSONAL PHILOSOPHY OF ACADEMIC ADVISING

David Freitag

Creating a written personal philosophy of academic advising requires thought, intro-spection, study, and clearly communicated personal objectives for advising. It takes time and commitment by those actively participating in the field. Although not an easy or quick process, documenting a personal philosophy can and should be done by all academic advisors.

The new advisor can take heart: An advisor's personal philosophy belongs to him or her alone and can thus take the form and content that best embodies individual preferences in prose and priorities for practice. Although the advisor should consider existing guidelines and include essential components, the philosophy mirrors her or his unique view. In addition, new advisors can expect to incorporate changes into their personal philosophy to demonstrate their increased understanding of advising, advisees, and their institution and unit. A living document, the statement of personal philosophy serves as a reference to which the advisor can return to draw inspiration and reconnect with the reasons for entering the field. The creation and maintenance of a personal advising philosophy helps an advisor become more effective now and in the future.

The Personal Philosophy Statement

Definition

A personal philosophy of academic advising is reflected in a positive, self-motivating statement of academic advising as the practitioner perceives it. The advisor uses the-ory as a foundation for approaches with students. The statement serves as an expla-nation for the reason to take on advising responsibilities, guides day-to-day decisions,

Adapted with permission from NACADA: The Global Community for Academic Advising: Freitag, D. (2011). *Creating a personal philosophy of academic advising.* Retrieved from http://www.nacada.ksu.edu/Resources/Clearinghouse/View-Articles/Personal-philosophy-of-academic-advising.aspx helps shape advising goals and objectives, and provides a solid basis for practice (Dyer, 2007).

Purpose

A personal philosophy of academic advising gives structure to advising sessions and provides "a sense of clarity and focus in day-to-day interactions with students and in long-term career goals" (Dyer, 2007, p. 48). It allows an advisor to incorporate theories of student development into daily work and "provides a clear rationale" for interactions with students (Dyer, 2007, p. 48).

Even if they do not realize it, every advisor already operates under a personal philosophy of academic advising. Each uses a selected (perhaps initially without intention) approach and method in practice. Awareness of one's own personal philosophy of academic advising enables the advisor to examine and improve relationships with and the outcomes for students. Therefore, all who advise students—such as staff, faculty members, graduate students, and undergraduate peers—should develop and express a personal philosophy of academic advising.

Content

Although an individual statement of academic advising philosophy differs from those of other advisors, the document often and justifiably includes common elements. For example, an advisor's philosophy should reflect the spirit of the NACADA Statement of Core Values of Academic Advising (NACADA: The Global Community for Academic Advising, 2005), the ethical code that guides the profession. Advisors need not directly reference the institutional or unit visions, values, missions, and goals in their personal statement; however, their articulation of advising, personal values, personal advising mission, and professional goals should not stand in opposition to the values featured in institutional documents or set down by NACADA.

A personal philosophy of academic advising should include a description of the approach(es), student development theories, and interaction strategies used in practice. The philosophy also can include an explanation of interest areas and ways in which the advisor uses (or intends to use) them. Advisor interest does not necessarily translate into a specialization; academic advisors should purposely acquire a broad knowledge base as well as identify specific topics that they find particularly applicable or intriguing. New advisors may explore issues that will advance their own self-development or the profession.

An advisor's personal philosophy should indicate the level of mastery to which the advisor aspires. David Freitag (2011) delineated four levels of professionalism advisors demonstrate through actions and behaviors: advising practitioner, emerging advising professional, academic advising professional, or academic advising scholar. An advisor's philosophy should affirm the choices made now and in the future to reach the classification of choice.

Creating a Personal Philosophy of Academic Advising

To create an effective personal philosophy, an advisor must build a solid academic foundation in advising and in student development. A new advisor can develop his or her knowledge base through classes, readings, and study. The New Advisor Development Chart (chapter 1) provides a comprehensive overview of the knowledge that the new advisor will need to master over the first three years in practice.

In addition to the chapters in this *Guidebook*, other resources provide additional exploration opportunities:

- *Academic Advising: A Comprehensive Handbook*, edited by Virginia N. Gordon, Wesley R. Habley, and Thomas J. Grites (2008), especially the following chapters:

  2—Theoretical Foundations of Academic Advising by Peter L. Hagen and Peggy Jordan

  5—Advising for Student Success by George D. Kuh

  6—Advising as Teaching and Learning by Drew Appleby

  7—Advising for Career and Life Planning by Paul Gore, Jr., and A. J. Metz

  21—Tools and Resources for Advisors by Pat Folsom

  22—Delivering One-to-One Advising: Skills and Competencies by Rusty Fox

- *Student Development in College: Theory, Research, and Practice* (2009) by Nancy Evans, Deanna Forney, Florence Guido, Lori Patton, and Kristen Renn

- Theories applicable to academic advising featured in the NACADA Clearinghouse: http://www.nacada.ksu.edu/Resources/Clearinghouse/View-Articles/Advising-Theory-Resource-Links.aspx

A new advisor may consider answers to the following questions helpful when developing a personal philosophy:

- What are my institution's and unit's published values, goals, and missions?
- What is the stated purpose of academic advising at my institution and in my unit?
- What are my strengths as an academic advisor?
- What excites me about academic advising?
- Do I feel an affinity for specific types of students?
- What topics related to academic advising interest me?
- What research projects related to advising am I interested in pursuing?
- What are my most developed advising skills?
- What legal or ethical situations do I expect to encounter most often in my caseload?

- What advising approaches do I use (or intend to apply) with students?
- Which theories of student development do I use or wish to learn?
- Which identity theories do I use or seek to investigate in relation to advising?
- Which typology theories do I use in practice or plan to explore?

Perhaps most important, the advisor should be able to answer the following:

- Why am I an academic advisor?
- How do I make a difference in the lives of students and colleagues?
- Do my students know their lives matter?

In the process of journaling, as described and advocated in chapter 17, advisors document thoughts and ideas upon reflection of practice or during study that may prove useful in shaping a personal philosophy of academic advising. The length of the statement matters less than the quality of ideas and their significance to the advisor. A one-page philosophy may suffice for many new advisors; others with more experience or who have developed multiple areas of interest and involvement may need multiple pages to fully convey their philosophy. New advisors should strive to develop an initial statement by the end of their first year. All advisors should review their philosophy statement throughout their careers, adjusting it to include new insights and interests.

To get the most benefit from the effort, an advisor should share and discuss the written personal philosophy of academic advising with colleagues and administrators. Through such discussions, the advisor can hone the skills and select the experiences that sharpen the philosophy statement. Through the process of creating, updating, reviewing, and sharing the personal philosophy of academic advising, the advisor will intentionally embrace those practices and theories that will benefit students.

References

Dyer, A. N. (2007). Advisement philosophy. In P. Folsom (Ed.), *The new advisor guidebook: Mastering the art of advising through the first year and beyond* (Monograph No. 16) (pp. 47–48). Manhattan, KS: National Academic Advising Association.

Evans, N. J., Forney, D. S., Guido, F., Patton, L. D., & Renn, K. A. (2009). *Student development in college: Theory, research, and practice* (2nd ed.). San Francisco, CA: Jossey-Bass.

Freitag, D. A. (2011). Freedom to choose: Advisor classifications and internal identities. *Academic Advising Today*, *34*(1). Retrieved from http://www.nacada.ksu.edu/Resources /Academic-Advising-Today/View-Articles/Freedom-to-Choose-Advisor-Classifications -and-Internal-Identities.aspx

Gordon, V. N., Habley, W. R., & Grites, T. J. (Eds.). (2008). *Academic advising: A comprehensive handbook* (2nd ed.). San Francisco, CA: Jossey-Bass.

NACADA: The Global Community for Academic Advising. (2005). *NACADA statement of core values of academic advising*. Retrieved from the http://www.nacada.ksu.edu /Resources/Clearinghouse/View-Articles/Core-values-of-academic-advising.aspx

GLOSSARY OF CONCEPTUAL TERMS

Patrick Cate and Marsha A. Miller

3-I career process model: Developed by Virginia Gordon (2006), a framework for helping students discover best-fit occupations and majors. In this approach, advisors inquire of students to reveal their preferences, inform them of relevant information, and integrate needed resources to help them decide upon a career path.

Academic advising approaches: Recognized ways to structure advising sessions as derived from varied theories in the social sciences, education, and humanities. Advising approaches are comprised of strategies (e.g., problem solving, decision making, career exploration) that help advisors efficiently work with students (Drake, Jordan, & Miller, 2013).

Advising is teaching: A term popularized by Executive Director Charlie Nutt, NACADA: The Global Community for Academic Advising, in the first decade of the 21st century. Proponents see academic advising as focused on student learning of a curriculum (topics advisors teach), with a pedagogy (methods for teaching), and for specified outcomes. Marc Lowenstein (2005) is frequently associated with this movement.

Appreciative advising: An academic advising approach derived from appreciative inquiry and other social constructivist theoretical foundations. It describes a six-phase process of advising. Jennifer Bloom, Bryant Hutson, and Ye He (2010) have researched, written, and presented extensively on this approach.

At-risk students: Students with characteristics, or a combination of factors, that indicate they may not persist to graduation (Harding & Miller, 2013).

Career advising: A collaborative process that "helps students understand how their personal interests, abilities, and values might predict success in the academic and career fields they are considering and how to form their academic and career goals accordingly" (Gordon, 2006, p. 12). Virginia Gordon is a recognized expert of career advising and has articulated models specifically applicable to undeclared students.

Career development theory: Donald Super's (1957) five-stage developmental process for making career decisions that serve as a foundation for the career development field. The five stages are growth, exploration, establishment, maintenance, and disengagement (see Denham, 2010).

CAS Standards: As explained by Eric White (2006), the Council for the Advancement of Standards in Higher Education (CAS) sets standards and guidelines for functional areas (e.g., academic advising, career services, registrar) in higher education. CAS Standards establish criteria expected through reasonable practitioner and institutional effort and diligence. The CAS Standards (2013) is one of three pillar documents in the advising field (the others are the Concept of Academic Advising and the Statement of Core Values of Academic Advising from NACADA: The Global Community for Academic Advising, 2005, 2006).

Competencies of academic advising: Delineated by the 2003 NACADA Task Force on Advisor Certification (NACADA: The Global Community for Academic Advising, n.d.) and based on the three components of advising, the five competencies include foundations knowledge (conceptual component), knowledge of student characteristics (informational component), career advising knowledge and skills (informational component), communication and interpersonal skills (relational component), and knowledge of advising applied at the local institution (informational component).

Completion agenda: A goal articulated by President Barack Obama (2009) in the State of the Union address. It challenges the United States to have the "highest proportion of college graduates in the world" (¶65) by 2020. Several higher education associations, a number of foundations, and several state legislatures have committed to this vision.

Components of academic advising: Three components of academic advising practice: (a) informational (knowledge advisors must master), relational (skills advisors must demonstrate), and conceptual (precepts advisors must understand). The components were first delineated by Wes Habley (1995); Jeffrey McClellan (2007) added two additional advising components: technology and personal.

Concept of Academic Advising (NACADA: The Global Community for Academic Advising, 2006): One of the three pillar documents of academic advising (along with the Statement of Core Values of Academic Advising [NACADA: The Global Community of Academic Advising, 2005] and the CAS [2013] Standards). The concept builds upon the advising-is-teaching movement to challenge campus leaders to define academic advising based on this document and advisors' roles as instructors who teach students to "make the most of their college experience" (Miller, 2013, ¶1).

Core Values of Academic Advising (NACADA: The Global Community of Academic Advising, 2005): A pillar document that purports ethics in advising. The Concept of Academic Advising (NACADA: The Global Community of Academic Advising, 2006) and the CAS (2013) Standards are the other two Pillars of Advising.

Developmental advising: Dialogue-based advising based upon student needs. Practice stems from student development theory and is epitomized by a "systematic process based on a close student–advisor relationship intended to aid students in achieving educational, career, and personal goals through the utilization of the full range of institutional and community resources" (Winston, Miller, Ender, & Grites, 1984, p. 19). Burns Crookston and Terry O'Banion first published their original concepts of developmental advising independently in 1972 and thus stand as the founding fathers of the movement. Crookston (1972/1994/2009) described developmental advising as

> concerned not only with a specific personal or vocational decision but also with facilitating the student's rational process, environmental and interpersonal interactions, behavioral awareness, and problem-solving, decision making and evaluation skills. Not only are these advising functions but . . . they are essentially teaching functions as well. (2009, p. 78)

O'Banion (1972/1994/2009) postulated that students in partnership with advisors initiate the advising process with exploration of life goals and continue through subsequent steps for exploring vocational goals, program choice, course choice, and scheduling courses.

Enrollment management: A strategic conceptual framework that aims to control the enrollment at postsecondary institutions through the use of admissions, marketing, and retention efforts.

Family Educational Rights and Privacy Act (FERPA) (U.S.) or Freedom of Information and Protection of Privacy Act (FIPPA) (Canada): Federal privacy laws that regulate the disclosure of a student's educational records to a third party, including parents (U.S. Department of Education, 2014). At most institutions, the registrar (in conjunction with legal counsel) determines privacy guidelines. New advisors should check institutional policies, which may entail stricter mandates than conferred by FERPA or FIPPA, before disclosing student information to any third party.

First-year experience (FYE): Description of 12-month matriculation period for full-time college students. Recognizing the significance of the first year on student retention, advisors look to increase persistence by providing specific, targeted assistance to first-year first-time students.

Graduation rate: The percentage of first-time full-time students who persist to earn a degree. In 4-year institutions, the undergraduate graduation rate is based on a four- or six-year time frame. At community colleges, the rate is based upon the percentage of entering students who complete an associate's degree within three years.

Hermeneutic advising: A humanities-based advising approach based upon the art of interpretation and used by some advisors to decipher, interpret, and understand students.

Holland-type indicator: The career development model based upon personality codes created by John Holland (1958): realistic (doers), investigative (thinkers), artistic (creators), social (helpers), enterprising (persuaders), and conventional (organizers). Some advisors use Holland codes from student results on a standardized instrument, *John Holland's Self-Directed Search* (PAR, Inc., 2013), to match personality types with corresponding work environments. Students utilize the resulting information to choose satisfying majors and careers.

Identity status theory: Paradigm by James Marcia (1966) based upon the work of developmental psychologist Eric Erikson (1902–1994). Marcia looked at four levels of identity directed by personal choice (decision-making status): diffusion (no identity crisis so decisions not eminent), foreclosure (students accept information without question), moratorium (currently in crisis and may be too confused to make decisions), and achievement (successful completion of a crisis and identity established).

Intrusive (proactive) advising: Originally termed *intrusive* advising as coined by Robert Glennen (1975). Now known as *proactive* advising, this strategy is identified with retention and persistence. Proactive advisors reach out to students, particularly those considered at risk for attrition, prior to their encounter with difficulties.

Learning-centered advising: An advising approach championed by Maura Reynolds (2013). Learning-centered advising focuses on students, the goals students establish, and the information they learn because they were advised.

Making the Most of College: Student Speak Their Minds: Book authored by Richard Light (2001) who explained academic advising as perhaps one of the most "underestimated characteristics of a successful college experience" (p. 81).

Models of advising/advising delivery models: The centralized, decentralized, and shared structures of academic advising delivery systems originally described by Wes Habley (1983). Marsha A. Miller (2013) suggested that in searching for like advising models one asks: "Who is advised?" "Who is advising?" "Where is advising done?" "How are advising responsibilities divided?" (¶5, 7–9). Kenneth Barron and Darcey Powell (2014) added a fifth question: "When are students advised?"

Motivational interviewing (MI): A counseling mind-set applied to academic advising by Judy Hughey and Robert Pettay (2013). MI focuses on developing intrinsic drive and resolving ambivalence. Advisors use MI particularly with students in difficulty or who are undecided and undeclared. (chapter 12)

Myers-Briggs Type Indicator (MBTI): Personality categorization developed by the mother–daughter team Katharine Briggs and Isabel Briggs Myers based upon the work of psychologist Carl Jung. Myers and Briggs based their indicator on preferences that relate to interests, needs, values, and motivation. Sixteen personality types emerge from answers to questions regarding four preference pairs: E/I (extravert/introvert), S/N (sensing/intuition), T/F (thinking/feeling), and J/P (judging/perception) (CPP, 2009).

NACADA: The Global Community for Academic Advising: Founded in 1977 and chartered in 1979 as the National Academic Advising Association. Today more than 12,000 advisors, administrators, counselors, faculty members, and other interested individuals belong to this worldwide educational association. NACADA is headquartered in Manhattan, Kansas, at Kansas State University.

National Survey of Student Engagement (NSSE): An organization that provides survey and related instruments for assessing the time and effort students devote to their educational activities and institutional initiatives to help students persist (National Survey of Student Engagement, 2015). Emeritus professor at Indiana University Bloomington and founder of the NSSE, George Kuh, also has published extensively on high-impact educational practices.

Persistence, retention, and graduation: Terms popularized by Ernest Pascarella and Vincent Terenzini (1991) in their seminal book *How College Affects Students*. These terms refer to institutional efforts to help newly enrolled students complete their educational goals.

Personal philosophy of advising: Each advisor's statement describing the theoretical, motivational, and overarching purposes that characterize his or her advising practice.

Pillars of Academic Advising: Three key documents that guide the practice of academic advising. These documents include CAS Standards (CAS, 2013), NACADA Concept of Academic Advising (NACADA: The Global Community for Academic Advising, 2006), and NACADA Statement of Core Values of Academic Advising (NACADA: The Global Community for Academic Advising, 2005).

Prescriptive advising: The advising approach largely practiced before, during, and immediately after World War II in which advisors selected information to share with advisees in a hierarchical manner. Considered useful in specific situations (e.g., for answering specific questions, such as "When is the last day to withdraw from class?"), prescriptive advising anchors the end of a continuum opposite developmental advising and the approaches that emerged in the late 20th century based on a multitude of theories from various disciplines.

Retention: The percentage of first-time full-time freshmen who return for their sophomore year. This figure is reported each year by an institution's registrar via reports to the U.S. Department of Education. Initiated in the early 1990s, retention discussions include efforts and challenges to keep students in postsecondary education, either at the same institution or at another, until they graduate (*persistence* and *completion*). Vincent Tinto's (1987) book *Leaving College: Rethinking the Causes and Cures of Student Attrition* first directed attention to retention and has been updated in various editions.

Self-authorship: A viewpoint on construction of knowledge that embraces the contextual nature and importance of knowledge integrated into sense of self. Baxter Magolda, a prominent scholar of self-authorship, "stresses the development of students' complex decision-making skills and their capacity to balance personal beliefs and values with critical evaluation of information" (Drake et al., p. xii). Self-authorship challenges college students to ask three questions: "How do I know?" (intellectual and/epistemology) "Who am I?" (interpersonal) and "How do I want to construct relationships with others?" (constructing relationships) (Baxter Magolda, 2004, p. 15).

Socratic advising: A method that encourages students to examine their own life, career, and educational goals. Using a critical-thinking paradigm, advisors ask probing questions based on previous student responses to gently push students to draw their own conclusions.

Stages of intellectual development: A nine-stage model to describe an individual's progression from simple to complex thinking. William Perry (1970) postulated that persons advance through stages from dualism (preference for single correct answer to any question), through multiplicity (knowledge as opinion), to committed knowledge (as constructed through critical thinking based upon values and experiences).

Stages of moral development: The six stages of moral development developed by Lawrence Kohlberg (1958, 1984). This continuation of cognitive psychologist Jean Piaget's development model includes the phases of obedience/punishment, self-interest, interpersonal relationships, social order, individual rights, and universal ethical principles.

Strategies of academic advising: Specific, coordinated tactics within a defined paradigm that advisors employ as part of an academic advising approach (Kimball & Campbell, 2013, p. 8). For example, an advisor using an intrusive advising approach contacts a student who has missed a test.

Strengths-based advising: An approach built upon "the premise that capitalizing on one's areas of greatest talent likely leads to greater success than investing comparable time and effort to remediate areas of weakness" (Schreiner, 2013, p. 106).

Success coaching: An offshoot of the advising-as-coaching approach that draws connections between leadership and personal life mentoring. Based on developmental-based theories, it provides students with practical strategies for use in creating and meeting personal (and academic) goals.

Theories: Conceptual frameworks routinely used in the practice of academic advising (e.g., student development, identity, personality). Theories applied to academic advising originated in the social sciences, education, and humanities. A unified theory of advising has not been established, and debate surrounds the appropriateness of a single paradigm for such a dynamic profession.

Theory of marginality and mattering: The argument that students must feel they matter to someone or some group at the institution to be retained. Originally posited by Nancy Schlossberg (1989).

Undeclared or undecided: Terms used to describe students currently attending a postsecondary institution who have not officially chosen an academic major.

Vectors of identity development: Seven areas of student progression: developing intellectual, physical, and interpersonal competence; managing emotions; developing emotional autonomy and recognizing interdependence; developing healthy interpersonal relationships; establishing identity; developing purpose; and developing integrity. Originally developed by Arthur Chickering in 1969, the vectors were updated in 1993 by Chickering with coscholar Linda Reisser.

References

Barron, K. E., & Powell, D. N. (2014). Options on how to organize and structure advising. In R. L. Miller & J. G. Irons (Eds.), *Academic advising: A handbook for advisors and students: Vol. 1: Models, students, topics, and issues.* Retrieved from http://www.teachpsych.org/Resources/Documents/ebooks/advising2014Vol1.pdf

Baxter Magolda, M. B. (2004). *Making their own way: Narratives for transforming higher education to promote self-development.* Sterling, VA: Stylus.

Bloom, J., Hutson, B., & He, Y. (2010). *The appreciative advising revolution!* Champaign, IL: Stipes.

Chickering, A. W. (1969). *Education and identity.* San Francisco, CA: Jossey-Bass.

Chickering, A. W., & Reisser, L. (1993). *Education and identity* (2nd ed.). San Francisco, CA: Jossey-Bass.

Council for the Advancement of Standards in Higher Education (CAS). (2013). *Academic advising programs.* Retrieved from http://standards.cas.edu/getpdf.cfm?PDF=E864D2C4-D655-8F74-2E647CDECD29B7D0

CPP. (2009). *Myers-Briggs Type Indicator.* Retrieved from https://www.cpp.com/products/mbti/index.aspx

Crookston, B. (2009). 1994 (1972): A developmental view of academic advising as teaching. *NACADA Journal, 29*(1), 78–82. (Reprinted from *Journal of College Student Personnel, 13,* 1972, pp. 12–17; *NACADA Journal, 14*[2], 1994, pp. 5–9)

Denham, T. (2010, February 26). *The 5 career stages.* Retrieved from http://blog.timesunion.com/careers/the-5-career-stages/385/

Drake, J., Jordan, P., & Miller, M. A. (Eds.). (2013). *Preface.* In J. Drake, P. Jordan, & M. A. Miller (Eds.), *Academic advising approaches. Strategies that teach students to make the most of college* (pp. ix–xv). San Francisco, CA: Jossey-Bass.

Glennen, R. E. (1975). Intrusive college counseling. *College Student Journal, 9*(1), 2–4.

Gordon, V. N. (2006). *Career Advising: An academic advisor's guide.* San Francisco, CA: Jossey-Bass.

Habley, W. R. (1983). Organizational structures for academic advising: Models and implications. *Journal of College Student Personnel 24*, 535–540.

Habley, W. R. (1995). Advisor training in the context of a teaching enhancement center. In R. E. Glennen & F. N. Vowell (Eds.), *Academic advising as a comprehensive campus process* (Monograph No. 2) (pp. 75–79). Manhattan, KS: National Academic Advising Association.

Harding, B., & Miller, M. A. (2013). *Cultivating the potential in at-risk students* (Pocket Guide No. 11). Manhattan, KS: National Academic Advising Association.

Holland, J. (1958). A personality inventory employing occupational titles. *Journal of Applied Psychology, 42*(5), 336–342.

Hughey, J., & Pettay, R. (2013). Motivational interviewing: Helping advisors initiate change in student behaviors. In J. Drake, P. Jordan, & M. A. Miller (Eds.), *Academic advising approaches: Strategies that teach students to make the most of college* (pp. 67–82). San Francisco, CA: Jossey-Bass.

Kimball, E., & Campbell, S. M. (2013). Advising strategies to support student learning success. In J. Drake, P. Jordan, & M. A. Miller (Eds.), *Academic advising approaches: Strategies that teach students to make the most of college* (pp. 3–15). San Francisco, CA: Jossey-Bass.

Kohlberg, L. (1958). *The development of modes of thinking and choices in Years 10 to 16.* (Unpublished doctoral dissertation). University of Chicago, Chicago, IL.

Kohlberg, L. (1984). *Essays on moral development: Vol. 2. The psychology of moral development: Moral stages, their nature and validity.* New York, NY: Harper & Row.

Kuh, G. D. (2008). *High-impact educational practices: What they are, who has access to them, and why they matter.* Washington, DC: AAC&U.

Light, R. (2001). *Making the most of college: Students speak their minds.* Cambridge, MA: Harvard University Press.

Lowenstein, M. (2005). If advising is teaching, what do advisors teach? *NACADA Journal, 25*(2), 65–73.

Marcia, J. E. (1966). Development and validation of ego identity status. *Journal of Personality and Social Psychology, 3*, 551–558.

McClellan, J. L. (2007). *Content components for advisor training: Revisited.* Retrieved from http://www.nacada.ksu.edu/Resources/Clearinghouse/View-Articles/Advisor-Training-Components.aspx

Miller, M. A. (2013). Structuring our conversations: Shifting to four dimensional advising models. In A. H. Carlstrom & M. A. Miller (Eds.), *2011 NACADA national survey of academic advising* (Monograph No. 25). Manhattan, KS: National Academic Advising Association. Retrieved from http://www.nacada.ksu.edu/Resources/Clearinghouse/View-Articles/Structuring-Our-Conversations-Shifting-to-Four-Dimensional-Advising-Models.aspx}sthash.GxuEcnKX.dpuf

NACADA: The Global Community for Academic Advising (NACADA). (n.d.). *Academic advisor competencies.* Retrieved from http://www.nacada.ksu.edu/Resources/Clearinghouse/View-Articles/Academic-advisor-competencies.aspx

NACADA. (2005). *NACADA statement of core values of academic advising*. Retrieved from http://www.nacada.ksu.edu/Resources/Clearinghouse/View-Articles/Core-values-of-academic-advising.aspx}sthash.4Lmg43na.dpuf

NACADA. (2006). *Concept of academic advising*. Retrieved from http://www.nacada.ksu.edu/Resources/Clearinghouse/View-Articles/Concept-of-Academic-Advising-a598.aspx}sthash.dz7WcHDi.dpuf

National Survey of Student Engagement (NSSE). (2015). *National survey of student engagement (NSSE): Survey instrument*. Retrieved from http://nsse.iub.edu/html/survey_instruments.cfm

Obama, B. (2009, February 24). *Remarks by President Barack Obama—as prepared for delivery: Address to joint session of congress*. Retrieved February 24, 2009, from http://www.whitehouse.gov/the_press_office/Remarks-of-President-Barack-Obama-Address-to-Joint-Session-of-Congress

O'Banion, T. (2009). 1994 (1972): An academic advising model. *NACADA Journal, 29*(1), 83–89. (Reprinted from *Junior College Journal, 42,* 1972, pp. 62, 63, 66–69; *NACADA Journal, 14*[2], 1994, pp. 10–16)

PAR, Inc. (2013). *John Holland's Self-Directed Search (SDS)*. Retrieved from http://www.self-directed-search.com/

Pascarella, E. T., & Terenzini, P. T. (1991). *How college affects students*. San Francisco, CA: Jossey-Bass.

Perry, W. G., Jr. (1970). *Forms of intellectual and ethical development in the college years: A scheme*. New York, NY: Holt, Rinehart, and Winston.

Reynolds, M. M. (2013). Learning-centered advising. In J. Drake, P. Jordan, & M. A. Miller (Eds.), *Academic advising approaches: Strategies that teach students to make the most of college* (pp. 33–43). San Francisco, CA: Jossey-Bass.

Schlossberg, N. K. (1989). Marginality and mattering: Key issues in building community. In D. C. Roberts (Ed.), *Designing campus activities to foster a sense of community*. New Directions for Student Services, No. 48 (pp. 5–15). San Francisco, CA: Jossey-Bass.

Schreiner, L. A. (2013). Strengths-based advising. In J. Drake, P. Jordan, & M. A. Miller (Eds.), *Academic advising approaches: Strategies that teach students to make the most of college* (pp. 105–120). San Francisco, CA: Jossey-Bass.

Super, D. E. (1957). *The psychology of careers: An introduction to vocational development*. New York, NY: Harper.

Tinto, V. (1987). *Leaving college: Rethinking the causes and cures of student attrition*. Chicago, IL: The University of Chicago Press.

U. S. Department of Education. (2014). *Family Educational Rights and Privacy Act (FERPA)*. Retrieved from http://www2.ed.gov/policy/gen/guid/fpco/ferpa/index.html

White, E. R. (2006). *Using CAS Standards for self-assessment and improvement*. Retrieved from http://www.nacada.ksu.edu/Resources/Clearinghouse/View-Articles/Using-CAS-Standards-for-self-assessment.aspx}sthash.mKN1Q7hU.dpuf

Winston, R. B., Jr., Miller, T. K., Ender, S. C., & Grites, T. J. (Eds.). (1984). *Developmental academic advising*. San Francisco, CA: Jossey-Bass.

FOUNDATIONS: THE INFORMATIONAL COMPONENT

Managing and delivering information constitute a critical aspect of advising, but the deluge of data can overwhelm a new advisor. The chapters in this section provide the tools that will help practitioners navigate the informational river that seems constantly in flood stage. Both professional and faculty advisors face many of the same issues and challenges. Therefore, they need to know the relevant information and manage it for maximum effectiveness while also demonstrating awareness of legal concerns and understanding the boundaries of their responsibility. To provide consistency in addressing the informational component of advising in part three and throughout other chapters in the book, the editors elected to use Linda Higginson's (2000) informational categories—institutional, external, student needs, and self-knowledge—as the organizational framework.

Reference

Higginson, L. C. (2000). A framework for training program content. In V. N. Gordon & W. R. Habley (Eds.), *Academic advising: A comprehensive handbook* (pp. 298–307). San Francisco, CA: Jossey-Bass.

5

THE NEW PROFESSIONAL ADVISOR

BUILDING A SOLID INFORMATIONAL
ADVISING COMPONENT

Jody Johnson

This chapter has a singular focus: to help new professional advisors get started in their careers, particularly in the areas of acquiring and managing advising information. Although advisors also need to understand the conceptual and relational aspects of their work, learning all of the information to know and reference stands as the most critical aspect of effective advising in the first year. The Concept of Academic Advising from NACADA: The Global Community for Academic Advising (NACADA) (2006) states that "the curriculum of academic advising ranges from the ideals of higher education to the pragmatics of enrollment"(¶8), and the advisor knowledge base falls within this range.

To complicate matters for the practitioner, this knowledge base varies substantially by institution; a community college in rural Kansas, a private university in Boston, a dental school in Canada, and a research institution in London require advisors to know different specific policies and procedures. However, certain standard practices and principles for learning and managing advising information apply to each setting.

The Concept of Academic Advising (NACADA, 2006) places teaching at the center of advising, which means advisors need a strong information base. Advisors may consider their own experiences when generating expectations for themselves as teachers. No one enjoys a semester with an instructor who is uncommitted to the knowledge of the discipline or who lacks facility in the details (or the broader concepts). When taking seriously the charge to educate students, advisors accept the responsibility to learn the advising information base.

Internal and External Information

In the first step for acquiring and managing advising information, new advisors must identify the kinds of knowledge that advisors commonly use. They may want to categorize information into knowledge about "internal institutional structures and functions" and the "external environment," as explained by Linda Higginson as a part of the *information component* of advising (2000, pp. 303–304). Concerning internal institutional knowledge, Higginson noted that advisors find themselves in a particular "environment composed of philosophical and historical underpinnings of the institution along with current structures and functions" (p. 303). New advisors may benefit by focusing on the word *environment* and thinking of themselves as an organism affected by the "conditions, circumstances, and influences" around them (Webster's New Twentieth Century Dictionary, 1968). Advisors who understand their surroundings and their responsibilities within it—the conditions, circumstances, and influences—can more easily identify the critical data they must acquire as well as methods for managing it.

For example, the structures (i.e., procedures and policies) at a decentralized institution may not apply uniformly or campus-wide. One academic unit may accept a D as a transfer grade; another unit may not. Through observation, new advisors discern this decentralized approach, consider its pervasiveness on campus, and watch for other manifestations of it. The list of Higginson's (2000) topics of internal structures and functions provides a starting checklist and a strong resource for advisors with little direction in a new position (Appendix A).

Certainly in the first year, advisors must gain competency in the basics of the internal environment, but they must acquire basic familiarity with external information as well. Sometimes the tyranny of schedules (e.g., back-to-back student appointments) or research (e.g., for program changes) restricts advisors within the boundaries of their institutions, limiting their time and causing them to focus too much on the local environment. Higginson (2000) underscored the importance of linking to the outer world and identified three components to which advisors need to connect: "the higher education community, the local community surrounding the campus, and the broad world of work" (p. 304).

The external knowledge necessary for advisors to learn depends on the specifics of their advising position. For example, community college advisors must gain some immediate familiarity with the institutions to which many of their students transfer. Advisors in a master's program need to seek data on doctoral programs as well as the complex arena of work and practice. Advisors working with freshmen should gain awareness of the local community to help their students engage beyond the institution (Appendix A).

Managing Advising Information

After identifying the key information needed, how does the new advisor approach the monumental task of organizing it? The work includes developing strategies for learning and organizing information for retrieval. The following four steps can help advisors master this twofold process:

1. Assess challenges to learn advising knowledge
2. Acquire advising information
   o Identify the best sources of information

     o Reflect on strengths in acquiring knowledge

     o Learn like students; learn from students

3. Organize information for an effective appointment

     o Develop a framework for advising information

     o Use technology creatively

     o Set up the office for information retrieval

     o Deliver knowledge effectively

4. Plan for practical, intentional self-development

See also Applications and Insights—Organizing the Chaos: Office and Computer, immediately following this chapter.

Assessing Challenges to Learning Advising Knowledge

The *2011 NACADA National Survey of Academic Advising* (Carlstrom & Miller, 2013) shows that advisors undertake unique responsibilities in settings with varying degrees of support and resources (Self, 2013). Some advisors are generalists, advising across the entire college or campus curriculum while others focus on specific majors or populations. Some advisors work in advising units with training programs; others practice in isolated situations, working individually or with a small staff. Regardless of their situation, new advisors can assess relevant information by answering the following questions on training, resources, and technology:

     o Does an existing training program provide information or do I need to find and create my own opportunities to learn? (If the latter is the case, the advisor can employ the New Advisor Development Chart in chapter 1 and suggestions in chapter 17 to identify typical types of information the advisor should know.)

     o Is the catalog available in a print version and updated infrequently (every two or three years), or is it online and updated regularly? Are degree checklists uniform in design or hodgepodges of styles, fluency, and accuracy? Advisors need to gauge the quality of each information resource and determine the accuracy and trustworthiness of the information associated with each.

     o How is relevant information stored and managed electronically? Are tools accessible for managing information or are some data buried deep in shared computer drives with cryptic folder titles? Advisors must keep up to speed on the latest technologies used on campus.

These questions do not encompass the only criteria new advisors might use to assess the information needed in their advising settings, but they serve as starting points for understanding the level of personal initiative necessary to learn the internal and external information associated with their advising circumstance.

Acquiring Advising Information

Identify the Best Sources of Information. In searching out quality updated data, the advisor must choose the best source. For example, the advisor may need to determine if the student needing information on degree audits should research the online catalog, fill out a check sheet made in the advising center, access an electronic degree audit, or look at a listing on the department web site.

In addition to reviewing institutional output, advisors interpret information produced by departments and support units, some of which exists in numerous places in various forms. For instance, a course repeat policy might be found on the registrar's web site and also posted in a formal online policy library. Academic units may issue a variation of the repeat policy on department web sites.

When faced with ubiquitous electronic and traditional formats in which information may appear in many forms, the advisor may find that other people serve as the best resources. Veteran advisors, supervisors, and faculty members can share the most appropriate wellsprings of information that they have uncovered over the years, which often prove more utilitarian than those offered in a formal training program. Seasoned advisors often possess a more nuanced understanding of rules, policies, exceptions, and course sequencing than the best impersonal research can reveal. Furthermore, they may have developed special expertise in a particular area; for example, one may be well versed in the details of academic probation while another grasps the intricacies of the curriculum.

However, even those without mentors or training programs can join forces to gain the information they need. Just as students in a college course find study partners, new advisors in the same cohort can work together and challenge each other to learn as much as possible. To tackle the overwhelming knowledge base, new advisors will first need to identify the information categories with which they struggle and seek out those known for their facility in those areas.

Some centralized campuses offer uniform, published information or streamlined technology such that advisors can deftly find the best sources of information on campus. When each academic unit chooses a different style or medium for presenting critical information or when technology remains underdeveloped and not implemented fully across campus, advisors must make discerning choices. With the help of the New Advisor Development Chart in chapter 1, advisors should identify the best campus sources from which to develop an advising library.

For a new advisor searching for basic, noninstitutional information, NACADA materials and other advising publications make good initial points of reference. For instance, a new advisor with limited knowledge of underrepresented student populations may need a primer to best address specific advisee questions and concerns from students of color. The advisor can look at the *Student Population* index at the NACADA Clearinghouse (http://www.nacada.ksu.edu/Resources/Clearinghouse.aspx) and find many applicable articles such as "Students with Specific Advising Needs" (Harding, 2008) and "Advising Students of Color and International

Students" (Clark & Kalionzes, 2008). A good reference book in addition to this guide-book will soon be published by NACADA: *Beyond Foundations: Becoming a Master Academic Advisor* (Grites, Miller, & Givans Voller, forthcoming). It will serve as a good piece with which to start a core resource library.

Reflect on Strengths in Acquiring Knowledge. Some advisors revel in details and facts; they may pride themselves in knowing every answer (and learning those answers as soon as possible). Others use their gifts to help students uncover the influences of their unique backgrounds and their personal goals, but may be a bit slower at recalling verbatim the prerequisites for a physics class or graduate programs in a particular field. Donald Clifton and Edward "Chip" Anderson (2006) referred to these unique talents as natural abilities that, when employed over time, become strengths.

In addition to specific strengths, advisors enter the field with varying perceptions of the job. The talents and viewpoints they offer make them stronger or weaker in particular advising competencies (conceptual, informational, and relational). Advisors often find motivation for developing their knowledge base in the realization that advising is teaching, and they recognize that a call to teach is a call to prepare.

Advisors must develop competency in all the conceptual, informational, and relational aspects of advising. Therefore, new advisors must deliberately give attention to any areas in which they do not show particular giftedness. For example, an advisor with a particular talent for synthesizing student narratives and connecting with others personally (the relational component) may need to spend additional time honing information-gathering skills to bolster the informational and conceptual aspects of practice.

Every advisor can learn and manage the necessary advising information, but only if they are completely honest about their various levels of proficiency. To adequately refine talents and develop needed skills, advisors must first determine their strengths. They can investigate the ways they organize and receive information and subsequently invoke those strategies to bolster weak areas. Practical tools, such as the *Myers-Briggs Type Indicator* (MBTI) (CPP, 2013), can help new advisors investigate their learning processes and apply them to acquiring advising information. Such an instrument, often available in human resource or career counseling units that staff experts in interpreting the results, allows a new advisor to articulate preferences for learning advising information. For instance, naturally intuitive advisors may want to explore connections beyond the training topic, often in an abstract manner, while those who are more sensory in nature prefer concrete details and likely focus readily on the topic at hand. The former advisor may want to study the philosophy behind a particular academic policy and its effects on students while the latter may seek mastery of the policy details. Both processes offer valuable ways of knowing, and eventually the advisor will pick up both the reason for and the details of the policy, but advisors' learning styles may reflect proficiency in one aspect over the other. Knowing their inclinations, advisors can acknowledge their learning style and the types of information that will challenge their ability to acquire and develop effective strategies for learning.

Learn Like Students; Learn From Students. Advisors dispense myriad instructions to students for learning: Review notes soon after class, develop a time-management system, find a tutor to help understand confusing material, and so forth. The same caveats apply to advisor learning as to student learning: Advisors should reflect on the practices they suggest to students and incorporate them into their own strategies for learning and maintaining the advising knowledge base. Advisors must understand that the efficacy of various learning strategies varies with the individual, so they, like students, can experiment with learning tools and organizational schemes to determine the strategies that work best for them.

Advisors can harvest useful information from student conversations, especially if the advisor has little familiarity with the institution. For example, when I was new to my current institution, I taught an academic skills seminar for students on probation. Intensive Elementary Spanish, a common course recommended for my advising pool, met in my classroom after my seminar. Even those whose high school Spanish preparation made them excellent candidates for the course found the class title daunting and expressed apprehension about enrolling in it. Each week as I left my seminar, I found students waiting in the hall for the Spanish class, and I seized this time to create an impromptu focus group where I could learn about the course. Every couple of weeks I chatted with the students about their performance in the class and thus developed a strong understanding of its content and structure.

Advisors can take advantage of the same type of learning that I garnered from the waiting Spanish students by asking questions in one-to-one advising sessions. Through my regular appointments, I frequently confirm the nature of course requirements or changes by inquiring "Is BIOL 100 still allowing students to drop the worst of five exams?" "Does the Leadership Seminar still require students to complete a service project for credit?" "Have the reading requirements changed for Western Civ I?" Advisors who ask students good questions in advising sessions can learn much about the expectations in a class as well as the academic preparation and study skills necessary to succeed in it. Of course, these student answers require more advisor exploration with vetted sources.

Indeed, advisors can gain a wide range of information from their conversations with students on those areas not reflected in official university documents, such as transition and student support issues. Some examples of information best garnered from students include

Transition issues

- o The nature of family communication
- o Cultural and family expectations
- o The experiences of transfer students
- o The most confusing procedures and policies on campus
- o The nature of life in various housing complexes
- o Student perceptions of requirements for a successful college experience

Academic and student support issues

- Detailed information about specific general education courses
- Individual professor expectations
- The most effective academic support services on campus
- Students' experiences at a particular support service office
- Frustrating policies or procedures that require advocacy for change
- The most meaningful program experiences (e.g., study abroad, research, service learning)
- The most confusing aspects of the computerized degree audit system

Organizing Information for an Effective Appointment

Well-organized information ultimately leads to a meaningful and productive encounter between the advisor and the student. The pace of the session is comfortable yet dynamic. The advisor has command of advising knowledge and transmits it easily for the strongest impact. In this shared time, the advisor works within a well-understood framework using technology, the advising space, and most importantly, powerful language, to support the student's educational journey.

Develop a Framework for Advising Information.   Advisors should invest adequate time to identify an information organization framework that fits their situation. The best web sites accommodate the most typical means of exploring and categorizing information. In discussing the "architecture of information" in their *Web Style Guide,* Patrick J. Lynch and Sarah Horton (2008, ¶2) offered the following five steps to organizing information adaptable for any knowledge base or format (e.g., paper-and-pencil or e-file):

1. "Inventory your content: What do you have already? What do you need?" Advisors should use the informational component of the New Advisor Development Chart in chapter 1 as a starting point for this exercise.
2. "Establish a hierarchical outline of your content and create a controlled vocabulary so the major content, site structure, and navigation elements are always identified consistently." Rather than feeling constricted by a controlled vocabulary, advisors who find and consistently use meaningful phrases enhance the usability and communicability of the information.
3. "Chunking: Divide your content into logical units with a consistent modular structure."
4. "Draw diagrams that show the site structure and rough outlines of pages with a list of core navigation links."
5. "Analyze your system by testing the organization interactively with real users; revise as needed." In context, the *real users* include other advisors and students.

Therefore, new advisors should collaborate with others to discover their favorite approach to organizing information and monitor the way interactions with students change when utilizing various organizational systems of information. They should evaluate the information management system after the first semester or year and make adjustments.

Use Technology Creatively. Technology pervades the advisor's daily life. Jeffrey McClellan (2007) sees it as such a strong force that he advocates that it be elevated to the level of the conceptual, informational, and relational components of advisor training. At the most basic level, new advisors can manage information with basic technology tools such as scanning and storing degree check sheets on a shared drive and proficiently using institutional web offerings. More sophisticated products, available at little or no cost, can accommodate storage and management of advising information.

For example, I started an office advising wiki using (a) free wiki software that functions like Wikipedia, (b) very limited informational technology support (I needed the staff only for setting up password access), and (c) the efforts of one administrative assistant who embraced the project. Through simple maintenance, this initiative developed into a tool that all staff can update as academic units provide new information. The updates are tracked automatically in an edit tracking section that identifies the advisor who made the latest change. Rather than duplicating check sheets or catalog information, the wiki allows staff to record supplemental details such as the nuances of program admission requirements, issues about course sequences, and policy clarifications.

A single advisor could initiate a wiki for individual or office use. Visual organizers often prefer using mind maps, and free or inexpensive software (less than $50) can typically meet their needs. Mind maps, first used for brainstorming, take related concepts and terms and use icons, pictures, and other visual imagery to help the brain connect the information. The software can display essential components of any information set, which can be saved for sharing and printing.

Others may choose to use a blogging web site as a content management system, as used by many institutions. This template-based approach allows people in individual units to handle content. Like the wiki, a blogging site can be adapted and protected by a password.

These three examples highlight a few of the strategic uses of technology and illustrate the power of simple tools combined with an innovative spirit for information management. Beginning advisors can find readily available resources to help them store and manage information. When financial resources allow, well-developed software tools can be purchased; however, in today's fiscal climate, advisors may need to demonstrate particular resourcefulness. Advisors should ask colleagues, technology support personnel, and supervisors about technology at their institutions and evaluate its possible use for information management.

Set Up the Office for Information Retrieval. New advisors need to consider their physical space for easy access and retrieval of information. This simple suggestion applies especially to new advisors who have not yet internalized or memorized information and will thus heavily rely on resources. In short order, advisors should determine and keep handy the print pieces used most frequently during appointments. Similarly, they should bookmark frequently visited web sites. Having information at their fingertips can help make new advisors feel more secure, especially in the first busy season of their careers.

New advisors also should ensure that the computer is situated so that students can see the screen; if possible, advisors should procure a large or dual screen that makes information clearly viewable during appointments. As James Eckerty (2011) has shown, office space sends particular messages to students in the advising session. A little time spent reflecting on physical space helps advising sessions flow more smoothly and productively.

Advisor competence in communication, including thorough use of tools and technology, affects the nature of the appointment. For example, referring to computerized advising tools or degree audits can bog down an otherwise well-paced discussion; typically these enterprise systems use fixed features accessible in a controlled and uniform fashion across the campus. Advisors may pull information from the tool in advance or add to it after the session, but sometimes the advisor's use of the tool consumes valuable appointment minutes or keeps students from learning about the mechanism itself. Therefore, new advisors can study the best method for incorporating such tools into the flow of the session, for example, by creating effective phrases to introduce screen progressions and otherwise educate the student while completing important tasks.

I actively question students about their previous use of the online tools used during advising to assess their ability or propensity to use them. I also suggest ways they can use the information created in the advising appointment independently.

Deliver Knowledge Effectively. Powerful language that effectively explains complex policies, requirements, or life situations involves the vocabulary and advising fluency that create meaningful advising sessions. At the 2008 Region VII NACADA Conference keynote address, Jennifer Bloom suggested renaming the "Plan B" conversation as "parallel plans" dialogue. Under either term, the advisor discusses alternative academic choices when a student's first choice might prove infeasible, but the turn of phrase reframes the negative perception of potential change into a positive image of possibilities. After the conference, I religiously used *parallel plans* to discuss backup strategies and found that it transformed the nature of my advising on the topic.

Sometimes new advisors have a firmer grasp on the advising knowledge base than they realize. Often they struggle more with formulating the words or phrase to explain the concept to the student than with their own understanding of a policy or situation. Employing the best expression culminates in more effective advising sessions and improved self-esteem for new advisors as they pave the way for transformational advising, not just in giving their students information, but also for fostering meaningful educational plans (Kincanon, 2009).

For example, veteran advisors develop brief descriptions of general education requirements that they can adapt to different majors and short descriptions that describe the essential elements of courses to help students select them appropriately. To develop phrases that effectively communicate information in an understandable and memorable way, new advisors can steal ideas from experienced advisors for use in dialogues about a policy or situation. Advisors who use language effectively make the most of their time with students and empower others to create meaningful educational experiences.

Planning for Practical, Intentional Self-development

Training programs often offer a blitzkrieg-like experience: a speed date with everyone and a crash course in all relevant information. When the training is completed (or if not offered), the advisor must commit to self-development. The New Advisor Development Chart in chapter 1 helps advisors know the critical informational elements of the first year of advising. The taxonomy outlined in chapter 1 can also help advisors set goals for self-development such that the advisor gives more than the correct answers and instead articulates complete and insightful answers (Johnson & Sallee, 1994). For instance, an advisor may accurately relate to a current student that the School of Business requires a 2.5 university GPA for application, but offers a more complete answer by explaining that admission can be competitive in a given semester and a higher GPA may be needed for acceptance. An advisor's insightful answer applies the correct and complete information (GPA requirement and competitive admission) to a student's academic performance and personal situation, helping the advisee better appreciate the viability of the academic choice: "The necessary GPA for application to the business school is at least 2.5, but it could be higher at any semester. With your GPA of 2.55, you may want to consider a parallel plan in the event your application is not successful." This approach provides the basis for establishing meaningful academic plans for students.

A plan for development can be as straightforward as setting a goal to implementing the suggestions on the New Advisor Development Chart (chapter 1); see also suggestions in chapter 17. The key elements of any plan are intent and self-initiation, but the specific suggestions for implementing a self-development plan may include:

o Determine a set amount and particular time each week to review a chosen category of information, such as degree requirements or enrollment policies.

o Seek out a mentor who has developed the ability to give insightful answers and ask their assistance to develop one's knowledge base.

o Keep in mind the dynamic progression of knowledge development—acquiring (learning), organizing (systematizing), and managing (refreshing like when conducting a computer search).

o Remember the objective: Be organized; the method one uses reflects a personal choice and is secondary to the goal.

o Keep a weekly log of questions that arise about the advising information base in a readily accessible computer or paper notepad, and set and keep an appointed weekly time to review the questions with colleagues and supervisors through the first year.

These simple steps include the elements of timeliness and personal support, and they provide a conceptual framework for a development plan. They also allow personal freedom to find an organization style that works for the individual. These steps represent self-initiated development that proves useful while establishing a pattern of independence. Supervisors and future employers appreciate this type of personal initiative.

Summary

Internal institutional structures and functions as well as the external environment are two essential domains of important advisor knowledge. Mastery of both takes time, but the foundational steps can set advisors on the path to mastering the art of advising. A methodical approach to identifying one's information needs, resources, and challenges in managing information allows the new advisor to set a plan for learning. Over time, as students of the profession, advisors develop language, style, and technology preferences that allow them to guide students skillfully through the college experience. The adoption of systematic learning and communication builds trust with advisees, credibility with campus partners, and recognition in the field. As new advisors grow into the role, they cultivate the advising knowledge base and build advising wisdom, gaining strong insight into the world of students and the institutions for which they advise.

Aiming for Excellence

o Observe an experienced advisor and write notes about the conference. Compare your notes with those of the veteran. How are they similar and how are they different? Discuss the reasons the experienced advisor included information that you did not.

o Observe veteran advisors at several points during your first year. Each time, reflect on your observations; specifically compare the salient points from your first-month observations with the issues that seem new or important after 9 or 12 months.

o Choose an academic program admission requirement, a support office (e.g., tutoring, student health), and a communication issue (e.g., advising a student on communication with parents about academic probation). Using the model of correct, complete, and insightful answers (New Advisor Development Chart in chapter 1), provide answers at each level for the items chosen.

o Identify any "philosophical and historical underpinnings" (Higginson, 2000, p. 303) of the institution that affect the way advising information is disseminated on campus. For instance, what role have faculty members played in advising, and how does that history influence the information available to advisors today? Is the commitment to technology on campus strong and innovative, or has it been limited and poorly developed? How do the current attitudes toward technology relate to daily advising?

o Select three advising colleagues to interview about the best sources for academic program information. Ask them to explain the ways they choose and integrate specific electronic and print resources in their advising sessions.

o Identify three policies, programs, or student situations that you have had trouble describing. Meet with three different advisors to discuss the specific language they use to explain these areas. Ask them about exact phrases or words that enhance and keep conversations with students flowing.

o Keep a log of information you learn from your students. What did you learn about specific courses? What was the academic profile of the student who provided you with new insights or information? What did you learn about life in residence halls? What did you learn about another department, office, or unit? How might you use student-generated information in future conversations with and referrals for advisees?

o Start a general education journal in a preferred platform (e.g., computer document, pencil-and-paper, etc.) to keep notes on general education information gathered from students and colleagues. Each semester identify five courses to learn about in greater detail. When meeting with a student taking one of the courses, gather information for the journal by asking them about the nature of the course (amount of reading, experiential components, professor expectations, students' initial perceptions vs. their course experience, nature of exams, specifics about content covered, etc.); you can also interview student peer advisors about these courses.

o Using the New Advisor Development Chart in chapter 1, choose two of the informational component categories and set dated milestones for reaching the year one level of competency.

o After six months in the advisor role, draw a diagram of how advising information is categorized at the institution. Use the image to determine the informational areas in which you lack confidence. Meet with a supervisor or more experienced colleague to discuss strategies for developing the weak areas.

o Make a list of five learning strategies to suggest to students. Determine a way to appropriate these same tactics into your daily advising routine. Reflect on your own progress each week.

○ Invite two other advisors on campus to meet and review the NACADA Concept of Academic Advising (NACADA, 2006), especially the curriculum section in paragraph 8 of the Introduction. Discuss it in terms of advising in the first year, identifying the items that might be the most difficult to learn or implement.

○ Take the *Myers-Briggs Type Inventory* (CPP, 2013). When meeting with a facilitator to discuss the results, focus on ways the outputs indicate individual learning styles and the best ways you can acquire and organize information.

○ Read Organizing the Chaos: Office and Computer and identify ideas to implement. After six months, evaluate your organizational efforts.

References

Bloom, J. (2008, March). [Parallel plans]. Presented at NACADA Region VII annual meeting, Branson, Missouri.

Carlstrom, A. H., & Miller, M. A. (2013). *2011 NACADA national survey of academic advising*. Retrieved from http://www.nacada.ksu.edu /Resources/Clearinghouse/ View-Articles/2011-NACADA-National-Survey.aspx

Clark, E. C., & Kalionzes, J. (2008). Advising students of color and international students. In V. N. Gordon, W. R. Habley, & T. J. Grites (Eds.), *Academic advising: A comprehensive handbook* (pp. 189–203). San Francisco, CA: Jossey-Bass.

Clifton, D., & Anderson, E. (2006). *StrengthsQuest*. New York, NY: Gallup.

CPP. (2013). *The Myers-Briggs Type Indicator (MBTI)*. Retrieved from https://www.cpp .com/products/mbti/index.aspx

Eckerty, J. (2011). *"Approachable" "intimidating" "unprofessional" "credible": What do our offices say about us?* Retrieved from http://www.nacada.ksu.edu/Resources /Clearinghouse/View-Articles/Office-Design-Research-Study.aspx

Grites, T. J., Miller, M. A., & Givans Voller, J. (Eds.). (forthcoming). *Beyond foundations: Becoming a master academic advisor*. Manhattan, KS: NACADA: The Global Community for Academic Advising.

Harding, B. (2008). Students with specific advising needs. In V. N. Gordon, W. R. Habley, & T. J. Grites (Eds.), *Academic advising: A comprehensive handbook* (pp. 189–203). San Francisco, CA: Jossey-Bass.

Higginson, L. (2000). A framework for training program content. In V. N. Gordon & W. R. Habley (Eds.), *Academic advising: A comprehensive handbook* (pp. 298–307). San Francisco, CA: Jossey-Bass.

Johnson, J., & Sallee, D. (1994). Marketing your college as an intangible product. *Journal of College Admission, 144* (Summer), 16–20.

Kincanon, K. (2009). *Translating the transformative: Applying transformational and self-authorship pedagogy to advising undecided/exploring students*. Retrieved from http://www.nacada.ksu.edu/tabid/3318/articleType/ArticleView/articleId/647/article.aspx

Lynch, P., & Horton, S. (2008). *Web style guide* (3rd ed.). Retrieved from http://webstyleguide
.com/wsg3/3-information-architecture/2-organizing-information.html

McClellan, J. L. (2007) *Content components for advisor training: Revisited.* Retrieved from
http://www.nacada.ksu.edu/Resources/Clearinghouse/View-Articles/Advisor-Training
-Components.aspx

NACADA: The Global Community for Academic Advising. (2006). *NACADA concept of
academic advising.* Retrieved from http://www.nacada.ksu.edu/Resources/Clearinghouse
/View-Articles/Concept-of-Academic-Advising-a598.aspx

Self, C. (2013). *Who advises? Implications for practice based upon answers to the 2011
National Survey of Academic Advising.* Retrieved from http://www.nacada.ksu.edu
/Resources/Clearinghouse/View-Articles/Implications-of-advising-personnel-of
-undergraduates-2011-National-Survey.aspx

Webster's new twentieth century dictionary, unabridged (2nd ed.). (1968). [Environment].
New York: NY: The World Company.

Applications and Insights
Organizing the Chaos: Office and Computer
Pat Folsom, Jennifer E. Joslin, and Franklin Yoder

Organizing the Office

An organized physical space helps advisors keep important information easily obtainable in advising sessions. We offer suggestions that will also keep the clutter off the desk.

For those using paper files or who work in a paper-based office:

- Create paper files for majors, offices, and programs using the broadest category possible and order topically or alphabetically. Files can be in a desk drawer or notebooks. Some may find color coding through labels or folders helpful for quick access.
- Weed out files annually.
- Keep commonly used forms on the desk in an organizer that also houses pens and pencils.
- Always keep a number of empty folders with blank labels on hand so new information about a new major or program can easily be added to the filing system.
- Create a phone log on a simple legal pad. Write a date in the column each morning and the name of the advisee who called or was called as well as the purpose for the call. Jot down critical information on the call; later transfer to advising notes. If follow-up is needed, highlight or place an asterisk or checkmark by the entry.
- Use sticky notes to personalize handouts or for writing reminders about a student for use in advising notes.
- Place projects unrelated to advising (and their related materials) inside a drawer or file or otherwise out of an advisee's sight.

Organizing the Computer

As with physical space, the advisor must maintain organized electronic files. The following strategies, which parallel those used to keep the office organized, will keep communications and electronic files readily retrievable:

- Create mailboxes for majors, offices, and programs using the broadest category possible (e.g., academic programs). Within the broad category mailboxes, add specific files (e.g., to academic programs add natural sciences, biology, biochemistry, chemistry).

- o Place electronic files for majors, offices, and programs on the computer desktop.
- o File topically or alphabetically.
- o Weed out outdated files every semester.
- o Use the highlight feature, if available on the computer system, to draw attention to e-mails with outdated material. This strategy will save an enormous amount of time when searching for old e-mails to delete.
- o Handle incoming e-mails one time: Read them and then file or delete them.
- o Rename the e-mail subject line so it matches the organizational system, which will help with fast retrieval.
- o File or delete sent items at the end of each day.
- o Delete inbox items weekly.
- o Create a follow-up mailbox for items that demand quick responses.
- o For e-mail containing important information that will be continuously and frequently used (e.g., information outlining or detailing new requirements, policies, and procedures), cut and paste text into a word-processing program and create a quick reference tool or handout.
- o Bookmark the web sites most commonly used with advisees.
- o Check bookmarks each semester for broken links or outdated material.
- o Save and reuse responses to questions students frequently ask.

Adapted with permission from NACADA: The Global Community for Academic Advising: Folsom, P., Joslin, J., & Yoder, F. (2007). Organizing the chaos. In P. Folsom (Ed.), *The new advisor guidebook: Mastering the art of advising through the first year and beyond* (Monograph No. 16) (p. 57). Manhattan, KS: National Academic Advising Association.

Applications and Insights

Advisor Checklist of Questions: Institutional Information to Learn in Year 1

Stephen O. Wallace and Beverly A. Wallace

To gain functionality and confidence, new advisors must acquire basic understanding of their institutional environment, the role of academic advising on their campus, and their students. They can gain this understanding by researching answers to the following basic questions about the institution:

o What is the mission of the institution?

o What is the organizational structure of the institution?

o Where are important offices located on campus?

o What is the advising delivery model for my unit?

o Who advises?

o How are advisees assigned to advisors?

o What are my responsibilities as an advisor?

o What are the advisees' responsibilities?

o What do administrators, colleagues, and students expect from advisors?

o What relevant advising technologies—such as institutional web sites, degree audits, early warning appointment scheduling systems, and communication networks—are available?

o Where can I access informational publications, such as the institution's catalog, student handbook, or advising guidebooks?

o How often are specific institutional publications updated?

o How does an advisor know which catalog to use for a specific student?

o What is the institution's policy on the release of student information to other advisors, instructors, and parents?

o What is FERPA (or FIPPA)?

o What are the institution's drug and alcohol policies?

o What are the institution's student judicial affairs policies?

o What opportunities for advisor professional development are available?

6

THE FACULTY ADVISOR

INSTITUTIONAL AND EXTERNAL INFORMATION AND KNOWLEDGE

Stephen O. Wallace and Beverly A. Wallace

Ready or Not—Pop Quiz!

There is a knock on the door. A student enters and asks, "Professor Taylor, do you have a minute?" Dr. Taylor, a first-year faculty advisor, welcomes the student and asks, "How may I assist you?" As the student responds, "You're my advisor, and I have a question about. . . ." The professor, known across campus for dynamic classroom teaching and content expertise, experiences heart rate increase, squirms uncomfortably in the desk chair, and attempts to mask uncharacteristic nervousness with a smile.

Sound familiar? Even during scheduled advising sessions, when a student raises a question, poses a problem, needs information, or seeks assistance, the encounter often feels to the advisor like an unannounced pop quiz in which correct answers and appropriate information must be immediately provided to meet a student's expectation. Conscientious faculty advisors know that their performances on these quizzes may result in significant consequences. The student's level of satisfaction—even persistence and graduation—as well as the faculty advisor's own professional reputation and advancement may depend, in part, by his or her answers on the quizzes.

The faculty advisor bears responsibility to provide accurate information, and new faculty members quickly discover that there are enormous amounts of information they need to know to be effective academic advisors. Many first-year faculty advisors, especially those without previous training or experience as academic advisors, face a steep learning curve. The seeming demand to know everything can leave a faculty member feeling overwhelmed, and new faculty advisors, in particular, may become frustrated if they feel ill-prepared for the recurring pop quizzes. Many new faculty advisors frantically seek help in gaining the necessary knowledge and skills to excel during their first year and beyond.

Ready or not, the pop quizzes come and come and come. New advisors can face these challenging tests with confidence if they fully appreciate three liberating insights: (a) Learning the information an advisor needs to know depends on experiential and developmental processes (see chapter 1); (b) the pop quizzes are open book; and (c) no advisor is expected to be an in-person, on-call Siri, who can provide instant answers to any and every question students ask. Rather than provide inaccurate information to the student, however, advisors without a vetted answer need to acknowledge their limits and admit "I don't know" and then give the student a correct answer as soon as possible. This honest interchange can provide a valuable learning moment for both the student and the advisor. No advisor knows all of the answers, but each does need to learn the questions to anticipate and where the answers can be found.

In this chapter, we provide an overview of the unique role that faculty members fill as academic advisors and the broad scope of knowledge they must gain to develop into advisors of distinction. We then focus on a strategy that faculty advisors can use to aim for excellence in the first year. Recognizing that acquiring the needed knowledge is a developmental process, we provide suggestions to assist new faculty advisors in identifying the needed information in the first year, ways to obtain and manage this information, and the steps necessary to maintain growth as advisors.

We encourage readers to use the sample questions provided in Applications and Insights—Advisor Checklist of Questions (chapters 5, 6, 9, 10, and 13) as study guides to prepare for the upcoming pop quizzes. As with any study guide, the lists of questions are not inclusive, and not all queries apply to every setting. Advisors will need to add items as they identify them. Rather than memorize generic, canned answers, faculty advisors should formulate their own responses as appropriate for their institutions and the needs of the students they advise. New faculty advisors can use this self-assessment tool to gauge their progress in understanding some of the basic information they need to know. In addition, they should make use of the New Advisor Development Chart in chapter 1 to design a strategy for continuous professional development and to chart their progress in achieving advising excellence.

The Unique Role of the Faculty in Academic Advising

Academic advising is an integral component in the mission of higher education institutions of all types—2-year, public and private bachelor, master, and doctorate, and proprietary institutions of varying sizes—and is delivered by diverse individuals who fill various roles, such as faculty members, professional advisors, academic coaches, graduate assistants, and others (Carlstrom & Miller, 2013). While advisors may function within diverse environments, all academic advisors face the intense challenge to deliver quality advising in response to the specific contexts of the institution and the changing needs of their students.

Advising personnel and their practices vary according to the type and size of the institution, but faculty academic advising remains an integral component in fulfilling the mission of a majority of institutions of all types (Carlstrom & Miller, 2013). The unique role of the faculty in academic advising corresponds to institutional mission, size, student population, and faculty status. Faculty members work within many on-campus advising delivery models, such as faculty-only, supplementary, split, and dual (chapter 2). Some faculty members advise as part of their contractual obligations while others willingly volunteer.

Advisor experiences and perceptions may differ among those who carry a full-time or reduced instruction load and advise as a part of their teaching responsibilities and those with faculty status but who carry no teaching loads, as well as between faculty advisors in tenure and nontenure track positions. Similarly, faculty members who advise only majors in their academic departments likely experience their roles differently from those who advise students in majors across campus or undeclared students (Wallace, 2013, ¶7).

The use of faculty advisors offers distinct benefits for the advancement of the institution, success of students, and personal and professional development of advisors. Margaret King and Thomas Kerr (2005) noted that

> the advantages of using faculty are their program and course knowledge, their knowledge of related career fields, the respect they hold within the institution, the cost to the institution, and the fact that research shows a clear relationship between student interaction with faculty and student retention. (p. 320)

Faculty members bring unique perspectives to their roles as academic advisors. For example, faculty advisors offer experiential insights into classroom expectations, rationales for program structures, course requirements, and institutional policies. Faculty advisors have gained in-depth knowledge about course content and can help students select appropriate courses that support their evolving academic and career goals. Furthermore, faculty members use and build on their rich history of experiences to inform and assist students with opportunities for research, continuing education, and career development.

In the current economic climate in higher education, faculty members will likely assume greater roles in delivering academic advising. Therefore, the question shifts from "will faculty serve as frontline points of contact for student concerns and questions?" to "how effective will they be in responding to the questions, needs, and concerns of the students they encounter?"

Faculty Academic Advising: A Dynamic, Multidimensional Process

New faculty advisors express diverse and complex attitudes and perceptions toward academic advising as shaped by the individual's appreciation of quality advising, expectations for advisors, and the advisor's level of confidence to succeed in the role. These attitudes and perceptions are typically formulated during the faculty member's first-year experiences as an advisor. Therefore, new faculty advisors must develop a positive understanding of the role that faculty members fill as academic advisors.

Many faculty members cannot devote themselves full-time to the art of advising as do professional advisors. Instead, their advising duties are one of the multiple complex responsibilities they must manage (Wallace & Wallace, 2010). New faculty advisors with instructional responsibilities often feel overwhelmed by institutional demands to demonstrate excellence in teaching, conducting scholarship, performing service, and managing sizeable advising caseloads. In addition, they face expectations to keep students and parents happy such that undergraduates continue flowing through the pipeline from enrollment to graduation. Most new faculty members desire to excel in each of their areas of responsibility and are confident that their academic preparations have adequately equipped them for their instructional and research duties. However, many lack previous knowledge or experience as academic advisors and struggle with feelings of uncertainty about their competency in this new role. Their levels of anxiety may also be heightened by misperceptions of the expectations for new faculty advisors.

Several popular myths about the nature of advising and the role of faculty advisors, if embraced, can heighten the levels of concern and frustration experienced by new faculty advisors. The primary falsehood suggests advising is easy—that anyone who cares about students and can impart some basic information can be a good advisor. In reality, quality advising requires more than a kind disposition and good intentions.

Some institutions promote a similar myth: Because faculty members can teach, they can advise. Faculty members, as educators, often readily value those elements of advising that embody essential components of quality teaching, but they must recognize that quality academic advising is a dynamic, multidimensional process that demands the development of a unique set of knowledge and skills.

To lessen any unfounded concerns and to better understand the nature of advising, new faculty advisors may benefit from learning about the ideas and history that undergird modern academic advising (chapters 2, 4, and 9). One quickly ascertains that quality faculty academic advising is a dynamic, multidimensional process informed by several relevant theories. In fact, no single theory drives advising best practices. Instead, effective academic advisors incorporate an array of theories borrowed from the social sciences, education, humanities, and student and career development. To gain a richer appreciation for the field of academic advising and the role of faculty advisors, all advisors can and should gain familiarity with the multiple theories that inform the practice of advising—a rather daunting challenge that cannot possibly be accomplished in an advisor's first year.

We recommend that new faculty advisors begin by adopting a first-year learning goal of attaining an understanding that places advising into a meaningful context—advising as teaching. This paradigm focuses on educational processes and students (Drake, 2013). Within this paradigm, rather than viewing advising as an unwelcomed add-on to a faculty member's heavy load of responsibilities (Wallace, 2013, ¶9), effective faculty advisors appreciate advising as a key component of the teaching–learning interaction. In their advising-as-teaching roles, faculty members do not merely serve as on-call information booths; they recognize that effective advising involves more than imparting information on course curriculum and registration issues. They esteem the value of quality academic advising in empowering students to assume ownership of their educational experiences.

Components of Quality Academic Advising

Wes Habley (1995) advanced the ongoing conversation on the elements that constitute quality academic advising by identifying three essential categories of knowledge and skills:

- o conceptual—the advisors' understanding about the nature of advising, the institutional advising environment, advisees, and the nature of the advising relationship;
- o informational—the information that advisors need to know and provide in accurate detail to students; and
- o relational—the skills and attitudes advisors must establish and maintain in the advisor–advisee relationship.

Habley (1995) explained the importance of these advising underpinnings: "Without understanding (conceptual elements), there is no context for the delivery of services. Without information, there is no substance to advising. And, without interpersonal skills (relational), the quality of the advisee/advisor interaction is left to chance" (p. 76). While he clearly identified each component as essential to quality advising, Habley (1995) also made clear that information comprises the substance of quality advising and provides the framework for the conceptual and relational dimensions.

Because faculty advisors face an enormous challenge in attaining or knowing the access points for the information students need to achieve their educational goals, we turn to Linda Higginson's (2000) framework that outlines the substantive information that advisors need to know in four basic categories: the internal (institutional) environment, the external environment, student needs, and advisor self-knowledge. In this chapter, we focus on the internal and external information that faculty advisors must attain and touch on student-centered advising; for more information on self-knowledge, see chapter 10.

The Internal Environment

Faculty advisors function within diverse environments and face intense challenges to deliver quality advising responsive to the specific contexts of their institutions and the changing needs of students. To comfortably execute their roles as advisors, faculty members must quickly grasp a basic understanding of their institution and its culture, which is cultivated through the institutional mission and goals, the campus social and political climates, and available resources. The institutional culture is reflected in the definition and mission of academic advising, the model for advising delivery, and faculty roles and responsibilities.

Specifically, faculty advisors must learn the systems and structures that direct institutional operations. They must know the technological systems used in advising and registration; academic programs; curricular requirements; policies and procedures;

special populations and support services; and institutional rules, regulations, and organizational structures that affect student learning experiences (Higginson, 2000).

Student-Centered Advising

Advisors assist students in designing and achieving appropriate personal, academic, and career goals. To achieve these objectives, they must assist students in identifying options and exploring alternatives to make appropriate decisions, evaluate personal and academic strengths and weaknesses, and develop skills needed for successful completion of the degree. To be effective in this endeavor, advisors must assess and address students' individual needs. Before advisors can identify students' needs, they must first know the students.

Valuable information about advisees can be extracted from the institution's student information system, so advisors need to learn to navigate and access information from it. However, more important than getting up to speed with institutional technology, the faculty advisor needs to take the time to listen to advisee narratives, which will often reveal insights into the student's areas of excitement and concern.

The types of information new faculty advisors should learn will vary according to the personal and academic developmental levels of their students. In general, first-year students present different needs than do upper-level students. For example, first-year students likely need to focus on entry-level major requirements, the general education program, basic university procedures (e.g., declare a major or drop a course), and important dates and deadlines. Third- or fourth-year students may initially look to major and graduation requirements, then turn their attention to specific data on certification requirements, internships, or graduate school or professional program application processes. Likewise, students with declared majors need different information than do undeclared students.

Smaller cohorts also challenge advisors with unique issues. For example, adult students and returning student veterans, who bring a wealth of knowledge, experience, and depth of character to campus, present issues unlike those of many traditional-aged students. First-generation college students, without the advantage of parental or personal knowledge of the college experience, may struggle with the general goals and vocabulary of higher education, as well as navigation of the specific institutional system. In addition to identifying the general needs associated with the student's cohort, the faculty advisor must recognize the student's individual characteristics and respond to his or her specific needs.

The External Environment

The external environment of postsecondary institutions has evolved from local and regional concerns to global connections. As a result, education extends beyond the classroom to prepare students for spheres outside their immediate world. Faculty advisors can link students to external arenas through their established professional and disciplinary networks and other referral sources and services. In practice, they often use their connections and knowledge to combine academic pursuits with real-world applications and settings, such as service learning opportunities, cooperative education programs, and internship experiences.

Through their personal knowledge and experiences with various aspects of the external environment, faculty advisors also assist students in identifying options for major fields of study and prepare them for new, emerging career fields. They can pair students' personal and academic interests to specialized concentrations within a career field, such as business, social services, law or medicine, as well as help them identify and prepare for acceptance into appropriate graduate programs.

The external information advisors need corresponds to their unique institutions and positions. For example, faculty advisors in community colleges must rather quickly ascertain knowledge about the transfer process and course articulation policies of the institutions to which students often transfer. Those in vocational training institutions must gain familiarity with employment outlook projections and the skills essential for job placement. Faculty advisors in teacher education programs must know state and regional certification requirements, as well as the school systems and associated administrators where the students may apply for placement. Effective faculty advisors of graduate students know available research and grant opportunities and can suggest appropriate professional associations. Even those advising freshmen need enough awareness to help them engage with the local community or find resources outside the institution.

All advisors need to be knowledgeable about external resources to enrich students' academic experiences and make appropriate referrals for community engagement, as well as for continuing educational or career exploration and development. In addition to assisting students in achieving their academic and professional goals, advisors frequently assist students with broader concerns not adequately addressed through campus resources; for example, advisors may need to refer students for assessment of personal abilities, access to mental health services, connection with religious interests, or help with family, legal, or financial matters.

After hearing the broad realms and complex details learned and embraced by faculty advisors who best advise students, new faculty advisors may be inclined to panic. Therefore, we remind the new advisor that gaining knowledge in context takes time and requires engagement in this developmental process. The first step involves the realization that although they must strive for excellence, first-year advisors are not expected to know all and be all. Achieving excellence in advising compares to gaining fluency in a foreign language (Folsom, Joslin, & Yoder, 2005) or mastering the steps to a rhythmic dance (Wallace & Wallace, 2010): It takes time, and it takes practice. As when undertaking any incremental goal, the advisor must determine the basics to mark realistic milestones for acquiring knowledge in the first year.

Thriving in the First Year: Mastering the Basics

Those new faculty advisors who identify the basic information most important for their students set themselves up to thrive in the first year. Through talking to their students and other advisors, new faculty advisors can identify the questions most often asked. Popular student queries often begin with these key phrases: "What are the requirements for . . . ?" "How do I . . . ?" "Where do I go to . . . ?" "What is the deadline for . . . ?" "What do I do about . . . ?" "Can I . . . ?" Of course, the answers advisors give must relate to the contexts, assisting students to effectively function within their institutions and achieve their educational goals.

Applying Internal Information

All first-year faculty advisors should acquire basic understanding of their institutional environment, including the role of academic advising, the responsibilities for the faculty advisor, and students in the cohort advised. The following checklist provides the general information areas for which advisors will need to research the specifics applicable to their situation:

- o institutional policies, regulations, procedures, and deadlines that students must know;
- o campus resources that provide assistance to students, such as disability offices, tutorial or learning labs, student organizations, career development programs, student health centers, and services for specific student populations;
- o the advising delivery model including features such as advising personnel, process for advising assignments, and advisor and advisee responsibilities; and
- o available advising resources and relevant advising technologies, such as institutional web sites, online degree audits, and communication networks, as well as institutional student information, course registration, early warning, and appointment scheduling systems.

In addition to learning the sources of information, new faculty advisors must create a method for easy, convenient access to it. They may bookmark important web sites as well as obtain hard copies of available informational publications, such as advising and program student handbooks, and the institution's catalog. For specific questions to ask about the institutional environment, see the Applications and Insights—Advisor Checklist of Questions: Institutional Information to Learn in Year 1 after chapter 5. For specific help with managing information, see chapters 5 and 16 as well as Applications and Insights—Organizing the Chaos: Office and Computer at the end of chapter 5.

Assisting With Student Educational Goals

The types of information that advisors need to assist students are linked to three basic components of student success:

- o navigating the institutional system,
- o making appropriate academic decisions, and
- o maximizing use of available resources.

Navigating the Institutional System. To make it through the graduation pipeline, college students need to know the language of higher education and the processes for undertaking tasks on campus. Therefore, first-year faculty advisors should be able to explain the institutional policies, procedures, dates, and deadlines that are most important, utilized, and likely to affect students' academic progress. This set of knowledge includes policies that determine a student's academic standing and progress, such as those that relate to academic probation, dismissal, and readmission; requirements to maintain financial aid and NCAA eligibility; the procedure for declaring or changing a major or minor; student course registration; and the acceptance of transfer credits.

Advisors also must learn appropriate referral resources for specialized expertise, such as maintaining financial aid eligibility. Because complex institutional, state, and federal policies make up the full scope of many referral sources, a faculty advisor should not be expected to grasp the details of all of the programs and regulations; therefore, to ensure that students receive the correct information, advisors must be ready to refer them to the appropriate campus and community sources. See Applications and Insights—Advisor Checklist of Questions: Teaching Students to Navigate the Institutional System at the end of this chapter.

Helping With Academic Decisions. To succeed in college, students must design realistic academic goals and develop the decision-making skills that enable them to achieve those goals. To assist students in making informed decisions, learning objectives for first-year advisor should include

- ability to identify available programs and provide an overview of the requirements (with the aid of an advising handbook and other available resources) for the academic programs of study, majors, minors, and areas of concentration. Faculty advisors must articulate basic information about programs outside of their own department such as requirements to be accepted into a major. They also must know the critical points of contact for the student to receive more information. Faculty advisors should admit shortcomings and offer referrals accordingly; "I can't help you because that is not my department" is never an appropriate response.
- familiarity with the institution's policy on minors. Are students required to declare a minor? If so, what minors are available? What is the procedure to declare one?
- competency in helping students with postbaccalaureate goals, such as medical or law school. To assist these students, faculty advisors need to know the most appropriate programs to prepare the student to pursue such post-undergraduate goals and to assist the student's explorations for advanced studies, using appropriate referrals as necessary.
- proficiency in employing resources to find course descriptions and information on course sequences with increasing commitment of this information to memory.

- o facility in explaining the rationale for the institution's general education program and outlining the various categories and options of appropriate general education courses.
- o aptitude for placing students in specific courses, such as those restricted to certain majors, appropriate for honors students, and that satisfy developmental-level placements.

Encouraging Student Use of Resources. Effective advisors understand the value gained by college students who avail themselves of appropriate resources. To advance this self-help behavior in students as they strive to achieve their personal, educational, and career goals, advisors need familiarity with often-used internal and external resources. They must demonstrate knowledge of services for academic assistance (e.g., tutoring or student–athlete assistance programs), ability assistance (e.g., Office of Disability Services), and career development (e.g., part-time job fairs and internships). Advisors must also know how to link students with appropriate campus student organizations and programs to advance their engagement with the institution and local volunteer opportunities and events that encourage students to connect with their new community. See Applications and Insights—Advisor Checklist of Questions: Teaching Students to Use Resources in chapter 10.

In addition to knowing the services and points of contact for resources available on and off campus, first-year advisors must learn

- o the symptoms indicating that a student may benefit from special services. Advisors can refer to the students' academic records, feedback from course instructors, students' self-reports, and consultation with the institutional offices that serve students with special needs. Faculty academic advisors without counseling backgrounds should seek training on assessing student needs through the institution's counseling, health, career development, or learning centers and new faculty development programs.
- o the Family Educational Rights and Privacy Act (U.S. Department of Education, 2014) policies that ensure the student's right to confidentiality (chapter 8).
- o the relational skills to encourage resistant students to seek needed services (chapter 11).

Mastering and Managing Information

Quality academic advising demands a unique set of internal and external information. Even those who accept that, over time, they will master needed advising knowledge frequently cite information overload as a major challenge. New faculty advisors can face the demands for information and unannounced pop quizzes with confidence by employing a strategy to master and manage the amount of information they will need to process and learn.

Step 1. Identify Needed Information

The New Advisor Development Chart (chapter 1), combined with the sample questions and strategies offered in part three of this *Guidebook,* relates the scope of the internal and external information first-year faculty advisors need to know and manage. New advisors should craft a set of questions pertinent to their institutions and advisees. They can start their personalized list by listening to and asking students about their concerns and by inquiring of peer faculty advisors, professional advisors, and others engaged with students about the issues they regularly encounter.

Step 2. Identify Sources of Available Information

Faculty advisors must seek out and embrace the internal institutional resources delivered electronically and in print. They should seek the wealth of informational resources offered throughout the institution through the campus, academic department, advising center, or other advisor networks. Any who lack formal support for development and guidance on advising (Carlstrom & Miller, 2013) can garner knowledge and institutional understanding from experienced advisors (chapter 17). In institutions utilizing a shared advising model, faculty members can lean on professional advisors for answers to important questions.

Specific information on typical student concerns appears in traditional institutional resources, such as the course catalog, student handbook, and advising guidebooks, as well as Frequently Asked Questions (FAQs) sections of program and department web sites. In addition, faculty members should make contacts with and stay abreast of web sites offered through the offices of the registrar, admissions, and closely related academic departments.

In addition, in today's cyber world, advisors and students have unprecedented access to information provided throughout the external environment. Faculty advisors can find vetted answers to almost any student question through professional association web sites, such as the Clearinghouse from NACADA: The Global Community for Academic Advising. In addition to the Clearinghouse, NACADA provides excellent sources of information about advising and advisor development: *Academic Advising Today* and the *NACADA Journal* are open access venues that offer, respectively, practice- and research-based articles. Faculty advisors at all levels of experience should be encouraged to attend national and regional conferences where they can receive updates on new theories and practices, obtain new perspectives, and experience rejuvenation. New advisors should also participate in e-mail lists related to their personal advising goals and interests.

Step 3. Create an Advising Resource Tool Kit

New faculty advisors can take solace in the realization that the recurring quizzes are open book. Therefore, each advisor should create a readily accessible set of resources and a cheat sheet that include needed information. Helpful resources can be found in hard copy and electronic formats, such as

- the institutional catalog, student handbook, and departmental advising guidebooks. However, at many institutions, students are accountable to meet the policies and requirements in place at the time of their acceptance as degree-seeking students. As programs and policies change, institutional publications, in print and electronic formats, are periodically updated; therefore, advisors must ensure that they are providing accurate information to their advisees.

- a list of student FAQs with answers. New advisors should consolidate known FAQs and answers from the various sources they have uncovered. In addition to providing handy access, the list, whether kept as an electronic file or printed copy, must reflect current institutional and student information. The questions might remain the same, but the answers may change along with adjustments in institutional policies, programs, and procedures.

- contact list for key people in important offices across campus including name, office location, phone number, and e-mail addresses.

- copies of the campus map with key locations identified to distribute to students.

- bookmarked links to valuable resources for advisor development, such as those from NACADA.

Final Lessons for First-Year Faculty Advisors

Effective Advisors Are Continuing Learners

The art of academic advising reflects dynamic processes practiced in a continuously evolving academic environment with a changing student body. Faculty advisors must keep up with modifications in university policies, programs, advising resources, and advising best practices or they risk employing ineffective advising methods that misguide students with outdated information. Ongoing development is implicit in the concept of advising as an art (chapter 1); therefore, ongoing advisor development is critical to the effectiveness of the advisor (Wallace & Wallace, 2010; chapter 17).

Effective Advisors Are Teachers

Students accustomed to information available at their fingertips often unrealistically expect instant answers to their questions. In addition, Wallace (2007) noted that some students depend upon their advisors for quick answers such that the advisor's office resembles an information booth with a revolving door, often with the same students returning with the same questions. Advisors must overcome the sense of satisfaction in fixing a student's problem, dispel any pride in being known as the go-to person for quick answers, and dissuade students from such dependency. The reliant student's behavior may feed the advisor's ego, but fails to empower the student.

Faced with the demand to provide accurate, on-the-spot information, the new advisor's heart may start racing, especially if the answer does not immediately come to mind. Rather than panic, the advisor as teacher needs to remember that in the advising office, just like in the classroom, a primary objective should be to teach students to take responsibility for their decisions. By modeling the process of finding the answer, not just giving the answer, both the new advisor and the advisee learn: The former adds to the advising tool kit and the latter gains greater understanding of the issues and rationales of policies and procedures. Instead of exulting in the ability to provide the answer, the faculty advisor who embraces advising as teaching observes with satisfaction as the student discovers the answer. Advisors can extend this gratification as they witness students taking ownership of their educational experiences and developing critical skills transferable to other dimensions of their lives. In addition, faculty advisors reduce the number of unannounced pop quizzes they encounter such that they can invest more time in effectively advising students and in professional development activities.

Effective Advisors Demonstrate Competence

As all teachers know, a perfect score on a pop quiz does not necessarily translate to proficiency in the topic of the test. Likewise, although first-year faculty advisors must initially focus on learning the basic advising procedures on their campuses, the needs of their students, and the important information and resources available to address those needs, they must continuously engage in learning about advising and about the advisor's role in assisting students with their educational goals. All advisors need a professional development plan that fine-tunes the craft of advising and leads to a deeper understanding and application of advising strategies. This plan should include topics such as best practices, student development and career development theories, and the use of technology (chapter 17).

Ultimately, advisors need to acquire the knowledge to teach students how to successfully navigate the institutional system through the completion of a desired program of study.

First-year faculty advisors need to realize that excellent academic advising, like teaching, is an art and a science, and becoming masterful advisor requires progress through a developmental learning process (Folsom, 2007). The New Advisor Development Chart (chapter 1) provides a road map for the advisor's journey. The taxonomy provides implicit short- and long-term goals that serve as guideposts: a starting point and destination, as well as checkpoints to document and gain insight into the advisor's growth toward excellence.

Pop Quiz—Ready!

There is a knock on the door. A student enters and asks, "Professor Taylor, do you have a minute?" Dr. Taylor welcomes the student and asks, "How may I assist you?" The student responds, "You're my advisor, and I have a question about. . . ." It is pop quiz time. Dr. Taylor, prepared and with advising resources at hand, confidently smiles.

Aiming for Excellence

o Chart milestones in learning information for becoming an effective advisor. In your first year, to identify current areas of knowledge and those that must be acquired, use the questions and strategies in the Applications and Insights, especially the Advisor Checklists of Questions on Institutional Information to Learn in Year 1, Teaching Students to Navigate the Institutional System, Student Information to Learn in Year 1, and Teaching Students to Use Resources. Then at the end of your first year, use these as post-tests to assess growth. This self-assessment should be repeated in each continuing year.

o Identify internal (institutional) and external sources of information that provide answers to the questions students may ask. For quick access to needed information, bookmark the most useful electronic sources and obtain hard copies of available institutional publications with basic information tabbed and highlighted.

o Construct a FAQs list by consulting with other advisors, reviewing existing lists, and listening to students. Maintain it as an evolving, dynamic document to ensure the relevancy and accuracy of the questions and answers.

o Review the file of an advisee with an upcoming appointment. Based on information gleaned from the file, how will you greet the student and open the conversation?

o Generate descriptions of the programs, majors, and minors offered through the institution and meet with the department chair or program director to discuss the information that students interested in these areas should know.

o Use the New Advisor Development Chart in chapter 1 to design a professional development agenda that includes attending at least one national or regional NACADA conference, participating in available institutional training opportunities, and reading current articles on the theory and practice of advising.

o Design and implement a method to assess your effectiveness as a faculty advisor. This could include soliciting student feedback through surveys and peer observations of advising sessions.

o Does your institution create and maintain a demographic and academic profile of its students? (Admissions and registrar personnel as well as web sites may present or possess student data.) If it does, use it to learn about the students who attend your institution and specifically those you advise. In what ways do your advisees fit into the student profile at the institutional level? How do they differ from the majority cohorts?

References

Carlstrom, A., & Miller, M. A. (2013). *2011 NACADA national survey of academic advising* (Monograph No. 25). Retrieved from www.nacada.ksu.edu/Resources/Clearinghouse /View-Articles/2011-NACADA-National-Survey.aspx

Drake, J. K. (2013). Advising as teaching and the advisor as teacher in theory and in practice. In J. K. Drake, P. Jordan, & M. A. Miller (Eds.), *Academic advising approaches: Strategies that teach students to make the most of college* (pp. 17–32). Manhattan, KS: National Academic Advising Association.

Folsom, P. (Ed.). (2007). *The new advisor guidebook: Mastering the art of advising through the first year and beyond* (Monograph No. 16). Manhattan, KS: National Academic Advising Association.

Folsom, P., Joslin, J., & Yoder, F. (2005). *From advisor training to advisor development: Creating a blueprint for first-year advisors.* Retrieved from www.nacada.ksu.edu/Resources/Clearinghouse/View-Articles/Training-Blueprint-for-New-Advisors.aspx

Habley, W. (1995). Advisor training in the context of a teaching enhancement center. In R. E. Glennen & F. N. Vowell (Eds.), *Academic advising as a comprehensive campus process* (Monograph No. 2) (pp. 75–79). Manhattan, KS: National Academic Advising Association.

Higginson, L. C. (2000). A framework for training program content. In V. N. Gordon & W. R. Habley (Eds.), *Academic advising: A comprehensive handbook* (1st ed.) (pp. 298–307). San Francisco, CA: Jossey-Bass.

King, M., & Kerr, T. (2005). Academic advising. In M. L. Upcraft, J. Gardner, & B. O. Barefoot (Eds.), *Challenging and supporting the first-year student: A handbook for improving the first year of college* (pp. 320–338). San Francisco, CA: Jossey-Bass.

U.S. Department of Education. (2014). *Family Educational Rights and Privacy Act (FERPA).* Retrieved from http://www2.ed.gov/policy/gen/guid/fpco/ferpa/index.html

Wallace, S. (2007). Teaching students to become responsible advisees. *Academic Advising Today,* 30(3). Retrieved from http://www.nacada.ksu.edu/Portals/0/ePub/documents/30_3.pdf

Wallace, S. (2013). Implications for faculty advising. In A. H. Carlstrom & M. A. Miller (Eds.), *2011 NACADA national survey of academic advising* (Monograph No. 25). Retrieved from http://www.nacada.ksu.edu/Resources/Clearinghouse /View-Articles/Implications-for-faculty-advising-2011-National-Survey.aspx

Wallace, S., & Wallace, B. (2010). Training faculty advisors. In J. Givans Voller, M. A. Miller, & S. L. Neste (Eds.), *Comprehensive advisor training and development: Practices that deliver* (Monograph No. 21) (pp. 53–59). Manhattan, KS: National Academic Advising Association.

Applications and Insights

Advisor Checklist of Questions: Teaching Students to Navigate the Institutional System

Stephen O. Wallace and Beverly A. Wallace

To answer questions such as the ones that follow, first-year advisors must know institutional policies and procedures as well as important dates and deadlines:

- How many credits must a student carry to be considered full-time?
- What GPA is required to maintain satisfactory academic progress?
- What are the processes associated with academic probation and reinstatement to good standing?
- What is the policy on academic dismissal? Readmission?
- How many credits must a student complete to remain eligible for financial aid?
- What are the NCAA regulations for a student-athlete to remain eligible?
- How does a student declare or change a major or minor?
  - What are the deadlines for declaring or changing a major?
  - Must students fulfill specified requirements, such as GPA or prerequisite courses, to be eligible to declare a specific major?
  - What are the regulations for declaring a double major? Double minor?
  - What are the institution's course registration procedures?
- When do students register?
  - What must students do before they are permitted to register?
  - How do students register for courses?
  - How do students change their schedules?
  - How do students drop or withdraw from a course?
  - How do students request permission to register for a course that is restricted or closed?
- What is the course availability?
- Are some courses restricted to certain populations of students (e.g., upper-division, certain majors)?
- What prerequisites must students satisfy?
- Are some courses offered only during certain semesters?

- o How does a student request permission for course substitutions?
- o Does the institution offer off-campus or online courses?
  - o What are the requirements, if any, for a student to be eligible to register for online or off-campus courses?
  - o Is the number of extended courses limited per semester?
  - o Do all extended courses contribute to graduation requirements or is the number restricted?
- o What is the institution's placement testing policy? For new students? For transfer students?
- o What institutional policies apply specifically for students placed in developmental-level courses?
- o Can students test out of a course for credit?
- o What transfer credits are accepted from other schools?
  - o Is the number of transfer credits applicable toward graduation limited?
  - o What grade is required for a transfer course to be accepted for credit?
  - o What is the procedure for determining whether the transfer course is credited toward the student's program of study or as an elective?
  - o What transfer course grades are factored into the student's GPA at the receiving school?
- o What is the institution's or unit's policy for accepting standardized testing (e.g., AP or CLEP) scores for course credit?
- o What is the institution's course repeat policy?
  - o What restrictions, if any, are placed on repeat courses? For example, how many times can a student repeat a class necessary for graduation?
  - o How are repeat grades factored into the student's GPA?
  - o Can a student repeat a failed course at another institution and transfer it back to satisfy program or graduation requirements?
- o What is the deadline to apply for graduation?
- o What processes must a student undertake to withdraw from the institution without jeopardizing readmission?

7

CAREER ADVISING

THE INTERSECTION OF INTERNAL AND EXTERNAL INFORMATION

Dorothy Burton Nelson

All advisors receive career-related questions from students, such as "What is the best college major for me?" "What career(s) can I enter with this major?" and "What do I need to do to get accepted by my desired professional or graduate school?" Many students equate decisions about college majors to career choices (Gordon, 2006). Even advisors who focus primarily on academics need enough information to respond to career-related questions and address assumptions. Advisors transitioning from a purely curricular perspective to one that incorporates career advising must appropriately assess information and guide students through the complexities of integrating knowledge about themselves, the workforce, and career-related decision making. Minimally, advisors demonstrate familiarity with the skills employers seek, describe ways the college curriculum builds these skills, and provide information or referrals that will expand students' comprehension of the job prospects in their field so that they can make informed educational and career decisions. To enhance their overall effectiveness as agents of long-term student success, advisors must know the basic components of career advising.

Building a Knowledge Base for Career Advising

This chapter focuses on the internal (or institutional) and external informational needs for effective career advising. Internal information includes knowledge about academic programs; curricular requirements; policies and procedures; special populations and services; institutional rules, regulations, and organizational structures; and technologies used in advising and registration. That is, it advances advisor efforts in moving students into, through, and out of the institution (Higginson, 2000). For career advising, external information includes data on the workforce, labor market, and economy as well as supply and demand shifts, internships, professional associations and schools, job search strategies, and so forth. New advisors should note that two additional types of information contribute to effective career advising: knowledge of the student's characteristics and an understanding of decision-making dynamics (Gordon, 2006; Holland, 1973; O'Banion, 1972/1994/2009; Parsons, 1909).

Obtaining and Managing Information for a Career-Advising Model

Career advising most fully integrates internal and external information for students (Higginson, 2000). Therefore, to advise students effectively regarding careers, advisors must possess both a full understanding of and the facility to access internal and external sources of information. Advisors may use a career-advising model as a framework to help them identify the essential information they need to learn and subsequently deliver to students. Although a number of good career-advising models assist advisors, in this chapter, I focus on a modification of Virginia Gordon's (2006) 3-I process.

In *Career Advising: An Academic Advisor's Guide*, Gordon (2006) described the competencies and the knowledge bases necessary for those who engage in career advising. The 3-I model focuses on understanding students and their advising needs, identifying the resources that best inform the career-advising process, and undertaking the necessary steps for helping students integrate information into an action plan for effective career decision making. The 3-I framework is composed of the following interactive and continuously used components:

○ inquire,

○ inform, and

○ integrate.

Inquire

Through the inquire phase of Gordon's (2006) 3-I model, advisors gain an understanding about students, including insight into their situations and informational needs. Advisors enter this phase at the beginning of the advising session or when students present with problems or questions. In this information-gathering process, both advisor and student ask and answer questions that span students' academic and nonacademic lives, such as personal, financial, or institutional concerns. This complex interaction typically extends over several advising sessions. New advisors must recognize advisee questions that appear related to academics but reflect career concerns:

○ Is this the right major for me?

○ What can I do with this major?

○ Is this the right major for getting a job in _____?

○ I really don't find my _____ classes interesting.

○ I've been thinking about changing majors.

These inquiries and statements, among others, suggest that students are experiencing career-related information deficits (Gordon, 2006, p. 49) such that they do not see ways occupations relate to a chosen college major. Specifically, they may lack informational or experiential knowledge about occupations that interest them. Furthermore, they may not know how to acquire relevant data about careers. The collaborative process encourages the advisor and advisee to sort through the student's issues, concerns, and questions as they determine the precise information needed for effective decision making or issue resolution.

Inform

In the inform phase, the advisor helps the student acquire self-awareness about occupations of interest and the educational requirements for the related major. Like the inquiry component, it involves collaboration: Although students can surf the Internet to obtain career-related information, Alice Reinarz and Nathaniel Ehrlich (2002) found that students comprehended this retrieved data better by working with an advisor. Students gain self-knowledge by employing instruments that elicit information about their personality and other characteristics, such as interests, abilities, and values as well as personality type. Therefore, advisors can help students by connecting them with resources that reveal aspects of their personalities and other characteristics.

Career assessment tools may help clarify students' personality profiles, which further aid advisees in determining realistic career and academic directions. The occupational aspect of the inform phase also involves student use of resources to generate career options commensurate with their personality profile or assessment results. Such tools may yield many occupations of potential fit or interest, but advisors can help students narrow down the options to those with the highest levels of congruence to personality assessment results. In addition, advisors direct students to additional information about occupations. In the inform phase process, students' potential college majors often emerge.

The inform phase requires the development of the most extensive and complete integration of internal and external knowledge bases by advisors and may represent the most challenging phase for new advisors without prior training on or experience with career advising. Seasoned career advisors can readily select the appropriate career assessment and prepare individuals for, administer, and interpret formal or informal assessments such as the *Myers-Briggs Type Indicator (MBTI)* (CPP, 2009a; The Myers-Briggs Foundation, 2014), *John Holland's Self-Directed Search* (PAR, Inc., 2013), and other interest inventories (e.g., COPS [EDITS Online, 2012], or the *Strong Interest Inventory* [CPP, 2009b]). Veteran career advisors also display knowledge about multiple career exploration resources (print, electronic, and experiential) and connect students to the most appropriate ones for their unique searches. Finally, they know the characteristics of students who have demonstrated success in specific majors and can use that insight to connect other students to potential majors.

During their first year, new advisors learn academic requirements as well as the nature of major course work as they gain familiarity with the characteristics of students successfully completing specific majors (internal information). If their advising responsibilities relate primarily to academic concerns, they should learn to recognize career-related questions (see inquiry phase) as well as communicate the location of on-campus career-related services (e.g., for assessment, exploration, resume writing, experiential learning opportunities, and job search readiness and strategies as well as interviewing and placement).

New advisors benefit from knowing a few career exploration resources. The largest and most credible body of workforce information, the U.S. Department of Labor, categorizes and condenses pertinent occupation information into user-friendly databases, including the interactive O*Net Online. Additional resources include the *Occupational Outlook Handbook* (OOH) (online and hardcopy) by the U.S. Bureau of Labor Statistics (n.d.). Both OOH and O*Net rely on ongoing research and data collection on an array of workplace information. For example, specific job description entries include data, collected over a 10-year period and projected for the upcoming decade, on work tasks, environments, and locations; projected growth or decline of hiring; technological influences; experience and educational requirements; wages; special features; and so forth. The entries are based on general trends in the workplace that affect all occupations as well as those specific to a particular line of work and related occupations.

New advisors begin to grasp the ways skills gained in academic programs prepare students for various occupations and the ways competencies required for specific occupations connect to academic majors. However, because the breadth and depth of knowledge required for mastery of the inform phase may overwhelm them, advisors should remember that they do not bear sole responsibility for answers to student questions; in fact, their ability to make proper referrals to campus and community reflects best practices.

After they view themselves with a more objective, realistic perspective and can connect their characteristics to suitable occupations, students should demonstrate more comfort with and excitement about choosing a college major or place more energy in their current major because they can initiate planning with the end goal in mind (Covey, 1990). Guiding students through this phase can be one of the most exciting and meaningful components of the career-advising process.

Integrate

In the integrate phase, advisors and students examine, evaluate, and synthesize the information they have acquired (Gordon, 2006). The information that students have gained about themselves, suitable occupational options, and related college majors provides the foundation for this phase, but students must apply their knowledge to make decisions regarding a career or major. Gordon (2006) noted that the decision-making characteristic of this phase links both of the previous parts of career advising. Students, explicitly or not, make decisions on a daily basis, including the option of declining to choose. Some students remain unmoved in the integrate phase; therefore, new advisors must recognize the dynamics that expedite or inhibit the decision-making process and should note behaviors such as reticence, dependence, or negativity.

Until the point of decision difficulties, advisors may not have recognized under-currents of internal or external influences affecting the student. Inhibiting factors, such as family pressures, economic shifts, and workforce supply and demand fluctu-ations as well as levels of career self-efficacy and clarified self-concept, among oth-ers, may impede the career decision-making process (Sampson, Reardon, Peterson, & Lenz, 2004). According to the Sampson et al. (2004) readiness model, career decision-making inhibition factors fall into two categories: capability and complexity. Capabil-ity factors are internal to the person and delay or impede career decisions. Complexity involves environmental factors, or dynamics external to the person, that curb readi-ness to move forward. Indecision related to internal or external pressures may indicate the need for referrals to other campus support services, such as a counseling center or career services office.

In addition to an extensive internal and external knowledge base, advisors work-ing in the integrate phase must understand the decision-making process; therefore, they may benefit from identifying a decision-making framework to guide their prac-tice. Robert Lock (2004) identified five decision-making coping styles that can help advisors to identify obstacles and to encourage student management of them in the decision-making process:

- *Unconflicted adherence* is typified by little consideration of options and a resistance to explore based on preference for the known, familiar, and comfortable.

- *Unconflicted change*, also characterized by little purposeful deliberation or exploration, is often seen as arbitrary or impulsive change when the decision maker acts according to a gut feeling.

- *Defensive avoidance* involves exaggerated anxiety such that decisions are delayed, exacerbating stress levels and perpetuating a vicious cycle.

- *Hypervigilance* may logically follow defensive avoidance for those facing the immediacy of decision making. Hypervigilant decision makers tend to panic over imminent decisions, characterized by redundant and obsessive thought processes. Quite often, fear of negative consequences serves as the precipitating culprit. All important decisions may evoke a certain level of worry, which typically elicits caution and thoughtfulness.

- *Vigilance* is characterized by attentiveness and caution, a demonstrated understanding that action allows one to manage and reduce inordinate affective responses, such as anxiety. Vigilant decision makers understand timeliness and the need to take certain risks. (pp. 310–312)

Advisors can certainly teach vigilance in decision making. Specifically, they can serve as role models and managers for making healthy and productive decisions (Lock, 2004). To engage students in the vigilant decision-making process, advisors use tools that will demystify impending decisions. For example, when asking a student about career and academic concerns, the advisor should use a system for recording student issues as clearly and accurately as possible. As conversations progress, written documentation captures thoughts and ideas that contradict or confirm prior information; moving data from the compartments of the mind to the printed word creates a powerful means of seeing patterns and confusion. Tools, such as worksheets, matrixes, and computer record-keeping systems, increase clarity and reduce redundancy, thus promoting effective decision making.

The vigilant decision-making style emerges in Gordon's (2006) 3-I model. In the inquire phase, advisors help advisees see the impending decisions so they can set up the next logical step: brainstorming options and gathering necessary information for choosing. Finally, in the integrate phase of the 3-I model, advisors model assessment and evaluation of information such that the student can determine ensuing consequences of potential decisions. Becoming a vigilant decision maker requires focus on rational thought and separation of fantasy from fact.

Decision making and action may appear to be culminating events for a person engaged in the workforce exploration process, but decision making is neither a disconnected, an isolated, nor a one-time activity, nor does it necessarily yield a stable outcome that terminates the process. For this reason, phases in Gordon's (2006) 3-I model are interactive and interwoven; each component can be revisited at any point in the career exploration process. In the integrate phase, the advisor may need to return to the inquire and inform phases to gather more information about the student, workforce, or other factors.

Decision-Making Follow-Up

Students may make career decisions relatively early, before taking many classes in their major or participating in firsthand experiences, such as internships in their chosen fields. For example, a pre-medical student shadowing a doctor may reconsider the desire to tackle the stress they witness in a medical practice. Advisors help students evaluate the effectiveness of their decisions and goals by monitoring their academic progress and discussing the positive or negative impacts of experiential learning experiences on their decisions. Advisors also assist students in navigating through their remaining college years, making necessary adjustments to their academic plans as necessary.

As students gain more decision-making experience, advisors can track their academic progress to suggest timely and important adjustments to goals and academic plans as well as gauge the appropriateness of the original decision. Over time, advisors must gain in-depth knowledge about academic requirements, course sequencing, prerequisites, and course availability (internal information) for the major as well as courses required for students' occupational or postgraduate goals (external information). They also recognize signs of student struggle in majors, such as poor grades, withdrawals from major classes, avoidance of major course work, and lack of progression in the field of study, as well as better performance in elective or non-major courses.

Career-Advising Interviewing Techniques

Each phase of the career-advising process—inquire, inform, integrate as well as deciding, mapping, and tracking—involves a complex advising interaction requiring strong interviewing skills. New advisors can use an established career interviewing construct by Norman E. Amundson (2003) to guide them in these interactions and gain a better understanding of their students. Amundson identified five lines of questioning to help advisors interview students regarding careers.

- Elicit the idea or belief component of understanding by asking questions that reveal the student's thoughts and situations: "What concerns do you have about your academic plans?"
- "Gather confirming and disputing evidence" about information previously gleaned from a student: "Can you identify any reasons that you should not pursue the_____ field?"
- "Seek information about concept development"; that is, determine the development level of the student's ideas: "How long have you considered this field?"
- Determine social supports for making career decisions: "How did your parents/friends/spouse respond to your thoughts?"
- Determine both positive and negative impacts of the decision by helping the student evaluate and confirm decisions: "What do you see as the positives of making a career change at this time?"

This interview process can be an exploration and discovery process for the student and advisor such that it clarifies the type of additional information that may be needed. The basis of Amundson's (2003) interviewing technique involves toggling back and forth to reveal confirming and contradictory evidence (pp. 104–107).

Career Advising in Action: A Case Study Using Gordon's 3-I Model

The dynamics involved in career advising may present challenges for advisors who lack formal career-advising training, but all advisors benefit from a basic understanding of career advising. The case study presents application of Gordon (2006) 3-I career-advising phases: inquiry, inform, integrate, and follow-up. For each phase, the necessary advising knowledge, as characterized by Higginson (2000), and the interview techniques of Amundson (2003) are identified.

Gordon's (2006) 3-I Model	Amundson's (2003) Five Lines of Questioning and Higginson's (2000) Internal and External Knowledge for Advisors
Phase: Inquire	
The week before registering for spring classes, Reggie meets with an advisor. In the meeting, Reggie expresses lack of clarity about a major, is "burned out" with school, and wants a semester of "easy" classes before making a decision about a major. The advisor, Dom, notices that the grade report showed adequate progress but did not reflect Reggie's abilities. Dom asks if they could put aside scheduling concerns for a minute and talk about Reggie. Specifically, Dom asks about Reggie's most pressing career-related concerns and any career goals past or present. Reggie had thought about being a teacher, but had recently rejected that idea.	**Elicit the idea or belief presented by the student:** *"What concerns do you have about your career plans?"* Recognizes career-related issues Uses knowledge about academics (or majors) to recognize risk statements by students
Dom probes Reggie about the aspects of teaching once considered attractive as well as the reasons this option no longer is under consideration. Reggie had liked the idea of working with children, enjoyed helping at a preschool, looked forward to extended time off over the summers, but expresses discouragement based on many complaints from teachers about low pay and national or state mandates that limit their ability to work effectively with children.	**Gather confirming and disputing evidence:** *"Can you identify any reasons that you should not pursue the_____ field?"* *"Explain your doubts about going into this field."* **Seek information about concept development:** *"What were the most attractive features to you?"* *"What caused you to begin doubting your decision?"*
In response, Dom asks Reggie to consider learning more about the field of teaching and other career fields. Dom also suggests that Reggie undertake a career assessment to learn more about personal interests and identify strengths and talents. Reggie agrees and completes an informal screening version of *John Holland's Self-Directed Search*, a personality assessment.	**Advisor knowledge needed:** Identifies appropriate assessments (external) and career exploration (external) If advisor is not conducting the assessment, refers student to appropriate office (internal)

Phase: Inform	
After Reggie completes the Holland screening, Dom reviews the output, noting that all six Holland personality types make up Reggie's personality structure, but with the Social-Artistic-Conventional typings emerging as dominant. Dom explains that the interests and social personality type are associated with helping professions; specifically, artistic types are drawn to situations in which they are free to create and express themselves, and conventional types like to work within structure and predictability.	**Gather confirming and disputing evidence:** *"What qualities or characteristics do you possess?"* *"What would make you a good _____?"*
Reggie expresses happy surprise by these results, noting that some of these personality traits would have remained unexplored without the assessment, but they seem to fit extremely well.	**Seek information about concept development:** *"What were the most attractive features to you?"*
Dom further explains that using the Holland code to seek jobs highly correlated with the personality type increases the likelihood of job satisfaction. Reggie begins gathering information about occupations.	**Advisor knowledge needed:** Adapts *John Holland's Self-Directed Search* results to occupational choices (external)
Reggie has access to many career search resources, but Dom recommends O*Net Online because it is easy to use, can be accessed from Reggie's residence hall, and is current and accurate. Dom shows Reggie how to access the site and how to enter the dominant Holland types to start the search. Reggie finds that using all three dominant types as input yields only four jobs, but that reducing the Holland types to two results in a huge list. Dom notes that Reggie must go through the larger list and write down the job titles that sound interesting. Reggie finds five titles, but other than elementary school teacher, the titles seem unfamiliar. Dom points out the hyperlink associated with each title, which can be used to find out more about each job. Dom suggests that Reggie use a worksheet so that the same information (educational and experiential requirements, flexible time, job security, and wages) is documented for every job title written down. Reggie makes another appointment after completing the search process.	Connects to tools for learning more about careers (external)

Phase: Integrate	
When Reggie returns, Dom asks about the most attractive jobs found to date. The information made Reggie feel very positive about teaching. Upon Dom's request for an explanation, Reggie reports discovering that although working with behavioral problems drove some teachers away from the field, other teachers cited this work as challenging and exciting.	**Determine the social supports:** *"Have you discussed your concerns or ideas with anyone?"*
In addition, two other jobs on the list sounded interesting and also required a degree in education. Dom and Reggie outline the positives and negatives of the jobs explored. Dom asks if Reggie has enough information to make a decision, and Reggie responds in the affirmative with the intention to declare an education major.	**Advisor knowledge needed:** Helps develop decision-making skills (conceptual/relational) **Determine both positive and negative impact of the decision:** *"What are the consequences you will face when making this decision?"* *"Can you accept those consequences?"* *"Is there anything you can do to minimize the consequences?"*
Dom discusses the timing of Reggie's decision, while also asking about other concerns that might warrant waiting a while—possibly taking time to reflect and identify other questions or concerns before moving forward.	*"Explain the benefits of making the choice right now versus waiting awhile."*
Reggie does not feel more time is necessary, and so Dom describes the process for declaring a major and locating the requirements for it in the institutional online catalog. Dom then instructs Reggie to read the information very carefully, jotting down questions for their next advising session.	**Advisor knowledge needed:** Explains institutional procedures and policies (external)
Phase: Follow-Up	
Reggie and Dom meet again to develop a plan to graduate with an education major and to select specific classes for the upcoming term. Dom indicates a desire to meet with Reggie until graduation to discuss career and academic goals as well as address any obstacles or challenges Reggie may face.	Uses institutional resources and knowledge of course sequencing to create a plan to graduation (internal) Identifies risk factors or challenges associated with major (internal and external)

Note. John Holland's Self-Directed Search (SDS) (PAR, Inc., 2013); *O*Net online* (U.S. Department of Labor, n.d.).

Summary

Career advising makes meaning of academia. The extensive information needed for delivering effective career advising spans internal or institutional dynamics as well as external, or workforce, factors (Higginson, 2000). Using a student-centered career-advising model allows advisors to effectively identify knowledge areas to master, organize, and manage. Using an established framework for interviewing in combination with a career-advising model helps ensure that new advisors ask students questions that move them toward making informed, appropriate college-major and career decisions.

The ultimate goal of career advising, however, involves more than finding and accessing career information. It hinges on helping advisees transform information into knowledge applicable to their decision making (Carr & Epstein, 2009). Academic programs become alive and meaningful to students fortunate enough to engage with advisors in discussions that involve more than curriculum topics (Glennen & Vowell, 1995). In addition to helping students meet goals, this process contributes to an exciting and challenging career for advisors.

Aiming for Excellence

o To connect and become comfortable with career development and career advising, first accept that everyone goes through the process. Writing about your own career journey may help you connect with others sorting out the same or similar issues. It will also help you connect with tasks involved in career advising. Begin by writing your own career autobiography and consider the reasons you liked or disliked certain jobs. Identify the most satisfying work-related experiences. Think about influential people in your work choices and pinpoint the reason they exerted an impact. Determine career-related questions or struggles that remain unanswered or unresolved. Identify obstacles overcome or in your current path.

o Conduct a scavenger hunt on campus to discover the available career-related resources. Visit identified units to learn more about their role, scope, and mission. Ask permission to observe or audit one or more career classes to build your career knowledge base.

o Sign up with Career Services to learn about the career development process as students experience it. Become familiar with the assessment instruments used and the educational requirements (if any) for administering them to students. If pencil-and-paper assessment tools are not used, request access to any online career assessment and exploration programs used by your institution (e.g., Focus 2, Kuder, SIGI[3]). Pretend to be in the process of making important decisions: You may reconnect with an ignored calling.

o Practice administering one of your favorite assessments with a willing colleague (or family member). Your practice should include helping students prepare for the assessment, administering the instrument (if part of the advising role), interpreting the results, and helping the person understand ways to use the output in making important decisions. Investigate information sources that can help answer the ubiquitous question "What can I do with a degree in___?" Review the data until you can easily name 5 to 10 of the most common jobs associated with any given major and typical employer types (e.g., federal or state agencies, retail stores, private firms, major hospitals, hotels and restaurants, entertainment). Become familiar with key personality characteristics for each of the common jobs because they relate to high levels of job satisfaction.

o Become a member of NACADA to gain access to all published and online materials. Join an electronic mailing service (e.g., Listserv) that deals with career advising and development to communicate with a broad community about situations, concerns, and questions. Share and compare best practices. Networking with others across institutional types proves an ancillary benefit as you become a recognized commodity in a professional organization. Get involved!

o Register in a career development course with the aim of equipping academic advisors with career-advising skills.

References

Amundson, N. E. (2003). *Active engagement: Enhancing the career counseling process* (2nd ed.). Richmond, BC, Canada: Ergon Communications.

Carr, D. L., & Epstein, S. A. (2009). Information resources to enhance career advising. In K. F. Hughey, D. Nelson, J. K. Damminger, & B. McCalla-Wriggins (Eds.), *The handbook of career advising* (pp. 146–181). San Francisco, CA: Jossey-Bass.

Covey, S. R. (1990). *The 7 habits of highly effective people: Powerful lessons in personal change*. New York, NY: Simon & Schuster.

CPP. (2009a). *The Myers-Briggs Type Indicator (MBTI)*. Retrieved from https://www.cpp.com/products/mbti/index.aspx

CPP. (2009b). *Strong Interest Inventory*. Retrieved from https://www.cpp.com/products/strong/index.aspx

EDITS Online. (2012). *COPS Interest Inventory*. Retrieved from http://www.edits.net/2010-04-05-16-32-27/18-cops.html

Glennen, R. E., & Vowell, F. N. (1995). Selecting, training, rewarding, and recognizing faculty advisors. In M. L. Upcraft & G. L. Kramer (Eds.), *First-year academic advising: Patterns in the present, pathways to the future* (Monograph No. 18) (pp. 69–74). Columbia: University of South Carolina, National Resource Center for the Freshman Year Experience & Students in Transition.

Gordon, V. N. (2006). *Career advising: An academic advisor's guide*. San Francisco, CA: Jossey-Bass.

Higginson, L. C. (2000). A framework for training program content. In V. N. Gordon & W. R. Habley (Eds.), *Academic advising: A comprehensive handbook* (pp. 298–308). San Francisco, CA: Jossey-Bass.

Holland, J. L. (1973). *Making vocational choices: A theory of careers*. Englewood Cliffs, NJ: Prentice-Hall.

Lock, R. D. (2004). *Taking charge of your career direction: Career planning guide, Book 1* (5th ed.). Belmont, CA: Thomson Brooks/Cole.

The Myers-Briggs Foundation. (2014). *The Myers-Briggs Type Indicator*. Retrieved from http://www.myersbriggs.org/

O'Banion, T. (2009). An academic advising model. *NACADA Journal, 14*(2), 10–16. (Reprinted from *Junior College Journal, 42*, 1972, pp. 62, 63, 66–69; *NACADA Journal, 14*[2], 1994, pp. 10–16)

PAR, Inc. (2013). *John Holland's Self-Directed Search* (SDS). Retrieved from http://www.self-directed-search.com/

Parsons, F. (1909). *Choosing a vocation*. Boston, MA: Houghton Mifflin.

Reinarz, A. G., & Ehrlich, N. (2002). Assessment of academic advising: A cross-sectional study. *NACADA Journal, 22*(2), 50–65.

Sampson, J. P., Jr., Reardon, R. C., Peterson, G. W., & Lenz, J. G. (2004). *Career counseling & services: A cognitive information processing approach*. Belmont, CA: Brooks/Cole.

U.S. Bureau of Labor Statistics. (n.d.). *Occupational outlook handbook*. Retrieved from http://www.bls.gov/ooh/

U.S. Department of Labor. (n.d.). *O*Net online*. Retrieved from http://www.onetonline.org/

Applications and Insights

Occupational Exploration Worksheet

Dorothy Burton Nelson

Occupational Title: _____

Three primary, daily work tasks for this occupation:

1. _____

2. _____

3. _____

Technology tools or innovation unique to the occupation: _____

_____

What math courses will provide the necessary background for this occupation?

_____

What other courses are listed in the "special knowledge" section that are also included in your curriculum?

_____

In the skills and abilities section, which of the listed skills are among your strongest?

_____

_____

Which of the listed skills and abilities are those you will have to work to develop?

_____

_____

What Holland interest code is associated with the occupation?

_____

Which work styles come easiest to you?

_____

Which work styles do not come easily to you?

_____

List the specific training, education, and qualifications needed for entry in this occupation:

Training:

_____

Education:

_____

Qualifications:

_____

How many people currently work in this field?

_____

Explain the demand or lack of demand for employment in this field.

_____

What is the job outlook?

_____

What is the median salary?

_____

Name some related occupations:

_____

Write a statement of how this occupation is or is not a good fit for you. Explain in detail.

_____

_____

_____

Note. Reprinted with permission from Dorothy Burton Nelson.

8

LEGAL ISSUES IN ACADEMIC ADVISING

Matthew M. Rust

Bodies of law provide some of the most important and complicated areas of institutional and external knowledge that new advisors need to learn. Academic advising does not necessarily bear as many high-risk legal concerns as other areas of the university (e.g., admissions, disability services, athletics, technology transfer, and so on), but the new advisor must develop familiarity with the legal frameworks that affect practice. Indeed, the confidential and trust-based nature of the advising relationship requires that advisors remain current on the policies and procedures in place to protect students' legal rights and to fulfill institutions' legal obligations. Specifically, new advisors need to know the laws, regulations, and institutional policies related to (a) privacy of student information, (b) liabilities created by advisors as agents of the institution, and (c) equal rights and due process for students.

This chapter does not provide specific legal advice but imparts knowledge about general rules within some of the legal frameworks that most directly affect academic advising. Although this general guidance focuses on American law, the final section places this discussion in a global context with particular attention on general distinctions from Canadian legal traditions. After reading this article, new advisors will likely feel more confident in recognizing potential legal issues in their advising practice so they can appropriately consult the relevant policies, administrators, or counsel to ensure legal compliance in their specific situations.

Confidentiality and Privacy of Student Information

Advisors regularly view, handle, and discuss personal information maintained in students' institutional records. The documentation ranges from innocuous contact information to demographic and academic performance data. In the United States, a web of federal and state privacy laws as well as institutional policies protect this personal information.

The Family Educational Rights and Privacy Act

U.S. advisors must familiarize themselves with the primary federal privacy law applicable to them: the Family Educational Rights and Privacy Act (FERPA) (U.S.

Department of Education, 2014). A federal funding statute, FERPA is implemented through regulations from the U.S. Department of Education Family Policy Compliance Office. It predicates receipt of federal funding dollars (e.g., for research or student financial aid) on institutional compliance with the privacy protections FERPA mandates. The statute was originally enacted in the wake of the Watergate scandal and prompted by fears over the presence of personally identifiable information stored on computers. Despite the original intent, the statute and the regulations used for implementations have not always kept up with technological advances (Humphries, 2008). Consequently, legislators and regulators have periodically reacted to the changing educational environment with revisions to the statute and regulations that necessitate commensurate changes in advising practices.

Education Records.   FERPA applies to the personally identifiable information maintained by institutions in the education records of any student—regardless of age—who is in attendance at the institution. The implementing regulations specify that

> attendance includes, but is not limited to—(a) Attendance in person or by paper correspondence, videoconference, satellite, Internet, or other electronic information and telecommunications technologies for students who are not physically present in the classroom; and (b) The period during which a person is working under a work-study program. (34 C.F.R. § 99.3, 2011)

Universities and colleges may define the beginning of "in attendance" for FERPA purposes through institutional policy. This date will fall after the point of admission but no later than the day the student first attends a class, in person or from a distance, at the institution (Rooker & Falkner, 2013). FERPA protects from disclosure most of the information that advisors access within student education records. One notable exception exists. Advisors may disclose directory information maintained in an education record if the student has not requested that it remain private (Campbell, Cieplak, & Rodriguez, 2012). Directory information includes names, street and e-mail addresses, and phone numbers. It also includes participation in recognized activities and sports, dates of attendance, academic major, class standing, degrees and awards received, and—as of the 2012 regulatory updates to FERPA—student identification numbers unless the number alone (e.g., not in combination with a password) could lead to third-party access of an educational record. Although FERPA allows the release of these forms of directory information, advisors should consult appropriate administrators, such as the registrar or retained legal counsel, to determine whether state privacy laws or institutional policies prohibit the disclosures that FERPA permits.

Disclosures.   New advisors make the safest assumption by treating all student information as private and only disclosing it in accordance with the institution's procedures for the release of student data. Advisors may communicate FERPA-protected information under the following fairly typical circumstances: (a) the student gives consent, (b) an education official has a legitimate educational interest in it, (c) tax dependent status is verified, and (d) in the event of a health or safety emergency.

Consent-Based Disclosures. In the most likely cases, advisors release student record information to a third party after the student has explicitly consented to the disclosure. For example, a student who decides to keep a parent informed about academic progress may consent to the advisor sharing private information with that parent. In such a situation, the student consent should be written, signed, and dated. The release should also specify the purpose of the disclosure, which records may be shared, and the persons to whom disclosures may be made (Campbell et al., 2012).

In addition, regulatory updates from 2008 require institutions to utilize reasonable methods to authenticate the identity of any third party who requests the disclosure of education records. Institutions often comply with this mandate by adding a password to the student consent documents. The student then shares the password with the parent or other individual specified in the consent form. If the components of consent are met—including the authentication of the third party's identity—FERPA allows the release of the education records.

Disclosures to School Officials. In another fairly common situation, advisors provide student information to school officials with a legitimate educational interest in the student's data. Under FERPA, the scope of legitimate educational interest likely includes any employees with whom an advisor may share student information such as faculty, professional, and undergraduate peer advisors; clerical staff who support the work of advisors; and administrators. Because FERPA does not define the qualifications for this legitimate educational interest exception, advisors should consult institutional resources on FERPA compliance; some institutions develop policies that specify the personnel who have a legitimate educational interest in protected information from a student's education record.

Disclosures Based on Tax Dependent Status. In the instance that a student declines to sign or revokes consent to disclose records, the parent may request access to the records, under FERPA, by proving the student's status as a tax dependent of the parent. However, most advisors likely do not assess tax dependent status, and institutions may have trained employees in the registrar's office to receive and examine tax documents to determine a student's tax dependent status. Advisors need to know the proper office to handle inquiries about tax status.

An important point related to parental access is that FERPA protection applies to all students—regardless of age—attending the institution. New advisors, in particular, may not realize that parents of students under the age of 18 must qualify through consent or tax dependent status to access the student's education records.

Disclosures Under the Health and Safety Exception.   Regulatory updates to FERPA in 2008, largely in response to the tragic deaths at Virginia Tech caused by a troubled student, clarify that an advisor may release private information upon learning that a student has articulated a threat posing significant danger to him- or herself or to any other person. The advisor "may disclose information from education records to any person whose knowledge of the information is necessary to protect the health or safety of the student or other individuals" (34 C.F.R. § 99.36, 2008). In the analysis of a potential health and safety exception to general FERPA nondisclosure rules, advisors should consider whether they learned of the threatening behavior through an education record (e.g., an e-mail from the student) or simply from an in-person conversation. FERPA does not apply to the latter situation because a conversation does not qualify as an education record (Family Policy Compliance Office, 2006).

Many campuses have developed threat assessment teams as recommended by the governor's report following the Virginia Tech tragedy; these teams receive non-emergency information about troubling behaviors and work to determine any risk they pose to safety or security (Dunkle, Silverstein, & Warner, 2008). New advisors should familiarize themselves with the campus threat assessment team and how best to access and utilize it.

In addition to encouraging advisors to report troubling behavior to threat assessment teams, institutions frequently employ institutional policy that makes advisors mandatory reporters of information pertaining to sexual assault. As a result, advisors need to know the procedures for reporting a sexual assault to the institution. Even in places without an institutional or state mandate, FERPA permits advisors to report threatening behaviors and statements from students through the health and safety exception. In this regard, advisors have more flexibility to disclose confidential conversations (which are not FERPA-protected educational records) or e-mail messages (which likely are educational records) than licensed medical and mental health providers are afforded under their professional confidentiality obligations and medical record privacy laws (Tribbensee, 2008).

Students' Right to Inspect Records.   Students have a right to examine their own educational records under FERPA. Many institutions feature information systems that provide students with on-demand access to the databases that hold education records through password-protected web portals. However, students have a right to inspect other records not associated with the institutional system, such as notes kept by an advisor in the advisor's office. FERPA specifies a sole-possession record exception to this right to inspect, but it only applies to records that only a single university employee, such as an advisor, can access. Therefore, any information made available in any way to colleagues, custodians, or technical support staff, such as that on disposed paper or typed in a word-processing file, falls outside the sole-possession exception. Therefore, advisors should assume any recorded advising notes will not qualify as sole possession but will be considered an education record subject to inspection by the student to whom the record pertains.

State Privacy Laws

Most advisors at U.S. institutions of higher education pay attention to FERPA, but new hires may not realize that state privacy laws often require greater protections of student information than mandated by FERPA (Nicholson & O'Reardon, 2009). For example, some states require encryption for any names and identification numbers electronically transmitted. Under FERPA, these data constitute directory information that generally can be disclosed. Some state laws require institutions to monitor the data security practices of third parties with access to education records (e.g., those used to administer student surveys); FERPA does not require this vetting.

Some states have passed laws that impose strict criminal or tort liability for even single instances of private data released for unauthorized reasons. Strict liability means that a breach of privacy makes the institution liable; plaintiffs or prosecutors need not prove intent or negligence on the part of the institution. In contrast, FERPA threatens the loss of federal funding if an institution's policies and practices fail to substantially comply with FERPA after it has received notice of the problem from the Family Policy Compliance Office and has been given a reasonable time to comply (Zick & Levinson, 2009); however, this ultimate punishment has never been handed down from the U.S. Department of Education (Daggett, 1997).

Likewise, institutions need not fear tort liability under FERPA. In response to a situation in which students felt their FERPA rights had been violated, *Gonzaga v. Doe* (2002) clarified that students do not have an individual right of action under FERPA, which means they cannot sue institutions for violations of FERPA protections. However, some states have enacted long-arm statutes that make their data privacy laws—which do often grant individual rights of action—applicable to out-of-state universities that admit or enroll their students (Nicholson & O'Reardon, 2009).

These various examples illustrate that FERPA provides a baseline of privacy protection minimums, but it does not require institutions to comply with the patchwork of stricter privacy laws evolving throughout the various states. The complex web of state privacy laws means that advisors must check regularly with the institution's FERPA compliance officers (likely the registrar or general counsel) to determine whether any new laws require new procedures for the protection of student information.

Advisors as Agents of the University

Advisors act on behalf of and subject to the control of the universities that employ them, making them agents of the university under the common law doctrine of agency. This legal tradition dates back to the 12th century in England through centuries of court opinions and legislative adjustments. Agency law will vary from state to state, but it remains relevant to advising practice. Under agency law, advisors—the agents—are able to create liability for the institutions employing them—their principals—without necessarily creating liability for the advisors themselves. Liability in these cases most likely arises through contract or tort law (Hynes & Loewenstein, 2008).

Liability in Contract Law

Courts predominantly view the relationship between students and the higher education institutions they attend as contractual in nature (Kaplin & Lee, 2013). However, the terms of this academic contract are not always clear. Courts have upheld arguments that the express and implied terms of the academic contract need not be neatly contained in a single academic bulletin, but often originate from a variety of sources (*Aronson v. University of Mississippi*, 2002). Agents can change the terms of the contracts their principals enter into (Hynes & Loewenstein, 2008). Academic advisors, as agents of the university, can potentially alter the terms of the academic contract between the student and institution through the concept of apparent authority within agency law. Academic advisors may or may not have the actual authority from their institution to change degree requirements or academic policies. However, as advisors teach students this institutional knowledge and inform them of updates to out-of-date bulletins, students come to reasonably rely on academic advisors for the most accurate information regarding the academic contract. From the student's perspective, the advisor possesses the authority, as an agent of the university, to inform the student of changes to the original academic contract. Consequently, a student who—to his or her detriment—has reasonably relied on academic advising that ultimately turned out to be inaccurate might try to enforce the changed terms of the academic contract under the agency law concept of apparent authority.

Institutions often take measures to minimize the chances of advisors or other agents mistakenly changing the terms of the academic contract through their apparent authority. These measures typically include frequent reminders to students that the academic bulletin, or other official document, represents the authoritative statement of degree requirements and academic policies. Furthermore, the clarifying material states that students must take responsibility for knowing and following these requirements.

Despite such disclaimers, students might sue for breach of contract when they believe that degree requirements or academic standing policies were changed to their detriment. In such situations, courts have traditionally shown great deference to the institution, believing that college faculty and administrators are better situated than the courts to understand academic decision making. However, a recent dissenting opinion from the U.S. Supreme Court has led some commentators to conclude an evolving decrease in this trust and therefore anticipate less deference from the judiciary toward the decisions made by university educators (Hutchens, Wilson, & Block, 2013). That is, courts may diverge from the past and apply ordinary concepts of contract law to disputes arising in the academic context; in these cases, the courts could interpret ambiguities associated with contract terms in favor of the student and against the interests of the university. As agents of the university, advisors should carefully communicate degree requirements and academic policies to students to avoid student confusion over the terms of the academic contract.

New advisors, in particular, should check with academic administrators about the documents considered the final authority on degree requirements and academic policies. For example, a student who finds conflicting requirements on an electronic advising audit, in the official university bulletin, and in degree requirement checklists on paper handouts, may very likely turn to an advisor to determine the proper authoritative text. Advisors who vet the proper sources of information can also suggest prompt resolution of poorly articulated policies and procedures in an effort to protect both the students and the institution.

Liability in Tort Law

In addition to communicating about the academic contract, advisors—as agents—may create liability for their institutions through missteps in tort law, specifically educational malpractice (also known as negligence). In tort law, malpractice claims typically consist of four elements: a duty of care, breach of that duty, causation (a link between the breach and happenings to the person bringing the claim), and damages to the person bringing the claim. A claim of advising-related educational malpractice would likely be based on the argument that advisors have a duty to provide to students accurate and timely institutional knowledge of educational opportunities and requirements. Therefore, if an advisor breaches this duty of care and thereby causes a student to experience damages, such as costs incurred through an extra year of classes, the student might be able to hold the institution liable under an educational malpractice claim.

In the United States, students have experienced mixed results in pursuing educational malpractice claims in the courts. In *Byrd v. Lamar* (2003), the Alabama Supreme Court heard a claim, similar to educational malpractice, in which an academic advisor repeatedly assured a student, Byrd, that courses required for a degree would be offered in a sequence that would allow the student to graduate within four years of transferring to the institution. Byrd alleged that the advisor knew all along those course offerings were not planned. A New York Appellate decision allowed students to proceed on a negligence claim against a professional college that had promised its chiropractic program would prepare students for licensure examination in all states, when in fact the students were ineligible to sit for all states' exams upon graduation (*Enzinna v. D'Youville College,* 2011).

Some malpractice claims represent scenarios unrelated to degree requirements. In *Nova Southeastern University v. Gross* (2000), the court found that an institution must take reasonable care in ensuring that students are not assigned to potentially unsafe off-site practicum or internship locations. Additionally, *Rinksy v. Trustees of Boston University* (2010) allowed a negligence claim by a social work student who, in the midst of an internship required for her degree, complained to university supervisors that a client at the internship site was touching and stalking her. The supervisors allegedly chastised the student for being uncommitted to the social work profession and did not reassign her to a different internship setting. As a result, the student claimed, the harassment continued.

Other students have not been as successful in bringing educational malpractice suits. In *Hendricks v. Clemson University* (2003), the plaintiff student-athlete sued because of athletic eligibility lost after following incorrect academic advising, but the court dismissed the claim finding the university did not have a duty to advise correctly (duty being one of the key elements of any negligence claim). In fact, courts frequently cite the lack of an established duty of care for university educators when they reject educational malpractice claims brought by students (Kaplin & Lee, 2013; Tokic, 2014). However, as states get more involved in the curricular matters of institutions, this trend may shift. For example, some states have enacted legislation in which degrees must be attainable within four years such that "effective" advising and mandated individualized degree maps be available to all students (see, e.g., Tex. Edu. Code §§ 61.070, 61.077; Ind. Code § 21–12–14). The courts in these states now have legislatively set standards of care for institutions, and students might rely on these standards as the duty element in educational malpractice claims.

New advisors can work to reduce potential malpractice liability through a few reasonable steps: vet institutional information, refrain from overstating the value of opportunities or field of study, promote only programs endorsed by the institution, and pursue professional development. Advisors should not promise course availability unless they can turn to a reliable, documented commitment from the department that offers the course (e.g., a published semester-by-semester schedule of offered classes). Likewise, they should know the marketability of a degree or the level of professional preparation it affords. New advisors should check their understanding of the applicability of a degree to a student's intended professional goals. They, along with their experienced peers, should continue to engage in frequent conferrals with the institution's career and preprofessional school advisors to ensure they grasp the realities associated with degree and program opportunities. Advisors should only promote those experiential learning opportunities (e.g., internships, service-learning, study abroad) that have been vetted by institution officials for appropriate educational quality and student safety. Furthermore, as states continue to legislatively impose duties on institutions of higher education, advisors should seek out campus-level discussions and training on compliance with any new laws that affect their work.

Equal Rights and Due Process

Equal Rights

In the United States, the federal constitution and civil rights legislation afford certain guarantees of equal rights to college students. These rights, frequently clarified in court decisions concerning admissions, affect the work of academic advisors. As with all functional areas of higher education, the academic advising profession is attuned to the diverse backgrounds of the various students who attend colleges and universities.

Presentations or publications related to culturally competent advising serve as core resources for advising (see, e.g., NACADA: The Global Community for Academic Advising, 2014). Advisors must remain mindful of protections afforded to classes of individuals who have traditionally experienced discrimination, particularly students of color.

The Fourteenth Amendment to the U.S. Constitution contains a clause that guarantees "equal protection of the laws"; this clause prohibits racial discrimination at public postsecondary institutions. At private colleges and universities, federal civil rights legislation, including Title VI of the Civil Rights Act of 1964 and 42 U.S.C. § 1981, prohibit such discrimination (see Kaplin & Lee, 2013). Four U.S. Supreme Court cases, all of which dealt with university admissions practices, have clarified the equal rights guarantees of these laws: *Fisher v. University of Texas at Austin* (2013); *Gratz v. Bollinger* (2003); *Grutter v. Bollinger* (2003); and *Regents of the University of California v. Bakke* (1978). Although these cases addressed race-conscious affirmative action admission plans, their guidance applies to retention-related practices in higher education, including academic advising (Coleman, Palmer, & Richards, 2005). These cases establish the constitutional permissibility of race-conscious practices in university programs narrowly tailored to ensure that

o students are not selected for program participation based solely on race; rather, race is one of a number of factors considered for eligibility.

o program administrators adequately consider available race-neutral alternatives to achieving the educational goals of a diverse student body.

o the program does not unduly harm majority students.

o the program is of limited duration with plans to terminate it as soon as is practicable. (*Grutter v. Bollinger,* 2003)

New advisors need not attempt to apply the four-factor test to determine the legal viability of a potential race-conscious advising practice. Instead, they should consult their institution's legal affairs office when considering development of or participation in an existing advising-related program created or executed in light of a student's race. No one should tailor a course of study or make program recommendations for students based solely on their race or ethnic background.

Due Process

Students also enjoy certain due process rights that affect the work of academic advisors. At public institutions, due process rights spring from the Fourteenth Amendment to the U.S. Constitution, which prohibits the arbitrary deprivation of property by the government. Students at public institutions have a property interest in their continued enrollment that cannot be taken away without adequate due process (e.g., notice and an opportunity to be heard). Although due process rights apply to both academic- and misconduct-related dismissals, courts usually do not look for as many procedural safeguards in the case of academic dismissals. Instead, the Supreme Court has held that courts should defer to academic judgments made at the institution unless a substantial departure from academic norms was indicated, the student was not made aware of academic deficiencies, or the academic standards had not been applied fairly (*Board of Curators of the University of Missouri v. Horowitz*, 1978; *University of Michigan v. Ewing*, 1985).

At private institutions, students do not enjoy constitutionally protected due process rights; however, courts have required private institutions, in general, to follow the academic dismissal procedures and policies they have established and under which students have agreed to enroll as per the academic contract (Kaplin & Lee, 2013). Therefore, regardless of the institutional types that employ them, new advisors need to know the academic probation and dismissal policies and procedures in place at their institution and make good faith efforts to inform students of these rules and processes.

Legal Issues in a Global Context

To introduce applicable, global legal theories to the many colleges and universities throughout the world that provide academic advising proves an impossible endeavor. However, recognizing that legal obligations vary from one country to another, the United Nations has compiled a listing of the general proper purposes, functions, and typical activities of academic advising, and the United Nations Educational, Scientific and Cultural Organization (2002) encourages leadership at institutions throughout the world to consider this resource as they develop and assess their student affairs programs and services. The laws and case studies discussed in the preceding sections focus on federal and state law in the United States, but the following general rules should help new advisors across the globe translate these principles into their own country's legal framework.

Common Law and Civil Law Traditions

Most of the systems of law throughout the world can be roughly grouped into common law or civil law traditions, or some mixture of the two (Fine, 2001; Palmer, 2012; Smits, 2006). In common law countries, such as England and the countries it colonized, including the United States, laws are derived mostly from a long tradition of court decisions with deference to prior precedent. Modern common law countries have codified and refined many court decisions through constitutions, statutes, and regulations. However, court decisions continue to play a primary role in the interpretation and application of legal theories. All of the legal concerns discussed in relation to the United States likely exist in some fashion in any common law country.

In contrast to the reliance on judicial precedent of common law states, civil law countries (most of Europe and Latin America) look almost entirely to legislation for their bodies of law. In this regard, judicial decisions in one case do not necessarily control application of the law in other cases, meaning judicial decisions on novel issues will not create new law. Civil law countries likely have some version of U.S. legal doctrines discussed herein (i.e., privacy, agency, equal protection, and due process), but contractual issues and tort duties in civil law countries typically derive from very specific statutes rather than a tradition of court opinions that might develop differently throughout the countries' jurisdictions. Therefore, advisors in civil law countries may have more clearly defined duties spelled out in their sources of law, making interpretation less complicated than the case-based approach to contract and tort laws that guide the practice of advisors in common law countries.

Canadian Law and Advising

Canada maintains a mixed jurisdiction system of laws derived from the common law and from the civil law traditions (Canada Department of Justice, 2013). While the majority of Canadian provinces and territories are based on a common law tradition, the province of Quebec—with its sustained ties to the French language and culture—has kept a truer form of civil law in the midst of a mostly common law country (Smits, 2002). For this reason, advisors in Quebec look to the civil code for guidance on not creating liabilities for their institutions. In the rest of the country, however, advisors would consult territorial common law, usually contract law.

> Most legal actions against [Canadian] universities by staff or students are for alleged breach of contract. Another common law base for suing universities is Tort Law, primarily on the grounds of negligence, liability, and defamation. However, there have been few tort-based cases in Canada, only a small number of which have been successful, even if courts recognize in principle that universities are liable for action of their agents, including faculty and staff. (Schuetze, 2013, p. 68)

A further important difference between Canadian and U.S. law regards federalism. While Canada's legal system includes a federal and provincial–territorial distribution of legislative power, it diverges remarkably from that of the United States. Field (1992) observed that—ironically—"each [country's] system has evolved to be more like the plan for the other." That is, the Canadian government was intended to be dominated by a strong central government, but historical developments led to greater provincial powers. In the United States, the historical constitutional plan emphasized states' rights, but a strong federal government has instead emerged. The differing privacy laws that govern academic advising practice in Canada compared to those affecting U.S. advising illustrate these two notions of federalism. In the United States, for example, the federal privacy law, FERPA, applies to all institutions—public or private—that receive federal dollars (for research, financial aid, and so forth). In Canada, however, the federal privacy law, the Personal Information Protection and Electronic Documents Act,

> does not apply to the core activities of ... universities. By core activities we mean those activities that are central to the mandate and responsibilities of these institutions. A ...

university . . . may become subject to the Act when it engages in a non-core commercial activity. (Office of the Privacy Commissioner of Canada, 2012, ¶8, 10)

This edict from the Privacy Commissioner means that Canadian academic advisors look almost entirely to provincial or territorial legislation to find the privacy laws applicable to their institution. The Office of the Information Commissioner of Canada (2014) hosts a helpful web directory of the provincial and territorial offices that enforce these privacy laws, typically known as Freedom of Information and Protection of Privacy Acts. These offices' sites provide interpretive guidance and recent legal decisions that can help Canadian advisors seeking to comply with their provincial privacy laws. For further reading on laws affecting Canadian practice, advisors benefit from consulting Lazar Sarna and Noah Sarna's (2007) *The Law of Schools and Universities,* which examines Canadian education law.

Summary

The legal and regulatory environment within which academic advisors must operate creates complexities and concerns not easily negotiated by a new practitioner. However, new and experienced advisors alike can take heart that the most salient areas of law for academic advisors can be grouped into three manageable categories: (a) privacy of student information, (b) liabilities potentially created by advisors as agents of the institution, and (c) equal rights and due process for students. Furthermore, after reading this chapter, advisors should feel more assured about their familiarity with the most important general principles from these three areas. Most important, they should feel confident in knowing when legal issues are likely to arise in advising practice and in knowing when to consult relevant institutional policies, administrators, or legal counsel. Equipped with this knowledge, advisors are well-prepared to help protect the legal rights of their students and discharge the legal duties of their employing institutions.

Aiming for Excellence

o Identify whether your institution has a university legal affairs office (sometimes called the "office of general counsel") or instead relies on a local law firm kept on retainer. Ask an administrator about whether and how your office should obtain legal advice.

o Seek out FERPA and related privacy law training available at your institution, particularly noting any web pages maintained by the registrar's office regarding FERPA compliance policies.

o Determine whether your state privacy law or institutional policies require record maintenance where FERPA does not, or conversely, whether they prohibit disclosures that FERPA permits.

o Verify the document that constitutes the final authority on degree requirements when conflicts of information arise between the bulletin, online degree requirements listings, paper checklists, electronic degree audits, and any other institutional publications.

o When promoting experiential learning opportunities (e.g., internships, service-learning, study abroad), ensure you refer students only to institutionally vetted programs.

o Seek out institutional training on how to comply with any new state-imposed mandates regarding academic advising.

o Ask your colleagues and administrators about whether any general counsel–approved race-conscious advising practices are in place at your institution. Be careful to follow any such guidelines that have been approved by university attorneys.

o Ensure you are in compliance with the process your institution sets for academic dismissals; inform students facing dismissal of their due process rights.

References

34 C.F.R. § 99.3 (2011).

34 C.F.R. § 99.36 (2008).

Aronson v. University of Mississippi, 828 So. 2d 752 (Miss. 2002).

Board of Curators of the University of Missouri v. Horowitz, 435 U.S. 78 (1978).

Byrd v. Lamar, 846 So. 2d 334 (Al. 2003).

Campbell, E., Cieplak, B., & Rodriguez, B. (2012). *Family Educational Rights and Privacy Act (FERPA): FERPA for colleges & universities.* Retrieved from http://www2.ed.gov/policy /gen/guid/fpco/pdf/postsecondary-webinar-presentation.pdf

Canada Department of Justice. (2013, April). *Where our legal system comes from.* Retrieved from http//www.justice.gc.ca/eng/csj-sjc/just/03.html

Coleman, A. L., Palmer, S. R., & Richards, F. S. (2005). *Federal law and recruitment, outreach, and retention: A framework for evaluating diversity-related programs.* New York, NY: College Board.

Daggett, L. M. (1997). Bucking up Buckley II: Using civil rights claims to enforce the federal student records statute. *Seattle University Law Review, 21*(1), 29–67.

Dunkle, J. H., Silverstein, Z. B., & Warner, S. L. (2008). Managing violent and other troubling students: The role of threat assessment teams on campus. *Journal of College and University Law, 34*(3), 585–636.

Enzinna v. D'Youville College, 2011 WL 1733907 (N.Y. App. Div., 4th Jud. Dep't 2011).

Family Policy Compliance Office. (2006, February 15). *Letter to Montgomery County Public Schools (MD) re: law enforcement unit records.* Retrieved from http://www2.ed.gov /policy/gen/guid/fpco/ferpa/library/montcounty0215.html

Field, M. A. (1992). The differing federalisms of Canada and the United States. *Law and Contemporary Problems, 55*(1), 107–120.

Fine, T. M. (2001). *American legal systems: A resource and reference guide*. Cincinnati, OH: Anderson.

Fisher v. University of Texas at Austin, 133 S. Ct. 2411 (2013).

Gonzaga v. Doe, 536 U.S. 273 (2002).

Gratz v. Bollinger, 539 U.S. 244 (2003).

Grutter v. Bollinger, 539 U.S. 306 (2003).

Hendricks v. Clemson University, 353 S.C.449, 578 S.E.2d 711 (2003).

Humphries, S. (2008). Institutes of higher education, safety swords, and privacy shields: Reconciling FERPA and the common law. *The Journal of College and University Law, 35*(1), 145–216.

Hutchens, N. H., Wilson, K., & Block, J. (2013). *CLS v. Martinez* and competing legal discourses over the appropriate degree of judicial deference to the co-curricular realm. *The Journal of College and University Law, 39*(3), 541–565.

Hynes, D. J., & Loewenstein, M. J. (2008). *Agency, partnership and the LLC: The law of unincorporated business enterprises—Cases, materials, problems*. Newark, NJ: LexisNexis.

Kaplin, W., & Lee, B. (2013). *The law of higher education: A comprehensive guide to legal implications of administrative decision making*. San Francisco, CA: Jossey-Bass.

NACADA: The Global Community for Academic Advising. (2014). *Cultural issues in advising*. Retrieved from www.nacada.ksu.edu/Resources/Clearinghouse/View-Articles/Cultural-Issues-in-Advising.aspx

Nicholson, J. L., & O'Reardon, M. E. (2009). Data protection basics: A primer for college and university counsel. *The Journal of College and University Law, 36*(1), 101–144.

Nova Southeastern Univ. v. Gross, 758 So.2d 86 (Fla. 2000).

Office of the Information Commissioner of Canada. (2014, April 7). *Links*. Retrieved from http://www.oic-ci.gc.ca/eng/links-liens.aspx

Office of the Privacy Commissioner of Canada. (2012, December 12). *Fact sheets: Municipalities, universities, schools, and hospitals*. Retrieved from https://www.priv.gc.ca/resource/fs-fi/02_05_d_25_e.asp

Palmer, V. V. (2012). *Mixed jurisdictions worldwide: The third legal family* (2nd ed.). Cambridge, UK: Cambridge University Press.

Regents of the University of California v. Bakke, 438 U.S. 265 (1978).

Rinksy v. Trustees of Boston University, 2010 U.S. Dist. LEXIS 136876 (D. Mass. December 27, 2010).

Rooker, L. R., & Falkner, T. M. (2013). *2013 FERPA quick guide*. Washington, DC: American Association of Collegiate Registrars and Admissions Officers.

Sarna, L., & Sarna, N. (2007). *The law of schools and universities*. Toronto, Ontario: LexisNexis.

Schuetze, H. G. (2013). Canada. In C. J. Russo (Ed.), *Handbook of comparative higher education law* (pp. 63–85). New York, NY: Rowman & Littlefield.

Smits, J. M. (2002). *The making of European private law: Toward a Ius Commune Europaeum as a mixed legal system*. Antwerp, Belgium: Intersentia.

Smits, J. M. (2006). *Elgar encyclopedia of comparative law*. Cheltenham, UK: Edward Elgar.

Tokic, S. (2014). Rethinking educational malpractice: Are educators rock stars? *Brigham Young University Education and Law Journal, 2014*(1), 105–133.

Tribbensee, N. E. (2008). Privacy and confidentiality: Balancing student rights and campus safety. *The Journal of College and University Law, 34*(2), 393–417.

United Nations Educational, Scientific and Cultural Organization. (2002). *The role of student affairs and services in higher education: A practical manual for developing, implementing and assessing student affairs programmes and services*. Retrieved from: http://unesdoc.unesco.org/images/0012/001281/128118e.pdf

University of Michigan v. Ewing, 474 U.S. 214 (1985).

U.S. Department of Education. (2014). *Family Educational Rights and Privacy Act (FERPA)*. Retrieved from http://www2.ed.gov/policy/gen/guid/fpco/ferpa/index.html

Zick, K., & Levinson, R. (2009). Issues arising from application of new FERPA regulations. *Proceedings of the 30th Annual National Conference on Law and Higher Education*. Retrieved from http://www.stetson.edu/law/conferences/ highered/archive/media/higher -ed-archives-2009/document/ii-zick-issues-of-new-ferpa-regulations-pdf.pdf

Applications and Insights
Audit of Legal Issues in Advising Practice
Matthew M. Rust

Privacy and Confidentiality (FERPA and State Privacy Laws)

☐ Does your advising office have a FERPA policy?

☐ Does your advising office annually communicate FERPA policy to students and advisors?

☐ Does your advising office ensure that advisors consistently follow institutional FERPA policy?

☐ Does your institution's general counsel annually review FERPA policy?

☐ Specifically, does your general counsel ensure your office FERPA policies are in line with

    ☐ any new aspect of FERPA law or regulations?

    ☐ institution FERPA policy?

    ☐ state privacy laws applicable to your institution? (State law—common or statutory—may prohibit disclosures that FERPA permits, or it may require maintenance of records that FERPA does not.)

☐ Does your FERPA policy

    ☐ define the information to be included in and excluded from advising records? (Once data are included, they are FERPA protected until the record is destroyed.)

    ☐ give students an option to inspect and request to amend their advising records?

    ☐ provide students a means by which to give informed and voluntary consent to disclose their FERPA-protected education records?

☐ Does this consent form

    ☐ note the specific individuals or class of individuals to whom the education records may be disclosed?

    ☐ state the specific office or individual who may disclose FERPA-protected information?

    ☐ describe how long the consent remains in place? (Consent will be in place until the specified date or until rescinded by the student.)

    ☐ note the specific records that may be disclosed?

- ☐ list the purpose of the disclosure?
- ☐ contain a signature and date line? (This can be a digital form.)
- ☐ require authentication from specified individuals when they call, e-mail, or visit the advising office to gain access to FERPA-protected information (e.g., a password provided by student on consent form)?
- ☐ require advisors to maintain a log of all disclosures of FERPA-protected information? (This is not required when the disclosure is based on consent or when disclosing to school officials with legitimate educational interest.)

Advisors as Agents of the Institution (Contract and Tort Liability)

- ☐ Have you familiarized yourself with all the potential sources of terms that comprise the academic contract to which your students agreed with the institution?
- ☐ Specifically, have you reviewed and kept documentation of
  - ☐ promotional materials by which your advisees were recruited?
  - ☐ institutional bulletins under which your advisees enrolled?
  - ☐ published degree requirements check sheets?
  - ☐ paper- and web-based degree audits you have used to advise individual students?
  - ☐ student handbooks?
- ☐ Have you confirmed with the appropriate academic administrators about the listings of degree requirements deemed authoritative to resolve discrepancies among the various terms of the academic contract?
- ☐ Do you carefully and promptly inform students when changes are made to degree requirements or course offerings?
  - ☐ Do you maintain a record of these notices?
- ☐ Do you avoid making promises regarding future course offerings unless you have obtained reliable, documented commitment from the department teaching the course?
- ☐ Do you regularly consult institutional career and pre-professional school advisors to avoid overselling the career-related usefulness of a degree or program?
- ☐ When promoting experiential learning opportunities (e.g., internships, service-learning, study abroad), do you refer students to institutionally vetted programs?

☐ Do you regularly seek out institutional training on how to comply with any new state-imposed mandates regarding academic advising?

Equal Rights and Due Process

☐ Do you ever consider a student's race when deciding which advising approach to use or which educational opportunities to promote?

☐ If you make such decisions, do you regularly review this strategy with the institution's legal counsel specifically ensuring that the practice

    ☐ comports with any new jurisprudence regarding race-conscious practices?

    ☐ is based on factors other than race alone?

    ☐ renders greater effectiveness in achieving educational goals than a race-neutral approach?

    ☐ does not harm majority students?

    ☐ is of limited duration?

☐ Are you familiar with the policies and procedures by which your advisees might be academically dismissed from the institution?

☐ Do you make good faith efforts to inform your advisees about dismissal policies and procedures?

☐ Do you accurately and promptly inform your students of academic deficiencies in their work?

☐ Do you faithfully follow dismissal policies and procedures in whatever roles you play in the process?

9

INFORMATIONAL COMPONENT

LEARNING ABOUT ADVISEES—PUTTING TOGETHER THE PUZZLE

Susan Kolls

In preparation for this book, a review panel drawn from the NACADA: The Global Community for Academic Advising Publications Advisory Board, New Advising Professionals Commission, and Faculty Advising Commission closely examined the first edition of The New Advisor Guidebook: Mastering the Art of Advising Through the First Year and Beyond *(Folsom, 2007). They positively reviewed Susan Kolls's chapter on the informational component of advising (pp. 59–62). Although much of the technology has evolved since the chapter was first published, advisors still utilize powerful data-rich student information systems, advising notes, and communication management systems to contact and connect with students. The tools have changed, but learning about one's students remains critical for effective advising, and the process still resembles the job of putting together an old-fashioned jigsaw puzzle: It is completed piece by piece. Therefore, Kolls's chapter is reprinted here with permission and without change.*

Starting as a new advisor is like looking into a box of a 1,000 piece puzzle. The one who approaches the puzzle with a plan for putting all the pieces together completes the image with less frustration and delays than if the task is undertaken via haphazard trial and error. Likewise, new advisors who systematically seek out available information on students will find themselves seeing the big picture and efficiently helping their advisees.

New advisors spend many hours learning their institution: its structure, programs, policies, and procedures. A seasoned puzzle solver becomes as familiar with the picture on the box as with the pieces it contains. Similarly, the new advisor must inform themselves about their students to the same extent that they learn about their university. How do new advisors gain knowledge about their advisees? In [chapter 4

Reprinted with permission from NACADA: The Global Community for Academic Advising: Kolls, S. (2007). Informational component: Learning about advisees—Putting together the puzzle. In P. Folsom (Ed.), *The new advisor guidebook: Mastering the art of academic advising through the first year and beyond* (Monograph No. 16) (pp. 59–62). Manhattan, KS: National Academic Advising Association.

of the updated edition of the *Guidebook*], Roufs described how student development theory provides insights for developmental behavior that advisors may
encounter in the traditional college-aged population; this information will help advisors in their interactions with students.

In addition to theory, advisors need specific knowledge about the student population on their own campuses, the subgroup(s) of students they advise, and the individuals sitting across the desk from them. Acquiring this information is a bit like putting
together a jigsaw puzzle: The pieces are combined to create a whole that is greater
than the sum of its parts.

Student Data

According to the New Advisor Development Chart (Folsom, chapter 1), during their
first year on the job, advisors should gain a "data-based conceptual understanding
of [their] institution's student body." Most institutions collect information on students and may have an entering-student profile. This general view of the student body
accounts for measurable characteristics and can be used to answers these questions:

- What is the average SAT profile for students entering the institution?
- What is the average high-school rank and high-school GPA?
- What high school courses or units must be completed for admission to the
  program? How many, if any, students are admitted with deficiencies in the
  required units?
- How many first-year students have Advanced Placement, College Level
  Examination Program test scores, or college course work they completed in high
  school?
- How is quality of high school assessed?
- From where do the students come? What states and countries are represented?
- How many students receive need-based financial aid?
- What is the gender division of each entering class?
- What percentage of the campus population is underrepresented minorities and
  what are the numbers (percentages) for specific ethnic and racial populations?
- What is the ratio of commuters to residents?
- How many entering students are of traditional age? How many are of
  nontraditional age?
- How many students enter directly from high school and how many transfer into
  the institution? What types of institutions are sources for transfer students?

Statistics provide a unique portrait of an institution's students. Each of the quantitative factors has implications for an institution's academic programs and advising. A
predominantly residential, traditional-aged student population has different advising

and educational support needs than a predominantly commuter and nontraditional aged student body. The answers to the demographic questions create the edges or framework of the jigsaw puzzle.

After learning about the general campus population, new advisors can focus on gaining an "introductory level knowledge and understanding about institutional population and individuals" (Folsom, chapter 1, New Advisor Development Chart) for which they have direct advising responsibility. By comparing the data on their advisees to those of the campus-wide population, advisors gain insight into advisees' development and needs. For example, an advisor who has a large percentage of students without the standard high-school preparation will deal with different advising issues than an advisor who works in a department that draws primarily honors students. Advisors who work mainly with transfer students face different advising needs than those who work with first-year students.

First-year advisors also need to learn about the subpopulations within the campus population and within their own group of advisees. Subpopulations might include those at risk, honors students, people with disabilities, international students, underrepresented minorities, and student athletes. While advisors absorb the statistical information about the general student body and specific populations and apply the important advising theories they have learned, they still have much knowledge to acquire; that is, they are filling in the puzzle, but it is still far from complete.

The Individual Student: Gaining Experiential Knowledge

During the first years on the job, advisors work toward deepening their knowledge of students through data, and they are also beginning to understand the implications of applying this information. That is, by applying basic knowledge, they gain valuable experience that moves them toward developmental advising. How might an advisor learn more about an individual student than the data can provide? A number of information sources on continuing students are available, including the student's academic record (grade reports, current registration, and enrollment history). The grade report can reveal information to answer these questions:

o What is the student's overall level of academic achievement?

o Has the student ever been on probation or dismissed?

o Has the advisee changed academic direction?

o In which types of courses does the student excel? In which does he or she struggle?

o Has the student demonstrated a pattern of drops or withdrawals from courses?

The student's folder can provide a wealth of information. Current students may have their admissions application essays or completed admissions surveys on file. The admission essay, for example, may reveal both the student's interests and the challenges she or he may have overcome as well as issues her or his family may be facing.

The folder may have conference notes from previous advising sessions. Good notes are terrific resources revealing the decisions students have made and the discussions surrounding those decisions, problematic situations and how they were resolved, and the student's affect (e.g., being pleased or upset about academic performance). Good notes may answer the following questions:

- What has happened, for instance, since the student has arrived on campus?
- What happened on his or her way to the advising office?
- What has her or his academic experience been thus far?
- What were his or her expectations prior to arriving on campus? Have those expectations been met?
- How approachable does she or he find the faculty?
- What was his or her experience visiting other campus offices?
- How emotionally and financially supportive are the advisee's parents?
- Does the advisee know her or his resident advisor?

Student files may contain letters of reference, which are revealing in the choice of information that is articulated and that which is not included. They may also contain letters of appeal or communications from dean's offices. Learning as much as possible about a student's history prior to the advising session will result in better academic advising. Of course, the puzzle is not complete until the image can be seen, and the advisor's information store is not complete until he or she meets with a student. Even though a first-year advisor may still be mastering the knowledge necessary to answer basic questions, she or he can begin to develop sound relational skills, and of these, active listening may be the most important. With experience, advisors should become more skilled, able to assess specific needs through a few focused questions, and recognize when their questions need to take a different path. The authors of [part four of the updated *Guidebook*] illustrate in detail the building of relational skills.

Regardless of their institutional or specific knowledge about students on their campuses, new advisors can excel in creating a warm and inviting conference. "Students value warmth and depth in advising relationships" (Mottarella, Fritzsche, & Cerabino, 2004, p. 58).

Campus Environment

Imagine that the puzzle is now (nearly) complete for an individual student. Does the puzzle maintain its shape without support? No. The puzzle must sit on a table or a board, which provides a foundation that is analogous to the campus environment. It is important to assess the board or table upon which the puzzle sits before completing the piece. For example, one must ask if the table is big enough to support the puzzle or is it too large? In the same way, advisors must understand how a student fits into the campus environment, and to do that a new advisor must first become informed about their new campus.

Information about advisees and the way in which this group of students relates to the campus cannot be considered without focusing on the measures of one's campus. According to Upcraft and Kramer (1995, p. 17), the college "environment can have a powerful impact on students." By comparing the on-campus environment with the place from which the advisees have come, advisors already versed on the data about students generate a more complete understanding of students' potential advising needs and concerns.

The term *environment*, when applied to an academic institution, has multiple meanings. Of course the physical environment is important:

o Is the campus urban, suburban, or rural?

o What is the size of the institution?

o Do students find the campus aesthetically pleasing?

However, the term *environment* also includes the campus climate:

o Are the options for participation in student organizations and residence hall life varied, extensive, or somewhat limited?

o Are campus events well attended?

o Are all athletics, including intramural as well as National Collegiate Athletic Association–level sports, important aspects of student life?

o Is there a Greek system on campus? What percentage of students participates in it?

o Is the focus of Greek life social or academic?

o What is the level of student involvement in campus activities?

o Are there ample opportunities for student leadership?

o Does the campus provide a welcoming environment for diverse populations?

The number and types of prevailing opportunities contribute to the overall campus atmosphere. If a student is able to become involved, both quantitatively and qualitatively, his or her chance of experiencing academic and social success is higher than if the student remains uninvolved (Astin, 1985). Because typical advisor–student ratios are high, an advisor cannot be expected to know everything about individual students. However, by gaining knowledge about students, developmental theories, and expectations and then applying this knowledge student by student, she or he can quickly become adept at reading students as well as situations. In other words, by putting puzzle pieces in place, advisors can see the whole picture and better anticipate and address the challenges that they and their advisees may face.

References

Astin, A. W. (1985). *Achieving educational excellence: A critical assessment of priorities and practice in higher education.* San Francisco, CA: Jossey-Bass.

[Folsom, P. (2007). New advisor development chart. In P. Folsom (Ed.), *The new advisor guidebook: Mastering the art of academic advising through the first year and beyond* (Monograph No. 16) (pp. 16–21). Manhattan, KS: National Academic Advising Association.]

Mottarella, K., Fritzsche, B., & Cerabino, K. (2004). What do students want in advising? A policy capturing study. *NACADA Journal, 24*(1&2), 48–61.

Upcraft, M. L., & Kramer, G. (Eds.). (1995). *First-year academic advising: Patterns in the present, pathways to the future.* Columbia, SC: National Resource Center for the Freshman Year & Students in Transition.

Applications and Insights

Advisor Checklist of Questions: Student Information to Learn in Year 1
Stephen O. Wallace and Beverly A. Wallace

Advisors must know the students they seek to educate. In addition to gaining access to institutional data, new advisors should concentrate on gaining information that provides insight into demographic and personal factors that may impact student achievement such as student goals, personal background, cocurricular interests, and nonacademic responsibilities.

- What is the academic status of the students served?
  - What is the student's classification—freshman, sophomore, full-time, part-time?
  - What are the student's SAT and ACT scores?
  - What is the student's GPA?
  - What are the student's major and minor?
  - Does the student have any developmental placements?
  - What is the student's current schedule of courses?
  - What courses has the student previously attempted, passed, or failed?
  - In what types of courses does the student exhibit academic strengths and weaknesses?
- Is the student involved in any extracurricular activities, such as athletics, organizations, band, ROTC?
- Does the student work? Full-time or part-time?
- Does the student have family responsibilities?
- What is the student's background: hometown, high school attended?
- What are the student's interests and hobbies?
- What are the student's plans for continuing education or career?
- How competent is the student in the use of the institution's technology?
- Does the student present any individual needs or concerns that should be addressed?

Applications and Insights

Learning From Students

New advisors build their advising knowledge more quickly by learning from their students. They must listen attentively to information students volunteer and their responses to questions.

- Talk to student workers about life at the institution.
- Encourage students to express the truth about their experiences and be prepared to hear it.
- Inquire about the content of courses. What are students reading? What types of assignments are they doing? On what papers are they working?
- Ask about life in the residence hall if applicable.
- Query students about professors they like and why.
- Solicit information about student experiences with other offices. Did they walk in or have an appointment?
- Encourage students to discuss their likes and dislikes about the campus.
- Inquire about students' challenges with academics and campus life.
- Ask students about their biggest surprises in their academic and campus lives.

Adapted with permission from NACADA: The Global Community for Academic Advising: Folsom, P. (2007). Learning about the institution from students. In P. Folsom (Ed.), *The new advisor guidebook: Mastering the art of advising through the first year and beyond* (Monograph No. 16) (p. 60). Manhattan, KS: National Academic Advising Association.

10

DEVELOPING SELF-KNOWLEDGE AS A FIRST STEP TOWARD CULTURAL COMPETENCE

Karen L. Archambault

An effective advisor demonstrates the ability to work with each and every student who presents for assistance. To gain this proficiency, both new and experienced advisors benefit from exploring and developing their cultural competence—the behaviors, policies, and attitudes that allow for individuals to work effectively in cross-cultural situations (National Association of School Psychologists, n.d.). Cultural competence allows advisors to understand and appreciate both their own backgrounds and those of others, including those vastly different from their own.

Advisors educated in counseling or psychology may have received some training in cultural competence through their personal academic experiences. However, all advisors may feel unprepared to face challenges in relating with those whose circumstances and upbringing differ from their own. Negotiating these experiences requires a strong understanding of self—personal identity and background as well as limitations and biases. Advisors also need intimate knowledge of the institution as well as an appreciation for their students. Using self-knowledge as a foundation, this chapter offers an exploration on ways advisors can explore, accept, and overcome their assumptions to benefit their students.

Knowing and Educating Oneself

Evaluate One's Own Limitations

Blane Harding (2007) argued that, as important as it is to understand students, advisors must gain self-awareness as well. Some advisors may readily identify with visible or obvious areas of diversity in specific situations, such as gender, race, or sexual identity, but may be less conscious of the other ways in which they add to the diversity of their department or campus. A recent graduate, hired as the youngest staff advisor in the department, likely brings a unique ability to connect to traditional-aged college students. A newly hired advisor with significant prior work experience, however, may more easily relate with parents or nontraditional students. Similarly, an advisor with a distinct academic background, such as science or philosophy, may offer others in the unit a unique perspective on core curricula or major courses. Differences encourage diversity of thought, which in turn inspires students to think more broadly.

New advisors benefit from evaluating their own diversity, their comfort level with the uniqueness of others, and their personal limitations. Advisors who embrace campus diversity unequivocally but try to mask discomfort with those representing particular populations will likely struggle more than those who acknowledge biases and seek to improve their own understanding. For example, an advisor raised in a homogenous neighborhood and who later attended similarly homogenous educational institutions may feel nervous when working with others who express themselves in an unfamiliar way. Rather than hiding their uncertainty when communicating with people unlike past peers, the advisor would benefit from addressing the apprehension and seeking opportunities for growth.

Although one can and should appreciate the experiences of others, no one has ever truly walked in another's shoes. Advisors should show care, empathy, and respect, but must recognize that they will never experience life as lived by those distinct from themselves. By acknowledging gaps in diversity and asking for guidance from those with greater cultural competence, advisors can make significant progress toward their own cultural competence.

Recognizing Assumptions

Understanding one's experiences and bases of knowledge assists advisors in moving toward cultural competence. In another step, one recognizes his or her assumptions.

Relying on one's lived experiences beneficially informs a relationship with a student, but it can prove incredibly dangerous if underlying assumptions remain unquestioned. New advisors may base their premises on the undergraduate institution(s) they have attended. Those who experienced a rich residential and student life at a public 4-year university, for example, may presume that adult students undergo a less fulfilling education than those with residential experiences. Similarly, advisors who attended institutions focused on professional programs, such as engineering or business, may struggle to overcome negative attitudes about the value of the core curriculum at a liberal arts college and demonstrate difficulty explaining its value to students.

Unexamined advisor assumptions may prove more detrimental to the advising relationship when the student's personal life differs significantly from that of the advisor. For example, a Black, gay advisor who overcame significant challenges because of both racial bias and prejudice regarding his sexual orientation may assume that all White heterosexual students easily assimilate at college or that all gay students of color face issues similar to his own. A White female advisor from a background of economic privilege and exemplary academic achievement may not recognize that her expectations of first-year students do not match up with the advisees' experiences. For example, when meeting a freshman from an economically disadvantaged home and with an average academic profile, this advisor may not provide the in-depth academic information needed or ensure that the student knows about on-campus support services or the study strategies that bolster academic success.

In addition, advisors must not assume that all students with common life experiences fit into a particular mold, such as those related to age, educational experience, or veteran status. Assumptions inhibit the ability to recognize individual student differences and risk both the advisor–advisee relationship and the appropriateness of the information communicated; not all veterans on campus are experiencing post-traumatic stress disorder any more than all valedictorians are naturally brilliant and need no academic assistance.

Advisors must recognize that, like students, they are products of their experiences, education, and environment and that these backgrounds include personal assumptions (Harding, 2007). Advisors are not (and cannot be) experts on the real life of each and every individual student; in addition, to some extent, advisors can learn only that which students are willing to share. Therefore, the advisor must fill the gaps in a student's story by asking appropriate questions and subsequently proffer advice based on cultural competence.

Understanding the Institution

Much like people, institutions have unique individual characteristics. Not only do they vary by size, but also their curricula reflect foci that range from the small liberal arts colleges to large flagship institutions. Their mission, whether for career-focused for-profit institutions or developmental community colleges, often bespeaks their on-campus cultures. The more attuned advisors become to the environment around them, the more effectively they can identify and meet the needs of their students.

Lee Bolman and Terrence Deal (2013) described four lenses through which individuals can view their organizations: structural, human resource, political, and symbolic. Individuals who view their organizations through structural frameworks seek change through organization and hierarchy, and persons who view their organizations through a human resource framework seek change through empowerment and meeting employee needs. Coalition building and power shifts characterize political frameworks; individuals who embody symbolic frameworks seek change through inspiration, purpose, and rituals. New advisors benefit from understanding the dominant lens used by others in their new environments, because even those with an amenable viewpoint will often fail to shift the focus of those around them. Specifically, new advisors in a political landscape will need to discern the entities who hold power in an organization, but if they land in a human resource zone, they must learn the symbols, rituals, and shared history to effectively communicate.

The dichotomies clearly emerge in a comparison of two hypothetical large, private, research institutions established in the late 19th century. At one, a new advisor may hear that success depends upon working with specific powerful individuals at the institutional or departmental levels; at the other institution, the new advisor learns that success is associated with working collaboratively within and across departments.

Advisors may enter the employ of an institution with a different dominant framework than that of their previous employers or those they had attended as a student.

The sooner they can identify the dominant framework, the more quickly they can negotiate the new workplace. Two institutions that look identical on paper often feel dissimilar when experienced personally.

The answers to the following questions assist advisors in understanding not only institutional culture, but also ways they might fit into that culture: Are decision makers operating at a distance, or do they collaborate frequently with frontline advising staff? Is advising held in esteem at the institution? Do personnel consider concerns of underrepresented students? Advisors may perceive the needs of their students as invisible to decision makers who work at a distance and must creatively make the needs of their students heard, especially those not part of the institution's majority. For example, if an institution's leadership demonstrates disengagement toward diverse students, advisors may not garner requested resources, such as funds, space, or additional personnel to improve the campus services for special populations. Similarly, if it perceives advising as the mere process of assisting students in reading the catalog and registering for classes and therefore does not prioritize it, advisors may lack resources, such as funding for professional development or additional staff, needed to educate students more fully and personally. In an ironic twist, students in stark environments may need greater advising support to overcome institutional challenges.

Perhaps most important, an understanding of the institutional culture allows advisors to effectively support students by either encouraging or challenging the assumptions that students bring to their new environment, culture, and expectations. Advisors must recognize that the expectations of students may not comport with the manner in which the institution functions; therefore, to explain to students how the system works and their fit within it, advisors must possess knowledge of the institution.

Understanding Diverse Students

Several theories inform advisors about student development in the context of cultural competence. Donald R. Atkinson, George Morten, and Derald Wing Sue (1998) put forth the racial identity model, which suggests a transition from conformity to the majority culture through withdrawal from the dominant culture and finding balance between it and all aspects of one's own heritage.

Foundational theories for lesbian, gay, bisexual, transgender, and queer (LGBTQ) development include Vivienne Cass's (1979) homosexual identity development model,[1] which explains stages of sexual identity development, and Anthony R. D'Augelli's (1994) model, which suggests growth as a process, rather than linear stages, and identifies the need for development both individually and within communities of support.

Ethnic development theories, such as Vasti Torres's (2003) Hispanic identity model, discuss the manner in which the individual student sees her or himself as a part of a

---

[1] Although Cass's theoretical model has, in some ways, become outdated culturally, it remains foundational for understanding identity formation among the LGBTQ community.

particular cultural community. Torres encourages individuals to determine particular areas of identity and consider whether each characteristic is part of a larger perspective of personhood or is the sole identifying characteristic such that the person stands in isolation and fails to integrate into a larger campus culture.

Advisors should encourage students to develop across multiple levels of identity but also understand that different aspects of experience and identity may emerge at different points during the college experience. A review of chapter 4 will provide advisors with a variety of theoretical frameworks with which to learn about their students, ranging from paradigms of student involvement to those related to identity development and developmental learning.

Advisors also may benefit from a big-picture perspective. By becoming familiar with the overall demographics and entering characteristics of the students on campus, as well as personally observing various groups of students as they experience campus life, an advisor gains understanding of students and can connect them to the most appropriate resources. Theories of development, demographics, or observations cannot give advisors a full story of any individual student, but over time, as advisors gain experience with students and with their campus, they recognize similarities in the narratives that point to specific student needs. In this way, advisors can sometimes identify areas of concern, such as financial stressors, not specifically disclosed by the student. Chapter 9 and Applications and Insights—Advisor Checklist of Questions: Student Information to Learn in Year 1 provide frameworks in which advisors may consider student-related data, such as academic background and test scores, as well as prior advising interactions and demonstrated knowledge of the campus environment.

Despite the proven resources available, the best way for advisors to learn about their students is to listen to them. To address the complexity of advising interactions across differences, advisors can use a five-question framework as a helpful guide for facilitating revealing discussions.

Five Questions

To prevent assumptions from limiting their interactions with students, advisors must remain reflective and self-aware. They can accomplish this consciousness by considering common questions that encourage broad thinking about each individual student. Over time, each advisor develops an individualized process for evaluating students' needs and establishing positive relationships. Five questions, in particular, provide a framework for initiating the assessment of student needs and advisor presumptions.

How Does the Student's Experience Differ From My Own? To recognize the ways in which the advisee's life experiences differ from those of the advisor, the advisor should consider the ways that the student's diversity may have influenced his or her experience. Just as important, however, the advisor must acknowledge that those areas of advisee and advisor experiences overlap; perhaps the advisor and advisee differ in gender and race but come from similar areas of the country, or they are of the same gender and race but have had dramatically different educational experiences. Answers to this question help an advisor guard against making inaccurate assumptions.

Am I Making Assumptions About This Student Based Upon Both Visible and Invisible Areas of Diversity?   Everyone makes assumptions based upon diversity. When meeting someone who appears entirely different from oneself, an individual may assume that the other's life experiences will differ completely from one's own as well; conversely, a person may assume that someone with similarities to oneself has had life experiences nearly identical to one's own. For example, the LGBTQ-identifying advisor with a difficult coming out experience, including an unwelcoming family, may assume that the LGBTQ student mentioning family problems is experiencing difficulty coming out; in fact, other challenges in family dynamics, not related to LGBTQ issues, may be causing the student's concerns; for example, perhaps step-family conflicts or legal problems of a sibling create anxiousness in the student.

Similarly, advisors may inaccurately apply stereotypes and advise students inappropriately. For example, a student attending a university on a basketball scholarship may not be focused primarily on the professional draft, but may aspire to run a Fortune 500 company. Although seldom formed out of offense or hostility, assumptions based on typical patterns or cohort characteristics can prevent advisors from connecting in a genuine way with the student.

How Do My Assumptions About All Students on This Campus Seem to Fit or Not Fit This Student?   Advisors on campuses with a fairly homogenous population may apply assumptions about the study body as a whole to individual students. For example, at an institution where students usually seek paid work while attending classes, advisors may assume that all students must negotiate their education around the needs of employers. Conversely, if most students come from wealthy families, advisors may incorrectly presume that every student experiences privilege and need not worry about employment.

If an advisor assumes that every student has matriculated directly from high school to campus because most follow this pattern, the needs of adult students, transfers, and veterans may remain unexplored. Advisors must consciously ask how the needs of specific students differ from those of the majority of the campus population.

Even at institutions enrolling diverse cohorts, advisors may make assumptions about one advisee based upon conversations with numerous students who appear alike. For example, advisors may inaccurately presume that students associated with certain campus organizations, such as Greek life, share certain personal or demographic characteristics, such as extroversion or a middle-class background. Likewise, although students in certain majors typically show fairly similar academic interests and strengths, and many struggle in particular courses, the advisor must not assume, for example, that an engineering major will dislike or struggle in composition classes.

In addition, advisors should recognize that students who bring diversity to the campus share similarities with the larger study body. Advisors who embrace only a student's uniqueness may hamstring their own ability to truly understand the individual and may focus too much on the areas of differences when rendering advice.

What Student Characteristics Contribute to Academic Successes or Challenges? Advisors may inadvertently approach diversity from a place of deficit by solely considering the challenges an individual has or must overcome to achieve academic goals. Certainly advisors should not ignore any specific assistance a student needs based on unique identities; however, when assuming that the first-generation student, for example, will struggle because of lacking college role models, the advisor may overlook the hard work and earned resilience that a working-class student has demonstrated and can employ to reach academic goals. Similarly, advisors who presume that a student of a racial or ethnic minority will feel isolated on campus may not realize the extensive miles the student has logged in navigating environments where he or she is not part of the majority.

To avoid unhelpful assumptions, advisors must investigate the characteristics that have helped the student succeed or have created challenges for her or him. They should see (and encourage students to recognize) how diversity contributes to the strength and success of the institution. Advisors can speak to students about how differences in perspective expand and inspire each of them. Perhaps even more important, students whose higher education experience is comprised of interactions only with those like themselves are likely less prepared for a diverse workplace and world than those who have embraced the opportunity afforded by on-campus diversity.

What Types of Support Does This Student (and This Campus) Possess to Address Specific Areas of Diversity That He or She Represents? Students who represent areas of diversity that are rare on campus may feel isolated and can benefit from identifying individuals like themselves as well as a campus community that welcomes their uniqueness. Advisors benefit from familiarity with the ways that the campus encourages diversity.

Some campuses may have established formal units, such as multicultural or diversity offices, or support services, such as an office of disability resources or a transfer center. Some offer full programs of support for first-generation college students or for veterans integrating into civilian life. Others may host student organizations or offer informal groups. If few or none of these support systems exist on campus, the advisor and student should seek information about those in the immediate community to supplement on-campus services.

Using the Five Questions

The following case studies illustrate ways advisors gain cognizance of the influence of students' backgrounds and experiences through use of the five questions. They also remind advisors that, regardless of whether the student has been influenced by traditional or nontraditional experiences, she or he should not be defined by any one characteristic. Advisors should consider the questions as tools in a large box, useful for giving advisors the ability to pick and choose, as appropriate, for the individual students with whom they work.

Case Study 10.1

Melissa, a young Caucasian advisor at an urban research university, identifies as a part of the LGBTQ and Jewish communities. Her advisee, Bobby, a Latino freshman who chose the institution for its strong business program, begins to discuss the challenges he is facing in transitioning to the institution. "The big city," he says, "is very different from where I grew up." He expresses concerns that the changes he is experiencing, including those related to his own sexual orientation, would not be welcomed in his rural home community. "My dad said that in the city, 'all the liberals and the gays would push me away from Christ.'" Pointing to a picture of Melissa, her children, and her wife from her recent wedding, Bobby asks, "Is that your family?" Upon Melissa's confirming answer, he adds, "Maybe you are the right person to help me."

How Does the Student's Experience Differ From My Own?

For Melissa, Bobby's story might seem similar to her own, as they both identify, to varying degrees, with the LGBTQ community. Melissa's coming out experience, however, did not include the same kind of family challenges that Bobby faces. Bobby also presents other visible signs of diversity, including his ethnicity and religion. Melissa should acknowledge and appreciate any common issues they have experienced with regard to sexual orientation and also consider Bobby's unique story. She should not attempt to deemphasize Bobby's connection with the photograph of her family, but she should identify how this part of his identity fits within the larger picture of his early experiences on campus. Therefore, she asks Bobby to share more details about his integration on campus in the first few weeks or inquires about his support systems. To start the conversation, she encourages him to share about his new acquaintances and about life in a residence hall.

Am I Making Assumptions About This Student Based Upon Both Visible and Invisible Areas of Diversity?

Based on his comments, Melissa may assume that Bobby needs to connect to other LGBTQ students. However, she first must uncover the salient aspects of his identity as he sees them. For example, based on the reference to Bobby's father, Melissa may wrongly presume that Bobby is moving away from the church in which he was raised. Similarly, she may inaccurately assume he views his ethnicity secondary to his sexual orientation. To clarify the life roles important to Bobby, Melissa asks him directly about his faith community and whether he has found support on campus or has remained connected to anyone at his home church. Although advisors must remain cautious about extensive self-disclosure, especially early in an advising relationship, Melissa draws on her own experience in diverse communities to probe Bobby's connections to both the on-campus LGBTQ community and to social organizations that may feel genuine to him.

How Do My Assumptions About All Students on This Campus Seem to Fit or Not Fit This Student?

From her knowledge of other successful business students, Melissa may incorrectly presume that Bobby brings a strong academic experience consistent with success in the business program. In focusing on Bobby's visible or disclosed diversity, she must not fail to look into Bobby's academic record and recognize personal growth issues typical of a student away from home for the first time. In addition, Melissa may assume that students who come to this institution seek the benefits from the surrounding city; however, reflection on Bobby's words suggests that this new environment may seem intimidating to him and reflect a college choice unsupported by his family.

What Student Characteristics Contribute to Academic Successes or Challenges?

Melissa's interaction with Bobby should demonstrate an understanding of Bobby's challenges in finding areas of strength in his academic and his personal life. Furthermore, Bobby's initiation into city living may serve as a source of excitement that may encourage him to integrate socially or a source of frustration, or even fear, further isolating him from others on campus and distracting him from his academic focus. Although Bobby recognizes that his family of origin may not support his sexual orientation or his choice to attend an urban university, Melissa encourages him to explore his own choices, recognizing the pros and cons of each, and embrace the opportunity to reflect and make decisions independently.

What Types of Support Does This Student (and This Campus) Possess to Address Specific Areas of Diversity That He or She Represents?

Melissa should be aware of the support structures on campus not only for LGBTQ students but also for those of ethnic minorities and various faith-based groups. She might know of other students addressing issues of sexuality or exploring sexual orientation in an environment that includes nonsupportive families and home communities. She may also want to refer Bobby to religious communities known to welcome LGBTQ individuals to which Bobby could turn should his home church reject him or he feel compelled to leave it. Similarly, Melissa can connect Bobby with other ethnic students with whom Bobby might identify.

Certainly, on a personal level, Melissa can serve as a positive role model for Bobby, but she must ensure that he knows of other resources as well, including faculty members in his academic area. Finally, Melissa may suggest that Bobby meet with second-year students from his hometown region to help him integrate into the urban environment in a way that keeps him connected with his upbringing; she may want to confirm the level of association he has established with existing on-campus or community organizations. To further gauge Bobby's comfort level with an investigation of specific support groups for LGBTQ concerns, Melissa and Bobby may discuss with whom he has shared his sexual identity, possibly role-playing conversations in a way that promotes Bobby's ability to seek support networks on his own.

Case Study 10.2

Rahul works as an advisor at a community college in a small town. A first-generation American of Indian descent, he gained an interest in college advising when a career-ending injury caused him to lose an athletic scholarship and he took a work–study position helping in the advising center of his alma mater.

As he reviews his schedule for the day, Rahul sees the name "Maria Chu" on his list. When on campus, Maria, a traditional-aged first-generation student of Vietnamese ancestry, has always used crutches and the assistance of her mother, an immigrant who speaks very little English, to navigate the campus terrain. According to the appointment notes, Maria wants to discuss future plans for transferring. Upon their visit, after a few minutes of small talk, Maria asks about future options in light of her recent acceptance into the honor society.

How Does the Student's Experience Differ From My Own?

Rahul's experience with a personal injury helps him understand some of the practical issues Maria experiences in navigating the physical landscape of the campus. However, his temporary injury, and the devices he needed for mobility, do not equate to Maria's lifelong use of crutches and personal assistance. In addition, his experience as a first-generation American and son of immigrant parents certainly comports with Maria's role in her family, so he may relate to any pressures she may feel to succeed as a representative of the family. Finally, although not of the same national origin, Rahul identifies as an ethnic minority, and therefore appreciates that Maria's Asian heritage may make her feel isolated on campus.

Am I Making Assumptions About This Student Based Upon Both Visible and Invisible Areas of Diversity?

Rahul should not assume that he fully understands how Maria experiences life with a permanent physical disability, but he likely appreciates the extended time and effort she needs to reach her on-campus destinations. He might inaccurately assume that her goals will need to be tailored because of dependence upon her family. Because of his own experience, Rahul may also presume that Maria feels undue pressure from her family. Furthermore, due to the prevailing cultural differences among families in Western and Asian cultures, he may wrongly presume the extent of her mother's role in Maria's decision making. Finally, as Melissa does with Bobby, Rahul may need to determine the salient identities that affect Maria's point of view, and in addition, he should not assume that her use of physical assistance indicates the presence or absence of other disabilities.

To directly address Maria's concerns about transfer and her future, he must keep a proper perspective of all the diversity issues possibly associated with Maria's situation, but directly ask her about her prior experiences and her course work to determine her academic strengths and challenges. He also needs to ask Maria about the role her mother is to play in their discussions to indicate that he intends Maria to guide this interaction.

How Do My Assumptions About All Students on This Campus Seem to Fit or Not Fit This Student?

Working at a community college, Rahul likely has worked with diverse students in terms of age, ethnicity, academic backgrounds, and veteran status and with a wide variety of life experiences. He may simply expect all students to face some form of challenge and may see Maria's physical disability as no greater than that faced by other students. However, Rahul may consider Maria's mobility issues as more substantial than barriers to access that other students overcome; conversely, he may see them as inconveniences that pale compared to the issues faced by students without the family support that Maria enjoys.

Again, the role of family support could contribute to Maria's unique situation among students, and Rahul may assume that her mother's constant presence limits Maria's ability to connect independently with other students her age. Therefore, rather than presume a negative influence of her family, Rahul asks Maria about her social life on campus and friends.

Throughout their conversation he must solicit or listen for details about Maria's values and goals. Furthermore, rather than dwell on practical aspects of her mobility, Rahul must recognize that Maria has successfully navigated difficult environments in her life and like all other potential transfer students now needs trustworthy, accurate information on which to make an informed decision about her future.

What Student Characteristics Contribute to Academic Successes or Challenges?

Rahul realizes that Maria will need to address and obtain assistance with mobility wherever she transfers, and although all institutions receiving federal funding must comply with ADA mandates for accommodations, some institutions and situations will likely offer Maria more ease of accessibility than others. He must also recognize that Maria exhibits a great deal of resilience to meet the goals she sets for herself.

Although her current dependence on her mother for mobility may present a potential stumbling block to independence, family support in all realms of her life, which eludes many students, may prove valuable to Maria's academic success. Therefore, Rahul helps Maria investigate her interests in careers and future education to assist her in determining the best options for her unique circumstances and to encourage her continued success.

What Types of Support Does This Student (and This Campus) Possess to Address Specific Areas of Diversity That He or She Represents?

Rahul knows that Maria must connect with the Office of Disability Resources on this and her new campus. Rahul must respect all aspects of Maria—the diverse and the typical, in total—and not solely focus on her disability; she certainly possesses the expertise on that aspect of her life. In addition to support staff who may assist with accessibility, Maria may benefit from connections with students who share other characteristics with her, such as those within the honor society, her major, or in a Vietnamese American student group. Rahul encourages her personal and independent growth through referrals and direct contacts on her behalf in areas in which she expresses an interest.

Case Study 10.3

Tim, an African American advisor, begins his first professional position at the historically Black college where he recently completed his bachelor's degree. At orientation, an African American woman named Tasha, who appears to be in her forties, approaches him and asks for assistance. Tim recognizes her name as one on his advisee list. Tasha immediately expresses concern about her decision to return to school: "Everyone looks so young—even you! You're young enough to date my daughter, and you're the one who's supposed to help me?" Tim is taken aback by her boldness when she asks, "Is there a way to change advisors to someone with more life experience?"

Of all the potential challenges to their advising relationship and Tim's ability to teach Tasha about the university, the college experience, and the curriculum, the most damaging would be Tim's buy-in to Tasha's presumption that his youth and limited life experience render him an ineffective advisor. Tim should embrace her boldness, which seemed initially offensive, as a virtue; furthermore, he can confront her presumptions because she has shared them. Although Tasha has more life experience, Tim need not shy away from serving as her advisor if he can trust in his training and education to help ameliorate the differences associated with their age difference. Therefore, Tim encourages Tasha to keep their first appointment, and Tasha agrees.

How Does the Student's Experience Differ From My Own?

Tim cannot fully understand Tasha's experience as an adult student enrolling in college after dropping out decades ago. However, he can certainly find other areas of identity with which he can connect with Tasha. Their similar racial identity may prove as important for their relationship as generational differences because Tim represents the success that Tasha seeks as a graduate of this institution.

He inquires about her choices for obtaining an education and choosing their shared institution. He also looks for other similarities to emerge, such as family characteristics or academic interests.

Despite attempts to find them, Tim uncovers few similarities with Tasha, but does not avoid her concerns about his age or act defensively about her assumptions on his experience level. Instead, Tim inquires about her future plans and perceptions of the strengths she brings to campus. He encourages her to elaborate upon her past successes and challenges and uses that information along with her stated goals to demonstrate both his ability and knowledge while helping her link to resources on campus.

Am I Making Assumptions About This Student Based Upon Both Visible and Invisible Areas of Diversity?

Tim learns that Tasha's family or her job has taken priority over her education, delaying her return to college. However, he must resist the temptation to think that these roles will continue to take priority over her education. He must also avoid assumptions about Tasha's ability to complete the course work because she has not attended college in recent years. Depending upon his experience with other adult students on the campus and in light of her negative reaction to the ages represented at orientation, Tim may make assumptions about Tasha's ability to find others with whom she can connect, but he must remember that other potential areas of diversity, her race and gender, place her in the majority at this particular historically Black college. In addition, despite the similarities that Tasha shares with the student body, Tim must not discount the other areas of invisible diversity that Tasha may possess, such as the compounding reasons she did not complete her education earlier (e.g., a divorce, caretaker to parents, and so forth) or academic challenges (e.g., test anxiety) undisclosed to Tim.

How Do My Assumptions About All Students on This Campus Seem to Fit or Not Fit This Student?

Although a new advisor, Tim draws on his time as a student at the institution to determine ways Tasha can fit into the larger campus environment. Despite knowing that students at this institution form cliques in residence halls, leaving adult students and commuters out of certain social circles, he also recognizes that students connect primarily on the basis of academic interest, making them welcoming to students regardless of age and background. Therefore, he encourages Tasha to seek like-minded acquaintances in her classes.

In addition to his personal experience, Tim looks at institutional data indicating that most current students choose this institution to link with others based upon racial identity, and Tim knows that Tasha chose the institution based upon its proximity to her home and family. With the combination of insider and data-driven knowledge, Tim may be uniquely positioned to help Tasha's personal growth by suggesting the points of assimilation and differences that may emerge in unexpected ways: Tasha may find more relationships with young people based on academic interests than she will with other, perhaps older, students primarily connected through their racial identity.

What Student Characteristics Contribute to Academic Successes or Challenges?

Tasha may think of her age as a disadvantage because it seems to separate her from the majority of the campus's students. Likewise, her family commitments differentiate her from her classroom peers. However, the sacrifices made for her family may inspire her to succeed in a way that challenges her classmates, and her life experience helps her link classroom lessons to the real world. Her racial identity, especially combined with her generational status, may allow her to connect to the history of the institution, and possibly to the faculty, to bridge any gap created by age. In fact, her lived experience in the local community may help her communicate a perspective about the historically Black college and surrounding region that may resonate with others seeking to more fully understand the heritage they share at the institution and in society.

What Types of Support Does This Student (and This Campus) Possess to Address Specific Areas of Diversity That He or She Represents?

Tim investigates whether this campus has a support group for adult students or an active women's center. He also encourages Tasha to rely on prior relationships through which she gains support. He recognizes the strength that Tasha's family may provide and suggests that Tasha seek connection to these less conventional resources for college success.

Summary

No advisor, regardless of experience, can fully prepare for every student who walks into an appointment. However, all can work toward understanding their own strengths and challenges with regard to cultural competence. Furthermore, advisors can ensure that their understanding of their institutions and the manner in which others within it embrace (or fail to embrace) diversity allows them to support more effectively the students in their charge. By using a systematic approach to working with all students, new advisors develop a skill set that enables them to meet advising learning goals while gaining important experience that furthers their own development in understanding and educating diverse students.

Aiming for Excellence

o Attend activities and events both on campus and in the community that represent a broad range of cultures, including your own. Demonstrate to students the value you place in cultural competence by being visible at events in which you appear to be an outsider.

o Seek mentors in areas where you lack expertise. If new to an institution, find a mentor with significant institutional memory as well as those within other departments with whom you can effectively partner.

o Do not assume that your mentor will guide the relationship; ask questions such as "What do you like most about working here?" "If I have a good idea about something, who do I talk to about it?" and "How do advisors get involved in decision making?" to identify institutional and unit strengths and challenges as well as the influential formal and informal leaders on campus.

o Speak with students, both your advisees and others around campus, about their experiences. Find out the good and poor sources for student advocacy.

o Work with those who are marginalized to bring their concerns to the forefront.

○ Attend or start an advisor reading group. Suggest not only articles that reflect diverse subject matter, but also authors who exhibit uniqueness in race, ethnicity, gender, sexual orientation, and background.

○ Share and gain knowledge across institutional lines. Find faculty members, paraprofessionals, and administrators to speak at your next department meeting or in-service.

○ Be vulnerable. Admit to gaps in your knowledge so you can learn more. If your personal experience does not include exposure to specific groups, ask those responsible for educating and mentoring these cohorts about the history of the group, student needs, and opportunities for involvement.

○ Review NACADA resources, including both the NACADA Clearinghouse and the Commissions and Interest Groups specific to student populations to learn about various student cohorts.

○ Select one of the case studies presented in this chapter. For each of the five questions, develop questions that will elicit solid information from the student and will improve your understanding and advice to all students.

○ Many institutions have established professional development programs or diversity offices that offer workshops dealing with cultural competency or global cultural awareness. After attending a workshop, make a list of the skills and ideas helpful in your advising practice. Identify two skills or ideas to implement immediately. In your journal, record the ways in which your new tools are working. Revisit your list on a monthly basis and continue to implement skills and ideas until you have gone through your entire list. (Folsom, 2007, p. 107)

○ Request that the person in charge of advisor training and development invite a diverse group of students to discuss their experiences at your institution as well as identify the assistance they seek from advising (Folsom, 2007, p. 107). Where no advisor training and development exists, consider inviting students to an informal feedback session (offer snacks).

○ Consider whether your office is welcoming to all populations. What can you do to make your office welcoming to all student populations? (Folsom, 2007, p. 107)

References

Atkinson, D. R., Morten, G., & Sue, D. W. (1998). *Counseling American minorities: A cross-cultural perspective* (5th ed.). Boston, MA: McGraw-Hill.

Bolman, L. G., & Deal, T. E. (2013). *Reframing organizations: Artistry, choice, and leadership* (5th ed.). San Francisco, CA: Jossey-Bass.

Cass, V. (1979). Homosexual identity formation: A theoretical model. *Journal of Homosexuality, 4*(3), 219–235.

D'Augelli, A. R. (1994). Identity development and sexual orientation: Toward a model of lesbian, gay, and bisexual development. In E. J. Trickett, R. J. Watts, & D. Birman (Eds.), *Human diversity: Perspectives on people in context* (pp. 312–333). San Francisco, CA: Jossey-Bass.

Folsom, P. (2007). Aiming for excellence: Suggested advisor development activities. In P. Folsom (Ed.), *The new advisor guidebook: Mastering the art of advising through the first year and beyond* (Monograph 16) (p. 107). Manhattan, KS: National Academic Advising Association.

Harding, B. (2007). Relational skills: Establishing cultural credibility. In P. Folsom (Ed.), *The New advisor guidebook: Mastering the art of advising through the first year and beyond.* (Monograph No. 16) (pp. 97–99). Manhattan, KS: National Academic Advising Association.

National Association of School Psychologists. (n.d.). *NASP Resources: Defining cultural competence.* Retrieved from http://www.nasponline.org/resources/culturalcompetence /definingculture.aspx

Torres, V. (2003). Influences on ethnic identity development of Latino college students in the first two years of college. *Journal of College Student Development, 44*(4), 532–547.

Applications and Insights
Advisor Checklist of Questions: Teaching Students to Use Resources
Stephen O. Wallace and Beverly A. Wallace

First-year advisors need to know available services offered throughout the campus and community, the referral processes, and follow-up procedures.

- o What campus referral sources and services are available?
  - o What accommodations are provided for students with disabilities?
  - o What academic assistance and student support services are offered?
  - o What programs or services assist students on academic probation to regain satisfactory academic standing?
  - o What health and wellness services and programs can students access?
  - o What specialized services and programs, such as those serving specific cohorts (e.g., a women's center or veteran's groups), are available?
- o Who should a student contact (name, location, phone) if they have questions about:
  - o student registration?
  - o an official transcript?
  - o transfer or withdrawal from the institution?
  - o a grade dispute?
  - o issues with a course professor?
  - o problems with a fellow student?
  - o their student account?
  - o financial aid regulations?
  - o campus organizations and clubs?
  - o career exploration and development?
  - o internships?
  - o service learning projects?
  - o concerns related to sexual harassment or abuse?
  - o available referral sources and services?

VOICES FROM THE FIELD

ADVISING INTERNATIONAL STUDENTS

Yung-Hwa Anna Chow

Internationalization of higher education, although no longer a new phenomenon to academic advisors, may operationally vary according to region. Many European countries focus on internationalizing curricula, while investment attracts foreign students to and from China. In the United States, postsecondary institutions focus on promoting study abroad programs and building branch campuses overseas, and British colleges and universities are dedicated to recruiting foreign students and establishing business and research relations abroad (Layton, 2012). In this Voices From the Field, I examine the reasons for the international flow of students, the impact of internationalization on U.S. postsecondary institutions, and ways academic advising can positively influence the experience of international students studying in the United States.

The latest data from the United Nations Educational, Scientific and Cultural Organization Institute for Statistics (2014, ¶2) stated that "In 2012, at least 4 million students went abroad to study, up from 2 million in 2000, representing 1.8% of all tertiary enrollments or 2 in 10 students globally." Central Asia is the largest source of international students, with China, India, and Korea the top sending countries from this part of the world. The top destination countries are the United States (18%), the United Kingdom (11%), and France (7%).

The increase in international students follows several worldwide trends, including specific, differentially perceived postsecondary educational experiences and the increased globalization opportunities associated with them. Specifically, in 2009 and 2010, the Institute of International Education conducted a survey of over 9,000 prospective study abroad students in four major sending regions (including India, Brazil, United Kingdom, and South Africa) and found that 76% of the respondents agreed with statements suggesting that the United States offers a higher quality higher education system than do their home countries (Chow, 2011).

In addition, international experience plays a significant role in the education and future employment opportunities of many students. In 2008, Phil Gardner, Linda Gross, and Inge Steglize, for the Collegiate Employment Research Institute, reported that more than 45% of employers surveyed in the United States found that recent hires with international experience stood out and excelled beyond their peers in areas of understanding cultural differences in the workplace; interacting with people who hold different interests, values, or perspectives; adapting to situations of change; and so forth. According to Gardner et al. (2008), many employers around the world cite the ability to speak a second language and experience abroad as preferred qualifications for prospective hires.

Although some students can afford to study abroad through family funding or scholarships to experience general personal and professional growth, others receive funding to pursue a foreign education for very specific purposes. For example, the Saudi Arabian Cultural Mission to the U.S. (2013) sponsors students to study in a field that meets economic or social needs of Saudi Arabia. Many advisors work with students in majors that require or strongly encourage a study abroad experience before graduation.

Value of International Education

Internationalization in higher education presents a myriad of benefits as well as obstacles that affect universities worldwide. On the positive side, meaningful interactions between domestic and international students can offer lifelong benefits to participants and the campus culture. In a Duke University study of survey data from 5,675 former students, researchers found that students who had substantial engagement with peers from abroad related well to people from different backgrounds, were better at "synthesizing and integrating ideas and information," and were "also more likely than their peers to question their own, and society's, beliefs" (Fischer, 2013, ¶6–7). U.S. students can develop this positive relationship when interacting with international students on their home campus or in study abroad situations overseas.

However, on the negative side, college campuses must determine and apply the best ways to integrate international students from many dissimilar nations so that both domestic and incoming students can create and benefit from meaningful interactions. To contribute positively to the challenges imposed by a changing student dynamic, including the impact created by the influx of international students and increased interest of domestic advisees in study abroad programs, advisors need to increase their cultural competency.

Five Questions

Due to the current state and projected growth of internationalization in postsecondary institutions, educators must prepare for working with students from environments different from those in which they were raised. In chapter 10, Karen Archambault suggests that advisors can address five questions to gain practical cultural competency. Both new and seasoned advisors can apply Archambault's questions to their conversations with international students.

How Does the Student's Experience Differ From My Own?

Few similarities characterize most U.S. advisors and international students. Advisors with direct experience as international or study abroad students may share some experiences with advisees from overseas, but those without any international experience may need to settle on improving visualization about life in another country by taking college-level courses that increase understanding and improve communications, such as a second language class.

Although often open and flexible to new encounters, international students will experience culture shock, language difficulties, and homesickness while navigating through a new education system on an unfamiliar campus. Therefore, advisors should strive for empathy and picture themselves in the students' situations. As advisors study other countries and consider the challenges of their advisees, they can increase their cultural competence by keeping the following questions in mind:

o How might I react to living in a place where communication is a constant struggle?

o How might I internalize separation from family or friends for an extended period of time?

Am I Making Assumptions About This Student Based Upon Both Visible and Invisible Areas of Diversity?

When working with international students, advisors quickly recognize the cultural customs or norms that differ from the domestic U.S. experience, but they also discern that they cannot possibly know all of the different ways people interact around the world nor assume that stereotypical generalizations will provide either appropriate or helpful guidance. For example, many Chinese international students come to the United States with an unclear understanding that plagiarism, as defined by Western standards, carries severe punishment in U.S. institutions, but this generality does not mean that all international Chinese students copy and paste their research papers (Galinova & Giannetti, 2014).

Although advisors must recognize differing general cultural viewpoints and practices (e.g., U.S. professors consider sharing homework answers dishonest behavior, not examples of cooperation and helpfulness), each international student presents individual perspectives and experiences, and the advisor must take time to learn about each student's home country and each individual's attitudes toward them. They can use the following questions to drive an inquiry about the experiences that shape their students' current worldview:

o What are some traditional holidays and why are they significant?

o What was it like to attend school in _____?

How Do My Assumptions About All Students on This Campus Seem to Fit or Not Fit This Student?

The experiences of international students uniquely vary from those of domestic students on campus. Those new to the United States present different needs and expectations, making them inherently unlike the American cohort. Therefore, new advisors should gain familiarity with areas that do not apply to citizens, such as basic immigration policies; for example, they need to know that international students cannot enter the United States more than 30 days prior to the start of the semester. With understanding of this law, advisors appreciate that incoming international students must assimilate very quickly to a new home and culture before classes start and will realize their international advisees benefit from connections to campus student organizations that put them in touch with students from their home region or country. Advisors also need to introduce them to domestic students, and those who have traveled to the international students' home countries, in particular, may serve as effective peer mentors.

What Student Characteristics Contribute to Academic Successes or Challenges?

Advisors can effectively address student characteristics applied to education by looking at the work of Pierre Bourdieu (Bourdieu & Passeron, 1970/1990), who defined *cultural capital* as previously acquired knowledge necessary to successfully navigate in a particular environment. Bourdieu theorized that cultural capital may be reflected in different learning styles. For example, in American culture, educators profess and reward critical thinking and analytical reasoning. However, students from other regions, particularly in the East, may have been primarily taught the value of memorization and thus consider knowledge of a volume of information in detail more important and practical than the principles associated with Western thought (Galinova & Giannetti, 2014). In fact, some students may copy or duplicate important class material in memorizing it because they consider knowledge communal in nature and addition of their own original ideas as an expression of arrogance (Friedman, 2010, ¶8). This preference for memorization and humbleness often undergirds the problems with plagiarism experienced by Chinese international students, who have spent years memorizing, verbatim, to demonstrate the type of learning considered most appropriate in Chinese schools (Friedman, 2010; Galinova & Giannetti, 2014).

Advisors must remember that international students have developed their own cultural capital that they bring with them. Students' adaptability and demonstrated respect for the cultures and norms of others exemplify the type of competency that domestic students can emulate. In fact, these contributions from international students have inspired colleges and universities to recruit them as a means of engendering diversity on campus.

Advisors play a role in enriching learning for all students and promoting cross-cultural interactions of international and domestic students. The idealized campus includes internationalization that does not involve students necessarily leaving campus to study abroad; instead, the educational system increasingly capitalizes on international students' prior experiences.

Consistent with these goals for internationalization for domestic students, advisors must assist advisees who possess relatively little cultural capital by giving them the necessary tools to improve their academic skills. Even the least experienced advisors can contribute to this goal by determining the type of information and learning style that fits each student and situation. Specifically, they can encourage international students to take classes that promote academic skills such as critical thinking and analysis. Once students have acquired these attributes for success in their new institution, they will be able to demonstrate their own cultural capital in the classroom setting.

What Types of Support Does This Student (and This Campus) Possess to Address Specific Areas of Diversity That He or She Represents?

Karen Doss Bowman (2012), in an article on integrating international students into the university campus, stated that despite specific goals set by college administrators, meaningful interactions between domestic and international students remain relatively rare. To foster growth of all students, she recommended cross-cultural training for advisors, efficient transfer agreements between U.S. and international institutions, employment of bilingual counselors, and establishment of living–learning communities that encourage exchange between international and domestic students. To this end, advisors can ask superiors or colleagues the following questions to identify units with effective practices that benefit international students:

- Which departments offer clear transfer agreements with international institutions?
- Where can advisors find on-campus bilingual counselors or translators?

In addition to learning about existing resources, advisors need to collaborate with those in well-developed programs to familiarize themselves with the specific issues of international students on campus. They also need to take advantage of offerings, such as work-life educational workshops and lectures, that prepare advisors as good global citizens. NACADA offers a myriad of resources such as webinars, articles, and the Global Engagement Commission for advisors seeking to learn about international students and study abroad benefits. Advisors who attend regional and national conferences to learn and present about experiences with international students, proven programs, and ways to integrate study abroad into major curricula contribute to the promotion of the internationalization that best prepares students for the globalized world.

Summary

The shrinking global community demands that students embrace internationalization in higher education. As a result, academic advisors must move away from a service-oriented role to adopt that of a teacher (NACADA: The Global Community for Academic Advising [NACADA], 2006), and they need to do it consistently with pedagogy critical to advising. As stated in the Preamble of the Introduction to the NACADA Concept of Academic Advising (NACADA, 2006),

> Academic advising is integral to fulfilling the teaching and learning mission of higher education. Through academic advising, students learn to become members of their higher education community, to think critically about their roles and responsibilities as students, and to prepare to be educated citizens of a democratic society and a global community. Academic advising engages students beyond their own world views, while acknowledging their individual characteristics, values, and motivations as they enter, move through, and exit the institutions. (¶7)

Because of international student mobility and the ever-increasing demands to produce informed and critically aware citizens, advisors must equip themselves to educate unique student populations. The learning process necessary for this endeavor will benefit not just advisees but new and seasoned advisors alike.

Aiming for Excellence

- o Meet with an advisor in international programs to learn about the populations coming to campus: the top sending countries, the most popular majors, and the extent to which web sites or other public offerings are translated for parents.

- o Familiarize yourself with immigration processes, regulations, and documents.

- o Attend any workshop or presentation about information on international students and their home cultures.

- o Identify international student organizations on campus and participate in their cultural activities and events.

- o Research top majors for international students on your campus to see if they offer resources designed to help international students; for example, do they train and select international peer mentors or offer writing assistance?

- o Ask admissions and the registrar about the application of international transfer credits and any transfer agreements in place for specific countries and international universities.

- o Take advantage of NACADA and other advising resources. Read *Academic Advising Today* and NACADA Clearinghouse articles on international students. Join the Global Engagement Facebook page, and attend presentations on international students at regional and annual conferences.

o Ask international students about their experiences on campus. Specifically inquire about key events and situations: orientation, availability and accessibility of contact personnel in international programs, and level of connection on campus. Obtain their suggestions for improving their U.S. college experience. Share constructive feedback with those in a position to enact change.

References

Bourdieu, P., & Passeron, J-C. (1990). *Cultural reproduction and social reproduction* (2nd ed.) (Trans. Richard Nice). London, UK: SAGE. (Original work published in 1970.)

Bowman, K. D. (2012). Beyond the comfort zone. *International Educator, 21*(2), 56–59.

Chow, P. (2011, May). *What international students think about U.S. higher education: Attitudes and perceptions of prospective students in Africa, Asia, Europe and Latin America.* New York, NY: Institute of International Education.

Fischer, K. (2013, June 7). Interacting with international peers in college may confer lasting benefits. *The Chronicle of Higher Education.* Retrieved from https://chronicle.com /article/Interacting-With-International/139683/

Friedman, P. (2010, May 26). China's plagiarism problem. *Forbes Magazine.* Retrieved from http://www.forbes.com/2010/05/26/china-cheating-innovation-markets-economy -plagiarism.html

Galinova, E., & Giannetti, I. (2014). *Advising international Chinese students: Issues, strategies, and practices.* Manhattan, KS: NACADA: The Global Community for Academic Advising.

Gardner, P., Gross, L., & Steglitz, I. (2008, March). *Unpacking your study abroad experience: Critical reflection for workplace competencies* (CERI Research Brief 1-2008: Collegiate Employment Research Institute, Vol. 1, No. 1). Retrieved from http://studyabroad.isp.msu.edu/people/unpacking_brief.pdf

Layton, H. (2012, December 13). *How do you define internationalization?* Retrieved from http://chronicle.com/blogs/worldwise/how-do-you-define-internationalization/31114

NACADA: The Global Community for Academic Advising (NACADA). (2006). *NACADA concept of academic advising: Introduction.* Retrieved from http://www.nacada.ksu.edu/Resources/Clearinghouse/View-Articles/Concept-of -Academic-Advising-a598.aspx

Saudi Arabian Cultural Mission to the U.S. (2013). *Mission.* Retrieved from http://www.sacm.org/AboutSACM/Mission.aspx

United Nations Educational, Scientific and Cultural Organization. (2014). *Global flow of tertiary-level students.* Retrieved from http://www.uis.unesco.org/education/Pages/international-student-flow-viz.aspx

PART FOUR

FOUNDATIONS: THE RELATIONAL COMPONENT

The relationship forged between student and advisor directly affects the nature of advising interactions. Especially when delivering difficult news to students, advisors must invoke relational skills that maintain trust with the student and integrity in the advising relationship. Contributors to this part of the *Guidebook* analyze the role of effective communication and provide frameworks for fostering a strong bond that holds even in the most challenging situations. In addition to helping new advisors understand the value of developing their relational skills, the chapters highlight tips for putting these skills into practice.

11

EFFECTIVE COMMUNICATIONS SKILLS

Peggy Jordan

Communication involves an exchange of information and ideas between two or more people. It may include verbal, nonverbal, written, and electronic interchanges. Communication between advisor and student begins with the first face-to-face meeting or earlier if written or electronic means were used to contact the student.

Effective communication is not a passive process. It requires alertness, energy, critical-thinking skills, and introspection. It is characterized by advisors who convey information, ideas, and feelings accurately and understand the information, ideas, and feelings of the student. Essential to good advising, effective communication can be learned.

Susan Barnett, Scott Roach, and Martha Smith (2006) found that using advanced communication skills will exert a positive impact on advising; they constitute the tools advisors use to perform their jobs as they provide information to students about classes, degree plans, college policies, and personal issues. As in most professions, advisors build their communication tools gradually by reading as well as observing, reflecting, and modeling seasoned advisors. If advisors lack fundamental effective communication skills, they cannot perform their jobs. Richard Light's (2001) often quoted statement, "Good advising might be the single most underestimated characteristic of a successful college experience" (p. 81), hints at the importance of effective communication. In fact, Hadyn Swecker, Mathew Fifolt, and Linda Searby (2013) found student retention increased 13% for every meeting with an advisor. This finding validates the contention that the advisor–student relationship, which is built on effective communication skills discussed in this chapter, influences a student.

Listening and Self-awareness

An active and complex process, effective listening involves awareness of both self and others. To be a good listener, one must develop skills of active listening and interviewing (or questioning). Effective listening results in understanding.

Self-awareness includes cognizance of one's own physical and emotional states, physical behaviors, and personal biases.

Physical State

An advisor's physical state might manifest itself in the following thoughts:

- "I have a headache."
- "My eyes itch because of allergies."
- "My neck is sore."
- "I am starving! When am I going to lunch?"

These unpleasant physical states can show on a person's face, behavior, or voice tone: frowning because of a headache or neck pain; eyes watering from allergens; lack of focus due to hunger.

Emotional State

Advisors may feel scared, nervous, happy, sad, excited, or angry. These emotions are unlikely to be related to the advisee; however, students may perceive an advisor's emotions as personally directed toward or in response to them.

For example, in my first year in advising I experienced an encounter with a colleague that left me angry. I will always remember the poor student who came to me immediately after the encounter. He apologized for every question he asked. Although I kept saying, "No, you're fine," he sensed my anger and frustration (even though I thought I had hidden it). Finally, I apologized and explained that he had accurately recognized my emotional state. I told him that my anger had nothing to do with him but was the result of an incident that I was having trouble putting out of my mind. I promised to give him my undivided attention for the remainder of his appointment. From that moment, we were able to address his agenda rather than mine.

Advisors cannot always hide the human issues and concerns that encroach upon their day. When students assume that nonverbal displays are directed at or inspired by them, the advisors must give a brief explanation of the distraction: "I'm sorry. I was thinking about an issue I'm having, but I will stop"; "I don't mean to ignore you. My child is home sick and I worry that her dad is texting me about her. That's why I keep looking at my cell phone." Upon realizing that the advisor has not communicated in the best possible way, and no human perfectly engages another, she or he must open up in honesty to the student affected by the behavior.

Denial is one of the worst enemies of an advisor. If unable to acknowledge his or her own internal state, the advisor has no chance of ameliorating the effect(s) it may have on communication with students.

Physical Behaviors

Physical mannerisms may have a positive or negative impact on communication. To complicate matters further, the culture may dictate the interpretation of some mannerisms. Positive physical behaviors in most western cultures include

- o smiling when greeting a student;
- o maintaining good posture, which promotes breathing and alertness and suggests positive interest;
- o making eye contact (cultures vary in how eye contact is interpreted; deference to authority figures may be shown by looking down; some cultures may view too much direct eye contact as aggressive);
- o using facial expressions such as smiles and head nods; and
- o maintaining an open posture (without crossing one's arms or legs), which communicates openness.

Mannerisms that are distracting or bring a negative response should be avoided. These may include

- o looking at one's watch;
- o fidgeting;
- o demonstrating inattentiveness with actions such as pencil tapping, rubber band snapping, and so forth; and
- o answering the phone while with a student.

The advising session should be an oasis for students where their thirst for information, acceptance, and understanding is quenched. The advising office is one place the student should be able to relax and let down her or his guard; a place where the student is welcomed rather than tolerated, accepted rather than evaluated, and stimulated to grow rather than encouraged to stay the same. To provide a safe place, the advisor must know the student and the appropriate questions for and expected behaviors of that individual.

Personal Biases

The advisor's goal is to listen without judgment, but everyone has developed biases. When advisors recognize their own preconceived ideas or biases, they stand a better chance of keeping those ideas from interfering with their relationships with advisees. If advisors ask students to look at themselves honestly, they must be committed to examine their own thoughts and feelings with honesty as well. The limits of an advisor's self-understanding may also diminish his or her understanding of students' feeling and experiences. Furthermore, advisors cannot change attitudes and behaviors that interfere with student success if they are unaware of their own biases and idiosyncrasies. For example, when advisors hear a description of themselves from several people (students, colleagues, supervisor), even if they do not agree, the advisors owe it to themselves and their advisees to consider the possibility that the information is accurate. Excellence in advising comes from minds open to new ideas, including about oneself, as well as about students.

Other-Awareness

Other-awareness, or awareness of the student, is a second component of listening. Before the student says a word, advisors are aware of the student's physical presence: height, weight, age, ethnicity, dress, and cleanliness. They are also aware of their own reaction to these characteristics. Advisors should also be aware of students' facial expressions, muscle tone (relaxed, tense, nervous), and body position (leaning forward, looking down, turned away). All of these describe body language or nonverbal communication. To check for mixed messages, an advisor should note student's words and determine whether they match the nonverbal information presented. Kathi Mestayer (2013, p. 38) explained, "The exchange of nonverbal signals in conversation creates a constant feedback loop, one that can both reinforce communication and escalate miscommunication." She explained that nonverbal communication is learned over time and based on a person's culture, ethnicity, gender, age, language, regional identity, and other factors. In addition, socioeconomic status, sexual orientation, educational achievement, family structure, religious beliefs, health status, and various "challenges and ableness" contribute to one's world view (Cunningham, 2003, ¶3).

New advisors, in particular, can learn about making assumptions about others from Karen Archambault's discussion of cultural competence in chapter 10. They may also benefit from looking at the listing by Kris Rugsaken (2006) on the meanings of behaviors in various cultures.

Leigh Cunningham (2003) and Archambault (chapter 10) both stressed the importance of looking beyond generalizations about various groups. Instead, advisors should pay attention to their reaction to a person's unique view of the world, especially if it differs from those not previously encountered. Cunningham said, "We can come to the place that we, for the most part, seek to comprehend before we judge, and offer thoughtful, responsive understanding and respect more often than reactive judgment" (¶10).

Barbara Lamont (2005) provided an instructive example of possible miscommunication. For example, she warned advisors that often Japanese students give polite and respectful responses, but leave the office without an understanding of the information offered. These students' deference to authority figures may manifest as listening, and their lack of questions may incorrectly indicate that the advisor had clearly communicated to them. In fact, the student may be confused and frustrated.

A student may have developed a preconceived idea about the advisor because of biases as well. Advisors should not take exhibitions of bias personally, but rather, use the opportunity to familiarize themselves with the student better. Although advisors should help all students, domestic and international, appreciate and develop their cultural competency, they must honor the histories and norms that inform the student's world view. That is, with a full appreciation for diversity, advisors need to accept the specific levels of development and social understanding of each advisee.

Empathy is a powerful aid in understanding others. When individuals put themselves in another's position, they can understand more easily how the other person may feel. Advisors have responsibilities to others in the institution who do not always allow them to satisfy a student's request, but they should understand the frustration, sadness, or anger the student may feel. Maturity and self-confidence enable advisors to appreciate a student's feelings without becoming personally offended or responding defensively.

Active Listening

Active listening involves one's whole being. It requires more effort than just signs of paying attention. It includes visual cues of listening, such as making eye contact, keeping cultural variations in mind, and leaning slightly forward. The facial expressions reflect the statements of the other conversant and include nodding the head, raising an eyebrow, or looking surprised. Active listening also inspires reflective questioning or statements meant to invoke consideration, such as, "So, you want to major in education, but you don't know the area or level you want to teach."

Statements such as "And that makes you feel anxious" show reflection of feeling. Advisors employing active listening make use of clarifying questions to check understanding of the student and to offer supportive statements. Advisors may summarize the student's narrative to convey understanding and to give the student the opportunity to hear his or her own questions or concerns. This invitation for reflection may help the student clarify salient issues.

Because a listener can process information much more rapidly than a speaker can produce it, advisors are able to organize the messages given by students and make a mental list of clarifying questions and hypotheses concerning a student's needs. However, this processing advantage can place an obstacle to good communication as well. Advisors whose minds are racing ahead may answer the student's question before the advisee has completely stated it. Advisors must allow the student to finish talking, even if the advisor thinks he or she has heard the same story from other students.

Clarifying Questions

Asking questions is part of the listening process. Advisors put students' words, tone, gestures, and body language together to guess at the meaning of the communication exchange. The advisor's supposition is only a guess until the advisor checks her or his understanding with the student. Clarifying statements may begin with phrases such as

- o "So, what you want is . . ."
- o "Let me see if I understand your question . . ."
- o "What I hear you saying is . . ."

If the student says, "No. That's not what I mean," the advisor has the chance to try again, maybe with a statement such as "Help me understand." The speaker and the listener bear equal responsibility for the relationship, and if one stops trying to communicate, the exchange is lost.

Critical Thinking

Skill in interviewing can elicit valuable information from students. The simplest situations are those in which the student asks information-based questions: "What does my grade-point average need to be to get off academic probation?" or "What are the prerequisites to the business program?" Typical information-oriented training programs equip advisors to handle these types of questions, but new advisors sometimes feel ill-prepared to deal with students whose questions fall outside the parameters of their training programs.

For example, advisors may see students who do not ask a specific question and may not know the reason they are in an advising office. Open-ended questions, which require more than a *yes* or *no* response, elicit the best information and help move the conference forward. Good initial questions are

- o "How did you happen to come here?"
- o "What do you expect will happen here?"
- o "What do you hope to accomplish here?"

Sometimes students give tangential explanations, and well-conceived clarifying questions can be used to get at the heart of the issues. However, even after restating the advisee's response, the advisor must remain comfortable with silence as a student may need time to process his or her thoughts about the issues that inspired the meeting with an advisor. Brief moments of quiet time also allow an advisor to reflect on the student's affect. A student who appears sad, anxious, or angry may welcome the opportunity to talk about the feelings creating the reaction.

When advisors learn to be skillful interviewers with abilities in different kinds of inquiry and in unhurried listening, they offer students the opportunity to grow conceptually and eventually evaluate circumstances to make their own decisions. If the advisor does not question students in a way that stirs their cognitive capabilities, students miss an opportunity to become independent thinkers and masters of their own destinies. Such skill is one of the hallmarks of advising as teaching.

Dealing With Complex Questions

Complex student situations—such as those in which a student is trying to gain admission to a professional program, to get off academic probation, or to maintain a C average each semester—may require an advisor to use advanced communication skills. In chapter 3, Joanne Damminger gives a concise guide to ethical decision making for advisors. She explains the special challenges in giving students bad news or delivering complex information. All the ethical guidelines maintain the need for honesty. The advisor does the student no favor by masking the reality of a situation. Difficult information should be delivered fully and accurately, but with empathy. For example, after informing a student that admission to a special degree program was denied, the advisor should encourage the student to explore options such as seeking admission the following semester, working on the grade point average, or taking additional courses to make admission in the future more likely.

Sometimes the advisor cannot ethically suggest the student pursue the original plan and may need to help the student seek alternate degree paths. In the worst-case scenarios, the student must cope with dismissal from the institution due to poor performance or academic misconduct (faculty advisors, in particular, may deal with the latter and thus prepare for such incidences accordingly).

In the face of unpleasant realities, some students react with denial, depression, or anger. They may project blame onto a variety of people, including the advisor, who must remain calm and allow the student to appropriately air concerns. While acknowledging the advisee's feelings, the advisor can plant seeds of encouragement that may germinate when the student can better understand and deal with the unchosen changes to educational plans. Advisors in these difficult situations can inspire students in their personal growth, providing referrals as appropriate to more specific help, such as a counseling or job placement center. However, as with students whom the institution seeks to retain, acceptance and any necessary transformation remain the work of the individual.

Strong advising skills help educators inspire students to see their situations, options, and themselves more clearly. Through advisors' effective listening and interviewing, students may gain better understanding of their own feelings, assumptions, beliefs, and abilities. Students achieve this cognizance at different rates, depending on their maturity, level of self-awareness, and capacity to accept responsibility for making their own decisions. Advisors and students can then work together to help students make the best possible choices and progress toward their goals.

Referral Skills

Good communication skills are evident when academic advisors effectively handle questions or face student situations that are beyond the scope of their own expertise. Referrals are important for two reasons: Advisors cannot know everything, and the trust that allows students to open up in an advising conference can also lead to advisor dependence. Therefore, it is not only best for the student but also emotionally healthy for the advisor to acknowledge her or his limitations and refer students to other resources when appropriate; yet seldom do new advisor training programs address the art of referral. To learn more about making appropriate referrals, a new advisor can turn to organizations that track the growing mental health needs of incoming college students. (See also chapter 13.)

The American College Health Association offers a nationwide survey of students at 2- and 4-year postsecondary institutions. In 2012, it reported that approximately 30% of college students reported depression deep enough to interfere with daily functioning. Depression can be a short-term, situational, or long-standing condition. Students with depression or who experience other mental health issues should receive professional intervention.

Depression may be the most common mental health issue advisors encounter, but it is not the only one. According to Linda Castillo and Seth Schwartz (2013), the majority of serious mental illnesses manifest themselves in late adolescence or early adulthood. Along with the common college transition issues, students present with relationship problems, developmental issues, anxiety, depression, suicidal ideation, and personality disorders. For example, Sherry A. Benton, John Robertson, Wen-Chih Tseng, Fred B. Newton, and Stephen L. Benton (2003) found that students seen in college counseling centers today are diagnosed with more complex and severe problems than the students seeking treatment in the 1990s.

Academic advisors are often among the first to observe symptoms of mental health problems. Some signs of emotional or psychological distress include the following:

- extreme weight loss,
- evidence of self-abuse (e.g., cuts, burn marks, welts, or bruises),
- evidence of alcohol or drug abuse,
- lethargy,
- withdrawal,
- disorientation,
- problems with concentration,
- a sense of hopelessness,
- anxiety,
- pressured speech (speech that is rapid, almost nonstop, and difficult to interrupt),
- delusions or hallucinations, or
- preoccupation with thoughts of death.

Advisors are neither responsible for counseling nor qualified to counsel students; therefore, advisors who suspect that a student is experiencing a mental health issue should always follow the protocol established by their office or unit. This may include referring the student to a campus or community mental-health counselor. The first step toward making an effective referral is to listen to and establish rapport with the student. By responding as a compassionate listener, the advisor confirms the student's decision to approach an advisor for help, which may encourage the student to follow up with a referral. Some appropriate responses to a student who presents with a mental health issue include the following:

o "I'm sorry you're having a difficult time."

o "I'm glad you chose to talk about this."

o "It is clear that you are struggling with this."

Advisors may clarify the problem or the area of distress and share, in the context of the student's disclosure, the advisor's observations about the student's behavior with regard to these issues. For example, by observing, "I've noticed that you have lost a lot of weight" or "You seem distracted," advisors can give the student an opportunity to share important information. After telephoning ahead to alert the counseling staff, the advisor may walk a student to the counseling office. New advisors may want to ask a senior advisor to assist in interviewing a student and making a referral.

New advisors must respect that the decision to follow through on any referral remains with the student. Unless they present a danger to themselves or others, students cannot be forced to seek help, even if it would be in their best interest. When needed, first responders, such as security, medical, or police personnel, may be called to protect the student or others. Advisors should learn the university procedures for helping students in crisis. Many institutions have implemented crisis teams that approach certain difficult situations.

In most cases, the advisor relies on policy statements and his or her best judgment when deciding whether to refer a struggling student to mental health services. However, an advisor should always refer a student who expresses concern about alcohol or other drug use or reports being abused or committing abuse on another. New advisors should seek out information about their responsibilities to report a potential situation of abuse as well as policy and protocol at their institution, especially where these topics are not covered in a training program.

Regardless of the type of referral, advisors should prepare students for the information they will receive from the provider. By following up with the student, the advisor generates another opportunity to reinforce the student's corrective action or to make other suggestions for students dissatisfied with the referral.

Electronic Communication

Although some advisors and advisees primarily seek face-to-face communication, specific information, such as appointment dates and deadline reminders, can more clearly and conveniently be given by e-mail or other electronic media. Degree plans, school policies, schedules, and calendars are appropriately communicated through web sites. Advisees taking classes solely online may live miles off-campus and must choose to interact by phone, e-mail, or social media. Others prefer the accessibility, privacy, and ease of communicating through technology (chapter 16). The new advisor needs to learn about any policies the institution has implemented specifically regarding electronic communication, and regardless of the number or extent of such mandates, should always maintain a professional, working relationship with the student. Whether advising with students face-to-face or through electronic media, advisors need to ensure their effectiveness as educators and agents of student growth.

Realistic Expectations

New advisors must be realistic about their skills. Advisors at all levels are continuously learning, but the first year can be particularly daunting for new advisors; they need to consult with and refer to more experienced advisors. Because advising is important and has a very direct impact on students, new advisors are often anxious. They ask themselves:

- ○ "What do I say and how should I say it?"
- ○ "What if I don't know all (or any of) the answers?"
- ○ "What if I make mistakes?"
- ○ "What if my supervisor doesn't like how I work?"
- ○ "What if students are not satisfied with me?"
- ○ "Can I ruin a student's whole life with a mistake I make?"

While advising is important, there is no requirement that advisors must be perfect.

Consulting with a more experienced peer is an excellent way to gather information and learn different styles and approaches to advising. All advisors, new and seasoned, must have the courage to be themselves, accept their own uncertainties, make mistakes, and figure out corrective actions.

Typically, advisors are evaluated by supervisors and by students, but they should reflect on their own relational experiences during the first year and perform a self-evaluation. Applications and Insights—Checklist for Listening, Interviewing, and Referral Skills, immediately following this chapter, provides items to heighten advisors' awareness of behaviors and attitudes that affect their work with students. By evaluating their own behavior and effectiveness with students, advisors can continue learning, developing, and growing. With self-evaluation comes the opportunity to fill in deficits and shore up weak skills. Through the communication skills of listening, interviewing, and referring, advisors can impact the lives of students.

Aiming for Excellence

Self-reflection

o What is your best communication skill? How did you learn it or develop it?

o Which of your communication skills needs the most improvement? How did you learn or develop it? What are your plans to enhance it?

o What part of advising is the most difficult for you to relate to students?

   o Which aspect of listening is most difficult for you?

   o Which aspect of interviewing is most difficult for you?

   o Which aspect of referring is most difficult for you?

   o Which could be improved?

   o What strategies would you use for improvement?

o Ask a colleague or supervisor to answer the preceding questions about you. Make a plan for change based on the feedback you receive. Consider attending a NACADA workshop, researching the NACADA Clearinghouse for more information, shadowing another advising professional, and participating in other enrichment activities.

Recall

Think about a verbal interchange you experienced with a teacher (college or high school), advisor, administrator, or supervisor in which you felt genuinely understood. Think about the behaviors the listener displayed to make you feel understood. Do you currently incorporate these behaviors in your own communication with advisees? Add those and other actions of your mentor to create a communication skill bank.

Pick a Model

Interview an individual whose communications skills you admire to gain a better understanding of effective communication techniques. The following questions may yield important insights:

o How did you learn the communication skills you practice?

o What do you keep in mind when communicating with others?

o Do you still struggle with some aspects of communicating?

o What strategies do you use to continue improving your communication skills and outcomes?

Ask to shadow the person to study his or her interactions. Afterward, write a personal reflection listing behaviors you would like to incorporate into your own interactions.

Communication Circle

Write 7 to 10 words or phrases that describe your communication style. Then draw a circle and divide it, as in Figure 11.1, according to the amount of time you spend using that aspect of communication in a typical advising session (the segments will not be equal).

Did any pattern surprise you? What would you like to change about your circle?

Telling Lies (Group Exercise)

o Create a set of lies to describe yourself as an advisor.

o Share the lies about yourself as an advisor with a partner, creating as much of a false persona as possible.

o Explain your feelings about the persona you depicted in the created lie.

o With other participants discuss the following questions:

  o What similarities exist between the real and created persona?

  o What characteristics of the real or made-up advisor may describe expectations for advising, the institution, or society?

o To the extent you feel comfortable, share the lies that may reflect professional goals or setbacks.

Figure 11.1. Communication circle

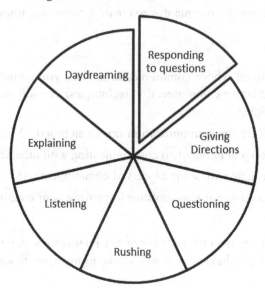

Advising Award

Imagine you were nominated and received a national advising award (NACADA's Outstanding New Advisor Award or Outstanding Advisor Award) based on your superb relational skills. Write mock letters of recommendation from the perspective of a student, a peer, and a supervisor who know your communication skills. Are there important skills, not mentioned in the letters, that you lack or upon which you could improve? How will you learn to improve or expand your competencies?

Some institutions offer professional development programs or have diversity offices that present workshops dealing with relational issues. Workshop topics may include handling difficult people and mediating disputes, among others. Try to attend one workshop a semester even if it does not directly address academic advising situations. For example, Dealing with Difficult People may be designed for supervisors or managers; however, the skills addressed may be directly applicable to advising. After attending a workshop, make a list of the skills and ideas to implement in short- and long-term practice. Record the ways in which your new relational tools are working. Revisit your list on a monthly basis and continue to implement skills and ideas until you have gone through your entire list.

References

American College Health Association. (2012). *American College Health Association–National College Health Assessment II: Reference group executive summary fall 2011*. Hanover, MD: Author.

Barnett, S., Roach, S., & Smith, M. (2006). Microskills: Advisor behaviors that improve communication with advisees. *NACADA Journal, 26*(1), 6–12.

Benton, S. A., Robertson, J. M., Tseng, W. C., Newton, F. B., & Benton, S. L. (2003). Changes in counseling center client problems across 13 years. *Professional Psychology: Research and Practice, 34*(1), 66–72.

Castillo, L. G., & Schwartz, S. J. (2013). Introduction to the special issue on college student mental health. *Journal of Clinical Psychology, 69*(4), 291–297. doi:10.1002/jclp.21972

Cunningham, L. A. (2003). *Multicultural awareness issues for academic advisors*. Retrieved from http://www.nacada.ksu.edu/Resources/Clearinghouse/View-Articles/Multicultural-a84.aspx

Lamont, B. J. (2005). *East meets west—Bridging the academic advising divide*. Retrieved from http://www.nacada.ksu.edu/Resources/Clearinghouse/View-Articles/East-meets-West—Bridging-the-advising-divide.aspx

Light, R. (2001). *Making the most of college: Students speak their minds*. Cambridge, MA: Harvard University Press.

Mestayer, K. (2013). Mixed signals. *Hearing Health Magazine, Spring*, 36–39.

Rugsaken, K. (2006). *Body speaks: Body language around the world*. Retrieved from http://www.nacada.ksu.edu/Resources/Clearinghouse/View-Articles/body-speaks.aspx

Swecker, H., Fifolt, M., & Searby, L. (2013). Academic advising and first-generation college students: A quantitative study on student retention. *NACADA Journal, 33*(1), 46–53.

Applications and Insights
Advisor Checklist for Listening, Interviewing, and Referral Skills
Peggy Jordan

Advisors can rate themselves on skills for each category. They may also ask a colleague to shadow them (with the student's permission) and offer feedback on these skills.

Advising Communication Skills	Never	Almost Never	Sometimes	Almost Always	Always
Greeting					
I welcome each student on arrival.					
I make sure my office is comfortable and private.					
I express caring, interest, and acceptance by words and gestures throughout the meeting.					
Listening					
I am aware of my physical and emotional states and how these states may look to others.					
I am aware of my personal biases and the impact of such biases on others.					
I maintain eye contact (when appropriate) and communicate involvement with facial expressions.					

Advising Communication Skills	Never	Almost Never	Sometimes	Almost Always	Always
I monitor my own mannerisms so I do not distract students from tasks at hand.					
I pay attention to what the student says and how it is said.					
I put myself in the student's shoes.					
I listen without criticism or judgment.					
I am open to new ideas.					
I give the student my complete attention.					
Interviewing					
I ask the student's reason for the meeting.					
I encourage the student to do most of the talking by asking open-ended questions.					
I use words familiar to the student.					
I avoid information overload.					
I focus on the student's questions rather than having a set agenda that I follow with all or most students.					

Advising Communication Skills	Never	Almost Never	Sometimes	Almost Always	Always
Rather than making decisions for students, I explore options with students and let them make informed decisions.					
I allow the student to fully tell his or her story before attempting to come up with a solution.					
I acknowledge my limits.					
I ask others for help if needed.					
I am familiar with campus resources.					
I make sure the person to whom I have referred the student is available, and I walk the student to the appropriate office if necessary.					
I follow up with student.					

Reprinted with permission from NACADA: The Global Community for Academic Advising: Jordan, P. (2007). Learning about the institution from students. In P. Folsom (Ed.), *The new advisor guidebook: Mastering the art of advising through the first year and beyond* (Monograph No. 16) (p. 91). Manhattan, KS: National Academic Advising Association.

Applications and Insights

Good Questions to Ask Advisees

- How are things going for you this semester?
- What has been the most challenging for you?
- What surprises have you had?
- What might have contributed to the surprise (challenge, outcome, etc.)?
- How might you do things differently next semester?
- What strategies have you tried?
- What have you learned about yourself?
- Have you developed any new interests or insights?
- How do your choices of extracurricular activities represent potential interest areas?
- What activities also define your skills?
- Based on your experience, what advice would you give to new freshmen?

Reprinted with permission from NACADA: The Global Community for Academic Advising: Folsom, P. (2007). *Good questions to ask students.* In P. Folsom (Ed.), *The new advisor guidebook: Mastering the art of advising through the first year and beyond* (Monograph No. 16) (p. 112). Manhattan, KS: National Academic Advising Association.

12

ACADEMIC ADVISING APPROACHES FROM THEORY TO PRACTICE

Jayne K. Drake

[Academic advising] needs flexible, eclectic practitioners able to adapt their advising strategies in accordance with the needs of their students. Being married to a single approach to academic advising, advisors potentially disregard the diverse ways in which students learn and presume a single, linear developmental path that is clearly more idealistic than realistic.

—Ezekiel Kimball and Susan M. Campbell (2013, p. 6)

Academic advising is recognized as an intentional, collaborative practice that supports and cultivates students' academic, personal, and career interests. It helps students make meaning of their world and helps shape their values, beliefs, and experiences. Students are influenced by their social, cultural, and academic backgrounds and so interpret their experiences in ways particular to them. Therefore, one standard approach to advising does not fit all students or situations. To promote student satisfaction and success, professional and faculty advisors, tutors, and advising administrators around the world must adapt their advising practice to the individual needs of their students. By seeing the student in front of them, advisors understand and respond to student diversity and difference, and they adapt advising approaches based on an understanding of student development theory.

In chapter 4, Kim Roufs notes that the field of academic advising has evolved based on approaches and strategies from a number of interdisciplinary theoretical perspectives, primarily those anchored in the social sciences, education, and the humanities. Theories specifically applicable to advising come from an understanding of the critical importance played by establishing relationships and encouraging the well-rounded development of all students. These developmental approaches inform and influence advising practice and student success.

This chapter illustrates selected developmental strategies as described in the second book of the academic advisor core resource library series: *Academic Advising Approaches: Strategies That Teach Students to Make the Most of College* (Drake,

Jordan, & Miller, 2013). The editors and contributors of *Approaches* explained that the strategies are grounded in the learning-centered nature of advising:

> Students are learners who establish a partnership of responsibility with their advisors and who ultimately take charge of their own academic, personal, and professional progress. Building relationships and encouraging this holistic development of all students are key elements in all of the described approaches. (Drake et al., 2013, p. ix)

In this chapter, the approaches are summarized in context for the new advisor.

Prescriptive Advising

The long-held view of prescriptive advising places the advisor squarely in the role of repository and disseminator of information on curricular matters, institutional rules, regulations, and processes. It situates the student as a passive receptor of information rather than an active participant in the advising process. Since the 1960s, when research on student development theories began to emerge, this-do-as-I-say approach has increasingly been dismissed as a single all-encompassing method of advising students.

However, current experienced practitioners recognize that prescriptive advising remains a solid strategy when a student needs specific direction (e.g., enrolling in a mandatory English class to remain in good academic standing). In addition, some student populations—such as international, first-generation, at-risk, exploratory, and military veteran students—often respond well to the instruction that prescriptive advising offers. In the same way that classroom teachers impart the subject matter, data, concepts, and ideas initially as part of the learning process, advisors, too, deliver the informational necessities as a way to engage students in knowledge building and active learning. Often these critical data get students in the door and provide the platform from which to discuss matters more directly related to their development as successful students.

> While no one will argue that a prescriptive model should be employed in isolation or adopted as the sole approach to student advising and learning, it is, nevertheless, an important and necessary element in the teaching and student-centered learning process that defines academic advising. (Drake et al., 2013, p. x)

Developmental academic advising serves as the foundation on which advising approaches are based. In chapter 4, Roufs traces the positions and influences of developmental theorists Burns Crookston (1972/1994/2009), Terry O'Banion (1972/1994/2009), William Perry (1968), and Vincent Tinto (1993), among others, whose separate observations form this groundwork; their research on intellectual, social, and ethical development extends well beyond prescriptive advising approaches to include the importance of advisor understanding of many different student populations and their participation in the academic experience and the broader campus environment.

Advising as Teaching

If advising is teaching, and the result is learning, then the advisor must be a good teacher.

—Marc Lowenstein (2005, p. 72)

Research in instructional pedagogy provides the foundation for the concept of *advising as teaching,* a term that provides a durable and versatile perspective for viewing the advisor as teacher and student as learner. One of the first advising professionals to delineate the skills, communication competencies, and attitudes that teachers and advisors share, Carol Ryan (1992) encouraged faculty members to view advising as a basic element of their teaching and advisors to view teaching as a basic element of their advising. The case of Terry illustrates Ryan's point.

A professor specializing in 17th- through 19th-century American history, Terry has been asked by the department chair to teach an undergraduate course in medieval British history. To prepare a class so distinct from the current research, publications, and teaching previously undertaken, Terry first reads the primary and secondary texts, then determines the appropriate information for the course level, organizes the material, creates a syllabus, and hopes for the best.

Terry's approach should sound familiar to experienced advising professionals. Indeed, in Table 12.1 faculty and professional advisors will find the relevant advising-as-teaching parallels. Professional advisors should use the *Teaching* comparisons to heighten their awareness of ways that treating advising as a complex subject can strengthen their work with students. Faculty advisors should see the parallels between preparation for their *Advising* interactions with students in their office and preparation undertaken for the classroom and value them as equal.

With that preparation done, Terry must now consider ways to communicate the material in the classroom. Table 12.2 shows how communications in the classroom and in advising appointments look like one another.

Table 12.1. Skills used in teaching and advising

Teaching	Advising
Researching the subject matter	Knowing institutional policies, procedures, programs of study, and referral resources
Planning and organizing course material	Preparing for advising meetings (e.g., organizing materials, reviewing notes, etc.)
Creating a course syllabus	Creating an advising syllabus

Table 12.2. Communication in teaching and advising

Teaching	Advising
Present subject matter clearly	Share information with advisees clearly
Establish dialogue with students in the classroom	Lead student to interact with the advisor
Demonstrate effective listening skills, not simply be a talking head	Listen to advisees, paying attention to both verbal and nonverbal cues
Encourage students' participation in their own learning	Guide students to be self-directed and autonomous
Give students feedback on their progress	Work together to regularly evaluate students' goals and progress toward goals
Help students learn to analyze and solve problems	Assist students in decision-making skills; do not make decisions for them

In the process of developing the medieval British history course, Terry also considers several strategic questions:

o What do I want students to be able to do or know as a result of learning in my course?

o How do I help students achieve this student learning outcome?

o Specifically, what materials, advice, or background information should I provide?

Terry understands that establishing the learning goals or outcomes for students constitutes an integral element of preparation for the new course. Using the same questions prior to an advising session, Terry demonstrates the type of goal setting and support that works as well in the advising office as it does in the classroom.

Terry's duties as an instructor do not stop at the classroom door. Educators must treat students with respect and concern, demonstrate accessibility and availability outside the classroom, offer regular encouragement, and serve as a role model. Good teaching, as with good advising, involves intentional processes that cannot be left to chance. Educators in the classroom and advising office attend to careful planning, accounting for different learning styles and providing clear expectations and goals for students. The parallels between the skills, the communication competencies, and the attitudes necessary for quality teaching and academic advising are striking.

In a sweeping definition of advising as teaching, Joe Cuseo (2012) explained that the good advisor is like the good teacher who

> helps students become more aware of their distinctive interests, talents, values, and priorities; who enables students to see the "connection" between their present academic experience and their future life plans; who helps students discover their potential, purpose, and passion; who broadens students' perspectives with respect to their life choices, and sharpens their cognitive skills for making these choices. (¶15)

In this regard, advising is also guiding. It is defined by a shared responsibility for student learning and growth, with advisors challenging and supporting students as they develop into self-authored adults.

Proactive Advising

[Proactive advising blends] the practices of advising and counseling into a form of student intervention that allows advisors to provide students information before they request or realize they need it.

—Jennifer Varney (2013, p. 137)

Intrusive advising—now known as *proactive advising*—rests on the premise that an institution should not wait for students to fall into academic difficulty before making contact with them. Advisors play a key role in motivating students to seek out campus services and resources before a student faces a crisis. The process involves intentional interactions and relationship building between advisors and (especially at-risk) students. As Jennifer Varney pointed out in *Academic Advising Approaches* (Drake et al., 2013), proactive advising does not mean coddling; it describes a directed, focused effort to assist students in seeking and obtaining the assistance needed to achieve academically, thereby creating a stronger incentive to meet educational goals. Through active interpersonal engagement, the advisor can assist students in cultivating informed, responsible decision making that will help to raise the probability of their academic success.

In her *Academic Advising Approaches* chapter, Varney (2013, p. 350) offered proactive advising solutions to a typical appointment scenario (Case Study 12.1).

Case Study 12.1: Using the Proactive Approach

A first-generation sophomore, Riley, comes to an advisor, Skylar, and says, "I am having trouble in two of my classes. I don't understand what the professor is talking about in one of them, but it's a required course for my major. The other is only a gen ed course, but I keep getting low grades on the writing assignments. I always got good grades in writing in high school. If I do poorly, this will lower my GPA, and I just got off academic probation last term. I want to stay in my major, but I don't know if I can pass this one course and that would really disappoint my family. What do you suggest I do?"

Skylar has determined to use a multifaceted approach to help Riley navigate this situation. Skylar must ascertain if the low grades are a result of poor writing skills, as Riley suggests, or possibly stem from misunderstanding of the material and assignments. Once the root of the problem is identified, Skylar can give

Riley the most appropriate help. Using a proactive approach, Skylar also antic-ipates the need for the tutoring center and other academic support services, and with Riley's permission, telephones people in these offices, introduces Riley, and provides appropriate background information. Riley wants to stay in the major, so Skylar suggests meetings with peer mentors or similarly experienced students in the major; these students may help Riley by sharing any similar experiences, especially with regard to overcoming academic struggles. Finally, Skylar sched-ules communications with Riley at regular intervals in a specific and detailed plan (days, time, and method of contact), as well as outlines expectations of information that Skylar should make available for discussion. By helping Riley understand the root causes of the situation and some strategies to overcome the challenges, Skylar has introduced Riley to proactive strategies to use when other adverse situations arise.

Adapted by permission. From J. Varney, Scenario I (p. 150), in J. K. Drake, P. Jordan, & M. A. Miller (Eds.), *Academic Advising Approaches: Strategies That Teach Students to Make the Most of College* © 2013 by Jossey-Bass.

Strengths-Based Advising

A strengths-based approach encourages [students] to capitalize on their unique gifts to become the best version of themselves and gain the most they can from their college experiences.

—Laurie A. Schreiner (2013, p. 117)

Utilizing the strengths-based approach, advisors focus on the students' talents that will lead to the greatest success rather than trying to remediate areas of weakness. By emphasizing their own talents, students likely engage more intensely in the learning process. In her chapter in *Academic Advising Approaches,* Laurie Schreiner (2013) explained that advisors can play an important role in helping students transform their talents into strengths. "By identifying and nurturing students' strengths as well as highlighting areas of existing competence, advisors in supportive relationships with students motivate them to become engaged in the learning process" (p. 107).

Schreiner (2013) outlined the strengths-based approach in a sequential five-step process:

1. Identify students' talents.

2. Affirm students' talents and increase awareness of strength.

3. Envision the future.

4. Plan specific steps for students to reach goals.

5. Apply students' strengths to challenges. (pp. 109–111)

Unlike proactive advising, in which one looks at the students' problems, strength-based advising is used to intentionally explore student potential. "Strengths-based advisors do not initiate the conversation by bringing up the areas where students are struggling. Instead, they focus on positive topics to help students identify specific academic tasks in which they have achieved some success" (Schreiner, 2013, p. 116).

Using a strengths-based approach, Skylar would take a different tack in the scenario presented by Riley. For instance, in response to Riley's issues with two classes, one in which the professor seems confusing and the general education course marred by poor grades on writing assignments, Skylar asks: "What classes seem easier to you?" See Case Study 12.2 for an example of a strengths-based advising session as reprinted, in part, from *Academic Advising Approaches* (Drake et al., 2013).

Case Study 12.2: Using the Strengths-Based Approach

[. . .] Riley replies, "I'm getting good grades in my public speaking and psychology classes."

Skylar asks for elaboration: "What specific academic tasks do you do well in those classes?"

"I think it's easy to participate in class discussions and group projects, and I am pretty good at giving talks. . . . I like psychology class, especially writing the reflective journal entries about class topics."

Skylar digs deeper, asking a series of questions that begin with "Which strengths are you using when participating. . . ." and following with specific instances Riley has mentioned: "in class discussions?" "engaged in group projects?" "giving oral presentations?" "writing journal entries?" Finally, Skylar asks Riley to summarize: "What energizes you when you're doing these things?"

Expressing an ability to relate well with other people and persuade them to engage in an activity, Riley responds readily, "Getting up in front of people, telling stories. I understand what makes people tick . . . and I'm fascinated by why people do what they do." Riley describes the enjoyment of thinking about and analyzing everyday phenomena.

Skylar asks, "How are the difficult classes different from psychology and public speaking?" Riley explains that in the difficult classes the professors lecture and do not utilize any group projects or class participation. Based on Riley's additional comments, Skylar surmises that the projects require analytical and research-based writing rather than reflective journaling. Wanting Riley to invent ways to use personal skills in challenging situations, Skylar follows up by asking, "Which of your strengths might be useful in those classes?"

"Well, maybe I could study with other students in the class and create my own group experience."

Acknowledging this as a good start, Skylar pushes for more ideas: "What can be done to understand the professors better? Have you been in this situation before—where it was really important to understand someone but you had difficulty doing so?"

Riley laughs before explaining, "Definitely! When I took my first job and my boss was from Korea, I had trouble understanding his English at first."

"So what did you do to understand him?"

"I watched his gestures and listened to his tone of voice."

"Why not use the same technique in the classroom?" Skylar advises Riley to watch the instructor's body language to determine the important points, which are likely to be on an exam.

"What else did you do to understand your boss?"

"I learned the job by listening carefully and by asking questions of the workers who had been there awhile. It took some time to figure him out!"

"Exactly!" Skylar exclaims. "The more you listen carefully and watch body language, the easier it will be to understand your professors. Also, I suggest writing down key words to look up after class, and be sure to read the assigned text and discuss it with others before class. You'll find the same strategies that worked for you in your first job are likely to work in these classes as well."

Skylar than changes tack: "What about those papers that require analytical, research-based writing? How do you prepare your speeches, particularly the persuasive ones?"

"I spend a lot of time searching the Internet for evidence to support my arguments."

"This strategy should help you with analytical papers too. Why don't you prepare your papers as if you're making an oral presentation? Record yourself making the presentation and then transcribe it. Take the transcript to the Writing Center for help in organizing it into a research paper."

Before leaving the office, Skylar agrees to organize a group of friends in the course with the unclear instructor and arrange for them to meet the day before each class to talk about their assigned reading and compare notes from previous lectures. Skylar offers to e-mail the following week to check on Riley's progress with these plans and to set up another appointment to talk about choices for a major.

Motivational Interviewing

[Motivational Interviewing] is built on the . . . principles of unconditional positive regard, respect for the advisee, and support of self-esteem as the advisee examines the need for change and the motivation to engage in the change process.

—Judy Hughey and Robert Pettay (2013, p. 68)

With the motivational interviewing (MI) approach, advisors encourage change in students' behaviors by helping them identify issues obstructing their academic or personal growth and then give them support as they overcome resistance or ambivalence to change. In *Academic Advising Approaches* (Drake et al., 2013), Judy Hughey and Robert Pettay (2013) offered a research-rich and detailed statement of the principles, strategies, and outcomes of the MI process that involves engaging, guiding, evoking, and planning (p. 68).

The advisor must first engage students to determine if MI will yield the desired result. Guiding involves "identifying a change goal, setting the agenda, and if necessary, giving information and advice—but only with student permission and in a way that honors the student's autonomy" (p. 68). The heart of the MI process involves evoking student "change talk" through, among other strategies, advisor use of positive open-ended questions and encouragement for considering options for change. Planning consists of setting goals, developing an action plan, and soliciting commitment from students.

The strategies used for Scenario I take on a different hue when MI techniques are applied. For example, in response to Riley's concerns about the general education class and the allegedly inarticulate professor, Skylar employs MI to probe and prompt as means to both solicit information and encourage Riley's detailed assessment of the obstructions to academic success. See Case Study 12.3 for an abridged version of the case study offered by Pettay and Hughey (2013, pp. 76–78).

Case Study 12.3: Using the Motivational Interviewing Approach

[. . . .] Using a nonjudgmental tone of voice and demonstrating genuine interest, Skylar engages Riley in a discussion of goals, issues, values, behaviors, as well as the need and motivation to change. First, Skylar could begin the session using one of the following suggestions, with the goal of setting the agenda and clarifying the presenting issues for Riley:

- Tell me about your ultimate career goal. What do you see as your strengths?
- Describe your passions [. . . .]
- What are your academic goals? Specifically, what is your goal for a grade in each of the courses?
- What is your ultimate career goal?

Skylar could specifically start with the rating: "On a scale of 0 to 10, with 0 being not at all important and 10 being very important, how important do you think it is for you to improve your academics and earn at least a B in each course?" If Riley responds by saying "9," Skylar would follow up with: "What keeps it from being a 10?" and "What would it take for you to get to 10?" A response of "10" means that Riley probably has a good understanding of the need for change and is open to continue the discussion toward implementing it [. . . .]

[During the discussion on behavior modification, Riley acknowledges that partying has taken time and attention away from studying.] Skylar makes evocative statements [. . .]

"I hear you saying that all of your friends party. Partying helps you to relax, not to think about the troubles you are having in your courses, the stress of school, and the disappointment you feel about your grades. You enjoy drinking with your friends because it is more fun than sitting in your room studying for courses you do not enjoy. It sounds like you might be afraid of being lonely if you stay home studying while others are out drinking [. . .] or partying is making you feel more anxious about your courses and the reality of being forced to leave school for academic reasons [. . . .]

"On one hand, I hear you saying you realize if your grades do not improve you will likely have to leave school. On the other hand, you enjoy partying with your friends during the week. And, you believe there is a direct correlation between partying during the week with your friends and your grades [. . . .]

- What is the worst thing that would happen if you stopped partying on weeknights?
- What is the best thing that could happen if you stopped partying on weeknights?
- Close your eyes and consider for a minute what your life would look like if you changed these behaviors exactly as you want?"

[. . .] Change is difficult. Sometimes afraid of failure, students choose to maintain ineffective, familiar behaviors rather than risk adopting new behaviors with unknown consequences. The advisor can help by expressing optimism in the student's ability to be successful in the change process.

Specifically, Skylar should validate Riley's courage to reject peer pressure and acknowledge the hard work necessary to make changes. Skylar might consider using some of the following inquiries with Riley:

- o What difficult goals have you achieved in the past? What strategies did you use to be successful with those goals? Could you tell me more about that?
- o What strategies worked for you last semester?
- o What would you like to see changed this semester?

Advisors need to affirm the good decisions the student has made in previous semesters. When they do not achieve the expected academic success, students sometime feel embarrassed and appreciate affirming statements from an advisor.

Students are more likely to engage and sustain change if they have strong self-efficacy. Advisors can reinforce self-efficacy by prompting students to articulate their own successes [. . . .]

Specifically, Skylar may employ thought-provoking inducements with the goal of bolstering Riley's self-efficacy for change:

- o There are pros and cons to making behavior changes in your life. To achieve your goals, it seems that you might need to change your behaviors that are not working for you. [. . .]
- o What are the not-so-good things about change?
- o What won't you like?
- o How will this affect you?
- o What are the good things about change?
- o How will they affect you?

[. . .] Skylar would then seek to engage Riley in change talk [. . .]

- o There is usually more than one possible course of action.
- o I can tell you about what's worked for other people.
- o You are the best judge of what works for you.
- o I have some ideas about how you could improve your academic habits, study skills, and grades. However, I am interested in your ideas. What can you suggest?
- o What do you think best suits your learning preferences, strengths, passions, and interests?
- o What do you think you can or could do?
- o Which solution makes the most sense to you?
- o What happened the last time you tried to make a change in your behavior?
- o How will it be different this time?

> o Let's be specific with strategies for when the barriers block the way of success again.

[...After Riley responds, Skylar might conclude the conversation with]: "I can see your desire and willingness to adjust your behavior. Of course, the decisions to make the changes are yours to make. I am here to help and support you."

Adapted by permission. From J. Hughey and R. Pettay, Scenario I (pp. 76–79), in J. K. Drake, P. Jordan, & M. A. Miller (Eds.), *Academic Advising Approaches: Strategies That Teach Students to Make the Most of College* © 2013 by Jossey-Bass.

Self-authorship

A man should learn to detect and watch that gleam of light which flashes across his mind from within, more than the lustre of the firmament of bards and sages . . . Trust thyself. Every heart vibrates to that iron string.

—Ralph W. Emerson, "Self-Reliance"

As Janet Schulenberg (2013) stressed in her *Academic Advising Approaches* chapter, self-authorship theory helps advisors to understand students' self-reflective and decision-making patterns as they develop increasingly complex thinking and interpretive skills. The approach helps guide students to find and trust their own voices and translate their beliefs into action. It teaches them to think for themselves—how to learn rather than what to learn (Baxter Magolda, 2009, p. 2). "As students and advisors relate through conversations founded on a trusting, collaborative relationship, academic advising provides a critical venue in which students can partake in the iterative, cyclical, back-and-forth process of habitual self-authorship" (Schulenberg, 2013, p. 135).

Self-authorship is generally characterized by a person's movement away from dependence on authority figures, such as parents, teachers, and advisors, to establishing a sense of self in which the individual develops his or her own ideas, goals, values, and actions. The self-authored student finds a balance between personal and external expectations and obligations. Advisors support this developmental process through reflective conversations that both challenge and support the advisee.

Self-authorship theory helps Skylar recognize that Riley is dealing with dissonance. Rather than immediately offering solutions to resolve issues with the professor or the writing assignments—such as seeing the instructor during office hours, visiting the tutoring center, or resorting to the course drop policy—Skylar pauses to reflect on the advising that fosters self-authorship development. Case Study 12.4 illustrates the ways Skylar encourages Riley to practice complex thinking that incorporates personal interpretation of situations, beliefs and values, and relationships.

Case Study 12.4: Using the Self-authorship Approach

[. . .] Skylar initiates [. . .] a reflective conversation, asking Riley to identify the causes of present troubles, develop goals, and create action plans that help to meet those goals [. . . .]

- o What created the situation that got you into academic probation?
- o What changes did you make that helped you recover?
- o What major courses have you really enjoyed? What was it about those courses that made them such good experiences for you?

Through this reflective conversation, Skylar can help Riley recognize the importance of interpreting situations and taking actions that affect outcomes.

[. . .] Initially, Riley must separate the multiple aspects of the situation by focusing on one challenge at a time. The following conversation prompts may help Riley move in a new direction: [. . .]

- o What are you supposed to be learning in that class, and how does it relate to the rest of the major?
- o What about the class is making sense to you?
- o What do you mean by "not understanding the professor"?

Skylar may suggest that Riley list particular reasons for struggling in class and then brainstorm ways to overcome those challenges. As a collaborative partner, Skylar should offer suggestions and alternative explanations as warranted:

- o Let's see if we can figure out why this class is included in the major. . . . Let's look at the syllabus together to see what you're supposed to take away from it.
- o What did the instructor say to you when you spoke to him about this?

[. . .] After co-examining the situation with Riley, Skylar could shift focus to the next issue:

- o Let's talk about your gen ed class. What's going well for you in that class?
- o You say the writing assignments are the cause of your current challenge. What made you good at writing in the past? How is what's being asked of you now different from what was expected in high school?

Again, Skylar can use reflective conversation to help Riley identify the particular reasons for this struggle and brainstorm ways to overcome the challenges.

Finally, throughout the discussion, Skylar can help Riley to reflect on decisions, construct internally meaningful interpretations, and find empowerment to set goals and take action[. . . .] Particularly, students need to practice paying attention to their internal voices and give their own values and beliefs a prominent position in driving decision making. By providing good company, Skylar helps Riley examine motivations and separate inner and outer voices, thus increasing Riley's ability to mediate external pressures while focusing on the tasks that can be affected by action.

Reprinted by permission. From J. K. Schulenberg, Scenario I (pp. 131–133), in J. K. Drake, P. Jordan, & M. A. Miller (Eds.), *Academic Advising Approaches: Strategies That Teach Students to Make the Most of College* © 2013 by Jossey-Bass.

Summary

Institutional leaders around the world need to consider the conditions in which students thrive—the meaningful connections needed with students for proper support and advocacy to help students achieve academic goals and career aspirations. They must look at the diverse needs of the students in front of them to adapt their approaches to their own practice. With a broader understanding of scholarly theories, approaches, and strategies, new advisors have access to a wider array of literature than was ever available to those who entered advising years ago:

> Advisors should examine their arsenals of theories and philosophies related to advising to construct individual yet socially mediated meaning and to develop new tools and strategies to improve teaching, learning, and assessment. As a result of these efforts, advisors grow adept at helping students reflect and self-assess to create unique definitions of their own academic and personal educations. (Musser & Yoder, 2013, p. 195)

Aiming for Excellence

o Identify and review your notes for a specific advising session in which a student raised issues that warranted a prescriptive advising approach. Did the student subsequently ask questions that moved the discussion beyond simple, factual answers, requiring a different advising approach? If so, after reading this chapter, consider the approach(es) that may work best to respond to other questions and address the newly presented issues.

o According to a 2014 survey of 111 academic advising directors, 70% of campuses offer training for advisors to help them proactively reach out to students before small issues become big problems (Fusch & Phare, 2014, ¶8). Using information you have learned about the proactive advising approach, identify the proactive advising techniques that exist on your campus. Select techniques to implement in your own advising. Evaluate their effectiveness after six months and again after one year.

o Design questions that you can use in advising sessions to help students pinpoint their strengths. Determine the campus resources that offer assessments or programming to aid them in identifying their strengths and then help them match their strengths to majors and careers.

o Think of times when a student (or acquaintance) has maintained a familiar behavior that has proven ineffective. Based upon discussion of motivational interviewing, what strategies might help the individual break the cycle and achieve more success?

o Other than in relation to academics, when might students need to develop ideas, goals, values, and actions as well as find a balance between those and external expectations and obligations? Create a case study (or review the file of a student) using a student-generated topic other than one that describes struggling with a class. Apply self-authorship strategies in a response to the case study or student situation.

o Which of the advising approaches discussed in this chapter most resonated with you? Search the NACADA Clearinghouse (http://www.nacada.ksu.edu /Resources/Clearinghouse.aspx) for an in-depth look into that advising approach. Purchase or borrow the NACADA/Jossey-Bass book *Academic Advising Approaches: Strategies That Teach Student to Make the Most of College* (http://www.nacada.ksu.edu/Resources/Product-Details/ID/B15.aspx). Dig deeper into the advising approaches mentioned in this chapter and the others in *Approaches* to refine your practice. Use the Houston case study review questions and the case studies in Appendix B as well as case studies included in other chapters to build your skill in applying the approach you have researched.

References

Baxter Magolda, M. B. (2009). Promoting self-authorship to promote liberal education. *Journal of College & Character, 10*(3), 1–6.

Crookston, B. (2009). 1994 (1972): A developmental view of academic advising as teaching. *NACADA Journal, 29*(1), 78–82. (Reprinted from *Journal of College Student Personnel, 13*, 1972, pp. 12–17; *NACADA Journal, 14*[2], 1994, pp. 5–9)

Cuseo, J. (2012). *Academic advisement and student retention: Empirical connections & system interventions.* Retrieved from http://cpe.ky.gov/NR/rdonlyres/6781576F-67A6

-4DF0-B2D3-2E71AE0D5D97/0/CuseoAcademicAdvisementandStudentRetention
EmpiraclConnectionsandSystemicInterventions.pdf

Drake, J. K., Jordan, P., & Miller, M. A. (Eds.). (2013). *Academic advising approaches: Strategies that teach students to make the most of college.* San Francisco, CA: Jossey-Bass.

Emerson, R. W. (n.d.). [Quote]. Retrieved from http://www.goodreads.com/author/quotes/12080.Ralph_Waldo_Emerson

Fusch, D., & Phare, C. (2014). *What advisors are being trained in.* Retrieved from http://www.academicimpressions.com/news/survey-report-training-academic-advisors

Hughey, K., & Pettay, R. (2013). Motivational interviewing: Helping students initiate change in student behaviors. In J. K. Drake, P. Jordan, & M. A. Miller (Eds.), *Academic advising approaches: Strategies that teach students to make the most of college* (pp. 67–82). San Francisco, CA: Jossey-Bass.

Kimball, E., & Campbell, S. M. (2013). Advising strategies to support student learning success. In J. K. Drake, P. Jordan, & M. A. Miller (Eds.), *Academic advising approaches: Strategies that teach students to make the most of college* (pp. 3–15). San Francisco, CA: Jossey-Bass.

Lowenstein, M. (2005). If advising is teaching, what do advisors teach? *NACADA Journal, 25*(2), 65–73.

Musser, T., & Yoder, F. (2013). The application of constructivism and systems theory to academic advising. In J. K. Drake, P. Jordan, & M. A. Miller (Eds.), *Academic advising approaches: Strategies that teach students to make the most of college* (pp. 179–196). San Francisco, CA: Jossey-Bass.

O'Banion, T. (2009). 1994 (1972): An academic advising model. *NACADA Journal, 29*(1), 83–89. (Reprinted from *Junior College Journal, 42,* 1972, pp. 62, 63, 66–69; *NACADA Journal, 14*[2], 1994, pp. 10–16)

Perry, W. G., Jr. (1968). *Forms of intellectual and ethical development in the college years: A scheme.* New York, NY: Holt, Rinehart, and Winston.

Ryan, C. C. (1992). Advising as teaching. *NACADA Journal, 12*(1), 4–8.

Schreiner, L. A. (2013). Strengths-based advising. In J. K. Drake, P. Jordan, & M. A. Miller (Eds.), *Academic advising approaches: Strategies that teach students to make the most of college* (pp. 105–120). San Francisco, CA: Jossey-Bass.

Schulenberg, J. K. (2013). Academic advising informed by self-authorship theory. In J. K. Drake, P. Jordan, & M. A. Miller (Eds.), *Academic advising approaches: Strategies that teach students to make the most of college* (pp. 121–136). San Francisco, CA: Jossey-Bass.

Tinto, V. (1993). Leaving college: Rethinking the causes and cures of student attrition (2nd ed.). Chicago, IL: University of Chicago Press.

Varney, J. (2013). Proactive advising. In J. K. Drake, P. Jordan, & M. A. Miller (Eds.), *Academic advising approaches: Strategies that teach students to make the most of college* (pp. 137–154). San Francisco, CA: Jossey-Bass.

Applications and Insights

Advising Techniques

A *road map* is similar to a plan to graduation. It can include courses and other experiences, but it is used to emphasize that time is limited and goes fast. Through a road map, advisors can show that planning an approach to the academic experience can give the advisee the best possible pathway through the educational experience.

Role reversal exercises make for great conversation about the subjective experience of courses and how to decide which classes to take. When a student asks, "What courses should I take?" the advisor can say, "Let's reverse roles. If I were to ask you the same question, what would you say?"

By using a strategy called *ask why six times,* advisors can get at the heart of the issue. The first couple of questions are easy to answer, but by the fifth or sixth inquiry the student is challenged to dig deeper into [her or his] histories and strengths. For example, the advisor can ask a student "Why do you want to be an engineer?" If the student replies, "Because I like math?" the advisor should challenge with another "Why?" and may offer some direction: "What about math do you like? How does that connect to engineering?" The student may be led to answer that both math and engineering involve problem solving. Then the advisor asks "Why?" again in the form of "Why do you say that?" or "How do you know that both involve problem solving?"

This inquiry should get the student thinking about his or her own past experiences, particularly those that the advisee may not have considered important, and it allows the advisor to introduce another line of questioning: "Why did you like (or not like) that role?"

Reprinted with permission from NACADA: The Global Community for Academic Advising: Folsom, P. (2007). *Advising techniques.* In P. Folsom (Ed.), *The new advisor guidebook: Mastering the art of advising through the first year and beyond* (Monograph No. 16) (p. 112). Manhattan, KS: National Academic Advising Association.

Applications and Insights
Characteristics of Effective Advisors

- Enjoy students.
- Engage in attentive listening.
- Relate to advisees of many cultures, ethnicities, and educational backgrounds.
- Commit to accuracy and clarity.
- Convey openness and friendliness.
- Know their limits and make referrals accordingly.
- Demonstrate organization.
- Express caring and empathy.
- Offer reassurance, show trustworthiness, and inspire confidence.
- Possess good memory.
- Use good sense of humor.
- Deliver hard news in a caring way.
- Ask for help.
- Bring organization and order to a disorganized process.
- Serve as effective communicators.
- Demonstrate creativity and innovation.
- Remain calm in a crisis.
- Show patience; can wait for students to come to their own conclusions.
- Attend to detail.
- Select and use appropriate technology.
- Ask probing questions.
- Know the best time to present information to students.
- Act with fidelity as good colleagues and collaborators.
- Remain flexible and adaptive.
- Multitask.
- Learn quickly.
- Express nonjudgment.

Adapted with permission from NACADA: The Global Community for Academic Advising: Jordan, P. (2007). *Characteristics of effective advisors.* In P. Folsom (Ed.), *The new advisor guidebook: Mastering the art of advising through the first year and beyond* (Monograph No. 16) (p. 37). Manhattan, KS: National Academic Advising Association.

PART FIVE

DELIVERING ADVISING

Advising delivery situations vary widely across academe. Some institutions, or units within them, require one-to-one advising with regular appointments between students and advisors, while others lack resources for this type of advising. Building good advising systems in unique, and sometimes challenging, academic environments requires creativity and commitment. Contributors to this section examine some extant advising structures and offer insight into ways excellent advising can be practiced in all types of postsecondary settings.

13

ONE-TO-ONE ADVISING

Charlie L. Nutt

In one-to-one advising sessions advisors fully integrate and apply the conceptual, informational, and relational components of advising. This chapter, considered a classic in the field, was originally published in the first edition of Academic Advising: A Comprehensive Handbook *(Gordon & Habley, 2000) and is reprinted with permission. The editors' additions reflect changes that place the chapter within the context of this book and reflect new research or changes in practice since its initial publication.*

Academic advising at its very best is a supportive and interactive relationship between students and advisors. Susan Frost, in *Academic Advising for Student Success: A System of Shared Responsibility* (1991), states that this relationship is important for three reasons: "(1) advising, unlike most out-of-class activities, is a service provided to most students; (2) advising provides a natural setting for out-of-class contacts with faculty to occur; and (3) advising involves intellectual matters, the most important area of concern for students" (p. 10). Often the one-to-one relationship between the student and advisor is the only opportunity a student has to build a personal link with the institution; it thereby has a profound effect on the student's academic career and on the student's satisfaction with the institution. Chickering and Gamson (1987) state that frequent faculty–student contact is the most important factor in student motivation and involvement and can provide students with the support needed to get through the hard times and keep working toward academic success. Therefore, it is clear that the value of the one-to-one academic advising relationship to students' success cannot be underestimated.

Necessary Interpersonal Skills

The one-to-one relationship is often not developed, due to advisors' lack of clarity about the skills and competencies that are vital to the effectiveness of such academic advising. Advisors must of course have clear knowledge of the academic programs and

---

Adapted by permission. From C. Nutt, Chapter 15: One-to-one advising (pp. 220–227), in V. N. Gordon & W. R. Habley (Eds.), *Academic advising: A comprehensive handbook* © 2000 by Jossey-Bass.

curriculum requirements at their institutions. One of students' most stated expectations of an advisor is the ability to give accurate and correct academic guidance. However, effective communication is also key to the one-to-one academic advising relationship. Unfortunately, advisors find it easy to revert to being the "teller" or the "expert" in the relationship, focusing primarily on the information they have to deliver to the student. Instead, advisors must be aware that one-to-one academic advising must be built on shared communication, which requires a different set of skills than those required in a one-way communication, including communication skills, questioning skills, and referral skills [as well as competencies in applying advising approaches].

Communication Skills

Communication skills are perhaps the most important set of skills needed by advisors in building relationships with their advisees. Yet these are often the skills most overlooked in advisor training or development programs. Advisors must understand that listening effectively to both what their advisees are saying and what they are not saying is an essential communication skill in creating an environment of trust in the advising relationship. The communication skills that advisors should demonstrate are as follows:

1. *Establishing and maintaining eye contact with students* [as culturally appropriate]. Students must feel they have the undivided attention of their advisors if they are to communicate openly and honestly on issues of concern. In addition, maintaining eye contact with students can enable advisors to pick up on nonverbal clues that students may be giving that contradict their words. [In situations in which the advisor or the student feels that eye contact is inappropriate, advisors must rely on other relational skills to indicate open and honest communication practices and to appreciate nonverbal cues from students.]

2. *Avoiding the inclination to interrupt students with solutions before students have fully explained their ideas or problems.* Advisors often fall quickly into the "savior mode" instead of giving students the chance to express themselves fully, resulting in communication becoming only one-way.

3. *Being aware of body language.* Students can tell immediately whether an advisor is listening or not by the body-language message the advisor sends. Shuffling papers, allowing for distractions such as telephone calls, and facing away from the student are all nonverbal clues that the advisor is more interested in the daily routine than in the advising session. Advisors should also be aware of the body language of their students. Students can portray many feelings through their body language that they would never express openly. Folded arms, nervous gestures, slouched posture, or physically turning away from the advisor are all examples of body language that may indicate feelings of anger, frustration, or depression.

4. *Focusing on the content of students' words.* Advisors must listen to the words and phrases that students use in conversation. They must be sure they understand clearly the facts of the issues or problems being discussed. It is important that advisors ask leading or probing questions if necessary to be sure they have understood distinctly the content of the conversation.

5. *Focusing on the tone of students' words.* Listening is paying attention to both what is being said and what is not being said. Often the tone of students' words or their facial expressions are more important than what they are saying. Advisors should listen carefully to students' voice levels or the distinctions they make in order to pick up on issues of major concern. In addition, tone of voice can often indicate to advisors a student's state of mind or well-being.

6. *Acknowledging what students are saying through verbal and nonverbal feedback.* This may include simply nodding one's head or responding to students with "yes" or "I see."

7. *Reflecting on or paraphrasing what students have said.* After students have finished talking, advisors must demonstrate that they have been listening by repeating back in their own words what students have said. This provides students with the opportunity to clarify what they have said and to correct any misunderstandings.

Questioning Skills

In addition to having good listening skills, advisors must become adept at using questioning skills. Learning how to ask questions effectively in order to assist students is vitally important in the one-to-one advising relationship. The key to effective questioning is to focus the questions on the concerns of the student and not on the concerns of the advisor. Advisors must develop skills in using both open-ended and closed-ended questions. Open-ended questions are invitations to students to talk more openly about concerns or issues without feeling as if the advisor is setting the agenda of the session. One strategy for using effective open-ended questions is to phrase them in terms of the student's needs, wishes, or desires; that is, instead of asking, "How can I help you?" or "What can I do for you today?" ask the student, "What do you want to talk about today?" or "What issues do you have about next semester?" Such questions will begin to help students understand that their role in the advising process is as important as their advisor's role. A simple method for developing the skill of using open-ended questions is to ask, "Can this question be answered in three words or less?" Closed-ended questions are best used to gather factual information only. Although it is often important to ask such questions in order to be sure that the facts are gathered, they can also serve to foreclose on dialogue instead of extending the conversation. Advisors must be aware of the types of questions they are asking because questions are clues to students that advisors are truly interested in the students' feelings and concerns. Open-ended questions indicate interest in the student; closed-ended questions indicate interest in only the facts.

Advisors apply communication and questioning skills as they utilize advising approaches. Students rely on advisors to help them think through difficult situations, solve problems, or decide on courses of action. They seek perspective that will help them not only understand the issues they face but also analyze and evaluate possible choices. However, advising remains a collaborative practice (chapter 12). Therefore, advisors must model and teach critical thinking, problem solving, and decision-making skills in advising sessions.

Advising approaches provide frameworks for teaching and modeling critical thinking, problem solving, and decision making. Advisors who practice advising as teaching overtly and explicitly instruct students in these processes. They may use a number of advising approaches in a single session or for a particular student. For example, advisors may invoke prescriptive advising to outline the process for registering for the subsequent semester or declaring a major, then take a proactive approach to confront a potential problem and generate alternatives, and then switch to motivational interviewing to support the student in identifying and committing to behavioral modifications necessary to resolve the issue. The most appropriate approach depends on the student. As Jayne Drake noted in chapter 12, "By seeing the students in front of them, advisors understand and respond to student diversity and difference, and they adapt advising approaches based on an understanding of student development theory." Drake also observed that advising approaches, like advising, are based on "a shared responsibility for student learning and growth, with advisors challenging and supporting students." "Building relationships and encouraging this holistic development of all students are key elements in all of the . . . approaches" (Drake, Jordan, & Miller, 2013, p. ix).

Referral Skills

Last, to develop a one-to-one advising relationship with students, advisors must use referral skills. Effective referral skills depend on an advisor's listening and questioning skills because the first step in referring a student is to determine the student's problems and issues. Advisors often make the mistake of referring students on the basis of the advisor's own feelings or views rather than clearly listening to the students or asking effective questions to determine what the students' problems or issues may be. When this is the case, students may see such referrals as only a method of getting them out of the advisor's office instead of as genuine desire to assist students in the best way possible.

The first and possibly most important step in effective referrals is for the advisor to explain clearly and in an open manner why the student should seek assistance from another source. The advisor and student must have jointly determined the problem for which assistance is needed and then formulated a plan of action that includes the referral. Demonstrating effective referral skills requires advisors to have a clear understanding of the services available on campus and in the community. In addition, advisors will be able to explain the type of assistance the student needs as well as the qualifications of the persons or agencies to whom the student is being referred. Advisors should take the time to visit and become acquainted with all areas of the campus that can support their students in order to be effective in the referral process.

An effective referral always includes the name, location, and if possible, telephone number and e-mail address of a contact person at the office or agency to which the student is being referred. To increase the likelihood of a successful referral, the advisor should assist the student by scheduling the appointment or by walking the student to the appropriate office. Finally, effective referrals include following up with students on the referrals and assistance they have received. If the situation warrants, the advisor should contact the student shortly after the appointment to discuss the referral and to determine if the student needs additional assistance. In other instances, the outcome of the referral can be discussed in the next advising session.

Advisors who work with data-based tools that flag referrals for automatic follow-up must familiarize themselves with the student management system at their institution. They should contact students to determine the extent to which they learned and benefited from referrals. Not only does this inquiry help the advisor learn the most helpful resources for a particular circumstance, but the extra communication gives students the opportunity to share insights that positively affected their situation. Furthermore, failure to follow up may send a message that that the referral was not important or that the advisor is uninterested in the student's progress.

Developing the interpersonal skills of effective listening, questioning [using multiple advising approaches], and referral is vital for advisors in order for one-to-one academic advising to be successful. Although it is important for advisors to know the academic programs or requirements or the curriculum of the institution, such knowledge alone will not provide students with the level of academic advising they need for success in their academic careers.

The One-to-One Academic Advising Session

Having knowledge of the institution's programs and requirements and developing effective interpersonal skills for communicating and assisting students are only part of the successful one-to-one academic advising relationship. The advising session or interview with the student is vital to the advising process. Often the best intentions and well-developed skills of advisors are overshadowed by their lack of attention to the advising session itself. The advisor must clearly understand the essential components of the advising session: planning and preparing for the session and the content and process of the session. [They must also demonstrate effective means of ending the appointment with appropriate summaries, collaborative goal setting, and documentation.]

Planning and Preparing for the Advising Session

The area in which most advisors fall short is planning and preparing for the advising session. The first step in planning is to understand that for many students scheduling an appointment with an advisor is something they may not do without the advisor taking some proactive measures. Successful advisors include the initiation of contact as a vital component of their work. Communicating with advisees on a regular and consistent basis is the first step they take when planning for advising sessions. This communication may take the form of personal letters, telephone calls, postcards, or e-mail messages [as well as communication management system tools]. Communication begins early in the advisor–advisee relationship and continues until students have reached their educational goals. The communication might be to invite the students in for a session, to congratulate them on some success, academically or personally, to check on their academic progress, or simply to keep in touch. Whatever the method of communication or the purpose behind it, the goal is to establish ongoing contact as the basis for a quality relationship.

Second, planning for an advising session with an advisee involves the advisor learning as much as possible about the student. The advisor reviews academic history, test scores, educational goals, and other information sources that might be available. An important source of information is advising notes from previous sessions. These notes are invaluable in helping to set the agenda or content of an advising session. They can also be used to remind the advisor of things that still need to be accomplished by either the advisor or the advisee. Advising notes are also extremely important if an institution has an advising center model in which students see different advisors for each session. An advisor must have the advising notes from the previous advisor in order to conduct an effective advising session with the student. In addition, many advisors send questionnaires to advisees for them to complete and return prior to their first advising session in order to get a clear picture of the students, their academic and personal strengths and weaknesses, and their goals. This step is not only done before the initial advising session, however. A successful advisor reviews the information on his advisees prior to all scheduled advising sessions.

Joe Cuseo (n.d.) encouraged advisors to have students complete a pre-conference intake form that includes students' answers to questions in six general areas: personal background, future plans, personal abilities or aptitudes, personal interests, personal values, and advising expectations. A sample of such a new student planning form, used at Cloud County Community College (n.d.), is included in the Clearinghouse of Academic Advising Resources from NACADA: The Global Community for Academic Advising. In addition to giving advisors valuable information about their students, questionnaires or intake forms can increase the productivity of an advising session by enabling advisors to immediately address a student's concern or potential challenge.

Third, although spur-of-the moment advising sessions or advising-in-the-hall sessions are a part of the college environment, advisors should be proactive in stressing to students the importance of scheduling appointments in advance in order to provide the advisor with ample time to plan effectively for each session. This scheduling itself takes careful preparation. The advisor must have a clearly designated schedule for advising sessions that should be communicated to students each academic term. Again, this can be done through written communication, telephone calls, or e-mail messages as well as by posting a schedule on the advisor's door or in his or her office area. Appointment scheduling encourages students to plan and prepare for the advising session. If students must make appointments, they are less likely to walk in at the last minute expecting the advisor to make their decisions or solve their problems. Instead, they will arrive ready to play an active role in the advising session. However, this approach also requires advisors to have the courage and fortitude to reschedule appointments for drop-in students instead of dropping everything at the last minute to see a student. An advising session in which neither the advisor nor the student has had an opportunity to plan and prepare is limited in its productivity.

Fourth, the advisor must plan for uninterrupted time with the students during the advising session. Telephone calls should be put on hold or the phone should be taken off the hook. [Technology has contributed to the potential distractions: Advisors should disable pop-up messages, notification sounds, and other elements of e-mail and online communication systems.] Adequate time should be allowed for each appointment so that a student does not feel rushed. Also, the schedule should allow time for the advisor to make notes and take care of other actions that result from the advising appointment. In the busy environment of higher education institutions today, this is likely the most difficult part of planning for advising sessions. However, the effectiveness of any advising session is seriously jeopardized by not planning carefully to avoid interruptions, which suggest to the student that the session is not an important activity.

Finally, prior to each advising appointment, advisors must clear their desks and their minds. A work space piled high with stacks of paper may convey that the advisee has interrupted the advisor or that the advisor is too busy to focus on them. As Peggy Jordan (2007; chapter 11) has noted, advisors distracted by other events, such as the traffic jam during their morning commute or with the pressing and difficult needs of the previous student, may seem distant or upset such that the student feels like an intruder (or worse).

To provide every student with a quality advising session, it is clearly the responsibility of the advisor to plan and prepare adequately. Although this may be the most time-consuming step, it sets the tone for all sessions and can determine whether a session is successful or not.

Content and Process of the Session

Once the session has been scheduled, the advisor then focuses on the session itself—on its content and process. It is desired that all advising sessions have a clear purpose when they are scheduled so that the advisor and the student both understand what will be discussed and can move into the content of the session smoothly. It is also clear, however, that in colleges today this is not always possible. Therefore, the advisor must focus on the session content on the basis of prior planning and preparation, while at the same time be sensitive to the student's concerns.

The first component of any advising session is developing or quickly reestablishing rapport with the student. While developing rapport is critical to the success of the initial advising session, it must also be done for each subsequent session. Although advisors may wish to jump quickly into the content of sessions, they must first take time to greet students by name and make them feel comfortable. This can be done by asking general questions about their well-being, family, or classes or by reviewing the content of the previous advising session. This component underscores the importance of planning and preparing for the session because an advisor must be familiar with students' backgrounds and goals in order to initiate rapport. Students must be made to feel comfortable at the beginning of each advising session if they are to work collaboratively with the advisor on the topics or issues addressed during the session. Many advisors often overlook this step, but it can truly make the difference between a successful session and an unsuccessful session.

It is important that advising sessions have a clear agenda or flow in order to be effective in assisting students. First, the advisor and student should discuss the previous advising session. This is the time to discuss the results of any referrals, the outcome of any actions taken, and the student's academic progress since the last session. The advisor and advisee then move to the purpose of the current advising session. It is essential that both parties be clear about the primary purpose of the session as well as look at any secondary or underlying issues. Next is discussion of the issues or concerns that the student has brought to the advising session. This is when the advisor's interpersonal skills will be most important. For example, the student may state that the purpose of the session is to discuss withdrawing from a class, but on the basis of the student's body language, tone, and facial expressions the advisor may determine that the issue is much more than withdrawing; instead, it may actually be financial problems, family problems, or other issues. It is also important during this stage in the advising session to discuss the issues and concerns of the advisor, which may range from academic policies and regulations to academic difficulties of which the advisor has been made aware by the advisee's instructors.

Closing the Session

Finally, the advisor should carefully conclude the advising session by taking time to summarize the discussion that has taken place and to outline any plans of action that have been developed.

The advisor should close the session by asking the student if he or she has any final questions. In addition, as appropriate, the advisor may encourage the student to summarize decisions discussed and outline courses of action. To prompt, as necessary, for student articulation of their learning, advisors ask "What have we done today?" and "What are your next steps?" To reinforce the decision made, including those for action, students can send an e-mail of an appointment summary and action plans to themselves and the advisor. Some advisors use a student management system that automatically sends students a short evaluation of the appointment. Advisors should prepare students to receive this evaluation and encourage productive and constructive feedback that will improve all future advising sessions.

During the session, the advisor should make all appropriate referrals and assist the student in setting a time line for accomplishing any goals or plans. By failing to do this, an otherwise successful advising session may accomplish very little for the student or the advisor.

Finally, advisors must make notes about each advising session, preferably as soon as possible following the session. Advising notes document discussions, decisions, actions, and the student's reactions to key points made in the session. Good advising notes help the advisor follow up with students on unfinished business or referrals as well as prepare for subsequent advising sessions.

Advisor notes are considered educational records and thus subject to the Family Educational Rights and Privacy Act and other laws and policies that regulate their disclosure. Guidelines put forth by Missouri State University (2014) offer excellent suggestions for documenting advising sessions. New advisors must talk to their supervisors to learn the protocol for safely keeping and appropriately sharing, if necessary, advising notes.

Conclusion

The successful one-to-one advising relationship can be a major factor in a student's decision to remain in college and be academically successful. One-to-one advising relationships must first be built of the advisor's development of the interpersonal skills of communication, questioning, and referral. During the advising session, advisors must use these interpersonal skills to assist their students. It is the advisor's responsibility to keep the conversation moving and on target; this may include carefully asking open-ended questions and focusing on analyzing students' verbal as well as nonverbal clues. Advisors must avoid the tendency to out-talk students by allowing them time to discuss issues before responding. The advisor must also focus on accepting students' attitudes and feelings about an issue; students recognize when advisors do not value their problems and concerns, and next time they will not be as willing to be honest and straightforward in the advising session.

Advisors must recognize the importance of planning and preparing for an advising session and then follow a clear plan of flow during the session. This flow must include a clear look at previous sessions, discussion of the present issues and concerns, and a distinct summary and follow-up plan for future actions and sessions. It is clear that one-to-one advising provides students and advisors with the opportunity to build lasting and valued relationships that will positively affect students' academic performance and satisfaction with the institution.

Aiming for Excellence

o Ask your supervisor or a colleague to observe your advising session with a student (with the student's permission) and to record the conference as closely as possible. What patterns emerge? Are you doing all the talking? Did you really listen to the student? Which advising approaches did you use? Should you have asked more clarifying or probing questions? Ask your supervisor or colleague for suggestions to improve your relational skills and expand your use of advising approaches.

o At the end of your first semester of advising, review your advising notes for students who you had referred to other offices or resources on campus. Did they take your suggestion and seek additional resources? What additional information or approach might better encourage students to take action on your suggestions?

References

Chickering, A. W., & Gamson, Z. F. (1987). Seven principles for good practice in undergraduate education. *AAHE Bulletin*, *39*(7), 3–7.

Cloud County Community College. (n.d.). New student planning form.] Retrieved from http://www.nacada.ksu.edu/portals/0/Clearinghouse/Links/documents/New-Student -Planning-Conference.pdf

Cuseo, J. (n.d.). *How I use the advisee information card*. Retrieved from http://www.nacada.ksu.edu/Resources/Clearinghouse/View-Articles/Creating-a-new -student-intake-form.aspx

Drake, J. K., Jordan, P., & Miller, M. A. (Eds.). (2013). Preface. *Academic advising approaches: Strategies that teach students to make the most of college*. San Francisco, CA: Jossey-Bass.

Frost, S. H. [sic] Academic advising for student success: A system of shared responsibility. ASHE-ERIC Higher Education Report, no. 3. Washington, D.C.: George Washington University, School of Education and Human Development.

Gordon, V. N., & Habley, W. R. (Eds.). (2000). *Academic advising: A comprehensive handbook* (1st ed.). San Francisco, CA: Jossey-Bass.

Jordan, P. (2007). *Learning about the institution from students*. In P. Folsom (Ed.), *The new advisor guidebook: Mastering the art of advising through the first year and beyond* (Monograph No. 16) (p. 91). Manhattan, KS: National Academic Advising Association.

Missouri State University (2014). Advising note guidelines. Retrieved from http://www.missouristate.edu/advising/43164.htm

Applications and Insights
Conducting Individual Conferences
Pat Folsom

Prior to the Conference
o Clear your desk.

o Review the student's file.

o Organize resources and advising materials.

o Refocus from the task at hand or previous student.

Opening
o Meet the student in waiting area or outside your office.

o Disregard first impressions.

o Forget previous difficult advising situations.

o Initiate conversation with a positive, personal note.

o Smile: You may be the only adult the student runs into that day who is genuinely glad to see her or him.

o Use the student's name.

o Shake hands (if culturally appropriate).

o Early in the session follow up on a personal story or situation discussed in the previous appointment.

o Demonstrate attentiveness to the student's physical presence: "You look (tired, worried, happy, like the cat who swallowed the canary) today. What's up?"

Time Frames
o Establish the time frame for the appointment: "We have 20 minutes today. We must get you registered, but is there anything besides registration that's on your mind?" "I'd really like to be able to help you with that—let's make another appointment so we can really talk about it."

o Tell students when you are least busy and encourage them to stop by or make appointments during these times so you that you can devote more attention to their concerns.

o Follow up with e-mail assignments over the summer.

Conference
o Make a positive comment about the student or the student's progress in each conference.

- Explain the reason you are taking action or asking a question.
- Make sure the runaround or office-shuttle stops with you.
- Ask questions that elicit solid information.
  - Ease into the tough questions and issues: "Let's discuss prerequisite classes." Do not initiate this conversation with *you* language:
  - "Let's talk about your resistance to prerequisites" will put the struggling student on the defensive.
  - "Tell me about your current classes." Then, if a prompt is needed, introduce each class for discussion one by one.
  - To gauge the student's level of engagement, ask what he or she is reading and the assignments that are interesting.
  - "Tell me about how life is treating you." How is your relationship with your roommate(s)?"
  - "Money aside, parents aside, what would you, in your dreams, be doing?"
- Practice active listening.
  - Wait for the student to complete her or his question or thought before jumping in with a comment or response.
  - Restate or ask clarifying questions before responding to a student question or comment.
  - Appreciate and use periods of silence.
- Keep on track. "I'd like to come back to something you said. . . ."

Conclusion

- Summarize (or instruct the student to summarize) decisions and actions. Clarify the take-away message for the student for this appointment.
- Ask the student to write down any plans of action.
- Make sure all student concerns and questions have been considered (answered or given referral): "What question haven't we addressed today?" "Is there something else you would like to discuss?" End the conference on a positive, personal note.

Follow-Up

- Record notes from the advising session.
- Phone or send the student e-mail with information or answers to questions you promised them.
- Take a moment to note issues to cover at the student's next appointment.

Adapted with permission from Pat Folsom, Jennifer E. Joslin, and Franklin Yoder: From *Creating a Blueprint for Your First Year of Advising and Beyond* workshop conducted at NACADA: The Global Community for Academic Advisors pre-conferences of the annual meetings from 2004 through 2007.

Applications and Insights

Creating a Welcoming Advising Atmosphere

- o Make the office space comfortable and student friendly.
- o Clear the desk and be ready for the conversation; do not remain knee-deep in other projects when the student arrives.
- o Start and end on a positive, supportive note.
- o Extend genuinely warm greetings (be the friendly face in a place that is not always friendly).
- o Really listen.
- o Look at the student when talking, but recognize that students from other cultures may feel uncomfortable with continual direct eye contact.
- o Smile and ask a nonthreatening question.
- o Refer to one item from the previous conference so that students know they are remembered and valued.
- o Ask the student to express questions or concerns before launching into the advising agenda.
- o Ask the advisee to help set the meeting agenda.
- o Begin the conference by focusing on a positive; recognize student successes and use them as springboards to discuss areas for improvement.
- o Note details that are important to the student (e.g., summer plans, significant event mentioned in passing) and ask about them in subsequent conversations.
- o Use open-ended questions to keep the student an active participant.
- o Learn each student's nickname. Ask about life outside of academics: recent trips, family, siblings, hometown, and fun activities.
- o Use humor.
- o Remember what it was like to be 18 years old.

Adapted with permission from NACADA: The Global Community for Academic Advising: Folsom, P. (2007). Creating a welcoming advising atmosphere. In P. Folsom (Ed.), *The new advisor guidebook: Mastering the art of advising through the first year and beyond* (Monograph No. 16) (pp. 110–111). Manhattan, KS: National Academic Advising Association.

Applications and Insights
Making the Most of Limited Time With Students
Pat Folsom, Jennifer E. Joslin, and Franklin Yoder

- Create guidelines for answering student e-mails. Determine which questions or actions can be answered by e-mail and which require a face-to-face meeting.

- Create standard messages for common questions (e.g., drop/add procedures).

- Create a standard template that can be personalized and sent to students on probation.

- Create standard e-mails for common student contacts and outreach (e.g., contacting no-shows, asking student to contact advisor, or requesting student to make an appointment).

- Create a to-do sheet for students to complete during their appointments. The sheet can include common referral offices and relevant contact information (it also acts as a checklist for information that needs to be covered in an appointment).

- Review student's electronic or paper file (conference notes, grade report, current registration) before the student arrives for an appointment.

- When using paper recordkeeping systems, use sticky notes as reminders of topics or issues that should be discussed with the student in the future.

- When a student phones, create an e-mail note. While talking to the student, summarize the conversation, including web site referrals and other specific information. After hanging up the phone, send the e-mail to the student. Cut and paste the summary into electronic notes (or print and add to paper notes).

- Create a personalized advisor to-do list.

New advisors must master and integrate a wide breadth of information at significant depth. By being organized, they can keep communication lines open, appointments focused, and advisees informed even while still growing in the new advising position.

Reprinted with permission from NACADA: The Global Community for Academic Advising: Folsom, P., Joslin, J., & Yoder, F. (2007). Organizing the chaos: Organizing time with students. In P. Folsom (Ed.), *The new advisor guidebook: Mastering the art of advising through the first year and beyond* (Monograph No. 16) (pp. 54–55). Manhattan, KS: National Academic Advising Association.

VOICES FROM THE FIELD

TEACHING THE DECISION-MAKING PROCESS

Marsha A. Miller

In a key practice, advisors teach students to make good decisions (Steele, 2013, ¶2). Some people have never received instruction on making a decision; they just do it. As a result, some new advisors react with surprise when students approach them for help with the process. When confronted with a student struggling to decide, the wise advisor realizes that "the goal is not to just make a decision, but to learn how to make decisions" (Steele, ¶4).

Although some in academia think that students should have learned decision making long before they enter college, advisors need to recognize that some students have "never [been] allowed a part in the decision-making process" (Ellis, 2014, p. 45). For example, Ali explained to long-time advisor, Drew, that two of Ali's four roommates intended to move out of their shared apartment midway through the term; one is experiencing financial issues and the other is enrolling in a vocational program. After telling Drew about these developments, sharing worries over meeting the rent payment, and recanting reasons for declaring a pre-med major at summer enrollment, a panicked Ali concluded the narrative with the declaration: "Maybe I should move home too!" Drew quickly grasped that Ali's anxiety stemmed from the need to sort through layers of complexity and effectively make decisions.

Drew had read Virginia Gordon's (2007) chapter on undecided students and knew that advisors can teach the decision-making process by first ascertaining the strategies a student typically uses to make easy decisions (e.g., when and where to eat). Appreciating that a person's decision-making tactics can vary based on the nature of the choice, Drew recognized that Ali could quickly choose among mundane day-to-day options, but Ali's parents had always made the larger decisions, and in fact, had selected the pre-med major Ali had declared over the summer. Furthermore, they had expressed disappointment in the only key decision they had left to Ali: choice of roommates.

With some understanding of the process by which Ali made big and little decisions, Drew started to isolate and address the problematic issues. Drew implemented a systematic decision-making approach that includes eight steps:

1. Create a constructive environment.
2. Identify the issues.

3. Generate good alternatives.

4. Explore the alternatives.

5. Weigh the alternatives.

6. Help students to choose the best alternative.

7. Check the decision.

8. Communicate the decision. (Mind Tools, 2015, ¶5)

Drew had already created a welcoming, constructive, and nonjudgmental environment for discussions, and in this space, began asking Ali probing questions to identify the salient concerns and alternatives. Drew's questions and insights helped Ali organize the decision-making process and guard against skipping important steps. The pair identified two issues that needed prompt resolution: choice of housing and declaration of a suitable major.

After discussing alternatives, Ali realized that breaking the rent contract would create additional problems that could negatively affect future housing opportunities, so Ali opted to stay in the apartment and try to find other roommates to split the rent. Ali also decided to connect with the Financial Aid Office to research additional funding and check campus employment web sites. Furthermore, Ali chose to defend against any parental objections by first exploring all options before sharing the decision to stay in the apartment.

However, Ali's discussion about the parentally selected major revealed a more complicated state of affairs. By applying Norman E. Amundson's (2003) five lines of questioning (chapter 7), Drew actively listened to and gained a better understanding of Ali. Specifically, Drew dug into the ideas and beliefs that influenced the situation to discover that Ali's parents had chosen a pre-med major because an uncle makes good money as a practicing physician. However, Ali described quickly tiring of studying physical sciences, as was evidenced by a poor midterm grade in chemistry. With Drew's prompting, Ali described enjoyment in social science classes, such as psychology, and stated that, upon graduation, "I do not want to sit behind an office desk all day!"

Drew helped Ali make an appointment for career exploration and asked Ali to reiterate the steps to take before the meeting with the career advisor. Drew scheduled a follow-up session and also documented the career-meeting homework steps in an e-mail.

Three weeks later, Ali returned for the follow-up appointment and announced the finding of two new roommates and a part-time campus job. Ali's financial situation had improved, and the parental conversations about the apartment and the pre-med major had been productive. Furthermore, the career counseling session yielded four different career paths for Ali's further exploration: criminal justice, social work, marketing, and business management.

To advance the decision-making process, Drew suggested that Ali participate in thinking hats, an enlightening and creative activity described by The de Bono Group to help individuals having trouble weighing alternatives (n.d., ¶2). Specifically, Drew instructed Ali to picture white, yellow, black, red, and green hats (de Bono, n.d., ¶2) and then to mentally select the white (facts) hat to wear. Under the white hat and by accessing relevant materials, such as the course catalog and department web sites, Ali delineated information about each major under consideration.

Once the facts were listed, Drew asked Ali to don the yellow (optimistic) hat and explore the positives about each alternative major. Then Ali wore the black hat and played the devil's advocate, writing down the negatives for each study program alternative, including any poor outcomes possible from pursuing the related career.

Next Ali put on the red (intuition) hat and elaborated on the aspects of each major that felt like a good or poor fit. Finally, Ali put on the green (creativity) hat and considered the possibilities for each choice, including new avenues for personal or professional growth that could be created while studying or working in the chosen field.

By the time Ali finished trying on hats, one of the two business areas, marketing, looked most appealing. Drew and Ali subsequently explored course options.

The case of Drew and Ali illustrates that decision making can be stressful for advisees, but advisors can use proven decision-making tools to teach them ways to sort through a variety of vexing issues. At some point, all students make decisions that affect their scholastic and personal lives, but with the advisors' guidance in exploration, they learn to optimize their chances for making the best choices for their personal situation.

Aiming for Excellence

o In consultation with other advisors, list the problem-solving techniques and decision-making strategies that work best with students. Access applicable Clearinghouse resources at http://www.nacada.ksu.edu/Resources /Clearinghouse/View-Articles/Critical-thinking-resource-links.aspx.

o Discuss with colleagues common problems that students present and strategies for resolving those issues.

o Several contributors to this book offer strategies germane to helping students develop decision-making, problem-solving, and critical-thinking skills. For example, Dorothy Burton Nelson (Chapter 7) discusses Gordon's (2006) 3-I model and Amundson's (2003) five lines of questioning. In addition, Jennifer Santoro and Misti Dawnn Steward, in Voices From the Field—Career Advising: A New Paradigm (following chapter 4), examine use of core desires in decision making. During your first three years, practice using each of these strategies. Which models or strategies do you employ most effectively? Do your strategies vary according to the student and situation? Keep a log of your reflections to help you hone your skill in using these strategies.

References

Amundson, N. E. (2003). *Active engagement: Enhancing the career counseling process* (2nd ed.). Richmond, BC, Canada: Ergon Communications.

The de Bono Group. (n.d.). *Six thinking hats.* Retrieved from http://www.debonogroup.com/six_thinking_hats.php

Ellis, K. (2014). Academic advising experiences of first-year undecided students: A qualitative study. *NACADA Journal, 34*(2), 42–49. doi:10.12930/NACADA-13-001

Gordon, V. N. (2006). *Career advising: An academic advisor's guide.* San Francisco, CA: Jossey-Bass.

Gordon, V. N. (2007). *The undecided college student: An academic and career advising challenge.* Springfield, IL: Charles C Thomas.

Mind Tools. (2015). *How to make decisions.* Retrieved from http://www.mindtools.com/pages/article/newTED_00.htm

Steele, G. (2013). *Decision making: Interest and effort.* Retrieved from http://www.nacada.ksu.edu/Resources/Clearinghouse/View-Articles/Decision-Making.aspx

Applications and Insights

Checklist of Questions: Teaching Students to Make Academic Decisions

Stephen O. Wallace and Beverly A. Wallace

To persist to graduation, students need to create clearly defined academic goals and acquire decision-making skills that support the achievement of those goals. Therefore, advisors must answer questions about available academic programs and graduation requirements. First-year advisors can anticipate questions such as:

- What degrees and certification programs are offered?
- What academic programs of study (major/minor/concentrations) are offered?
- Do programs accommodate students with earned high school dual credit?
  - nondegree seeking students?
  - adult students through degree completion?
  - students pursuing noncredit, continuing, and professional education?
- What are the graduation requirements?
- How many credit hours must be earned for graduation?
- What GPA is required to graduate?
- How many credits must be earned at the institution for graduation?
- How many credits does a major and minor require?
- How is the general education program organized and what policies are associated with it? How many credits are required to complete the general education program?
  - What options satisfy the general education categories?
  - Do any majors or minors require specific general education courses?
  - What is the minimum passing course grade to satisfy general education requirements?
- Is a minor required?
- Is a foreign language course required?
- What are free electives and do any count toward the program of study requirements?
- What noncourse requirements must be satisfied for graduation?

14

GROUP ADVISING

Donald Woolston and Rebecca Ryan

In preparation for this book, a review panel drawn from the NACADA: The Global Community for Academic Advising Publications Advisory Board, New Advising Professionals Commission, and Faculty Advising Commission closely examined the first edition of The New Advisor Guidebook: Mastering the Art of Advising Through the First Year and Beyond *(Folsom, 2007). They give high reviews to the chapter on group advising contributed by Donald Woolston and Rebecca Ryan (pp. 119–123). The climate within which group advising is practiced has changed since 2007. Advisors choose from more delivery options such as one-to-one, group, and multiple forms of online venues. In addition, regional accreditation agencies require student learning outcomes for all areas including advising. This chapter, with its foundational approach to group advising—the concept, components, characteristics, and challenges—remains relevant. It is reprinted with permission and without change. In the subsequent chapter, Rebecca Ryan examines group advising within the current higher education climate.*

The practice of group advising is growing both in importance and frequency. Clearly, the group advising model is closer to teaching and further from counseling than is one-on-one advising, and it is a proven, effective way to meet some of the traditional goals of academic advising. The reasons to conduct group advising and some effective means of leading group sessions are offered.

Carried out the right way and for the right reasons, group advising is effective and has great potential to benefit students and advisors. When advisors are faced with large advising caseloads, it offers a pragmatic alternative to traditional one-on-one conferences, allowing advisors to present necessary general information in a group setting and freeing advisor time in individual conferences for developmental advising (see [Ryan & Woolston, 2007]; Silverson & Bentley-Gadow [2007]).

Nearly every school and college on the University of Wisconsin–Madison campus offers group advising. In some units, group meetings are conducted as a follow-up to orientation for new students; in others, they take place before registration to convey

Reprinted with permission from NACADA: The Global Community for Academic Advising: Wolston, D., & Ryan, R. (2007). Group advising. In P. Folsom (Ed.), *The new advisor guidebook: Mastering the art of academic advising through the first year and beyond* (Monograph No. 16) (pp. 119–123). Manhattan, KS: National Academic Advising Association.

key curriculum pointers and reminders. Because of the trend toward group advising, we predict that new advisors most likely will encounter group advising opportunities in their careers. The guidelines and information presented in this article are designed to make those opportunities positive and productive experiences for both students and advisors.

Understanding Group Advising

Group advising is an advising model in which a knowledgeable person leads a group of students toward a better understanding of common educational requirements, policies, and procedures as well as the relevant strategies for completing them. The group advising model is closer to teaching, more information focused, and further from counseling than is one-on-one advising. New advisors who have experience with classroom teaching will find it natural; those with training in counseling may not be as comfortable as their teaching peers.

Group advising is most effective under the following conditions:

o Advisors are knowledgeable and able to field a wide range of questions, present information clearly, and facilitate group discussion.

o Students have a common set of requirements. For example, group advising might be used to orient new students to major requirements or collegiate or university policies and procedures, prepare students for registration, provide information on study abroad or internship opportunities, or prepare students for the graduation process.

o The campus culture reflects an appreciation of advising. Students must view advisors and advising as useful. If a campus lacks a culture in which advising is valued, an advisor can hold the group meetings, and even require students to come, but he or she will be dealing with intractable groups of annoyed students, and little useful advising will take place. In a campus climate where students do not read their e-mail, do not open their posted mail, and do not frequent the same set of buildings and walk by the same bulletin boards, group advising might not work.

The successful group-advising model does not eliminate one-on-one advising. In a model similar to that for advising and registration during student orientation programs, crucial information that applies to all students is presented in small group settings, and individually relevant information is delivered through traditional one-on-one advising as needed.

To advisors who have conducted summer orientation advising, the group advising process may look familiar. Advisors need to think about the preparation and process of summer orientations that might apply to programs offered throughout students' academic careers. A step-by-step guide for creating a group advising session is presented in . . . [Applications and Insights—The Group Advising Session: A Step-by-Step Guide at the end of this chapter].

Characteristics of Effective Group Advising Sessions

Not all proceedings of a meeting between a group of students and an advisor constitute good advising practice. A perfunctory effort to follow the step-by-step guide in . . . [Applications and Insights—The Group Advising Session: A Step-by-Step Guide] will not ensure that the goals for the meeting will be met. Best practices are based on thoughtful planning and efficacious processes. They include the following:

○ extensive and timely notification. Advisors should use all means available, including e-mail, bulletin boards, residence hall personnel, instructors, student newspapers, and Listservs to inform advisees about the meeting. Reminders should go out within a week of the session dates and again on the days of the meetings.

○ thorough preparation. For some reason, "I don't know" is better accepted in an individual appointment with a student than in response to a question in front of a large group. Making up a specious answer is not a solution for addressing a confounding question; instead, being prepared for a wide range of questions is absolutely imperative. Therefore, new advisors may want to observe or assist at group advising sessions and field questions from one-on-one conferences before trying to conduct a session by themselves.

○ engaging materials. Handouts are essential: Students need concrete and tangible resources to follow during the meeting and for reference when they return home. Materials should be clear, concise, and visually interesting. Worksheets (e.g., trial class schedules) should be accompanied by very clear instructions.

○ a clear agenda. The advisor's name, contact information, and meeting agenda should be prominently displayed during the meeting. The documented agenda helps the advisor stay on task and conveys to students the plan and important substance of the session.

○ time for questions from the group. Even with thorough preparation, an advisor will not be able to discern in advance all possible questions. Do not ask students to break in with questions because they typically will not be comfortable interrupting the presentation. Likewise do not wait until the end to ask for questions because time may expire. Instead, pause frequently and ask, "Now, what's on your mind?"

○ time for questions from individuals. At the end of the group meeting, the presenter should expect a queue of students with questions that are too personal or specific for them to ask in the group setting. If the session is close to the advising office, the advisor can bring students back to the office and individually meet with each. If the office is nowhere near the group session, she or he should try to create a little space so that students waiting in line will not overhear discussions with other students. Handling these postsession questions will test a new advisor's ability to quickly and accurately assess each student's situation, ask key questions, and provide an appropriate answer.

o help. Assistants can distribute handouts as well as collect forms and sign-in sheets. They also can help answer student questions. The more students in the session, the more questions will be asked. One person can run a group meeting of 50 students or even more, but that one person cannot answer all the individual questions that such a meeting will generate. A cadre of peer advisors or help from colleagues (e.g., copresenters) can be a huge benefit.

o encouragement for students to follow up. In ideal group advising, many subsequent one-on-one appointments will be generated, but not one for every student. Many follow-up questions from students will come in the form of e-mails or even instant messaging contacts. The advisor should be sure that the advising appointment schedule allows for students who attended the meeting and subsequently want to confer via e-mail or appointment. Students will be discouraged if they follow up on an invitation only to discover that their advisor has no time available to meet with them.

o evaluation and feedback. Every student should leave with a handout. In addition, they should leave their names and student numbers with their advisor. These could be collected on a sign-in sheet or forms completed in the meeting. For example, if the group session is focused on preparation for registration, advisors might ask students to write down their course choices for the upcoming semester. This gives advisors the opportunity to gauge the effectiveness of the session and to catch and prevent potentially poor academic choices. As an alternative means to determine the information that students learned and the plans they will make as a result of group advising, advisors may have participating students evaluate the session.

Group Advising: Benefits for Students and Advisors

Experience with group advising can be an exciting part of a new advisor's career growth. It can provide insights into student behavior and choices. It works well for students too.

Benefits for Students

Group advising can open communications between advisors and advisees, ultimately increasing student participation in one-on-one conferences. All students are accustomed to a classroom setting; however, even via the ubiquitous and utilitarian e-mail, many students find connecting with an advisor to be intimidating. Other advisees find walking into an adult's office as foreign or intimidating as entering a skateboard park would be to their advisors! Even if advisors create a warm, welcoming atmosphere, some students will still feel uneasy about crossing that office threshold.

Other students may not be intimidated but are sincerely convinced that their advisor does not have time for nor interest in their issues. Especially during busy advising periods, advisors may experience students who begin with "I know you are really busy, but . . ." and who end the meeting with "Thanks for your time."

After intimidated or anxious students show up to a group meeting and find out that their advisor has just one head, reasonably normal socialization, and a sincere interest in their welfare, everything changes. Without that group meeting, some advisees would never have made the advising connection. The safe environment offered by group advising may be especially helpful for student populations with special needs. For example, international students, especially those with marginal English skills and unfamiliarity with the American higher-education system, may appreciate the chance to soak up information in a group session so that they need not worry about formulating properly worded questions or finding the best place to ask questions. Even students without language barriers may not know how to talk to an advisor, and academically at-risk students may be the least likely to come to one-on-one advising sessions. Perhaps a struggling student fears that the advisor will be disappointed or angry with him or her. Perhaps the advisee feels alone in the situation.

For students hesitant to approach an advisor, group meetings offer both the power and safety of peers. As international, introverted, or struggling students hear peers ask questions or receive resolutions to their problems, they realize that not only are they not alone in their concerns but that advisors are approachable and helpful. From that point, many of these reluctant students are empowered to take advantage of the full range of advising opportunities, including one-on-one advising.

In summary, advising models are like academic support models. Just as many students prefer study groups to individual tutoring, perhaps because they do not feel comfortable admitting that they do not have answers or know the questions to ask, many advisees will initially prefer to attend group sessions instead of individual advising meetings.

Benefits for Advisors

Through group sessions, advisors quickly gain a big picture perspective on the common concerns and problems of students. Group meetings give advisors information that allows them to improve future group sessions, improve individual advising appointments, and advocate for students by providing feedback on student concerns to appropriate departments and central administration.

Group advising also offers advisors the opportunity to engage in advising as teaching with the group session agenda serving as the course syllabus. Group sessions afford advisors an effective means for setting advising expectations for students as well as demonstrating the treatment that students might expect of advisors. The likely outcomes are better informed advisees and individual advising appointments that focus on crucial individual differences and unusual concerns.

Perhaps just as important to advisors, group advising can remove some of the monotony that advisors otherwise might experience from repeating the same basic information 10 times on the same day. A bored advisor cannot be an effective advisor.

Group Advising: Challenges and Pitfalls

As experienced advisors who have conducted both group and individual advising over many years, we are aware that group advising has special challenges for a new advisor. Specifically, the advisor must develop presentation skills, learn to handle negative groups, deal with time pressures, and encourage attendance.

Presentation Skills

Few if any advisors have public-speaking skills in their job description, but oratorical proficiencies are required when faced with group advising assignments. Eye contact, voice projection, animation, stage presence, and clear diction are crucial to the group advising mission. Observing more experienced advisors leading group advising sessions and thinking about effective classroom presentations will help the new advisor develop the necessary presentation skills.

Negative Group Dynamics

Especially when advising is mandatory, students can show up with nasty attitudes. In his 2004 contribution to *The Mentor*, Patrick Lynch told an engaging story about the trials of working with an uncooperative small group. The students' general ungraciousness created a tension that was punctuated by a particularly brazen student making cellphone calls during the session! Public speaking experts know, and advisors soon learn, that the session leader cannot counter ugly behavior with retaliatory remarks. Instead, humor, respect, and professionalism are the only ways to address rudeness and disrespect.

Time Pressure

After being in the business for a while, advisors will notice that eventually every good advisor becomes a busy advisor. Group advising adds to this phenomenon. After standing in front of a group of students and demonstrating knowledge, empathy, and availability, an advisor's calendar will fill up quickly. Advisees and even their friends who have heard good reports of the advising session will want to make appointments for one-on-one sessions.

Student Attendance

If students do not attend group sessions, then time and resources are wasted. However, regardless of the publicity offered, only three means compel students to show up to the meetings. In one method, attendance is made mandatory so that registration holds are only removed after students have signed into a session. The second way to ensure attendance is to refuse students individual appointments until they have attended a group advising session. The third method is to make clear that the meetings are a very good time investment. After 10 years of working out the logistics, the advising staff at the University of Wisconsin–Madison has found an effective combination of these tactics.

Summary: Group Advising as Teaching

If group advising sounds a little like education in general, it should, because indeed it (as well as one-on-one advising) is about student learning. Group advising has limitations and is more difficult to carry out effectively than one might think, but the payoff, we believe, is very probable. The likely outcomes are better informed advisees and more effective individual advising appointments where advisors and advisees can focus on crucial individual and unusual concerns rather than common information that applies to most students. We are quite sure that a new advisor will eventually encounter group advising opportunities and that the information in this essay will help her or him be effective in that role.

References

Lynch, P. (2004, October). A new adviser's journal: Group advising. *The Mentor.* Retrieved from http://dus.psu.edu/mentor/old/articles/lyn04oct.htm

Ryan, R., & Woolston, D. (2007). One-on-one advising conferences. In P. Folsom (Ed.), *The new advisor guidebook: Mastering the art of advising through the first year and beyond* (Monograph No. 16) (pp. 109–118). Manhattan, KS: National Academic Advising Association.

Silverson, K., & Bentley-Gadow, J. E. (2007). Managing a large advising caseload. In P. Folsom (Ed.), *The new advisor guidebook: Mastering the art of advising through the first year and beyond* (Monograph No. 16) (pp. 128–135). Manhattan, KS: National Academic Advising Association.

Applications and Insights

The Group Advising Session: A Step-By-Step Guide
Donald Woolston and Rebecca Ryan

1. Reserve rooms of the correct size well in advance of the advising session.

2. Notify students of upcoming registration dates and advising expectations (mass e-mails, posters, direct mailings, and web site announcements). Publish a list of group meetings. Make clear whether the meetings are required or optional.

3. Prepare handouts: curriculum guides, worksheets, and so forth.

4. Draft an agenda to guide the meeting.

5. Make or procure necessary forms (e.g., session evaluation and course selection forms).

6. Invite peer advisors or colleagues who may be willing to help.

7. Welcome the students as they arrive and thank them for their participation. Encourage their questions during as well as after the meeting.

8. Create a sign-in sheet if meetings are required. Students can sign in as they enter or leave the session.

9. Go through the agenda, pausing frequently for questions and carefully monitoring the group for signals that students may have questions or do not understand the information.

10. Ask for questions from the group. Be patient, but do not demand responses. If no questions are forthcoming, review points that experience has shown to be especially confusing. With some luck, a student will ask about a particular course, and other students can be asked to share their knowledge about the course (a collaborative process that cannot be conducted during one-on-one advising).

11. Leave time for individual questions; thank the group again for attending. Ask them to complete the evaluation form or hand in other forms completed during the session.

12. Make clear how students make appointments for follow-up one-on-one advising meetings.

13. Patiently answer individual questions. If time is too short to allow detailed explanations, give a quick answer and encourage individual students to make appointments for a detailed discussion of the topic.

Reprinted with permission from NACADA: The Global Community for Academic Advising: Woolston, D., & Ryan, R. (2007). Group advising [Figure 10]. In P. Folsom (Ed.), *The new advisor guidebook: Mastering the art of advising through the first year and beyond* (Monograph No. 16) (p. 120). Manhattan, KS: National Academic Advising Association.

15

GROUP ADVISING

AN UPDATE

Rebecca Ryan

Since the publication of the first edition of The New Advisor Guidebook *(Folsom) in 2007, multiple forms for advising delivery have emerged and are utilized in whole or in combination, such as one-to-one, group, and electronic (e-mail, Skype, and so forth). Additionally, those practicing advising and working in higher education have embraced student learning outcomes as means to drive the creation and implementation of advising activities and delivery systems. The evolution of their practice toward specific learning goals has validated a trend toward a more intentional and strategic consideration of the many ways advisors educate and support students. Furthermore, practitioners have embraced and scholars have researched multiple formats of student engagement to promote retention. This updated chapter addresses these issues.*

Every student interaction creates a positive opportunity for advisors to engage students in the educationally purposeful activities so critical to student success (Kuh, Kinzie, Schuh, & Whitt, 2005). Just as they master multiple approaches to effectively meet student needs (Drake, Jordan, & Miller, 2013; chapter 12), advisors must also master multiple ways of delivering advising. Group advising offers advisors an additional venue to the one-to-one appointment for engaging students, and through thoughtful discussions, those facilitating groups promote personal growth for participants. Therefore, new advisors should consider group advising as a useful way to reach advisees, teach them the importance of advising, and help them meet the student learning outcomes (SLOs) that contribute to their academic success.

Because new advisors, especially those without classroom teaching experience, may feel less comfortable conducting group advising sessions than working one-to-one with advisees, this chapter provides key information on facilitating positive and productive group advising sessions. To benefit from the suggestions, advisors need only a willingness to explore this advising option.

Benefits of Group Advising

Benefits for Advisors

Advisors who facilitate groups can proactively provide access, support, and information for students at key touch points during an academic cycle: for example, during orientation, while adjusting to campus, through enrollment, at drop and withdrawal deadlines, and upon preparing to go home over break. They also make intentional plans for SLOs or create an advising curriculum to meet the needs of their students. Even for those without large caseloads or stifling scheduling constraints, use of group advising can maximize advisors' time and ensure that commonly needed information is presented consistently to students. For example, advisors of pre-med students can focus individual sessions more productively after all the advisees who need the information have been introduced to the complex undergraduate requirements.

Just as advising must reach individuals in a meaningful way, the delivery must fit the unique attributes of the advisor, and some practitioners may discover that their relational strengths align more closely with group than one-to-one advising. Those who feel most comfortable with the content, format, and delivery of information within groups can tweak the group format to address a variety of student learning styles.

Benefits for Students

In addition to creating a safe environment (Woolston & Ryan, 2007, p. 121; chapter 14), well-executed group advising encourages the building of community. In *Making the Most of College: Students Speak Their Minds* (2001), Richard Light stated that "to learn from one another, students with different backgrounds and from different racial and ethnic groups must interact" (p. 190). Also pointing to the value of diversity, Nancy King (2000) noted that "students who participate in group advising appreciate the opportunity to interact with peers as well as with an advisor. The feeling of connectedness is a powerful by-product of the group experience" (p. 236).

The benefits of group advising accrue only when groups are implemented and facilitated effectively. Advisors can use a simple three-step process to create effective advising groups: identify advising SLOs, determine the most effective means of achieving these outcomes (e.g., advising one-to-one, in groups, or electronically), and planning for and creating group advising sessions.

Setting the Stage for Group Advising

Start With Goal Setting

Group advising requires thoughtful and thorough planning for SLOs; however, regardless of the specific objectives, some proven strategies help advisors ensure that group sessions meet advising goals and create positive and engaging experiences for students. For successful implementation of these strategies, advisors begin with the end in mind (Covey, 2013); that is, they identify a clear purpose for advising and their own objectives for practice. Many advising units have established mission statements and SLOs that guide practice. Those without this kind of reference will need to identify the desired session results or SLOs from their advising interactions. Advisors will later use these SLOs to develop an advising curriculum or syllabus for students that they can use in either one-to-one or group advising sessions. In developing these goals, advisors need to pose the following questions:

o What do I want students to know, do, and value as a result of advising (NACADA: The Global Community for Academic Advising, 2006)?

o How are the outcomes currently being met (or not)?

o How can I structure advising opportunities and access (content, format, and times) to best help students achieve the desired SLOs?

New advisors should begin this exploratory process by reflecting on the basic information students need and then identify three to five points of knowledge or skills that a student should demonstrate as a result of advising. As they gain experience, advisors can add more SLOs to their curriculum. Advisors should formulate the specific goals that relate to SLOs.

After advisors work through the complex task of determining key SLOs, they need to examine current advising practices and activities to determine the means and timing by which students achieve the identified SLOs. The information in Table 15.1 serves as a good example for this part of the advising planning process. SLOs are listed in the left-hand column of the table, and advising activities that contribute to the stated SLOs are listed horizontally across the table.

As they complete the table, advisors must consider advising activities for the entire year. In the process, they identify points in time for implementing activities and meeting students' most common informational needs. In addition, advisors use the table to examine the established patterns and address the following questions:

o Do students have sufficient advising opportunities to satisfy SLOs?

o Are all SLOs addressed within current advising practices?

Table 15.1. Learning outcomes for knowledge and their sources

Learning Outcome	Source for Achieving Learning Outcome					
	One-to-One Appointments	Orientation & Information	Web Site	E-mail	Facebook	Student Peers
Knowledge Gained From Advising						
Reasons to see advisor		X	X			X
Ways to contact advisor		X	X		X	X
The basic nature of academic expectations	X	X	X			
How to use the enrollment system	X	X		X		X
Skills Gained From Advising						
Proactively seek advisor			X		X	X
Explore course options and make selections	X					X
Engage in extracurricular experiences*	X		X	X	X	X

Note. *Skill-building extracurricular experiences include community service, internships, jobs, study abroad opportunities, student organizations, and so forth.

o Are the current formats for delivering services (e.g., one-to-one, group, electronic, oral, written) the most effective?

o When are the peak demands on my advising time and how can I maximize advising engagement opportunities during these periods?

o Are new technologies and alternative ways of providing advising accessible to all?

As they consider ways to ensure that advising efficiently maximizes opportunities to address SLOs, advisors need to remember that students belong to a larger campus culture and likely have multiple opportunities to engage in activities that also address SLOs and encourage their development, such as first-year interest groups, living-learning communities, residence hall workshops, first-year experience courses, and student leadership programs, as well as service learning and community service commitments. Therefore, advisors need not offer or plan all meaningful opportunities, which frees them to focus on the unique contributions that they can bring to students. Having completed a thorough review of the goals and available means of supporting SLOs, advisors can determine the most effective delivery of advising (e.g., one-to-one, in groups, or electronic format).

Selecting a Means of Delivery

The review of possible venues informs planners considering group advising topics and settings. Those facing time or space restrictions may find the following factors particularly important in creating and implementing advising delivery formats:

o advisor professional preferences and skills. What are the advisor's strengths: technology use? public speaking? event planning?

o student population and student culture. What are the students' preferences for receiving, processing, and discussing information? Does the advisee or group present unique partialities or needs? For example, do they share status as international, first-generation, or adult students?

o efficiency. What topics are more effectively and timely delivered one-to-one, electronically, or through a group session? As Donald Woolston and Rebecca Ryan (2007, p. 119; chapter 14) asked, do the students face a common set of academic requirements, policies, or procedures (e.g., transfer articulation), or do they need information on a common topic (e.g., career readiness)? A group advising session offers an ideal venue for advisors who have developed an advising syllabus and curriculum for students who all need similar information within an identical time frame (e.g., orientation).

o SLOs for advising. Which SLOs and content might be addressed best in an experience outside of an individual appointment? For example, upper-level students who need baseline information about considering, exploring, choosing, and applying to graduate programs may benefit from the broad, initial information offered in a group setting, which frees up one-to-one advisor appointments for specifically focusing on a student's unique situations, interests, goals, and so forth.

Creating Effective Group Advising Sessions

The creation of groups requires logistically and conceptually complex planning. Advisors need to commit a moderate investment of time in organizing and preparing to implement groups with the potential to deliver maximum student learning potential. In addition to securing support from the unit supervisor or administration head, advisors should address the following questions during the planning process:

- When do students need the information? Effective sessions offer advising when students perceive a need for the information. For example, a session designed to prepare students to register should be scheduled a week or two before enrollment, not months before students can contextualize the information.

- What personnel are involved? New advisors may feel more comfortable copresenting with an experienced colleague, and some veteran advisors invite experts from career centers or international student offices to offer sessions on specific opportunities such as internships and study abroad. Other campus partners, such as those in the career center or disabilities services, may share goals and SLOs with advising units, making them natural choices for guest presenters.

- Is the location of the session accessible to everyone? Best practices include consideration for those who may experience barriers to attendance. Obstacles are often unique to an institution's mission and student population. For example, when selecting the space, the planner must consider building location: Is it on or off campus? Is parking available? Is the location conducive to the group topic and expected attendees? Is the facility accessible to those with physical disabilities? Advisors should visit the designated space to ensure that those using wheelchairs can maneuver comfortably, and they need to make sure that advisees with sight or hearing disabilities can engage with the advising materials.

- Do the content and format of the materials sufficiently vary to accommodate different student development issues and learning styles of the group participants?

- Will the content and format effectively allow students to meet the determined SLOs?

- Does the session reflect the advising mission and philosophy embraced by the institution, the unit, and the advisors involved?

o Who can help with the planning and implementation of advising groups?
  Advisors in small units or sole practitioners should seek out campus colleagues
  who work with groups (e.g., admissions counselors, orientation staff, residence
  hall staff) or who hold similar advising positions elsewhere on campus to
  brainstorm ideas and discuss strategies for creating and facilitating groups.
  Membership in an advising organization offers opportunities for collaboration.
  For example, NACADA brings advising colleagues from all over the world to
  create useful publications and personal networks of advisors.

o What feedback will come from students? Students' positive and negative
  comments about their group advising experience provide advisors with insights
  about the extent to which SLOs have been met (or not).

Although characteristics of effective group advising reflect ongoing experiences of
advisors in groups that meet in a physical space, many of the considerations apply to
groups facilitated online. The technology emergence since the last *Guidebook* (Folsom, 2007) was published offers advisors a wide range of new options for creating
an online curriculum and advising groups. For example, students studying in different countries need to complete their course equivalency forms for their home campus
after they have started their abroad courses. Students needing to undergo a similar
process, regardless of destination country, benefit from support and FAQs provided
via a live, shared web chat as well as asynchronously to accommodate time zone differences. In addition, advisors can use student databases to sort students by major,
year, or other characteristics, such as internship and scholarship recipients, to form
groups.

Advisors directing online groups gain the same benefits—efficiency, variety, consistency, information about students, and teaching opportunity—offered by facilitating
in-person advising. That is, advisors can disseminate common information online to
students so that they can focus on each individual's goals and growth during private
(in-person or online) sessions as well as provide information at key points over time
to build on previously presented material.

In addition, information available at all times via the Internet meets students' expectations for round-the-clock access. Endres and Tisinger (2007) acknowledged this
growing student preference for alternative information outlets and proposed that
advisors embrace technology and utilize it in positive ways. Advising on demand
involves technology (web sites, podcasts, videos) that makes important information
always accessible to students.

Furthermore, advisors can use in-person and online groups to ease student anxieties
prior to an individual meeting (Endres & Tisinger, 2007). For example, international
students can read and learn information at their own pace without concerns about
misunderstanding the advisor's oratory or formulating a spoken response. Furthermore, online groups can assist students in generating camaraderie; many students

now bring with them a long history of interacting with technology to connect with others.

New advisors considering online advising groups should still work through the three-step process discussed: identifying advising SLOs, determining the most effective means of achieving these outcomes, and planning and creating the online groups. They also will find chapter 16, Advising Online, helpful as they plan and design advising delivery.

Summary

By conceptualizing advising delivery as an opportunity for student engagement, advisors consider new methods, tools, and approaches for meeting student needs and demands for advising as effectively as possible. The effort encourages a thoughtful process essential for best advising practice. New advisors soon recognize that learning transpires in multiple settings and through many approaches, including group advising. They attend to building new skills (e.g., public speaking) and careful planning, driven by SLOs, to create engagement opportunities that stimulate student curiosity and self-awareness. Many will realize that "experience with group advising can be an exciting part of a new advisor's career growth" (Woolston & Ryan, 2007, p. 121; chapter 14).

Aiming for Excellence

o Go on the campus tour for prospective students and make note of the questions they ask. Consider ways the information disseminated and the communication techniques used by the tour guide and other participants may apply to students attending a group advising session.

o Identify three to five simple concepts or facts a student should know as a result of advising. For example, "I want advisees to know the best way to follow up with me (e-mail, phone, etc.)" or "I want students to understand how to read their degree audit report."

o Find two or three other campus units with similar or identical learning goals for students and determine the content issues shared among you. Talk with colleagues from those departments to see if a group advising session could fulfill the need for all units. Specifically discuss both topics and format.

o Create a rough outline or syllabus that represents the academic year. Include group sessions that meet the needs of your students across different advising seasons and make note of student awareness about the different ways to access advising and other pertinent information. Consider ways to keep advisees informed and updated about all advising opportunities.

o Create a list of the top five most commonly asked questions in your one-to-one advising appointments and think about ways to address these inquiries within a group setting.

o Attend, as a guest, other group sessions (advising and non-advising) on campus, such as those offered by personnel in career or student support services, the graduate school staff, tour guides, and leaders of academic clubs and organizations. Make notes on the meetings and identify the formats and strategies that engaged the participants or audience.

o Use advising notes or confer with colleagues to develop questions that students with little experience at the institution or in the community (e.g., first-generation or international students) may not think to ask. Focus on common issues that could be addressed in a group advising setting.

References

Covey, S. R. (2013). *Seven habits of highly effective people: Powerful lessons in personal change.* New York, NY: Simon and Schuster.

Drake, J. K., Jordan, P., & Miller, M. A. (Eds.). (2013). *Academic advising approaches: Strategies that teach students to make the most of college.* San Francisco, CA: Jossey-Bass.

Endres, J., & Tisinger, D. (2007). *Digital distractions: College students in the 21st century.* Retrieved from http://www.nacada.ksu.edu/Resources/Clearinghouse/View-Articles/Advising-the-millenial-generation.aspx}sthash.Ec38eFsx.dpuf

Folsom, P. (Ed.). (2007). *The new advisor guidebook: Mastering the art of advising through the first year and beyond* (Monograph No. 16). Manhattan, KS: National Academic Advising Association.

King, N. (2000). Advising students in groups. In V. N. Gordon & W. R. Habley (Eds.), *Academic advising: A comprehensive handbook* (p. 228–237). San Francisco, CA: Jossey-Bass.

Kuh, G. D., Kinzie, J., Schuh, J. H., & Whitt, E. (2005). *Student success in college: Creating conditions that matter.* San Francisco, CA: Jossey-Bass.

Light, R. J. (2001). *Making the most of college: Students speak their minds.* Cambridge, MA: Harvard University Press.

NACADA: The Global Community for Academic Advising. (2006). *NACADA concept of academic advising.* Retrieved from http://www.nacada.ksu.edu/Resources/Clearinghouse/View-Articles/Concept-of-Academic-Advising-a598.aspx

Woolston, D., & Ryan, R. (2007). Group advising. In P. Folsom (Ed.), *The new advisor guidebook: Mastering the art of advising through the first year and beyond* (Monograph No. 16) (pp. 119–123). Manhattan, KS: National Academic Advising Association.

16

ADVISING ONLINE

Jeanette Pellegrin

A successful advising experience often inspires a student to reach his or her academic goal, whether it be a degree, a higher GPA for entry into a program, or a resharpening of a rusty skill. Traditionally, advisors have worked one-to-one and face-to-face with students in an office or advising center on a campus during the once-typical Monday-through-Friday work week (from 9 A.M. to 5 P.M. in the United States), but increasingly advisors and advisees alike see this traditional schedule as obsolete. As education and the world become increasingly digitized, the advising experience must also reflect the Information Age.

Today, most college students demonstrate proficiency in communicating electronically. According to the Pew Internet Project (2014a, 2014b), persons of traditional college age use social networking sites, particularly on mobile devices, more than others in the U.S. population. Students maintain social and professional networks through e-mails, texts, blogs, and various social media. They not only are accustomed to sending, receiving, and processing information electronically but also expect to have access and utilize these means of connection at will; that is, they expect to initiate communication at their convenience—any time of the day or night and any day of the week.

The Community College Research Center (CCRC) (2012a) at Columbia University maintains that effective advising must include "sustained one-on-one interaction between the student and the advisor . . . not merely in the first semester but throughout the college career" (p. 61), and certainly most advisors would agree. To maintain the necessary level of interaction, advisors connect with their students electronically at some point whether they share the same physical campus environment or not. In fact, some advisors work with students who live hundreds or thousands of miles away from the college campus, making traditional methods of advising impossible. Although in an ideal situation advisor and student connect through a combination of in-person and electronic communication, this circumstance does not always materialize. Advisors and advisees may maintain a relationship without the two ever meeting in person or hearing one another's voice.

Online advising encourages more efficient information dissemination than does the traditional session in which the advisor in face-to-face consultation with the student relies heavily on spoken conversations and printed handouts of program requirements, deadlines, and referrals to departments and buildings elsewhere on campus. In addition, as most experienced advisors know, "pre-engaged students who arrive prepared for advising sessions are, unfortunately, not the norm" (Ambrose & Ambrose, 2013, ¶75), and online advising can drastically reduce or even eradicate the problem of readiness because advising through electronic means, such as e-mail, allows for communication at a time when the student can most appreciate and learn from the information received from the advisor. For example, a student distracted by concerns over an upcoming test may not focus on scholarship information presented in an appointment prescheduled an hour before the exam, but may benefit from an e-mail that she or he can open when able to devote the proper attention to the information in it.

In the past, online advising was seen as a disadvantage based on the belief that creating a relationship between advisor and student via the Internet poorly substituted for the face-to-face interaction. However, electronic communication provides some distinct advantages not found in the typical in-person advising scenarios. For example, it gives both parties the opportunity to review responses and edit them for tone, scrubbing out inflammatory words and choosing more neutral ones if necessary. In addition, unlike in a spoken conversation, a response need not be immediate; instead, the advisor can carefully check for facts, and the student enjoys "more time to carefully consider and provide more detailed, thoughtful reflections than [he or she can] in a face-to-face environment" (Ambrose & Ambrose, 2013, ¶76).

Arguably, the absence or presence of visual cues constitutes the most important difference between traditional and online advising. A meeting with a student face-to-face usually allows the advisor to process visual and auditory information about the student, which in turn provides cues on gender, sex, ethnicity, nationality, age, and so forth, but an advisor working online often must rely solely on information gleaned through a combination of demographic information in the institutional database and written responses from the student. Although this lack of initial information may mean the advisor must do a little more homework in getting to know the student, the likelihood of bias may also be reduced. Sometimes not knowing a student's profile relative to the traditional student for a certain program, for example, can prove advantageous (chapter 10).

If the lack of visual cues becomes problematic, a vast array of electronic communications, such as Skype and Facebook, can provide an interface in real time. The advisor and student need only agree on which system to use.

Online advising may require a new mind-set and different approaches for an advisor to embrace. However, as Peggy Jordan pointed out in chapter 11, "Excellence in advising comes from minds open to new ideas, including about oneself, as well as about students." For this mode of engaging and informing students, advisors must know how to organize, prioritize, and personalize the student's online advising experience.

Organizing

Conceptualizing the Goal

Regardless of whether the advising is undertaken in a traditional face-to-face format or via electronic means, the purpose remains the same: to help the student reach his or her goal. Therefore, before all other efforts, both parties must understand the goal.

During the process of obtaining a goal statement, the advisor must ask: "Why is the advising undertaken electronically?" Is the use of electronic media at this point in the advising relationship mandated by the school or predicated by the type of program delivery?

If it is the student's choice, does the online format provide the desired convenience or privacy not afforded by an appointment in person? If the student indicates such a reason for online advising, a discussion of workload, jobs, and scheduling might be appropriate early in the relationship. A student who says "I don't have time" to meet with an advisor or who exhibits discomfort meeting face-to-face may be giving warning signals that the advisor needs to explore.

Although advisors need to accept that some students request to be advised online simply for the sake of convenience, they must wonder if the student thinks that only electronic media provide viable options for advising. Such a position gives the advisor information on which to base questions about distance learning, disabilities, special needs, and so forth. Donald Woolston and Rebecca Ryan's discussion in chapter 14 on the advantages of group advising reveals the reason some students prefer being advised online, at least initially: The "safe environment" provided by electronic communication

> may be especially helpful for student populations with special needs. For example, international students, especially those with marginal English skills and unfamiliarity with the American higher-education systems, may appreciate . . . that they need not worry about formulating properly worded questions or finding the best place to ask questions. Even students without language barriers may not know how to talk to an advisor, and academically at-risk students may be the least likely to come to one-on-one advising sessions.

Beginning the advising relationship electronically can help dismantle some barriers to communication.

If the advisor chose the mode of communication, he or she must ascertain the student's comfort level with being advised electronically; that is, does the student possess the comfort and skill with technology needed to participate adequately in advising through the Internet? Discussing academic goals and progress can induce enough stress for students without adding concerns over technology to the situation. The advisor must clarify the chosen method of delivery and determine whether it will be the only method utilized. For a productive advising relationship, both parties must know the best ways to communicate both for typical concerns and especially during crises.

Establishing the Contract

A new advisor must be especially careful to establish the student's reason for seeking (or sometimes being forced to seek) advising. Advisors working online engage with representatives of special populations, whose reason for taking college classes may vary widely from each other and the majority cohort of the campus. From the first communication, the advisor must determine the purpose of advising for the student. The new advisor needs to also reflect on ways the mode of delivery, in this case electronic, affect her or his advising goals.

As with face-to-face advising, the expectations, rights, and responsibilities of both the advisor and the student must be clarified, preferably in the form of a standardized policy statement that can be shared electronically and amended as needed. In devising such a contract, the advisor needs to initiate a discussion of long- and short-term goals as well as deadlines for required paperwork. Specifically, the advisor and advisee need to set expectations regarding timeliness in communication. For example, they may decide on a deadline of two working days for a response to an e-mail from either party. This contract not only gives the advisor and the student a clear set of parameters for the relationship but can also provide continuity for the student in the event of advising personnel changes.

Choosing the Method

The advisor and student must also decide upon the chosen communicative delivery method for the relationship. Are e-mails sufficient? Would a live chat or phone call be more beneficial? Perhaps the pair should set up webcam meetings. The choices for electronic communication change almost daily, so the pair must choose carefully for consistency and reliability. An electronic format available today and disabled tomorrow can lead to disaster. Therefore, the advisor must ensure that the format offers consistent availability, ease of information recovery, and confidentiality between advisor and student. If the electronic format does not provide both advisor and student equal ease of access and usability, give-and-take discussions will begin to dwindle and the advising relationship to wither.

Communicating the Information

While a spoken conversation lasts no longer than the time it takes to speak the words, an electronic conversation can last in perpetuity, giving both the advisor and the student a reference point so that they need not reestablish the specifics of their relationship or unchanged information with each interaction. This permanent access offers benefits and drawbacks; because the information given can last on record forever, the advisor must ensure that it is properly updated. An answer to a question that contradicts one previously provided or that varies significantly from a colleague's response may erode the student's confidence in the advising relationship.

New advisors in particular must make every effort to hone and grow their communication skills. Furthermore, because clarity and consistency remain key to a trusting partnership, they must learn to educate students with sufficient information at the appropriate level of detail and quickly learn to filter the data exchanged in dialogue so that the advisee is not inundated with too much information.

As they refine their own filtering skills, new advisors may benefit from the rule of thumb that suggests a sender provide no more than three important facts per e-mail, if possible, and limit each e-mail to a single subject. For example, in response to a student who wants to know the classes needed to complete a program and important financial aid deadlines, the advisor should send two short e-mails, one on each topic, rather than one long and complex communique. A reply such as "I'm going to respond to your question about program completion first. Then I'll email you about financial aid deadlines" alerts the student that the second question will be addressed in a separate communication.

Online venues establish useful means of disseminating standardized, nonpersonal information, such as program course requirements. In addition to uninterrupted access, they offer more convenience in making referrals than the traditional hike-to-find manner of old. Electronic links certainly encourage follow-up better than maps and directions to other on- or off-campus resources. Electronic communication also makes sharing student information among colleagues, as appropriate under the Family Educational Rights and Privacy Act (U.S. Department of Education, 2014) and other privacy policies, convenient.

Because few paper documents are typically used in online advising, the advisor must create an electronic file or advising portfolio for each student and remain absolutely fastidious and diligent in maintaining these files. The advisor who allows 200 answered but unfiled e-mails to pile up in the inbox clearly lacks organizational skills or priorities and may become embroiled in a long, embarrassing, and potentially costly data recovery process.

Prioritizing: Managing Caseloads

Advisors working electronically must carefully organize their daily routines to tend to all aspects of their caseloads. Advisors working in traditional face-to-face venues know who they will be seeing in the appointment and the length of the meeting, can review the student's file, and schedule time immediately after the meeting to document accomplishments made and those left to be completed. Advisors working solely via the Internet rarely can organize the day so simply: To keep all channels of communication open, they receive and return e-mails throughout the day (often many times with the same student), update blogs periodically, and monitor social media. New advisors may want to organize their time according to the type of communication monitored per day: three hours for e-mail communications, two hours for Facebook and Twitter posts, one hour for updating blogs, and so forth.

Because advisors and advisees can use so many different forms of electronic communication, the advisor must prioritize tasks and yet maintain flexibility. Prioritizing often comes down to determining consequences. An inquiry from a graduating senior who e-mailed yesterday may take priority over a nonemergency question e-mailed earlier from a sophomore. A quick e-mail to the sophomore promising an answer by the end of the week may suffice, and of course, the advisor must always follow through by the promised deadline. If phone calls went unanswered on Monday because of the volume of e-mails received over the weekend, then the advisor places returned calls at the top of Tuesday's to-do list.

Alternatively, advisors may set up their day with online appointments, setting aside specific blocks of time to correspond with specific students. As with those expecting return calls, students appreciate knowing the time of their appointment so they can look for a communique from the advisor. To prevent one or two students from monopolizing their time, advisors may want to set time limits on certain tasks such as phone calls and Skype meetings. Flexibility remains key to communicating effectively online.

New advisors should look for specific "key points in [the student] college trajectories" that typically do not constitute part of the day-to-day advising routine but require special attention, such as when students have advanced from the freshman and sophomore level to the junior and senior level, such that new course choices open up to them, or when a student is ready to enroll for the final credit hours required to complete a program (CCRC, 2013b, p. 76). Some schools have established an electronic alert system to let advisors know when these milestones are being approached or have been reached, but advisors without access to such a tool must track these important dates. Because all busy advisors can overlook less frequent but vital deadlines, new advisors, in particular, must organize and prioritize tasks carefully. They may find that creating a database or simple spreadsheets can help, and a wise advisor often turns to the institutional tech support office and fellow advisors for suggestions.

Personalizing: Building the Relationship

If "the appointment is the primary relational vehicle of advising" (Ryan & Woolston, chapter 14), then some may believe that the online environment inhibits the relationship between the advisor and student. They may think that the relational component suffers in online communication as emotions, such as warmth and cheerfulness, are replaced by a smiley face or silly emoticon. Although this concern may have rung true in the earlier days of electronic communications, students and advisors alike today show competency at texting, e-mailing, Facebooking, and tweeting all manner of emotions (both positive and negative).

Online advising need not and should not be impersonal. Simply responding to an e-mail with a friendly greeting and the student's name sets the desired tone. A response that begins with "Welcome, Dylan! I'm looking forward to working with you" promises an engaged advisor, whereas "Dear Student, We have received your enrollment request" reduces the advisee, with all his or her dreams and concerns, to a digitized entity. Advisors should strive to maintain a tone of professional affability with advisees.

Asking open-ended questions such as "What career do you plan to pursue with this major?" or "I see you struggled in your biology course last semester; can you tell me what prevented you from getting a higher grade?" encourages the student to continue the conversation and allows the advisor and student to learn more about one another. Advisors should always practice active listening skills. Applications and Insights—Advisor Checklist for Listening, Interviewing, and Referral Skills in chapter 11 provides an excellent tool with which to evaluate relational skills.

Although advisees may prefer maintaining an informal tone, advisors must not use jargon or unfamiliar colloquialisms because many students will not ask for clarification for fear of appearing unprepared or unknowledgeable. Furthermore, to develop a welcoming environment, the advisor should review the student's personal and academic information before beginning the conversation, as including a small tidbit of information gleaned in the review process can help break the ice and shows that the advisor has taken an interest in and remembers the student from past conversations.

Maintaining a Professional Network

New advisors, in trying to develop relational aspects of advising online with students, may inadvertently overlook their relationships with other professionals involved in helping students attain their goals. Advisors who advise strictly online must intentionally maintain their networks both within the institution and throughout academia to prevent both isolation and tunnel vision.

Because advisors form the front line for change, they must assiduously keep up with amendments to the policies and procedures of specific departments and the institution as well as the trends affecting the advising profession. They must know the best person to address a student's concern or who can proffer the best advice on advising matters.

Summary

Online advising can allow advisors and students to interact far more often than the all-too-common twice a semester scenario. Both students and advisors can continue the advising process at any time and in any location such that advisors must manage and prioritize a high volume and wide span of communications as well as personalize the relationship with students who they may never hear or see. Rather than being a disadvantage, well-organized and deliberately delivered online advising offers a myriad of benefits for both advisor and student that contribute to student success in many aspects of their college experience.

Aiming For Excellence

o Create a list of referral links with specific e-mail addresses of colleagues willing to help your students or who have specific knowledge your students will need. Using this strategy, students seek and meet another person with whom to connect (and with whom you can later follow up).

o Create a file with boilerplate e-mails for responses to common questions such as "When is the last day to withdraw from classes?" or "How do I log into my online class?" Name the e-mail response files appropriately for easy retrieval.

o Start a coffee klatch! Invite other advisors and other colleagues to an informal meeting once a month (week, semester, and so forth) to chat about challenges and triumphs in working with students at a distance.

o Join a NACADA Listserv, or other electronic mail board, for advisors working in distance education or one of the many other special interest groups. When confronted with a problem or troubling situation, you can look to the expertise of dozens, if not hundreds, of other advisors who have worked through similar issues.

o Start a best practices thread online. Send out an inspirational or informational e-mail to your network of fellow advisors and other supporters. For example: "I make note of my advisees' birthdates and send them short happy birthday greetings via e-mail." Encourage others to add to the thread and be sure to click *Reply All* to ensure that everyone on the mailing lists sees all the entries.

o Organize your day by utilizing an online calendar feature. Block off certain hours of the day for certain tasks; for example, 8:00 A.M. to 10:00 A.M.: answer e-mails; 10:00 A.M. to 12:00 P.M.: respond to Facebook and Twitter; 1:00 P.M. to 3:00 P.M.: review graduation petitions. This tactic ensures that all means of communication are being checked routinely.

References

Ambrose, G. A., & Ambrose, L. W. (2013). The blended advising model: Transforming advising with eportfolios. *International Journal of ePortfolio, 3*(1). Retrieved from http://www.theijep.com/pdf/IJEP97.pdf

Community College Research Center (CCRC). (2013a). *Designing a system for strategic advising.* New York, NY: Columbia University.

CCRC. (2013b). *What we know about nonacademic student supports.* New York, NY: Columbia University.

Pew Internet Project. (2014a). *Social media use by age group over time.* Retrieved from http://www.pewinternet.org/data-trend/social-media/social-media-use-by-age-group/

Pew Internet Project. (2014b). *Social networking fact sheet.* Retrieved from http://www.pewinternet.org/fact-sheets/social-networking-fact-sheet/

U.S. Department of Education. (2014). *Family Educational Rights and Privacy Act (FERPA).* Retrieved from http://www2.ed.gov/policy/gen/guid/fpco/ferpa/index.html

Applications and Insights
Advising Online: Advice From Advisors
Compiled by Jeanette Pellegrin from NACADA Distance Education
Listserv

"While we tailor the message to the specific learner, we use template information to ensure that all advisors are sending out consistent messaging or are responding in a like manner. When learners get consistent information at each point of contact, it helps to build trust." *Seritas Smith, Coordinator, Advising Services, Athabasa University*

"If you advise by phone, send a detailed follow-up e-mail so that the advisor and advisees are both clear on what was discussed." *Jeanne Mannarino, Assistant Director of Advisement and Evaluation, School of Nursing, Excelsior College*

"Keep detailed records of what you discussed so the person becomes more 'real' to you and you don't lose track of someone 'out there.' They may already feel somewhat alone." *Karen Wilson, Academic Advisor, University of Hawaii at Manoa*

"Don't try to be everything to every student: Share info and connect them with resources early on. . . . You want to place the responsibility in their hands to manage their educational goals so they can fully own their failures and success." *Rebecca Roach, TRiO Support Services and Academic Advisor, Labette Community College*

"Limit the time for a telephone advising appointment and be sure the student knows it." *Catherine Holderness, Interim Director, University of North Carolina Exchange Program*

"Listen critically; find out what the real question is, not just the question that's being asked." *Nicole Ballard, Program Advisor, California State University*

"Try to anticipate questions that the learner may not be asking. If there is need-to-know information, it should be provided to all learners, whether they have asked a specific question regarding that topic or not." *Serita Smith, Program Advisor, Athabasca University*

"Smile when you answer the phone!" *Paul Castelin, Student Advisory Coordinator, Boise State University*

"Join a support group . . . open to anyone doing distance learning–related things—administration, admissions, advising . . . share (your) best and worst stories and encourage each other personally." *Catherine Holderness, Interim Director, University of North Carolina Exchange Program*

"Identify your 'go to' people as early as possible, those who are doing jobs similar to yours that you can share reality checks with, and those in other units who perform different functions but whose work impacts the success outcomes of your students." *Nicole Ballard, Program Advisor, California State University*

PART SIX

ADVISOR DEVELOPMENT FOR FOUNDATIONAL MASTERY

Training approaches are important ongoing developmental processes, ranging from the nonexistent to fully developed long-term programs. In this section, the editors focus on components of adequate training, regardless of available resources, the nature of the institution, or the circumstances of the advising. In ideal situations, training programs include an initial focused period of instruction followed by periodic supplemental information and practice offered at critical times and extending throughout the first few years. Many institutions do not commit the resources to provide in-depth or long-term training, so advisors must develop self-directed training options for their own professional growth. Training programs of any type must help new advisors face complex unanticipated situations not addressed during their initial training.

17

ADVISOR GROWTH AND DEVELOPMENT

BUILDING A FOUNDATION FOR MASTERY

Franklin Yoder and Jennifer E. Joslin

In a comprehensive advisor training and development program, new advisors experience an initial focused period of training followed by periodic supplemental training that may extend over many months. The comprehensive training program must account for complex, unanticipated situations the advisors experience after the initial training. It provides tools for mastering advising at a foundational level and helps turn the novice into an excellent advisor. However, despite the critical ongoing nature of training opportunities for new and veteran advisors, they vary from the nonexistent to the fully developed long-term program.

Most advisors enter the profession without prior experience or training, and the type of training they receive depends upon the advising delivery structure of their institutions and the available resources. Some fortunate advisors will receive formal training that includes classroom-style instruction and interaction with other advisors and administrators dedicated to the training, followed by supplemental, ongoing training, as well as integration into a formal professional development program that offers ongoing support and learning. Others find themselves in the advising chair on their first day of work with a computer and little else. Between these two extremes, variations and incarnations of training scenarios abound.

Many institutions do not dedicate resources for comprehensive training programs, so advisors must embrace self-directed learning options. This chapter provides a framework for constructing training and development opportunities for new advisors regardless of available resources or advising circumstances. It explains the rationale for training that prepares advisors to master informational tasks and to understand both the concepts and relational art of advising as introduced in chapter 1 and articulated in all the other chapters of this *Guidebook*.

A Self-directed Training Plan

The New Advisor Development Chart featured in chapter 1 presents a framework for self-directed training. All comprehensive self-directed training plans include the three components of advising (Habley, 1987, 1995)—conceptual, informational, and relational—delineated in the Chart. Understanding the concepts that form the essence of advising, knowing academic and institutional information, and developing relational skills with students and colleagues all support the development of excellent practice (Habley, 1987). To become a master advisor, a practitioner not only gains proficiency in the foundational advising elements but also applies this knowledge in both predictable and unpredictable situations. As described in previous chapters, especially those in part three and in the New Advisor Development Chart, advisors must grasp the informational components necessary to provide accurate and timely information to students.

Informational Component

New advisors need to learn—or learn how to access—a tremendous amount of information: for example, requirements for majors, course sequences, and general education stipulations. They must also demonstrate functional application of technology tools, institutional policies, and resources for students. They cannot learn all the details in a few weeks or even a few months; in addition, the details will change, so they must continually revisit key topics.

Advisors also will need to discern arcane and rarely used minutia from critical, commonly needed data. Therefore, new advisors should not task themselves with extensive memorization. Instead, they should focus on ascertaining the location of pertinent information they expect to need, ways to organize it (electronically and physically), and opportunities to demonstrate their growing understanding and application of the material.

As the evidence shows (chapters 1, 2, and 12), an academic advisor does not solely help students select the courses required for a particular major or program, and new advisors will quickly discover that helping students develop their potential requires far greater understanding than can be acquired by knowing the basic facts. For example, Dallas needs a calculus course to participate in an advanced physics class. A veteran advisor, Shawn not only knows from memory the course Dallas needs but uses the inquiry as an invitation to ask a few clarifying questions. Dallas had initially declared a biology major, which does not require completion of calculus or advanced physics. Therefore, Shawn asks Dallas to explain this newly identified direction. Although Shawn readily takes the opportunity to learn more about Dallas, a new advisor, Adrian, may understandably use the appointment time to carefully sort through the information on calculus courses to ensure Dallas receives accurate advice. Adrian is appropriately invoking the knowledge gained in training: The advisor must never provide an unresearched answer and must know where to find the vetted source, such as a web site, handout, or other official notification, for answers to student questions. An effective new advisor, such as Adrian, knows and uses resources to answer the student with confidence. This repeated experience will help solidify the information such that, with due time and initiative, Adrian will deftly integrate the facts with the conceptual and relational advising components to help Dallas and others reach their emerging goals.

As illustrated in the scenario of Shawn and Adrian, as advisors develop skills, they better grasp course sequences, prerequisite structures, and specific requirements for each major. Advisors must, in reasonable time and predictable fashion, advance beyond mere proficient use of resources because students rely on more than their explanation of course requirements. Students need advisors' guidance through future semesters of a program of study, and course selection and planning, important parts of advising, do not encompass the conceptual components that advisors must demonstrate to help students reach their ultimate goal of graduation.

Conceptual Component

Knowledge about the functions of advising in higher education and the institution as well as the roles of advising in student academic and mental development comprises the heart of practitioner understanding. When advisors consider their work as integral to the broad developmental processes that promote student growth and success, and when they see it in the context of the academic mission of their institution and unit, they commit to professional development. They specifically seek to learn the skills that extend their abilities to tackle new and unpredictable circumstances. Through self-directed or formal training, they gain confidence confronting challenging situations. For example, when a course fits a particular major but the major appears unsuited for the student, the master advisor provides the proper information but then asks the student thought-provoking questions: "Do you enjoy this type of course?" "Is this major fulfilling your needs and meeting your goals as expected?" Advisors use probing inquiry to help students grapple with deeper questions of goals, motivations, and interests.

A well-designed training plan raises conceptual questions that encourage advisors to take a long view of their work (i.e., beyond imparting facts and picking courses) and appreciate the developmental aspects of student growth (e.g., ways the educational plan contributes to student development). New advisors learn to challenge students to consider their academic program as a holistic experience that builds a broad knowledge base, critical thinking skills, and experiential learning. As advisors push themselves to push their students, it seems increasingly clear that the checklist of requirements is a small part of advising.

In the course of their conversation, Shawn points out that Dallas needs to complete a literature class as part of the general education program. Dallas responds by asking "Why do I have to take a course that has nothing to do with my major? It will be a waste of my time, especially as I need to take more, not less, math and science if I want to go to grad school."

Shawn points out that successful scientists articulate ideas and communicate with others in the field. In addition, scientists must help laypersons understand essential concepts that affect the public sphere. In an alternative approach, Shawn could have answered Dallas with another query: "Why do you think the institution requires the literature course?" Good questions force students to reflect on their concerns from a different perspective.

An advisor may strike a nerve with a provocative question such that a student may reconsider academic choices made to date. For example, perhaps Dallas comes back fully enthralled with the once-hated literature class. Shawn may invoke Chickering and Reisser's (1993) seven vectors of development (chapter 4) to structure conversations that will help Dallas determine whether a science major still meets Dallas's needs.

If Dallas expresses increased anxiety or confusion, Shawn could apply Schlossberg's (1984, 1989) theories of transition and mattering (chapter 4). Armed with good theory, advisors, such as Shawn, will use good relational skills to help students through the inevitable transitions and show that advisees matter.

Relational Skills Component

Training featuring use of conceptually based inquiry and theory provides context to advising as both a practice and a profession. However, gaining the skills needed to invoke useful conceptually based questions may challenge new advisors. Although relational skills can be learned, they are not acquired through memorization or traditional academic study.

In structured training settings, role plays allow participants to experience and practice the techniques and strategies that support and encourage the conceptual and relational components. Colleagues act as students, parents, administrators, and advisors to illustrate and capture the dynamics of an advising appointment. Advisors working solo can ask a supervisor or personnel in human resources to engage in the activities.

The manner of delivery can have a greater impact on students than the information presented, so cultivating relational skills proves as critical as acquiring knowledge and understanding theories. Advisors must develop their listening skills, interviewing techniques, and acumen to nonverbal signals. In response to input from advisees, they must use appropriate words, tone, and expression (chapter 11). Advisors encounter students in challenging circumstances and engage in difficult conversations with them, and without an established level of mutual trust, the advisor risks alienating the student when sharing negative news.

The development and application of relational advising skills require finesse. Individual personalities directly influence the advisor–student dialogue, and particularly in sensitive situations, can strengthen or weaken subsequent communication. The subtleties of good relational skills require trainers to add more complexity to the activities and plans than the straightforward approaches they use to teach factual matters, such as the requirements for a major or a program, or conceptual aspects, such as theory.

Some people exude a welcoming personality that invites conversations; others thrive in task-oriented situations in which they may best deliver advising through modeling and student-learning activities. Conversational and activity-based approaches apply in specific situations (such as group or online advising; chapters 14, 15, and 16), but advisors without a natural affinity for one-to-one interactions must develop their communication skills, in part, to create the type of relationship that inspires student confidence.

In an ideal situation, the advisor has established trust with a student before imparting unwelcome news. To advise students who apply to competitive undergraduate majors or graduate-level programs, practitioners must be prepared to discuss the parallel plan (Bloom, 2008; chapter 5) with students. Therefore, advisors in training must find a way to learn, observe, and discuss relational components such as establishing a respectful relationship, demonstrating trustworthiness, committing to follow-up actions, communicating compassion and sincerity, and undertaking other functional behaviors that implicitly and explicitly show that an advisor takes responsibility and is committed to each advisee's well-being.

Quinn, a pre-medical student with a relatively low GPA, shows no awareness that medical school admission appears highly unlikely. Although new to advising, Ari has been trained in the tools to navigate this situation. Rather than telling Quinn to give up the dream of a career as a physician, Ari asks "What do you know about admission to medical schools?" Quinn's body language indicates surprise at the question. However, after addressing this question and Ari's probing follow-up queries, Quinn starts reassessing the situation. Ari never questions Quinn's performance or potential.

Helping the student identify critical issues through self-reflection, rather than offering a fact-laden lecture, keeps the focus on the issue at hand and prevents the student from shifting blame onto the advisor or others. Furthermore, the advisor's expressed patience, empathy, and sensitivity can make a difficult conversation easier and maintain trust between the advisor and the student.

Just as when learning the conceptual components, new advisors can turn to veteran advisors to work relational aspects into a training plan. For these observations and role plays, advisors ask supervisors, other advisors, or human resources personnel to illustrate a case that deals with difficult interpersonal situations or personalities. By observing real-life interactions or role playing, the new advisor should understand the way nuance and careful word choices can make a difficult conversation more palatable.

Developing a Training Plan

The Nature of Learning

Training needs to accommodate the progressive nature of learning and development. While most training programs fill a few short weeks, or at best, the first year, programs can be designed to function over an extended period to ensure that advisors receive the necessary information and help with honing skills. Although situations vary, advisors typically require as many as three years to achieve complete foundational mastery of all aspects of advising. Therefore, new advisors can expect to encounter new opportunities for personal and professional growth during their first several years, and effective training needs to account for their metamorphosis from novice to artist over time.

Therefore, to support professional development training, the topics and foci must match up with an advisor's progress. New advisors will feel overwhelmed with training that offers too much information too quickly but will tire of rehashing material already learned. Advisors and administrators can use Bloom's revised taxonomy (Anderson et al., 2000) to keep advisors engaged and moving incrementally toward new and more challenging goals (chapter 1). Just as the well-crafted advising session offers the challenge and support necessary for advisee personal and academic growth, well-planned training provides the same for effective advisor development.

Timing of Training

The initial training plan should introduce all of the key concepts of advising. It often focuses on information transfer because advisors need facts germane to the time period when they will see students (e.g., at orientation, before a deadline period, in the beginning of the semester); however, even at the rudimentary stages, training should illustrate the ways all three components come into play in any advising interaction.

Adults in a learning environment express unique educational needs (Joslin, 2010): They prefer training and meetings with direct relevancy and application to their work. In general, they present as "problem-centered learners who want to apply knowledge immediately" (Joslin, 2010, p. 97). These learning characteristics mean that an effective training plan combines timely, consistent, and accurate content with immediate application in advising situations.

Over the course of a year, advisors encounter a cycle of situations that call for unique content, knowledge, and skill requirements. The most effective training addresses a specific topic or situation shortly before the advisor encounters the expected situation. For example, at most institutions a flurry of students show up immediately before the deadline for dropping courses. Therefore, training on these course-drop issues and situations should commence a few weeks before the deadline, not at the same time the advisor must learn about fall orientation or registration.

Information received just in time appeals to adult learners and avoids the overload that characterizes a short-term, intensive program. Advisors putting together their own self-directed training should first meet with other advisors to determine important deadlines and the knowledge necessary to negotiate situations associated with them. Specifically, they ask:

- What do I need to know?
- What relational skills will I need?
- What is my role in these situations?

After the initial training period, advisors should continually revisit topics, especially after gaining time in the chair facing the student in front of them. Although new advisors seldom, if ever, feel fully prepared for their first meetings with students, they will find that this first experience provides a context for the material learned in training: A conversation with students about majors and courses makes the training information relevant and real, bringing clarity and immediacy that role plays in a controlled environment cannot create. In the process, advisors identify areas of insufficient knowledge and understanding exposed by a student's inquiry.

However, complex topics that students present require subsequent training before a new advisor can fully comprehend or address them. In situations beyond the scope of his or her training or experience, the advisor must refer students or consult with veteran advisors as time and circumstances permit.

Key Training Elements

Advisors work with others in centralized centers and independently in departments. Others serve as faculty advisors. Some institutions employ caseload-based assignments with required appointments; other advisors see students as they appear in the doorway. Faculty advisors often see only students in their department or college. Where formal advisor training programs exist, an administrator often designs and oversees training; however, new advisors of any status must engage in self-directed professional development, including on typical training topics. Although a beneficial tool for all advisors regardless of training opportunities, the New Advisor Development Chart (chapter 1), proves most critical for advisors who must entirely self-train.

Goal Setting and Benchmarking

Advisors who work in small units or as the sole advisor in their area may not enjoy the privilege of a training period or easy access to observation experiences (whether as observed or observer). For these advisors, self-reflection through a journal or extensive notes becomes an essential component of their training. If possible, the advisor should also cultivate a mentoring relationship, complete with regular meetings, with a more seasoned advisor. Working with a colleague with even a bit more experience provides a means for discussing problematic situations and past appointments. The collaboration with others ultimately serves the student who presents the immediate concern and who receives follow-ups from the new advisor after the appropriate fact-finding investigations and consultations. Future advisees will benefit from the advisor's ability to convey updated information and employ refined approaches.

Journals provide an opportunity to reflect and to note frustrations and successes; they also allow new advisors to measure their progress toward mastery. As advisors move deeper into the layers of advising complexity, their journal entries will chart their travels through new circumstances and learned approaches. When looking back through their writings, advisors often see the ways their understanding and handling of problems, which had seemed challenging only a few months earlier, have improved.

In addition to a journal, advisors should create a set of goals for themselves. The New Advisor Development Chart (chapter 1) explains realistic expectations for the end of one and three years. Therefore, an advisor should identify a goal in each of the advising components (conceptual, informational, relational) and use the New Advisor Development Chart to document checkpoints in each of these areas. Because new advisors possess various levels of ability, knowledge, and experience, each will choose unique starting points on the Chart. Periodically revisiting these goals and making new ones, advisors who return to the New Advisor Development Chart and Bloom's revised taxonomy (Anderson et al., 2000) can track their progress (chapter 1).

For example, an advisor sets an informational-component goal of learning and understanding the course sequence of a particular major within the first six months in practice. The advisor considers this goal reached when she or he can list the required courses in the proper order and explain the pedagogical reasons for the sequence. After meeting this objective, the advisor seeks to learn the exceptions associated with steps in this sequence and the ways they are handled (e.g., the reasons one may be approved by the department). For example, Harley changes from engineering to business and has completed several advanced math courses that differ from those required for business. Harley's advisor understands that much of the material in the courses overlaps and must ascertain whether substitution, as explained by the business college, will likely be approved. After conducting the appropriate research on exempting the student from the math requirement, Harley's advisor must investigate and communicate the process for pursuing the proper permission from the department.

A goal in the relational area may reflect learning to effectively organize a one-to-one advising session. The advisor with this objective reads chapter 13, and with the Applications and Insights—Conducting Conferences list in hand, watches experienced advisors conducting a session. The advisor then considers the aspects of her or his typical advising session that meet predetermined goals and those that need improvement.

Technology Use

Technology has eased some of the challenges for advisors whose units lack a formal training program. Computers give new advisors easy access to information, webinars, blogs, articles, and advising networks. Institutional web sites contain course information, departmental expectations, institutional policies, degree requirements, support service information, and directories. Learning about and becoming proficient in the use of these resources should be an integral part of any training plan. By systematically reviewing these various resources, new advisors can learn the information needed to advise students. Through observing, debriefing, and conversing with colleagues, viewing online demonstrations, and attending conference presentations, they learn to incorporate the tools into advising sessions with increasing ease.

By maintaining a focus on the conceptual, informational, and relational aspects of practice, new advisors can acquire and apply technology knowledge throughout various aspects of their professional development. For example, a new advisor may learn about a terrific career advising web site and tap into a colleague's knowledge to introduce information to students in the best way and at the best time. Eventually, new advisors too will seamlessly use electronic (and print) tools just like the veterans whom they have observed in practice.

Professional Development Opportunities and Materials

Even institutions that do not provide specific, long-term, or in-depth advising-specific training offer developmental opportunities that benefit new advisors. The topics can vary from managing time to dealing with difficult colleagues to understanding first-generation students. Not every workshop or human resources presentation will focus on topics that seem particularly germane, but advisors should consider the insights they may offer in terms of the relational or conceptual advising components. Some may prove particularly relevant and applicable to an advisor's specific circumstances.

The NACADA: The Global Community for Academic Advising (NACADA) web site and the links featured therein furnish a rich source of advising information that new and experienced advisors find relevant. In particular, the NACADA Clearinghouse of Academic Resources provides useful articles on a wide range of topics— from advising theory to the Family Educational Rights and Privacy Act to first-year students. New advisors will find these articles helpful because they deal with very specific topics that may not be discussed in depth within a department. The web site proves especially helpful to advisors working in isolation as it presents the collective wisdom of experts in specific advising areas.

Effective training programs implement a variety of learning environments. Those in self-directed or limited training programs may particularly benefit from web-based tutorials or printed materials. An excellent training program also includes case studies that describe real-life situations and thus create a context for the information advisors are learning.

Appendix B features sample case studies for use in advisor self-development plans, and following this chapter, Pat Folsom's Voices From the Field—The Case Study: A Powerful Tool in Self-development Plans offers ideas for incorporating case studies into training. NACADA offers video vignettes of common advising situations through which new advisors can witness interactions between advisors and students. The vignettes include discussion questions that encourage new advisors to think about the complexity of advising and ways to approach difficult scenarios.

Training should connect new advisors with other on-campus advisors because critical links to colleagues encourage shared information and advice. These relationships may prove vital for advisors working alone in a department or in their faculty office. As explained in regard to advancing conceptual and relational skills, new advisors gain much from veteran advisors, especially specifically appointed and committed mentors, when facing new and unusual situations.

On-Campus Resources

Regardless of the advising delivery structure (e.g., centralized in one location or in units across campus or at a distance), advisors must integrate into the campus culture. Advisors routinely refer students to people in on-campus offices, and some send them remotely by Internet (chapter 16), to address a wide range of issues. Offices of the registrar, financial aid, counseling, admissions, student health, and residence services as well as the unit that handles petitions for exceptions to institutional policies are among those that students use on a regular basis. Organizational structures may seem obvious to advisors, faculty members, and staff, but students often lack the experience or vocabulary to navigate the system effectively.

Advisors who understand and can communicate the campus organizational structure and personally know people in offices provide students with accurate and easy-to-utilize referral information. Furthermore, personal connections open up lines of communication that ease the transition to a new place or position (a source for information or informal debriefs), introduce potential team members for training or event planning (e.g., brown bag lunch hosts or guests), and identify allies for implementing necessary improvements in policies or procedures that affect students or employees (e.g., committees to address accessibility issues for disabled students or workers).

Knowledge and practical understanding of the campus gives legitimacy for a new advisor among students and colleagues. An advisor who can refer a student and describe in detail the office, its function, and the people with whom he or she will meet may alleviate a student's anxiety about the referral. The advisor demonstrates knowledge that, when proven accurate during the student's visit, builds credibility and trust.

The factors to consider when developing a training plan for oneself or others appear overwhelming. The New Advisor Development Chart (chapter 1) provides the best guide; it can be copied for personal use. The chapters serve as permanent resources for advisors to read and reread as they gain appreciation for the context. As the primary self-development tool, the Chart encourages advisors to set goals and document their achievements. It provides for self-reflection. It challenges. It keeps an advisor on track toward mastering the art of advising.

Sample Self-development Plan

Training provided shortly before an advising activity or event offers information when needed and thus exerts the most impact; therefore, new advisors benefit from creating a year-long calendar featuring important advising deadlines or intense work periods. To identify important advising times, advisors should consult with other campus advisors, supervisors, and institutional calendars (frequently housed with the registrar). A sample calendar is provided in Voices From the Field—Sample Calendar for a Year-Long Self-development Program following this chapter. Although not every institution schedules the advising events as listed in the sample, the noted activities are typical of those found in many institutions.

For each calendar entry, advisors should ask themselves the following questions:

o What do I need to know to complete this advising activity (informational)? The answer enables advisors to search for the appropriate internal and external information and to learn more about their students.

o What is my role in this advising activity (conceptual)? The answer helps advisors pinpoint their fit into their unit and institution. It also encourages reflection on ways theory applies to the specific advising event.

o What skills will I need (relational)? This question addresses process and delivery. Advisors need to identify the communication skills as well as approaches and strategies necessary to advise students in conjunction with the scheduled advising responsibility.

All good questions inspire new ones, and advisors can continue their preparation for specific advising events or time periods by referencing the Aiming for Excellence activities and related queries in most chapters of this *Guidebook*; these compilations by the authors and editors offer advisors ideas and strategies appropriate for using their advising calendar in self-training for scheduled advising responsibilities. During and after participating in the scheduled advising duties, new advisors should note the practices that yielded progress toward self-identified goals and those requiring refinement or replacement.

Armed with data secured from the experience and subsequent assessment of their own effectiveness at meeting objectives, the advisor sets goals for the next scheduled responsibility. In addition to the assessment notes based on the calendar, advisors should refer to their journals and conversations with more experienced advisors or supervisors. They then should apply their insights into the new situations that will require their growing expertise. Because advisors start preparing for one activity as soon as they have fulfilled their most recently scheduled obligations, advisors must deliberately set aside time for journaling and intentional conversations with colleagues. The process of seeking answers to the questions, conducting an appointment or facilitating a group, reflecting on the advising offered, returning to the Chart and Bloom's revised taxonomy (Anderson et al., 2000), then engaging in training activities to prepare for the next recurrence of the event completes a cycle that the advisor must repeat throughout the year for each salient point on the advising calendar.

Advisor Evaluation and Self-assessment

Self-designed training programs must include early and ongoing evaluation and assessment. Early feedback promotes corrective action as needed and provides learning guideposts for the new advisor and supervisor(s) who must understand the effectiveness of the training activities. Informal and formal evaluation can help steer new advisors in the proper direction before they get mired in unhelpful and unproductive practices (chapter 3). Small problems can easily be corrected if caught early.

At a minimum, new advisors should receive a review and evaluation annually. Ideally, during their initial year, their supervising administrator will observe several appointments and review each advisor's overall performance. If not scheduled, advisors can ask for this feedback within the first six months and request that it not constitute part of the formal review. New advisors should seek ongoing conversation and interaction with supervisors; they need the connections with the institution that only their supervisors and colleagues can provide.

In addition to supervisory evaluations, new advisors must conduct self-assessment using resources covered in this chapter. Their journals provide a means for measuring progress toward their goals. A mentor who serves as a sounding board and a source of feedback may offer an informal and perhaps less-threatening assessment than one given by the supervisor. The New Advisor Development Chart and Bloom's learning taxonomy (Anderson et al., 2000) provide easy and sound assessment tools for tracking professional development throughout the first three years. Regardless of the procedure, new advisors should periodically ask three questions that form the cornerstone of the self-development plan: What do I need to know? What role do I play? What skills must I acquire? The answers inform advisor progress, identify challenges, and document plans.

New advisors who wish to assess the effectiveness of their self-directed training activities should begin with the end in mind (Covey, 1990). That is, they develop the competencies necessary to thrive in the advising profession by first identifying the knowledge, actions, and values that define their role at the institution and in the unit. Once the outcomes have been described (based on the mission and goals of the position), the training program can be assessed after six months or one year. For those with responsibility for a program, this evaluation provides information for refining the effort for use by future advisors.

Case Study

Micah has completed a brief initial training program and is preparing to meet with incoming students during summer orientation. A new advisor, Micah cannot possibly advise with the mastery of an experienced advisor, but has looked at the orientation structure, topics, and advising expectations to determine the information needed, the advisor's role in the situation, and the skills most suitable for the meetings with students. Micah sits in the chair knowing the basic information about the majors for the caseload of advisees, feels comfortable with one of the advising approaches introduced in training (Micah identifies readily with the strengths-based approach), and knows that, for now, the role of helping students select courses, providing support, answering basic questions about the curriculum, and presenting a friendly, welcoming face encompasses the extent of the responsibilities expected from this first round of advising experiences.

Specifically, due to the training provided by the unit, Micah feels prepared to answer questions about course sequences, general education requirements, and other general academic questions. Micah realizes that most incoming first-year students, who make up the caseload, will lack familiarity with college curricula and major requirements; they may also feel nervous and worried. Micah, an extrovert who genuinely enjoys young adults, feels most confident in being able to recognize and ameliorate their anxiety.

As expected, Micah used the knowledge and skills acquired in formal training and self-directed research to answer many of the questions that students ask. However, a few advisees presented with unusual circumstances. Rene felt qualified for Honors English, but was told that special permission was needed to enroll in the course. Micah told Rene that more research was required to determine the exact procedure involved and committed to call Rene later in the afternoon with an answer. After the appointment, Micah promptly researched web sites for answers and then, to confirm the accuracy of the determined answer, called the advisor in the English department for confirmation. As a new advisor, Micah felt apprehensive about this first week on the job, but had facilitated positive encounters with and outcomes for students.

In a journal, Micah entered observations and reflections about this first advising experience as situations unfolded. Many entries reflect a sense of unpreparedness that other advisors had said to expect. Micah remembered to outline goals for the next set of advising sessions. (At the end of the year, Micah felt satisfaction and relief upon seeing the progress made during those first few months.)

With the first advising experiences completed, Micah continues to review the New Advisor Development Chart, setting new goals for relational skills to replace the rudimentary ones chosen for the summer. As the final drop deadline nears, Micah is a bit surprised by the number of students contemplating dropping a course. Although Micah has used the information, knowledge, and skill questions to prepare for advising during this period, unusual issues have emerged in several sessions that Micah could not quickly address. For example, several students asked Micah to render an opinion on whether a drop will negatively affect their path to graduation.

Rather than panic over these issues, Micah recalls the words of experienced advisors regarding this trying initial period. Therefore, despite struggles with answers to unanticipated questions, such as those regarding long-term implications of dropping a class or upsetting a sequence of courses within a major, Micah tries not to worry. However, at times, the sense of unpreparedness, to the point of ignorance, compels Micah to reconsider if advising was the best career path.

At times like this, Micah goes back to study the New Advisor Development Chart or seeks support from those who had initially offered encouragement during training. Micah has also started reading advising-related publications and participated in a few NACADA webinars. All these choices reassure Micah that all novice advisors who want to excel and reach master status struggle with similar feelings and concerns.

No advisor will know the answer to every question, and even the experienced practitioner will feel inadequate at times. However, new advisors, in particular, receive important reassurance knowing that their disappointments and limited practice fall into a normal range for all others who advise. Over time, Micah improves upon the self-development processes outlined in this book, tweaking them to match the needs of advisees, the unit, and the institution.

Summary

Self-directed training programs will vary depending upon resources and circumstances, but the content of such endeavors should offer consistent information, guidance, and evaluation. Regardless of the training structure, new advisors should gain an understanding of the three components of academic advising: conceptual, informational, and relational. Although mastery of these keys to advising takes years, successful training plans give advisors the tools to understand the basics of each area such that their progress toward mastery can be benchmarked and evaluated. Training programs should include support and feedback that will help new advisors avoid developing habits that limit their professional development.

Training immediately points new advisors in a productive, challenging, and ultimately satisfying direction. In today's technologically rich environment, any advisor can create a flexible, accessible, and effective training initiative. Students, advisors, and administrators will enjoy the benefits of an effective training program because well-advised students learn the tools to meet their own academic and personal goals.

Advisors should also know that many of the advising skills they acquire during training will continue to develop for years to come. No one learns the art of advising quickly nor reaches perfection, but the developmental process of learning to advise offers rewards and challenges as the benefits of the ongoing endeavor, pursued with vigor and intent, show in students who ultimately identify and reach their own learning goals and persist to graduation.

Aiming for Excellence

- o Keep an advising journal in which you note your successes as well as frustrations. Consider the reasons that certain appointments went well and others were disappointing.

- o Talk through successes and frustrations with a colleague or supervisor. Ask them how they would have handled specific student situations.

- o For charting your development as an advisor, revisit the New Advisor Development Chart at benchmark times, typically 3, 6, 9, and 12 months. At each benchmark, self-identify your status with regard to the conceptual, informational, and relational components of advising and set new goals for mastering each component.

References

Anderson, L. W., Krathwohl, D. R., Airasian, P. W., Cruikshank, K. A., Mayer, R. E., Pintrich, ... Wittrock, M. C. (2000). *A taxonomy for learning, teaching, and assessing: A revision of Bloom's taxonomy of educational objectives.* New York, NY: Pearson, Allyn & Bacon.

Bloom, J. (2008, March). [Parallel plans]. Presented at NACADA Region VII annual meeting, Branson, Missouri.

Chickering, A. W., & Reisser, L. (1993). *Education and identity* (2nd ed.). San Francisco, CA: Jossey-Bass.

Covey, S. R. (1990). *The 7 habits of highly effective people: Powerful lessons in personal change.* New York, NY: Simon & Schuster.

Habley, W. R. (1987). *Academic advising conference: Outline and notes* (pp. 33–34). Iowa City, IA: The ACT National Center for the Advancement of Educational Practices. Retrieved from www.nacada.ksu.edu/Portals/0/Clearinghouse/advisingissues/documents/AcademicAdvisingConferenceOutlineandNotes.pdf

Habley, W. R. (1995). Advisor training in the context of a teaching enhancement center. In R. E. Glennen & F. N. Vowell (Eds.), *Academic advising as a comprehensive campus process* (Monograph No. 2) (pp. 75–79). Manhattan, KS: National Academic Advising Association.

Joslin, J. E. (2010). Interactive group learning. In J. Givans Voller, M. A. Miller, & S. L. Neste (Eds.), *Comprehensive advisor training and development: Practices that deliver* (2nd ed.) (Monograph No. 21) (pp. 97–103). Manhattan, KS: National Academic Advising Association.

Schlossberg, N. K. (1984). *Counseling adults in transition: Linking practice with theory.* New York, NY: Springer.

Schlossberg, N. K. (1989). Marginality and mattering: Key issues in building community. In D. C. Roberts (Ed.), *Designing campus activities to foster a sense of community.* New Directions for Student Services, No. 48 (pp. 5–15). San Francisco, CA: Jossey-Bass.

VOICES FROM THE FIELD

SAMPLE CALENDAR FOR A YEAR-LONG SELF-DEVELOPMENT PROGRAM

Franklin Yoder

This sample year-long self-development program outlines possible components for an initial training period as well as ongoing training activities through the following 11 months. The program also includes advisor development programming in which new advisors can participate alongside experienced advisors. Training schedules and topics will vary depending on advisor responsibilities and when a new advisor assumes the position. Although this template is designed for new advisors for whom academic advising makes up a majority of their contracted duties, faculty advisors will find much within the list that will be helpful, not just in regard to advising duties, but also for getting to know the campus.

Ongoing Weekly or Monthly Activities

- A working partner (more experienced advisor) can answer daily questions and identify topics for ongoing training; therefore, schedule one-to-one training sessions with a supervisor or colleague to address individual training questions and concerns.
- Attend meetings for advisors of specific majors.
- Observe conferences and review record keeping of experienced advisors.
- Have a colleague observe you in a student conference and meet with that person to debrief.
- Regularly check the Aiming for Excellence activities in this book for training ideas.

Adapted with permission from NACADA: The Global Community for Academic Advising: Yoder, F. (2007). Sample year-long advisor training and development program. In P. Folsom (Ed.), *The new advisor guidebook: Mastering the art of advising through the first year and beyond* (Monograph No. 16) (p. 153–156). Manhattan, KS: National Academic Advising Association.

o Revisit and work through case studies to focus on specific training issues and to chart growth.

August

Initial Intensive Training Period

o Set up your office and ensure that you have technology access.

o Become familiar with relevant technology and its application for advising.

o Gain an overview of advising resources: degree audit, handbooks, web sites, and so forth.

o Tour institutional offices.

o Focus on needed advising information: general education program, placement (math, composition, foreign language, and chemistry), major and degree requirements, and institutional enrollment profile.

o Participate with colleagues in exercises that synthesize and apply information: schedule-building exercises, case studies, and role plays.

o Review students in your advising caseload.

o Outline September advising responsibilities.

September

Advising Issues: Dropping and Adding Classes, New Student Advising Meetings

ONGOING TRAINING

o Discuss unusual or difficult student situations with your supervisor or another advisor as needed.

o Connect with advisees and make student planning conference appointments.

o Stay informed on relevant seasonal advising issues, such as add–drop deadlines.

o Outline upcoming October advising responsibilities.

PROFESSIONAL DEVELOPMENT PROGRAM

o Attend a workshop (e.g., White Privilege video).

o Invite other campus offices to present to you and your colleagues (e.g., from the Director of the Office of Student Life).

o Attend advisor-led meetings on specific majors in which you specialize.

October

Seasonal Advising Issues: Student Planning Appointments, Midsemester Reports

ONGOING TRAINING

- Use quizzes, case studies (some from your caseload if applicable), and role plays to address informational and relational issues as well as difficult student situations faced in planning appointments.
- Train on advising responsibilities for students in academic trouble (e.g., those who received midterm grade reports).
- Outline upcoming preregistration advising responsibilities.

PROFESSIONAL DEVELOPMENT PROGRAM

- Connect with colleagues (e.g., on using the knowledge gained from having taught a first-year experience course to improve advising).

November

Seasonal Advising Issues: Drop Deadline, Withdrawal Deadline, Registration

ONGOING TRAINING

- Discuss informational and relational issues as well as difficult student situations with a colleague who has experience with the drop deadline and with registration appointments.
- Discuss with a colleague strategies for how to manage your caseload or student traffic during these busy times.
- Have a colleague review your record keeping and provide feedback.
- Outline upcoming December advising responsibilities.

December

Seasonal Advising Issues: Students Who Cannot Get Courses or Who Register Late

ONGOING TRAINING

- Meet with a supervisor or colleague for feedback on initial and ongoing training.
- Reflect on growth using the New Advisor Development Chart (chapter 1), a journal, exercises, or quizzes.
- Outline upcoming winter break and January advising responsibilities.

PROFESSIONAL DEVELOPMENT PROGRAM
- Schedule an end-of-semester social function with your colleagues.
- Coordinate a common reading with colleagues and discuss relevant issues.

January

Seasonal Advising Issues: Following Up on Grade Reports, Spring Semester Orientation Programs, Drop–Add Period

ONGOING TRAINING
- Have a colleague show you how to review first-semester grade reports, including when to contact students with academic or schedule problems and send congratulatory letters to dean's list students.
- Become familiar with professional growth opportunities and expectations.
- Review formal performance-review process with your supervisor.
- Outline upcoming February advising responsibilities.

February

Seasonal Advising Issues: Planning Appointments, Selective Admissions Follow-Up With Students, Students at Risk

ONGOING TRAINING
- Conduct formal conference observation and record-keeping review for performance appraisal.
- Engage in professional development within the unit or campus by joining committees or specialization groups.

PROFESSIONAL DEVELOPMENT PROGRAM
- Revisit the New Advisor Development Chart (chapter 1). In which areas do you feel progress is being made? Which areas still need work?
- Search the NACADA Clearinghouse of Academic Advising Resources (www.nacada.ksu.edu/Resources/Clearinghouse.aspx) to learn more about topics about which you lack adequate knowledge.
- Visit the events area of the NACADA web site to determine which upcoming NACADA events would be beneficial to your professional development. Talk with your administrator to determine procedures and funding to participate in these events.

March

Seasonal Advising Issues: Differences Between Semester/Term Planning and Working With At-Risk Students

ONGOING TRAINING

- Hold (or encourage) an advisor–supervisor meeting for performance appraisal.
- Attend group or individual training on registration procedures for summer session and the fall term.
- Engage in professional development activities outlined in February.
- Outline upcoming advising issues.

PROFESSIONAL DEVELOPMENT PROGRAM

- Schedule an advising workshop (e.g., a 2-hour session on "How to Listen So Others Will Talk").
- Continue to develop in the areas identified last month, returning to the New Advisor Development Chart (chapter 1) to evaluate progress.

April

Seasonal Advising Issues: Registration for Summer Session and Fall Term, Sending Students to Departments for Advising

ONGOING TRAINING

- Outline upcoming May advising responsibilities.

PROFESSIONAL DEVELOPMENT PROGRAM

- Continue to develop in the areas identified in February, returning to the New Advisor Development Chart (chapter 1) to evaluate progress.

May

Seasonal Advising Issues: Sending Students to Departments, Preparing for Summer Orientation Programs

ONGOING TRAINING

- Take the opportunity to reflect on professional growth using the New Advisor Development Chart (chapter 1), journal, and exercises.
- Attend intensive group or individual training (multiple sessions) on summer orientation programs for entering students: structure, responsibilities, preparation, review of placement, and advising role in orientation.
- Outline upcoming June advising responsibilities.

PROFESSIONAL DEVELOPMENT PROGRAM

○ Attend advisor meeting to debrief on spring semester advising issues and discuss potential changes in upcoming summer orientation.

○ Continue to develop in the areas identified in February, returning to the New Advisor Development Chart (chapter 1) to evaluate progress.

June

Seasonal Advising Issues: Grade Report Review, Summer Orientation Programs

ONGOING TRAINING

○ Complete intensive orientation-training sessions.

○ Debrief after first several orientation programs with trainer or working partner.

○ Have a supervisor or colleague review your orientation conference notes and course placement.

○ Observe experienced advisors giving presentations to students and parents.

PROFESSIONAL DEVELOPMENT PROGRAM

○ Revisit the New Advisor Development Chart (chapter 1). In which areas have you made the most improvement since February? Which areas still need work? Set professional development goals for the upcoming months.

○ Determine the types of development activities that will help you achieve your desired professional development goals.

July

Seasonal Issues: Orientation Programs for Entering First-Year Students

ONGOING TRAINING

○ Continue individualized debriefings as appropriate.

○ Hold final training and orientation debriefing to assess the first year of training and the specialized orientation training.

○ Develop goals for your second year.

PROFESSIONAL DEVELOPMENT PROGRAM

○ Attend an advisor workshop on difficult advising cases.

○ Continue to develop in the areas identified in June, returning to the New Advisor Development Chart (chapter 1) to evaluate progress.

VOICES FROM THE FIELD

THE CASE STUDY: A POWERFUL TOOL
IN SELF-DEVELOPMENT PLANS

Pat Folsom

A case study is one of the most powerful and versatile experiential learning tools in a new advisor's self-development plan. It offers advisors the opportunity to test their knowledge, consider their advising role in a specific situation, and try various advising approaches in a safe environment.

Case studies present real or hypothetical academic advising scenarios to illustrate typical advising situations or showcase specific issues that emerge in advising appointments. They provide facts and a narrative background on a specific student, which advisors use to identify the salient issues of an advising session. The advisors then describe orally, in writing, or through role play with others possible ways to conduct the session. They specifically identify the information to acquire, questions and approaches to employ, and referrals to make.

Through their engagement with case studies, new advisors synthesize and apply their skills and knowledge. Advisors employ case studies to practice

- applying advising approaches in specific situations.
- identifying theories that inform the advisor about a student or circumstance.
- identifying potential ethical and legal issues.
- generating ways to make students feel welcome.
- explaining clearly relevant policies and course descriptions.
- developing questioning techniques and referral skills.
- exploring their self-knowledge in a specific context.

Case studies also offer new advisors the means to take stock of their place in the development process and to chart their growth. Through case studies advisors can

- identify knowledge gaps and then seek activities or resources for further training and development.
- seek feedback from colleagues or supervisors on their responses to the scenario.
- compare and discuss responses with more experienced advisors.

o after several months work through the same case study without referring to their first responses until after documenting the new thoughts on the case; this process demonstrates tangible evidence of their growth.

Advisors may effectively approach detailed and complex narratives through a standard set of questions that creates a framework for focusing on salient facts and identifying critical issues. The questions also prepare advisors to identify the most appropriate follow-up inquiries, advising approaches, and potential referrals for the case. The Academic Advisor Certification Program at the University of Houston (Folsom, 2007, p. 165) offers such a set of questions:

1. What does the information given tell you about what might be issues for the student and what type of help he or she might need?

2. What do you want to know about this student and why? What are possible issues with this student that need to be addressed?

3. How do we go about helping this student?

4. What type of approach do you want to take with this student and why?

5. What are some of the referrals that might be made? What are some of the things you consider when determining whether or not the student is ready for these referrals?

6. What is the most effective way to make the referrals?

7. What university policies need to be explained to this student?

Appendixes B2 and B3 feature case studies on which readers can practice using this set of questions. Active engagement with case studies such as those featured in the appendixes and throughout the book offer powerful preparation to new advisors when facing students. In addition, case studies provide valuable benchmarks for those working toward mastering the art of advising.

Reference

Folsom, P. (2007). University of Houston: Academic advisor certification program: Case studies. In P. Folsom (Ed.), *The new advisor guidebook: Mastering the art of advising through the first year and beyond* (Monograph No. 16) (p. 165). Manhattan, KS: National Academic Advising Association.

Applications and Insights
Strategies for Handling Stress

- Laugh with colleagues.
- Talk to colleagues.
- Take a walk.
- Practice relaxation techniques: deep breathing, visualization, yoga, stretches.
- Celebrate both big and small happenings with your colleagues.
- Belong to a professional organization, such as NACADA, and attend a conference.
- Block off a lunch period.
- Keep a journal.
- Exercise.
- Take it day-by-day and appointment by appointment.
- Develop outside of work activities that bring relaxation: exercise, hobbies, travel.
- Take some time during the day to unwind: Close the door and read the paper, listen to music, do a crossword or Sudoku puzzle.
- Talk to other advisors and administrators to express concerns and frustrations.
- Keep organized.
- Have a realistic perspective of your job and yourself; no one can be everything to everybody.
- Keep things in perspective and recognize that even the busiest time in the advising cycle will end.

Reprinted with permission from NACADA: The Global Community for Academic Advising: Folsom, P. (2007). Strategies for handling stress. In P. Folsom (Ed.), *The new advisor guidebook: Mastering the art of advising through the first year and beyond* (Monograph No. 16) (p.152). Manhattan, KS: National Academic Advising Association.

Appendix A

Higginson's Informational Framework

In the first edition of *Academic Advising: A Comprehensive Handbook,* Linda Higginson (2000) identified four substantive groups that apply to the informational component of advising:

Internal institutional structures and functions "are in place to carry through the educational mission" of the institution (p. 303). Topics related to internal information include

> advising technology . . . accommodations for students with disabilities . . . academic
> information programs . . . cocurricular opportunities . . . course availability . . . degree
> program curricular requirements . . . policies and procedures . . . referral sources . . .
> registration procedures . . . and use of information sources such as transcripts and . . .
> standardized tests. (p. 303)

External environment concerns encompass "the higher education community, the local community surrounding the campus, and the broad world of work." Advisors need to familiarize themselves with "service learning experiences; employment outlook projections; professional associations and disciplinary societies; opportunities for graduate and professional continuing education; referral and information sources and services" (p. 304).

Student needs inform advisors about specific topics they must learn to help advisees in their personal and academic growth. For effective practice, advisors must gain knowledge about "universal student characteristics" as well as those related to each student. Topics to learn include students' "career and personal decision making, evaluation of multiple options, learning style, effective learning strategies . . ." as well as general areas such as "special population issues . . . test preparation strategies, and time management" skills (p. 304).

Self-knowledge reflects developing insights into the attitudes, beliefs, and knowledge that advisors bring to their working relationships. To develop self-knowledge, advisors should ask themselves

> What attitudes do I have about student behavior—about alcohol use, sexual involve-
> ment, and academic dishonesty? What knowledge and beliefs do I possess about inde-
> cision . . . of [a] major? What do I know and believe and what are my attitudes about
> students? (p. 304)

Reference

Higginson, L. C. (2000). A framework for training program content. In V. N. Gordon & W. R. Habley (Eds.), *Academic advising: A comprehensive handbook* (1st ed.) (pp. 298–307). San Francisco, CA: Jossey-Bass.

APPENDIX B

CASE STUDY TOOLBOX

Appendix B1

CASE STUDY REVIEW QUESTIONS

University of Houston Academic Advisor Certification Program

Case Study Review Questions

With each case study consider, make notes, and speak about the following questions:

1. What does the information given tell you about what might be issues for the student and what type of help he or she might need?

2. What do you want to know about this student and why? What are possible issues with this student that need to be addressed?

3. How do we go about helping this student?

4. What type of approach do you want to take with this student and why?

5. What are some of the referrals that might be made? What are some of the things you consider when determining whether or not the student is ready for these referrals?

6. What is the most effective way to make the referrals?

7. What university policies need to be explained to this student?

Reprinted with permission from NACADA: The Global Community for Academic Advising: Folsom, P. (2007). University of Houston: Academic advisor certification program: Case studies. In P. Folsom (Ed.), *The new advisor guidebook: Mastering the art of advising through the first year and beyond* (Monograph No. 16) (p. 165). Manhattan, KS: National Academic Advising Association.

Appendix B2

USING CASE STUDIES WITH A
SAMPLE EXERCISE

In this exercise, the University of Houston Academic Advisor Certification Program case study review questions (Folsom, 2007a, p. 165) guide a first-person discussion of The University of Iowa case study "Career Path" (Folsom, 2007b, p. 161), reprinted with permission from NACADA: The Global Community for Academic Advising. Case studies require advisors to ask questions, raise issues, and engage in problem solving with respect to specific advising situations. Advisors, depending on their experience and advising responsibilities, will take diverse approaches to problem solving for the scenario. The case highlighted in this appendix represents just one sample of the many possible ways to work through the case study.

Career Path

The Advising Center secretary tells Bill that Denise Butler has called to make an "emergency" appointment, even though it's finals week. "She said it was important," the secretary says, "so I brought you her folder. She'll be here in an hour." Bill reviews the folder. Denise, from a medium-sized high school, came to college as a pre-med major. Her ACT scores were English 18, Math 16, Reading 19, Science 19, with a Composite of 19 (SAT 860–880). She placed into remedial college algebra and took it the first semester but did not do well. She "couldn't understand the foreign teaching assistant." Denise complained bitterly that the situation was badly affecting her grade. Bill had referred Denise to the Math Department, where she was able to make a section change. Her grade still suffered, however, and unable to find a tutor and frustrated with the math lab, Denise ended up with a D– in the course.

In spring semester, Bill met with Denise frequently. At each meeting she had tentatively decided on a new major: first pre-dentistry, then pre-nursing, then pre-business. "I want something that's going to pay well; I can't see myself being poor," Denise reported.

At her spring registration appointment, Denise seemed to be settling in. She reported B's in her spring courses (general education), had visited the career development center, seemed firmly committed to a pre-business curriculum, and signed up for microeconomics and a business calculus course. There was "no way" she was going back to retake the algebra course in hopes of improving

---

the original grade. "I was good in math in high school," Denise reported. "If this school would get more American teaching assistants it would make a big difference."

Before long, Denise arrives, out of breath. "I really wanted to see you before I go home," she says. "You're going to kill me, but . . ." She's decided to change career paths, she reports.

Bill waits. He's thinking maybe she's decided to go back to pre-nursing (the choice before pre-business) after all. "That's fine," Bill says smiling. "Tell me what you have in mind."

"Well, I went to the Career and Placement Office again and did some more reading, and I think I really found what I'd like to do."

"Which is?" Bill asks.

"I really want to be a judge," Denise says.

Case Study Questions and Responses

What does the information given tell you about what might be issues for the student and what type of help he or she might need?

The case study raises several important advising issues. The student, Denise, apparently lacks information about careers as well as a framework or approach for making decisions. In addition, she appears to operate from an external locus of control; that is, she attributes her grade in math to forces outside of her control and does not choose majors based on personal strengths. Denise's comments regarding math indicate that her development may be categorized as dualistic (Perry, 1968), and she needs to advance her intellectual and emotional competence (Chickering & Reisser, 1993). She also may be at risk of leaving school because of her inability to realistically identify goals and her poor performance in a math class necessary to meet any of her articulated career goals.

What do you want to know about this student and why?

I want to compare Denise's entering academic record with the typical student profile created by the institution based on demographic data. The institutional profile will give me a good idea about the level of academic challenge Denise may expect from the students in her classes and the level of academic support she might need. Before tackling the discussion of calculus, I want to know more about Denise's frustration with the math lab, which may also reveal her stage of personal development. I also want to know Denise's grades in other classes. A course-by-course review of her academic achievement would enable me to discuss her academic strengths as we explore her sense of herself as well as her academic and career options.

I also want to know Denise's decision-making process for choosing majors. Is she taking advice from other students or her parents? Is she simply looking at income? What other factors does she consider important? Her answers to these questions will tell me about the developmental and decision-making support she needs. I can use Denise's input to determine the best advising approach to take. In addition, by answering these questions, Denise will be forced to think through her actions and decisions—important for her personal and academic growth. Finally, I want to hear her recollections of the career development center. Did she use resources, do an assessment, or meet with a career advisor?

I need more information about Denise the person too: her family (e.g., is she a first-generation student?), ways she spends her free time, as well as her social interactions, friendships, and involvement with on-campus activities. Knowing her preferences may help us work through decisions about majors, and (I hope) create a better advising relationship that will benefit Denise in the future.

What are possible issues with this student that need to be addressed?

To explore the numerous issues about majors, grades, and decision making I will need to schedule a number of advising sessions. I intend to start the sessions by addressing intellectual competence and decision-making capacities because their advancement will positively influence the solutions to the specific problems associated with grades and program of study.

How do we go about helping this student? What type of approach do you want to take with this student and why?

I could use Virginia Gordon's (2006) 3-I Model with Norman Amundson's (2003) five lines of questioning, as introduced by Dorothy Burton Nelson in chapter 7, or the more general decision-making process from Mind Tools (2015, ¶5) explained by Marsha Miller in Voices From the Field—Teaching the Decision-Making Process in chapter 13. I definitely would consider the Arthur Chickering and Linda Reisser (1993) questioning techniques described by Kim Roufs (chapter 4). I could also use strength-based advising (Schreiner, 2013) and possibly motivational interviewing (Hughey & Pettay, 2013) as Jayne Drake summarizes in chapter 12.

In narrowing down the choices of approach, I'm struck by Denise's flawed career-related decision making; she clearly lacks a specific paradigm or process for choosing. Therefore, I would first invoke the decision-making strategy from Mind Tools (2015, ¶5) and follow the strengths-based approach, which Denise can apply to multiple facets of her life. After we have established Denise's strengths and a baseline decision-making framework, I will probe deeper through Gordon's (2006) 3-I model using Amundson's (2003) five questions. Throughout our meetings, I will document Denise's progress in development through Chickering and Reisser's (1993) vectors, employing motivational interviewing if she resists changing her locus of control.

What are some of the referrals that might be made? What are some of the things you consider when determining whether or not the student is ready for these referrals? What is the most effective way to make referrals? What university policies need to be explained to this student?

I believe Denise would benefit more from the career center than in the past and thus will recommend multiple visits over time. For example, I would refer her to meet with a career advisor for an occupational assessment (e.g., *John Holland's Self-Directed Search* [PAR, Inc., 2013]) because the results could support my strengths-based approach. As we progress toward a defined direction for her major, I will suggest that Denise return to the career center to learn how to use its resources for researching various occupations. I might refer her for internship information and to learn resume writing and prepare for job interviews. For all referrals, I will describe the services, collaborate with Denise to develop a list of questions to keep the meetings or research on a specific goal, and provide a standard form on which she could write the results of her research or meetings.

In our discussion about math, I will explain to Denise the prerequisite structure for math courses as well as policies for retaking a course.

References

Amundson, N. E. (2003). *Active engagement: Enhancing the career counseling process* (2nd ed.), Richmond, BC, Canada: Ergon Communications.

Chickering, A. W., & Reisser, L. (1993). *Education and identity* (2nd ed.). San Francisco, CA: Jossey-Bass.

Folsom, P. (2007a). University of Houston: Academic advisor certification program: Case studies. In P. Folsom (Ed.), *The new advisor guidebook: Mastering the art of advising through the first year and beyond* (Monograph No. 16) (p. 165). Manhattan, KS: National Academic Advising Association.

Folsom, P. (2007b). The University of Iowa, case studies: Career path. In P. Folsom (Ed.), *The new advisor guidebook: Mastering the art of advising through the first year and beyond* (Monograph No. 16) (p. 161). Manhattan, KS: National Academic Advising Association.

Gordon, V. N. (2006). *Career advising: An academic advisor's guide.* San Francisco, CA: Jossey-Bass.

Hughey, K., & Pettay, R. (2013). Motivational interviewing: Helping students initiate change in student behaviors. In J. K. Drake, P. Jordan, & M. A. Miller (Eds.), *Academic advising approaches: Strategies that teach students to make the most of college* (pp. 67–82). San Francisco, CA: Jossey-Bass.

Mind Tools. (2015). *How to make decisions.* Retrieved from http://www.mindtools.com/pages/article/newTED_00.htm

PAR, Inc. (2013). *John Holland's self-directed search (SDS).* Retrieved from http://www.self-directed-search.com/

Perry, W. G., Jr. (1968). *Forms of intellectual and ethical development in the college years: A scheme.* New York, NY: Holt, Rinehart, and Winston.

Schreiner, L. A. (2013). Strengths-based advising. In J. K. Drake, P. Jordan, & M. A. Miller (Eds.), *Academic advising approaches: Strategies that teach students to make the most of college* (pp. 105–120). San Francisco, CA: Jossey-Bass.

Appendix B3

SAMPLE CASE STUDIES

University of Houston

Academic Advisor Certification Program Case Studies

Case Study 1: Lisa   Lisa is a first time freshman in July orientation. She indicates that she wants to be a biology major. Her SAT math score is 400 and her verbal score is 410. She will need to take remedial course work in math and English. She is anxious to schedule her classes because she is afraid classes are filling up.

Case Study 2: Robert   Robert is an 18-year-old student who transferred last semester to the 4-year university. Records show 18 semester hours with a 3.0 GPA from a local community college. Last semester at the university he earned two failing grades and an incomplete. He was exempt from TSI [Texas Success Initiative (admissions testing)] due to high SAT scores. He lists himself as a communications major. He comes to the advisor to discuss his classes for the next semester.

Case Study 3: Sam   Sam began his university studies as an electrical engineering major and was suspended. He was readmitted as USD [University Studies Division (for undeclared students)] and intended to pursue a business degree. However, his cumulative GPA is 2.00 instead of the 2.75 required for admission into the business program. He now has a USD dean's stop because he has earned 60 hours and must declare a major to enroll.

Sam took career assessment tests that showed he had an interest in social sciences. He took a variety of classes in the College of Liberal Arts and Social Sciences [CLASS] but could not narrow his focus. He has interest in non-CLASS majors as well. He is concerned about majoring in a social science because he will need to go to graduate school to earn enough salary for

Reprinted with permission from NACADA: The Global Community for Academic Advising: Folsom, P. (2007). University of Houston: Academic advisor certification program: Case studies; University of Alaska Fairbanks: Case Study; The University of Iowa: Case Studies. In P. Folsom (Ed.), *The new advisor guidebook: Mastering the art of advising through the first year and beyond* (Monograph No. 16) (pp. 160–165). Manhattan, KS: National Academic Advising Association.

his desired standard of living. Based on his GPA, graduate school may not be an option. He is desperate to complete his degree. He is also currently working 35 hours a week.

Sam is seeking advice about his options.

University of Alaska Fairbanks

Case Study

Case Study 1 Advisee:

Freshman Fall 2005 admit

Female

21 years old

No known disabilities

Fairbanks

Commutes to campus from her apartment

Alaska native

Works 20 to 25 hours a week at Denny's Restaurant

Financial aid package

Fall Schedule

17 Credits

ENGL 111X Midsemester Grade of F

MATH 107X Midsemester Grade of F

HIST 100X Midsemester Grade of D

ANTH 100X Midsemester Grade of D

BIOL 105X Midsemester Grade of B

The student wants to withdraw from ENGL and MATH and add two late-drop courses.

Case Study 2 Advisee:

Fall 2003 admit

Male

23 years old

Lives in residence hall

White (Caucasian)

Probation Fall 2003

Fall 2004 and Spring 2005

Completed 27 credits (Freshman)

2.00 overall GPA

Enrolled 13 credits Fall 2006

Mid-semester grades Fall 2006 F, C, F, C

The student needs to register for spring 2006 courses.

The University of Iowa

Case Studies

Father and Son When fall midterm grade notices came out, Buster Brown showed F's in every course in which he was enrolled. Jack, his advisor, waded through the loud music on Buster's answering machine to leave several messages, but Buster did not call back until a week after the deadline for dropping courses. He told Jack there had been an unexpected death in his immediate family, but now that he was back on campus and had a chance to talk with his instructors, he was sure things would be okay. Jack expressed sympathy and outlined Buster's options (repeating the course in hopes of improving the grade, withdrawal) and asked him to keep in touch.

Buster came to see Jack 2 weeks later, saying he wanted to withdraw his registration because he was too far behind and certain to fail all his courses. Jack explained procedures and asked him to confer with his parents.

Several days later, Dr. Hightower, Buster's father called. He informed Jack he was a professor in the Department of Psychiatry at the college of medicine elsewhere and wanted to know why Jack was advising his son to "drop out of school."

Jack explained that the Family Educational Rights and Privacy Act (FERPA) prevented discussion of the particulars of his son's case, but said he could explain the withdrawal procedure and the typical reasons why an advisor might suggest that a student withdraw his or her registration. Dr. Hightower said, "I understand completely. We have that at my school too. But we're both university people so we can ignore the Buckley Amendment." Jack reiterated that he'd need Buster's consent before discussing his case, but that he'd be happy to listen to anything Dad might want to say. He learned that Buster was Dad's stepson, had had a weak academic record in high school, had gotten into the "scrapes with authorities" that are typical of adolescent rebellion. Jack got Buster back into the office that day and explained the conversation with his father, and Buster immediately gave Jack permission in writing to discuss Jack's situation with his father. Jack appreciated Buster's consent, because he felt it would prevent Buster playing him off against his father; Buster could no longer claim Jack was making him drop out.

When Dr. Hightower phoned back later that day, Jack remembered his customer service training and was quick to say, "I'm sorry about the death in your family. It seems to have upset Buster." There was a silence on the other end of the line.

"What death?" said Dr. Hightower. The phone line hummed.

"You mean no one died?" Jack said. "Uh. Let's talk about academic support." Dr. Hightower seemed grateful to have some information, saying he knew they could work together to help Buster succeed.

Buster came back in January, very thankful to be back on campus. He seemed to understand that he'd been given the opportunity to start over, a second chance. Jack helped him choose courses carefully; they came up with an interesting schedule well suited to Buster's interests and abilities.

Every 2 to 3 weeks Buster came to see Jack to discuss his academic progress. They discussed topics he was studying and projects he was doing in his classes, long-range plans, and academic goals. His father also called once a month and Jack always reviewed these conversations with Buster. When Buster came to register for the following fall, he said he thought he'd get all A's and B's. "Okay," thought Jack, "there is hope." But when he got Buster's grades he saw straight F's. Jack checked the computer and discovered that Buster had bounced a check for [a] University bill.

Sean   Sean arrived at the university with an ACT composite of 31 and was admitted to the honors program. He came from a large high school and at summer orientation expressed an interest in political science. He said that while in high school he spent a lot of time volunteering at a local hospital and enjoyed helping people. He was personable although not especially outgoing.

Sean came to his initial meeting in September but did not return for his next scheduled appointment in October. He received midsemester notices of D's in philosophy, composition, and beginning French. When called, he said things were going well and he did not want to drop any classes. A few weeks later, Sean came in to register and he said things were still fine. When grades came out, Sean received an A in marching band, an A– in political science, and failed his philosophy, composition, and French courses.

Sean did not make a planning appointment second semester. He came in to drop two courses. When asked about the first semester, he said he had lost interest in several of his classes but things are going better now. Once he gets rid of these two classes, things will be fine. He said he would be back to plan for fall semester but he never returned. It is near the end of a long day during registration and the advisor just received a message that Sean has dropped in to be cleared to register.

What should the advisor say to Sean when he is squeezed in between the 3:20 and 4:00 appointment? What should Sean be told if he returns for a longer appointment? How can he be convinced that these appointments are important?

Trevor It is late on orientation day and Bill is about ready to see his final advising appointment, an entering first-year student. It's been a long day. Several complicated student cases have led to delays in each successive appointment. As he reviews again the folder for this final student, he notes that the situation seems to be fairly routine.

Trevor Johnson is a first-year student from a large Iowa high school. He is an exploratory major. He has no Advanced Placement or CLEP credit and straight-forward test scores: an ACT composite of 24 (the institutional average). At 19, the ACT Math subscore may be a problem. "Well, if Trevor's not interested in a math or science major, we can wait on the quantitative and formal reasoning general education requirement," thinks Bill. Trevor's high school class rank is a little below average: 190 out of 325 students. He had taken a fair amount of French in high school. Bill begins to imagine a schedule that will help Trevor ease into college: rhetoric (required) and a few general education courses—perhaps sociology, a historical perspective, or possibly a third semester of French, depending on his foreign language placement test score.

Trevor arrives, completed trial class schedule in hand. He's eager, wired. His eyes have a certain level of intensity about them. He begins to talk about his many interests: languages, travel, and skateboarding. Bill glances at the trial class schedule Trevor has placed on the table in front of him and reads it upside down, noting with dismay that the list of courses includes some surprises: Calculus I, Computer Science I, and first-year Russian! Bill realizes that Trevor hasn't stopped talking. "Anthropology is probably my first love," Trevor says, "so I'm going on a dig next summer." Trevor keeps talking as Bill nods and shifts the trial class schedule to read the rest of the list: upper level French and a history course. No rhetoric to be found. That makes 18 s.h. [semester credit hours] on his primary schedule when the limit for entering first-year students is 16 s.h. First-year Japanese and Hindi are on his course alternates list.

When Bill finally gets a word in and is able to ask a few questions, he finds that Trevor completed three semesters of high school French and performed at C level. His foreign-language placement test suggests that a review course is in order. Trevor admits to not being a "math guy" but is interested in computer science and will likely double major or minor in it—hence the calculus and computer science courses. Trevor notes that rhetoric just "didn't fit in my schedule," and says he's to do that second semester. Oh, and by the way, he's always wanted to learn Russian; he couldn't wait to get to the university to be able to take that course. Bill nods, sighs, and thinks about where to begin.

John   John is very upbeat at orientation. His high school academic profile is not outstanding, but his grades and test scores do not raise any red flags. John indicates that he would like to plan on a 5-year graduation plan with a more relaxed load each semester. John seems very happy with his first semester schedule that includes rhetoric, a history course, and a political science class. Two weeks into the semester his advisor, Mary, receives a form from the Student Disability Services office. Mary reads the form with a sinking feeling; apparently John has learning disabilities and will find challenging courses, among others, with heavy reading loads, heavy analytical content, and multiple choice tests. Mary is relieved to see that not all the challenges boxes are checked. She thinks back to orientation when John told her "I LOVE to read and history is my favorite subject!"

Mary begins to think about how to advise John. His interests are in history, political science, and philosophy. All of these areas will involve heavy reading schedules, yet this is where John indicates he will be happiest. Mary wonders if the extra year will provide the cushion John needs.

Mark   Loren is meeting with Mark, a student athlete, to discuss courses for the upcoming semester. Mark is an art major. During the conference, Mark reports being disgusted by his colloquium professor. When Loren asks why, Mark shouts "Because he is gay!" Colloquium is a required course that Mark cannot drop.

About 10 minutes are left in the appointment when Mark divulges this information and the two of them still need to finalize course selection. How should Loren work with Mark?

[Loren believes it is important to use some of that time to ask clarifying questions about Mark's comments.] Mark decides to deal with the situation and when Loren next meets with him, Mark says that he has enjoyed colloquium and has really enjoyed working with the professor. However, in the subsequent semester, during the third week of classes, Mark is in Loren's office to discuss dropping another art class because "the professor is queer."

What approach should Loren take with Mark? Are referrals appropriate? What if Loren is an advisor who identifies as lesbian, gay, bisexual, transgendered?

Second Language   Dot met Win at a transfer orientation program right before classes began in the fall. He had immigrated to the United States from Vietnam five years earlier and was coming to the university with an associates of arts degree from a community college. His grades were good: A's and B's in Intermediate Algebra, Fundamentals of Communication, Pre-Calculus I, Composition I, Elementary French, and Introduction to Philosophy. He also did well in five racquetball and weight conditioning physical education classes. He received D's in General Chemistry, Macroeconomics, and Calculus II.

Win was full of energy, speaking rapidly, smiling, and nodding at everything Dot said. When Dot asked him about his interests, she had difficulty understanding his pronunciation. Win tried to explain where he was working, repeating the name of the business several times. "Is it a restaurant?" Dot asked. "A store?" Win talked on, describing his life, and Dot had the sinking feeling that she understood about 1 in every 10 words.

Dot registered Win for Engineering Calculus and Principles of Chemistry. She referred him to the College of Engineering for permission to take the Engineering I course. She also explained that Win's English language skills would be evaluated by the English as a Second Language (ESL) program. Win nodded.

Three days later, Win returned without having obtained permission to enroll in Engineering I. He had his ESL report with him: He was required to take all five English classes. The evaluator had written, "Difficult to evaluate grammar due to pronunciation," with an exclamation point. Dot explained they would need to make room in Win's schedule for at least two of the ESL courses: pronunciation and grammar.

At midsemester, Win was doing less than satisfactory work in both his calculus and chemistry courses. He wanted to drop the chemistry and concentrate on calculus. This proved to be a good idea, because he eventually earned a B– in it. Dot also was delighted that Win also earned a B– in ESL Pronunciation, and a C+ in ESL Grammar.

Win wanted to attempt Principles of Chemistry again in the spring. Based on his fall grades, he obtained permission to take Engineering I. He also registered for the next three ESL courses. Dot began to relax.

In a week, Win returned, wanting to drop ESL Conversation and add Engineering Statistics. Dot told him he could not drop any ESL course, a university rule. He was not happy about this, saying "But it is a waste of my time." Dot explained that he needed to keep his grades up to be admitted to Engineering and that the ESL courses also would help him communicate more clearly. She added, "I often have difficulty understanding you. Do you understand me most of the time?" Win nods.

Win returns three days later, very upset. He has had a car accident. It takes a long time for him to explain this to Dot. He has many bills, he explains, but has quit his job to devote himself full-time to school. He feels depressed. "I have no friend," he says.

Dot tries to sort all this out. She calls the Office of Services for International Students, only to discover that Win is not classified as an international student. She refers him to an office offering academic support services for minority students and to the Financial Aid office. She realizes that she should have referred him to those offices long ago.

Win comes back to see Dot, having arranged for tutoring and having obtained additional loans. He wants to drop Engineering I and add two physical education classes. He is vehement about wanting Tae Kwon Do. This is the one class he really wants! He says sadly that when he is in trouble there is nowhere to turn. Dot feels alternately sympathetic and exasperated with him. She then suggests local churches, the organization of campus ministries, social service agencies, Vietnamese student organizations, and the university counseling service. "It sounds as though you need support, understanding, and someone to talk to. Someone who is more qualified than I am to help you." Win nods. Dot writes down a list of phone numbers for him.

Three days later, Win is back. He waves a drop slip at Dot and says very loudly that it is absolutely necessary for him to drop the ESL conversation class. Dot tells him that even if she were to sign the slip, he would not be able to get the other required signature: Students are not allowed to drop ESL courses. Win says he cannot continue because the instructor hates him. "She gives me low grades because of the color of my skin," he says. Dot says, more adamantly, that Win needs this course very much and that ESL instructors teach people of all colors. He says he is absolutely not going to return to class: "No, no and finally, NO!" Dot watches his face through all this. She sees that he now regards her as part of his many problems.

INDEX

A

Academic advising: approaches to, 95; communications in teaching and, 234; components and competencies in, 6–8, 96; concept of, 96; creating welcoming atmosphere for, 265; defining, 41; developing skills for, 9–11; educational malpractice claims related to, 165–166; encouraging student self-exploration, 88; ethics for, 55–56; foundation for, 51–52; global context for legal issues, 168–170; history of, 39–41; identity development and, 71–74; is teaching, 40, 95, 233–235; knowledge required for, 4–6; learning taxonomy for, 11–12; mastering art of, 3–4, 8, 9–11, 15; milestones for, 137–138; mission and vision for, 42–43; NACADA Pillars of Academic Advising, 42, 99; New Advisor Development Chart for, 8–9; organizational structures for, 45–46; personal philosophy of, 91–94, 99; practical techniques for, 247; promoting professional status of, 47–48; reporting channels for, 44–45; self-authorship for students, 75–76, 100, 242–244; shared responsibilities of advisor and advisee in, 68–69; Socratic, 100; strategies of, 100, 231–232; student departure theories, 71; student success and, 46–47, 132–134, 191, 193, 196, 198, 206–207; technology used in, 114; theory of student involvement, 70–71; using faculty for, 126–128; wiki for, 114. *See also* Advising delivery models; Career advising
Academic Advising Approaches (Drake, Jordan, and Miller), 47, 231–232, 235–237, 239, 242, 243–244, 245
Academic Advising for Student Success (Frost), 251
Academic Advising (Gordon, Habley, and Grites), 93, 251, 327
"Academic Advising Model, An" (O'Banion), 39
Academic Advising Programs (AAPs), 42, 46, 47, 56–57, 60, 63, 64, 65, 66, 96
Academic Advising Today, 135, 208
Academic goals, 133–134
Academically Adrift (Arum and Roska), 84
Active listening, 213, 217, 252–253
activities. *See* Aiming for Excellence activities
Advising: appreciative, 78–79; developmental, 67, 68, 97, 232; hermeneutic, 97; intrusive, 98;

learning-centered, 98; prescriptive, 99, 232–233; strengths-based, 100, 236–238. *See also* Academic advising
Advising delivery models, 32–34, 98; about, 98, 249; delivery methods, 32–34, 98; emerging forms of, 281; group advising, 273–280; one-to-one advising, 252–266; online advising, 289–298; selecting group advising, 284–285; 3-I model, 95, 144–148, 149–152. *See also* *specific models*
"Advising Students of Color and International Students" (Clark and Kalionzes), 110–111
Advising syllabi, 44
Advisor Checklist for Listening: Interviewing, and Referral Skills, 226–228
Advisor Checklist of Questions: Institutional Information to Learn in Year 1, 123
Advisor Checklist of Questions: Student Information to Learn in Year1, 126, 183
Advisor Checklist of Questions: Teaching Students to Make Academic Decisions, 271
Advisor Checklist of Questions: Teaching Students to Navigate the Institutional System, 140–141
Advisor Checklist of Questions: Teaching Students to Use Resources, 202
Advisor notes, 260
Advisors: admiring ease of master, 3; advice for, 79–80; advising student's with different life experiences, 189–190, 192, 194, 197, 205; assessing how to learn advising knowledge, 109; assessing own learning proficiency, 111; biases of, 215–216; career advising by, 83–84; challenges in group advising, 278–279; characteristics of effective, 248; communicating with remote students, 221–222; conducting individual conferences, 262–264; cultural competence of, 185, 199; designing students' academic goals, 133–134; developing referral skills, 219–221; discovering on-campus resources, 310; evaluating limitations in cultural competence, 185–186; finding best information sources, 110–111; finding student's core desired feelings, 84–85; gaining experiential knowledge about students, 179–180; gathering student information, 178–179; group advising benefits for, 277–278, 281–282; handling stress, 325; identifying knowledge needed for new, 107–108; knowing